Oxford AQA History

A LEVEL AND AS
Component 1

The British Empire c1857-1967

Robert J Carr
Sally Waller
and Prof. Anthony Webster

SERIES EDITOR
Sally Waller

OXFORD
UNIVERSITY PRESS

Great Clarendon Street, Oxford, OX2 6DP, United Kingdom

Oxford University Press is a department of the University of Oxford. It furthers the University's objective of excellence in research, scholarship, and education by publishing worldwide. Oxford is a registered trade mark of Oxford University Press in the UK and in certain other countries

British Library Cataloguing in Publication Data
Data available

978-0-19-835463-5

Kindle edition: 978-0-19-836392-7

10 9 8 7 6 5 4 3 2 1

Paper used in the production of this book is a natural, recyclable product made from wood grown in sustainable forests. The manufacturing process conforms to the environmental regulations of the country of origin.

Printed in Great Britain by Bell and Bain Ltd, Glasgow.

We have made every effort to trace and contact all copyright holders before publication, but if notified of any errors or omissions, the publisher will be happy to rectify these at the earliest opportunity.

From the author, Robert J Carr: Thanks to Ru and my Lycée students for sharing the journey.

The publisher would like to thank the following people for offering their contribution in the development of this book: Brian York, Sally Waller and Indexing Specialists (UK) Ltd.

Links to third party websites are provided by Oxford in good faith and for information only. Oxford disclaims any responsibility for the materials contained in any third party website referenced in this work.

Approval message from AQA

This textbook has been approved by AQA for use with our qualification. This means that we have checked that it broadly covers the specification and we are satisfied with the overall quality. Full details of our approval process can be found on our website.

We approve textbooks because we know how important it is for teachers and students to have the right resources to support their teaching and learning. However, the publisher is ultimately responsible for the editorial control and quality of this book.

Please note that when teaching the AQA A Level History course, you must refer to AQA's specification as your definitive source of information. While this book has been written to match the specification, it does not provide complete coverage of every aspect of the course.

A wide range of other useful resources can be found on the relevant subject pages of our website: www.aqa.org.uk.

Please note that the Practice Questions in this book allow students a genuine attempt at practising exam skills, but they are not intended to replicate examination papers.

Contents

Introduction to features   v
AQA History specification overview   vi
Introduction to the *Oxford AQA History* series   viii
Timeline   x
Introduction to this book   xiv

PART ONE: AS AND A LEVEL
THE HIGH WATER MARK OF THE BRITISH EMPIRE, C1857–1914
SECTION 1
The development of imperialism, c1857–c1890   1

1 The expansion of the British Empire in Africa   1
   British expansion in Africa   1
   The Suez Canal and Egypt   6
   Summary   10

2 Imperial and colonial policy   11
   India's administration and defence   12
   International relations, colonial policy and the scramble
   for Africa   16
   Informal empire   20
   Summary   21

3 Trade and commerce   22
   Trade and commerce   22
   The role of the chartered companies   28
   Summary   29

**4 Attitudes to empire – the role and influence of
   individuals   30**
   The role and influence of explorers   30
   The role and influence of missionaries: Christian imperialism 33
   The role and influence of traders   35
   The role and influence of colonial administrators   38
   Summary   40

5 Attitudes towards imperialism in Britain   42
   Attitudes to empire: the British government   42
   Party political conflict   43
   Attitudes to empire: the British public   46
   Summary   49

6 Relations with indigenous peoples   50
   The Indian Mutiny and its impact   50
   Relations with the Boers and Bantu peoples in southern
   Africa   54
   Summary   57

SECTION 2
Imperial consolidation and Liberal rule,
c1890–1914   59

**7 Consolidation and expansion of the British
   Empire in Africa   59**
   A new African empire   59
   Expansion in Tropical Africa   62
   Expansion in British South Africa   67
   Summary   70

8 Imperial and colonial policy   71
   Administration of India and Egypt   71
   Native policy   78
   International relations and colonial policy   79
   Summary   83

9 Trade and commerce   84
   Trade and commerce   84
   Summary   90

**10 Attitudes to empire – the role and influence of
   individuals   91**
   The role and influence of Joseph Chamberlain   91
   The role and influence of Cecil Rhodes   93
   Colonial administration   93
   Summary   97

11 Attitudes towards imperialism in Britain   98
   Imperialism – supporters and critics   99
   National efficiency   102
   The British Empire and popular culture   104
   Representations of empire   107
   Summary   109

12 Relations with indigenous peoples   111
   Challenges to British rule   111
   The Sudan   113
   The causes and consequences of the Boer War   115
   Summary   117

PART TWO: A LEVEL
IMPERIAL RETREAT, 1914–1967
SECTION 3
Imperialism challenged   119

13 Expansion and contraction of empire   119
   The impact of the First World War   119
   The League of Nations mandates   121
   The expansion and contraction of empire   124
   The impact of the Second World War   125
   British withdrawal from India and the Middle East   127
   Summary   132

14 Colonial policy and administration   134
   Colonial policy and administration in India, Africa and the
   Middle East   134
   British relations with the Dominions and the Statute of
   Westminster   139
   Imperial defence   141
   Summary   142

**15 Trade, commerce and the economic
   impact of war   144**
   Economic impact of the First World War   144
   Trade and commerce between the wars   146
   Economic impact of the Second World War   149
   Summary   152

Contents (continued)

16 Attitudes to empire – the role and influence of individuals   **153**

The role and influence of Gandhi   153
The role and influence of colonial administrators   156
Summary   160

17 Imperialist ideals   **161**

Imperialism and popular culture   161
Representations of empire   164
The extent of imperialist ideals   165
Summary   167

18 Relations with indigenous peoples   **168**

Protest and conflict   168
Colonial identity   172
The development of nationalist movements   173
Summary   176

SECTION 4
The winds of change, 1947–1967   **178**

19 Decolonisation in Africa and Asia   **178**

Africa   179
Asia   185
Summary   189

20 Colonial policy and administration   **191**

Colonial policy and administration   191
The Suez crisis and its impact   194
International relations   198
The Commonwealth   200
Summary   201

21 Trade and commerce   **203**

Trade and commerce   203
Post-war reconstruction   205
Summary   206

22 Attitudes to empire – the role and influence of individuals   **208**

The role and influence of nationalist leaders   208
The role and influence of colonial administrators   215
Summary   217

23 Post-colonial ties   **219**

Post-colonial political and economic ties   219
Migration   221
The residual impact of empire and cultural ties   226
Summary   230

24 Relations with indigenous peoples   **231**

Challenges to colonial rule in Africa and Asia   231
The growth of nationalist movements   232
Nationalist movements and reactions to them   233
Summary   241

Conclusion   **243**
Glossary   **245**
Bibliography   **249**
Acknowledgements   **250**
Index   **251**

Introduction to features

The *Oxford AQA History* series has been developed by a team of expert history teachers and authors with examining experience. Written to match the new AQA specification, these new editions cover AS and A Level content together in each book.

How to use this book

The features in this book include:

TIMELINE

Key events are outlined at the beginning of the book to give you an overview of the chronology of this topic. Events are colour-coded so you can clearly see the categories of change.

LEARNING OBJECTIVES

At the beginning of each chapter, you will find a list of learning objectives linked to the requirements of the specification.

SOURCE   EXTRACT

Sources introduce you to material that is primary or contemporary to the period, and **Extracts** provide you with historical interpretations and the debate among historians on particular issues and developments. The accompanying activity questions support you in evaluating sources and extracts, analysing and assessing their value, and making judgements.

KEY QUESTION

The six key thematic questions in the specification for this topic are highlighted to help you understand and make connections between the themes.

PRACTICE QUESTION

Focused questions to help you practise your history skills for both AS and A Level, including evaluating sources and extracts, and essay writing.

STUDY TIP

Hints to highlight key parts of **Practice Questions** or **Activities**.

ACTIVITY

Various activity types to provide you with opportunities to demonstrate both the content and skills you are learning. Some activities are designed to aid revision or to prompt further discussion; others are to stretch and challenge both your AS and A Level studies.

CROSS-REFERENCE

Links to related content within the book to offer you more detail on the subject in question.

A CLOSER LOOK

An in-depth look at a theme, event or development to deepen your understanding, or information to put further context around the subject under discussion.

KEY CHRONOLOGY

A short list of dates identifying key events to help you understand underlying developments.

KEY PROFILE

Details of a key person to extend your understanding and awareness of the individuals that have helped shape the period in question.

KEY TERM

A term that you will need to understand. The terms appear in bold, and they are also defined in the glossary.

AQA History specification overview

Part One content

The high water mark of the British Empire, c1857–1914

1 The development of imperialism, c1857–c1890
2 Imperial consolidation and Liberal rule, c1890–1914

Part Two content

Imperial retreat, 1914–1967

3 Imperialism challenged, 1914–1947
4 The winds of change, 1947–1967

AS examination papers will cover content from Part One only (you will only need to know the content in the blue box). A Level examination papers will cover content from both Part One and Part Two.

The examination papers

The grade you receive at the end of your AQA AS History course is based entirely on your performance in two examination papers, covering Breadth (Paper 1) and Depth (Paper 2). For your AQA A Level History course, you will also have to complete an Historical Investigation (Non-examined assessment).

Paper 1 Breadth Study

This book covers the content of a Breadth Study (Paper 1). You are assessed on the study of significant historical developments over a period of around 100 years, and associated interpretations or extracts.

Exam paper	Questions and marks	Assessment Objective (AO)*	Timing	Marks
AS Paper 1: Breadth Study	**Section A: Evaluating historical extracts** One compulsory question linked to two historical interpretations (25 marks) • The compulsory question will ask you: *'with reference to these extracts and your understanding of the historical context, which of these extracts provides the more convincing interpretation of…'*	AO3	Written exam: 1 hour 30 minutes	50 marks (50% of AS)
	Section B: Essay writing One from a choice of two essay questions (25 marks) • The essay questions will contain a quotation advancing a judgement, and <u>could</u> be followed by: *'explain why you agree or disagree with this view'.*	AO1		
A Level Paper 1: Breadth Study	**Section A: Evaluating historical extracts** One compulsory question linked to three historical interpretations with different views (30 marks) • The compulsory question will ask you: *'using your understanding of the historical context, assess how convincing the arguments in these three extracts are, in relation to…'*	AO3	Written exam: 2 hours 30 minutes	80 marks (40% of A Level)
	Section B: Essay writing Two from a choice of three essay questions (2 x 25 marks) • The essay questions require analysis and judgement, and <u>could</u> include: *'How successful…'* or *'To what extent…'* or *'How far…'* or a quotation offering a judgement followed by *'Assess the validity of this view'.*	AO1		

*AQA History examinations will test your ability to:

AO1: Demonstrate, organise and communicate **knowledge and understanding** to analyse and evaluate the key features related to the periods studied, **making substantiated judgements and exploring concepts**, as relevant, of cause, consequence, change, continuity, similarity, difference and significance.

AO2: **Analyse and evaluate** appropriate source material, primary and/or contemporary to the period, within the historical context.

AO3: **Analyse and evaluate**, in relation to the historical context, different ways in which aspects of the past have been interpreted.

Visit **www.aqa.org.uk** to help you prepare for your examinations. The website includes specimen examination papers and mark schemes.

Introduction to the *Oxford AQA History* series

Breadth Studies

The study of history concerns the study of change and continuity over time. Sometimes it is easy for you to over-concentrate on the former and forget that, for long periods throughout history, much remained the same. In undertaking a historical breadth study covering approximately 100 years of history, you will have the opportunity to reflect on the processes of change and continuity and, in so doing, come to appreciate what drives and hinders change and how historical development is a multi-faceted process.

The course of history brings together many different strands or themes, so, in order to understand any broad period as a whole, it is helpful to divide it into its various aspects or perspectives. This book reflects the AQA

Key Questions which address a range of perspectives. These Key Questions are given at the beginning of the book and regularly through the text of the chapters. The most common themes in all the questions relate to the differing political, economic and social developments, but sometimes they highlight the place of religion, ideology or cultural movements across time.

Sometimes specific individuals colour history, changing the course of events or affecting others for good or ill, and the **Key Profile** features in this book will help you to identify the major influences on the period you are studying.

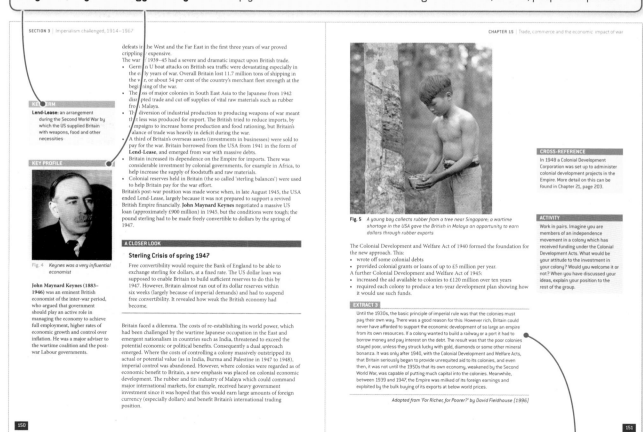

> **Key Term**, **Key Chronology** and **Key Profile** help you to consolidate historical knowledge about dates, events, people and places

▲ The British Empire c1857–1967

> **Extract** features support you with assessing the value of primary materials

While this book is designed to impart a full and lively awareness of a significant period in the history of one or more countries, far more is on offer from the pages that follow. With the help of the text and activities in this book, you will be encouraged to analyse past events, rather than merely learn to describe them. You will thus build up key historical skills that will increase your curiosity and prepare you, not only for A Level History examinations, but for any future study.

This book also incorporates passages of historical interpretation. These **Extract** features will encourage you to reflect on the way in which the past may be seen in different ways by academic historians and how the same factual evidence may support a variety of conclusions. The accompanying **Activity** features pose questions that are designed to stimulate debate on these interpretations. Suggestions for research also encourage you to read further and understand for yourself how history is a 'living' discipline and subject to constant revision.

The chapters which follow are laid out according to the content of the AQA specification, in four sections. Obviously, a secure chronological awareness and understanding of each section of content will be the first step in appreciating the historical period covered in this book. However, on reaching the end of each section, you should pause to reflect on the key questions posed and consider the 'big picture' which has emerged by that point, and the interpretations that have accompanied this. In this way, a broad and satisfying appreciation of history and historical processes will emerge.

Developing your study skills

You will need to be equipped with a paper file or electronic means of storing notes. Organised notes help to produce organised essays and sensible filing provides for efficient use of time. This book uses **Cross-References** to indicate where material in one chapter has relevance to that in another. By employing the same technique, you should find it easier to make the final leap towards piecing together your material to produce a broad historical picture. The exercises and research activities in this book are intended to guide you towards making selective and relevant notes with a specific purpose. Copying out sections of the book is to be discouraged, but selecting material with a particular theme or question in mind will considerably aid your understanding.

For students preparing for the AQA A Level examination, the essay questions posed in the examination will cover around 20–25 years of history or more. AS questions will also be broad, although there is no specific minimum timeframe for these. There are plenty of

examples of such 'breadth' **Practice Questions** in these books, both at AS in Part One and A Level in Parts One and Two of this book, as well as **Study Tips** and activities to encourage you to think about change, continuity, historical perspectives and interpretations. You should also develop timelines, make charts and diagrams, for example, to illustrate causation and consequence, analyse interpretations of key events, dissect broader developments thematically and identify the significance of major issues.

It is particularly important for you to have opinions on and be able to make informed judgements about the material you have studied. Some of the activities in this book encourage pair discussion or class debate, and you should make the most of such opportunities to voice and refine your own ideas. The beauty of history is that there is rarely a right or wrong answer, so this supplementary oral work should enable you to share your own opinions.

Writing and planning your essays

At both AS and A Level, you will be required to write essays and, although A Level questions are likely to be more complex, the basic qualities of good essay writing remain the same:

- **read the question carefully** to identify the key words and dates
- **plan out a logical and organised answer** with a clear judgement or view (several views if there are a number of issues to consider). Your essay should advance this judgement in the introduction, while also acknowledging alternative views and clarifying terms of reference, including the time span
- use the opening sentences of your paragraphs as stepping stones to take an argument forward, which allows you to **develop an evolving and balanced argument** throughout the essay and also makes for good style
- **support your comment or analysis** with precise detail; using dates, where appropriate, helps logical organisation
- **write a conclusion** which matches the view of the introduction and flows naturally from what has gone before.

While these suggestions will help you develop a good style, essays should never be too rigid or mechanical. This book will have fulfilled its purposes if it produces, as intended, students who think for themselves!

Sally Waller

Series Editor

Timeline

The colours represent different types of event as follows:

- Blue: economic/social events
- Red: imperial political events
- Black: international events
- Green: influence of individuals/ groups

1857
- Indian Mutiny (until 1858)

1858
- India becomes Crown Colony (formal Raj)
- Treaty of Tientsin obliges China to open more ports to Britain
- Burton and Speke discover Lake Tanganyika

1860
- Speke's expedition to locate source of Nile (until 1863)

1866
- Livingstone's third journey in Africa to look for source of Nile (until 1873)

1872
- Cape Colony granted responsible government

1873
- Onset of Great (Long) Depression
- Death of Livingstone

1874
- Gold Coast becomes a colony
- Stanley's expedition to search for source of Nile (until 1877)

1875
- Prime Minister Disraeli secures controlling stake in Suez Canal

1880
- First Boer War begins (until 1881)

1881
- Mahdi uprising in Sudan (until 1898)
- British defeated at Majuba Hill
- Pretoria Convention restores independence to Transvaal

1882
- Bombardment of Alexandria and occupation of Egypt

1884
- Berlin Conference (until 1885) discusses colonisation in Africa

1889
- British South Africa Company receives charter
- Rhodesia established
- Part of Nyasaland becomes a British Protectorate

1890
- Zanzibar becomes a British Protectorate
- Cecil Rhodes becomes Prime Minister of Cape Colony

1893
- Matabele War

1894
- Uganda becomes a Protectorate

1867
- Canada becomes a Dominion
- Diamonds discovered in South Africa

1868
- Colonial Society founded

1869
- Suez Canal opened

1871
- Stanley finds Livingstone
- Annexation of Griqualand West to Cape Colony

1876
- Victoria becomes Empress of India
- Anglo-French control of Egyptian finances

1877
- Annexation of Transvaal
- Delhi durbar
- Sir Bartle Frere appointed High Commissioner for South Africa

1878
- Afghan War begins (until 1880)

1879
- Zulu War begins (until 1880)

1885
- Gordon killed in Khartoum
- Indian National Congress formed
- Bechuanaland and Niger Coast protectorates established

1886
- Discovery of gold in South Africa
- Royal Niger Company receives charter
- Colonial and Indian Exhibition in South Kensington
- Anglo-German agreement over spheres of influence in East Africa
- First Indian National Congress Meets
- China recognises British control of Burma

1887
- Zululand becomes a Protectorate

1888
- Imperial British East Africa Company charter awarded
- Cook Islands become a British Protectorate
- Imperial Exhibition in Glasgow
- Sarawak, North Borneo and Brunei become British Protectorates
- Cecil Rhodes amalgamates Kimberley Diamond Companies

1895
- British East Africa Protectorate established
- Jameson raid

1896
- Joseph Chamberlain appointed Colonial Secretary
- Zanzibar War
- Rhodes resigns as Prime Minister in Cape Colony
- Formation of the Federated Malay states

1897
- Victoria's Diamond Jubilee
- Sir Alfred Milner appointed High Commissioner for South Africa

1898
- Battle of Omdurman and Fashoda incident
- Formal annexation of the Sudan
- Curzon becomes Viceroy of India

1899
- (Second) Boer War (until 1902)
- Anglo-Egyptian Condominium over Sudan

1900
- Ashanti War

1902
- Ashantiland incorporated into Gold Coast Protectorate
- Union of South Africa established

1903
- Chamberlain launches campaign for tariff reform

1910
- Union of South Africa becomes self-governing Dominion

1911
- Delhi durbar marks transfer of Raj capital
- Imperial Conference in London

1912
- ANC formed in South Africa
- Third Irish Home Rule Bill; Ulster Covenant signed to keep Ulster in Britain

1913
- Crisis in Ireland; Ulster Volunteers formed

1919
- Amritsar massacre in India
- Irish war for independence begins (until 1922); IRA formed
- Treaty of Versailles considers post-war mandates

1920
- Mahatma Gandhi becomes leader of Indian Congress
- British East Africa becomes Kenya
- Government of Ireland Act establishes a Northern Irish parliament (partition carried out 1921)
- Formation of National Congress of British West Africa

1922
- Creation of Transjordan
- Independence of Egypt
- Irish Civil War (to 1924)

1926
- Imperial Conference agrees definition of Dominion status

1935
- Government of India Act offers limited local government and separates Burma from India

1939
- Mobilisation of Dominion and Imperial forces to fight in Second World War

1942
- Fall of Singapore, Malaya and Burma
- Quit India movement established

1947
- Indian independence with partition to create Pakistan

1956
- Nasser nationalises the Suez Canal precipitating Suez crisis

1957
- Gold Coast becomes independent as Ghana
- Malay states become independent as Malaysia

1960
- Macmillan makes 'wind of change' speech to South African Parliament
- British Somaliland, Cyprus and Nigeria become independent

1961
- Sierra Leone, Tanganyika and British Cameroons become independent; South Africa leaves Commonwealth

1966
- Bechuanaland, Basutoland, Barbados and British Guiana gain independence
- HMS *Tiger* meeting between Wilson and Smith over future of Rhodesia

1967
- British evacuate from Aden which gains its independence

1905
- Partition of Bengal

1906
- Self-government restored to Transvaal and Orange River Colony

1907
- New Zealand gains Dominion status
- Mahatma Gandhi begins first non-violent resistance campaign in South Africa
- Indian National Congress splits
- Anglo-Russian Entente resolves differences over spheres of influence in Persia
- Baden Powell founds Boy Scout movement

1909
- Morley-Minto reforms in India

1914
- Outbreak of First World War
- Home Rule for Ireland (suspended for war)
- Egypt becomes a Protectorate
- Northern and Southern Nigeria united as Nigeria
- Protectorate established in Egypt
- Imperial troops assemble for war

1915
- Gallipoli landings involving ANZACs
- British support for an Arab homeland in return for their help in fighting the Ottoman Turks

1916
- Easter Rising in Dublin
- Home Rule League established in India

1917
- Balfour Declaration promises Palestine to Jews
- Imperial War Conferences
- Creation of Imperial War Cabinet

1929
- Onset of the Great Depression Colonial Development Act

1930
- Gandhi's salt march and disobedience campaign
- First Round Table Conference between Britain and India (until 1932)

1931
- Statute of Westminster gives Dominions constitutional autonomy
- Britain abandons gold standard

1932
- Ottawa Conference establishes imperial preference

1948
- Withdrawal from Palestine
- ANC win power in South Africa
- Ceylon and Burma become independent
- Communist insurgency in Malaya (Malayan Emergency to 1960)
- Ireland leaves Commonwealth

1952
- Mau Mau rebellion begins in Kenya (until 1959)
- Nkrumah becomes Prime Minister of Gold Coast
- Elizabeth II becomes Queen

1953
- Creation of Central African Federation combining Northern Rhodesia, Southern Rhodesia and Nyasaland

1954
- Withdrawal from Sudan begins (completed 1956)
- British troops removed from Egypt

1962
- Commonwealth Immigration Act
- Jamaica, Trinidad and Tobago, Uganda and Samoa all become independent

1963
- Kenya and Zanzibar become independent

1964
- Northern Rhodesia, Nyasaland and Malta become independent
- Zanzibar and Tanganyika combine to form Tanzania
- Ian Smith elected as premier of Southern Rhodesia

1965
- Creation of Commonwealth Secretariat in London
- Gambia, Maldive Islands and Cook Islands become independent
- Southern Rhodesia declares unilateral independence (UDI)

Introduction to this book

In 1857, Great Britain possessed a vast territorial empire which was spread across all continents of the world. Britain's possessions had eclipsed those of its former rivals – the Portuguese, Spanish and Dutch, who had dropped out of the competition for overseas colonies, and France, whose possessions were limited to Algeria and some islands in the Pacific. Germany, a country that was to become a rival in the 1890s, did not even exist as a united country in Europe until 1871. Although many Britons viewed the Empire with indifference and the pride felt later in the century had not yet manifested itself, there were, nevertheless, some high-sounding justifications offered for Britain's pre-eminence in the mid-century. **Blackwood's magazine** of 1843, for example, claimed that Great Britain had been 'destined by Almighty God to be the instrument for effecting his sublime hidden purposes with reference to humanity', while Lord John Russell, the aristocratic Liberal politician, put the reason for empire more bluntly (and perhaps more honestly), by declaring that, 'the loss of any great portion of our colonies would diminish our importance in the world'.

At its greatest extent, during the period covered in this book, the British Empire comprised over 13 million square miles and covered nearly a quarter of the earth's land-surface. It ranged from tiny islands to large land masses and was connected by an elaborate system of trade-routes and 'coaling stations'. Various maps are provided in this book to chart the expansion and contraction of the Empire.

Although the British Crown and Parliament exercised ultimate authority over the Empire, the actual business of governing varied. A **representative system**, with a royal governor and a local assembly, had been established in Britain's older West Indian colonies and in Canada, Australia, New Zealand and on the South African Cape. These '**colonies of settlement**' were so-named because they were peopled by white settlers who had usually gone to the colonies in search of land. From around the middle of the nineteenth century, these areas (although not the West Indies) moved to '**responsible government**'. This meant that they had their own government ministers who were answerable to their individual elected parliaments, in a system of government similar to that in Britain itself. Around the turn of the twentieth these internally self-governing colonies became known as **Dominions**. British authority over them was finally removed between 1926 and 1931, although the title 'Dominion' continued until after 1945.

Much of the remainder of the Empire was made up of **Crown colonies**. In 1857, these included areas which had been developed for trading purposes, such as Trinidad, Ceylon, various Pacific islands and parts of West Africa, and places like Gibraltar, Malta, Hong Kong and Singapore, which were naval bases or ports along the world's trade routes. The number of Crown colonies was set to expand in the later years of the nineteenth century as more of the African continent fell into British hands. The population in the Crown colonies was overwhelmingly non-European and therefore, to the nineteenth-century mind, incapable of self-rule. These colonies were administered directly by a governor appointed by the British Crown. It was only in the twentieth century that local legislative (law-making) councils were gradually established; most of these colonies gained full independence after the Second World War.

There were also territories in 1857 that were influenced by the British, even if not ruled directly by them. In these, British traders, backed by the powerful British Navy, which was the largest in the world, had established bases through conquest or advantageous deals with local rulers. Thus, much of Malaya had come to be controlled from Singapore and long stretches of the Chinese coast from Hong Kong. These areas are sometimes referred to as '**informal empire**' although in the later nineteenth century the term '**protectorate**' came into use for areas where rulers kept their own sovereignty but were 'protected' by the British Crown. Thus the lands of the Malay sultans became a 'Protectorate' in 1895; and Egypt, which Britain 'occupied' from 1882, was made a formal Protectorate between 1914 and 1922.

There was yet another type of rule added to the complex pattern of empire in the aftermath of the First World War. Some of the former provinces and imperial possessions of the defeated Turks and Germans were transferred, under the auspices of the peace-keeping body, the League of Nations, to Britain as '**mandates**'. These included Transjordan and Iraq, which were treated as protectorates, and Palestine and the German African colonies, which became Crown colonies.

Finally, there was India – 'the brightest jewel in the Crown' according to Disraeli in 1876, which had eclipsed the West Indies as the most important of Britain's possessions by the mid-nineteenth century. India stood apart from the rest of the Empire, not only because of its size, importance for trade, riches and immense population (expanded with the acquisition of the Punjab in 1849 and Lower Burma in 1852), but also because it had its own unique system of rule. Until 1858, India was governed by a trading company (the East India Company) on behalf of the Crown, and large parts of it (the **Princely States**) had been bound to the British Crown by treaties and thus were 'protected' in return. However, from 1858, the Crown assumed direct control – although the Princely States retained their status. India became known as the **Raj** and from 1876, British monarchs took the title Empress or Emperor of India. India was granted a limited form of representative government, but in practice, the British retained a firm grip until internal movements for independence forced change in the twentieth century. India and Pakistan gained independence in 1947.

Fig. 1   *British dignitaries visit the Maharajah of Cashmere in 1863*

While the British Empire was a confusing mix of self-governing dominions, Crown colonies, protectorates, mandates, the Raj and 'informal empire', its establishment and growth nevertheless led to the spread of British influence throughout the globe and helped to shape the world around us today. At its height, Britain was responsible for ruling 500 million people – more than a fifth of the world's population – and this position was retained until the Second World War. No country could experience such pre-eminence without being itself changed by the experience. Britain's interaction with its empire affected the British nation, economically, politically and culturally. Even after changed world circumstances and the rise of nationalism forced a period of decolonisation between 1947 and 1967, the imperial legacy remained a potent force.

This book seeks to enhance your understanding of the changes that took place in the British Empire in the years between 1857 and 1967, helping you to understand the politics of British rule, the economic impact of empire and the results of the interaction of peoples and cultures that emerged from this phenomenon. Obviously it is not possible to look at every part of the Empire in equal measure and this book concentrates on those areas that were given most attention by the British in each particular time period. Students with a specific interest in areas of the Empire that are not explored in depth here – for example British possessions in the Caribbean, in the Pacific or Malta and Cyprus in Europe – are encouraged to undertake individual case studies and link the experience of empire in their chosen area to the broader patterns investigated here.

As you read this book, you will be encouraged to think about the causes and consequences of British imperial expansion and contraction and examine for yourself the part played by individuals, groups and ideas in making the British Empire what it was. This approach should help you to develop an historical awareness that will enrich your understanding of the modern world.

You are invited to consider the following key questions as you work your way through this book; you will find them identified in the text too:

- Why did the British Empire grow and contract?
- What influenced imperial policy?
- What part did economic factors play in the development of the British Empire?
- How did the Empire influence British attitudes and culture?
- How did the indigenous peoples respond to British rule?
- How important was the role of key individuals and groups and how were they affected by developments?

There is plenty to learn and much to think about in the following pages. Try to approach your study in a spirit of enquiry. Look for the links and connections between developments in different parts of the world and at different times. Seek out further examples and explore the overlaps between themes such as political and economic developments. You should find much to absorb and fascinate you as you piece together past events and learn more about how the destinies of peoples and countries have been shaped by empire.

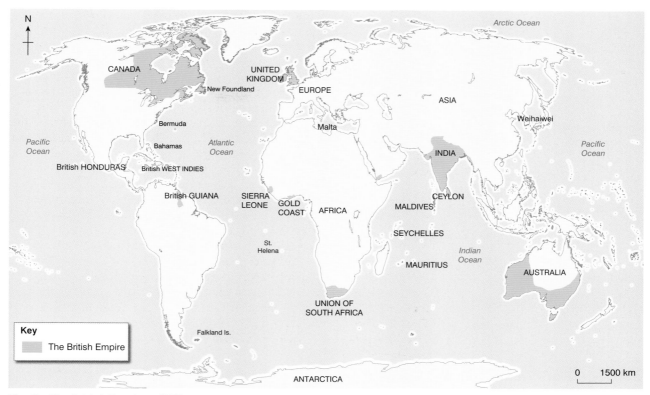

Fig. 2 *The British Empire c1857*

1 The development of imperialism, c1857–c1890

1 The expansion of the British Empire in Africa

EXTRACT 1

The international trading environment that had favoured Britain in the middle years of the nineteenth century was profoundly altered in the later years of the century by the growing political power of Britain's two traditional rivals, France and Russia. Britain also faced two new challengers, the United States and Germany. Moreover, rapid industrialisation had made the American and German economies increasingly fierce competitors in the markets that British manufacturers had comfortably claimed as their own. Even little Belgium had established a steel industry that challenged that of Birmingham. It was agriculture, however, that was the first to feel the full brunt of competition. The global spread of cheap and reliable railway and shipping systems allowed North American grain, Argentine beef, New Zealand butter, and various other agricultural goods to flood the British market, causing prices to plummet. The trade slump that began in 1873 seemed to many Britons a taste of things to come. Empire was regarded with renewed interest.

Adapted from *Britain and Empire 1880–1945* by Dane Kennedy (2002)

There is some truth in the traditional view that the British Empire was the product of a desire to seek out new foodstuffs and resources such as valuable minerals. However, the reasons for the growth of Britain's empire are actually far more complex than this. As you read this book, try to build up your own picture of what caused the expansion of the British Empire.

British expansion in Africa

British interest in Africa can be dated from the loss of Britain's American colonies at the end of the eighteenth century. The end of empire on the American continent sent the British on a '**Swing to the East**', looking for influence in Asia and Africa. Since Britain underwent a massive industrial revolution in the nineteenth century, steamships and weapons' production made it possible to establish footholds in these continents.

A CLOSER LOOK

The loss of the American colonies

By the eighteenth century, the British had a number of well-established colonies along the east coast of North America. However, disputes arose, partly because of the taxes that were imposed by Parliament in London over which the colonists had no control and partly because of colonial resentment at having to buy imports (tea, for example) from British merchants and to export goods (such as tobacco) to Britain. War broke out in 1775, between Britain and the colonial 'rebels' led by George Washington. The British were defeated and in 1783 the former colonies joined to form the United States of America.

LEARNING OBJECTIVES

In this chapter you will learn about:

- the expansion of the British Empire in Africa

- the establishment of the Suez Canal and British influence in Egypt.

ACTIVITY

Evaluating historical extracts

According to Extract 1, why was empire regarded with 'renewed interest' in the later years of the nineteenth century?

KEY QUESTION

As you read this chapter, consider the following key questions:
- Why did the British Empire grow and contract?
- What influenced imperial policy?
- What part did economic factors play in the development of the British Empire?
- How important was the role of key individuals and groups?

A CLOSER LOOK

The Swing to the East

Vincent Harlow, a prominent British historian in the early twentieth century, introduced the concept of a 'Swing to the East' to explain a shift in Britain's imperial priorities by the turn of the nineteenth century. He detected a change in British business and political interests away from the Western hemisphere towards both Africa and Asia. This outlook also marked a preference for trade rather than pure conquest and control.

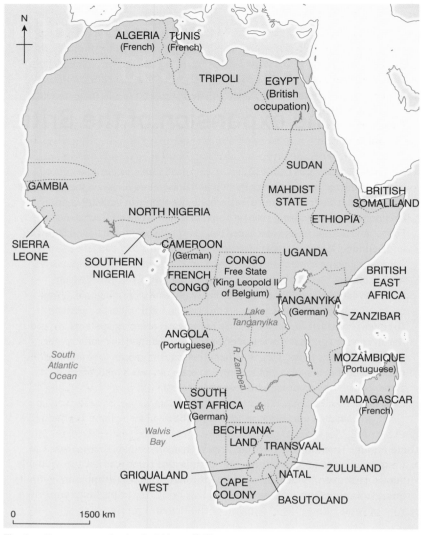

Fig. 1 *European territories in Africa c1890*

Reasons for British expansion in Africa

Fig. 2 *African ivory for sale – a very valuable commodity*

Trade and the economy

British merchants had traded with West Africa since the 1500s, largely as a means to acquire gold and ivory from elephant tusks. In the eighteenth century, however, the slave trade took precedence. By the time that Britain outlawed the slave trade in 1807, it had overseen the exportation of three million Africans to work in its American colonies and the British-owned plantations in the Caribbean as slaves.

Unsurprisingly, the key reason for British expansion in Africa during the second half of the nineteenth century was trade, or, more accurately, the prospect of further trade given the opening up of new routes inland and subsequent discovery of minerals and resources. Once materials, markets or routes had been accessed, further considerations emerged such as investment opportunities and strategic interests, which were very important in late nineteenth-century imperialism.

Some of the many reasons for British interest in expansion in Africa are given in Source 1:

SOURCE 1

From a British Foreign Office Memorandum on East Africa, 20 October 1884:

Apart from the mineral wealth which is believed to exist between the coast and the great lakes, there is an unlimited capacity for the production of cattle, cereals and all the usual articles of tropical trade. The climate is less unhealthy than that of the West Coast, and the great mountain ranges of Kilimanjaro and Kenya, situated between the lakes which give birth to the Nile and the fine harbours of Zanzibar, afford a European climate within easy reach of the coast, once roads are made. It is needless to dwell on the advantages of this to our navy, to our officials, and to traders. There is very good reason, too, for supposing that the natives are more naturally industrious than most of the West Coast tribes and that they would welcome the establishment of any Government strong enough to enforce good order and prevent the raids of the more turbulent tribes.

ACTIVITY

Evaluating primary sources

1. What reasons for interest in East Africa are given in this source?
2. How valuable would this source be for an historian studying the reasons for expansion in Africa?

In the second half of the nineteenth century, coal, iron and timber were sought in Africa in order to feed the demands of British industry. Conversely, as industrial productivity in Britain grew so did the need for sales markets. In this way a cycle of dependency developed whereby Britain sought African resources in order to manufacture goods, such as textiles and weapons, to sell back to Africa. This was particularly the case during the economic slump of 1873 to 1896, when Britain suffered from the **Great Depression**.

CROSS-REFERENCE

Trade and commerce from 1857 to 1890 are discussed in more detail in Chapter 3.

The Great Depression of 1873 to 1896 is outlined in Chapter 3, page 29.

Personal influence

Increasing trade led to a growth in the personal influence of British merchants in Africa. **Merchant-imperialists** such as George Goldie and Cecil Rhodes recognised and capitalised on new commodities and in the process found fame and fortune. British public and political interest in Africa was also stimulated by the great mid-century Victorian **explorers** who sought and traced the continent's waterways, publishing their findings, producing maps and spreading exotic tales of discovery and adventure.

CROSS-REFERENCE

The role and influence of merchant-traders is discussed in Chapter 4, pages 35–37. Their trading activities are covered in Chapter 3.

The role and influence of explorers is discussed in Chapter 4, pages 31–32.

Strategic factors

It is sometimes difficult to disentangle the commercial and strategic factors that led to colonisation. Britain's coastal interests in West Africa, for example, demanded protection, and a string of forts was built along the Gold Coast, as were coastal defences in Sierra Leone and Gambia. However, sometimes strategic interests predominated as, for example, in the establishment of a colony at the most southerly tip of Africa – the Cape. The temperate climate and deep water port of the Cape held advantages over other harbours and, in 1806, during the Napoleonic Wars, Cape Colony had been seized by Britain from the Dutch allies of the French. Cape Colony protected the sea route to the Middle East, China, Australia and, not least, India, thus giving Britain considerable power over the sea routes to the East.

Moral factors

The Victorian era was one of strong moral principles and, increasingly from the 1860s, Christian **missionaries** saw it as their duty to spread their faith among non-Christian – or, to their way of thinking, 'heathen' – peoples. Their view was that the Empire was a force for 'civilisation'. The most famous example of a missionary explorer is David Livingstone, who went to Africa in 1858 'to try and make an open path for commerce and Christianity'.

CROSS-REFERENCE

The role of missionaries and explorers, including David Livingstone, is covered in Chapter 4, pages 31–32.

ACTIVITY

What reasons for the spread of Empire are put forward in Extract 2?

EXTRACT 2

There was general agreement that the Empire was a powerful force for the spread of civilisation through trade and the imposition of superior codes of behaviour on its 'savage' inhabitants. There was a powerful body of Christian philanthropists who believed that these races could be raised to the standards of education and conduct which would place them alongside Europeans.

Subscribers to missions were encouraged to donate by pamphlets which outlined the depravity of the heathen. Lurid accounts were presented of idolatry and superstitions. From the Pacific and Africa came stories of tribal warfare, cannibalism, domestic slavery and thinly veiled details of sexual promiscuity.

Adapted from *The Rise and Fall of the British Empire* by Lawrence James (1999)

Other factors – adventure and exploration

Explorers were also motivational in the expanding African empire. By 1857, most of Africa had been mapped although the course of the Congo River was not charted by Europeans until 1867. It was the explorers who located vast reserves of raw materials, such as gold, palm oil and diamonds in Africa, which European merchants sought to exploit and trade.

A CLOSER LOOK

Explorers in Africa

Explorers had charted the Sahara in 1820, the Lower Niger River in 1830 and southern Africa and the Zambezi River in the 1850s. The source of the Upper Nile was recorded by Burton, and Speke (see Chapter 4 pages 49–50) in a series of expeditions between 1857 and 1868.

ACTIVITY

In a small group, choose a reason for the expansion of the British Empire in Africa and prepare a short PowerPoint presentation for the class. Presentations should include no more than two slides on the pre-1857 period and should concentrate on the motivation for expansion between 1857 and 1890.

The extent of British expansion in Africa 1857–90

Fig. 3 *A French cartoon on the 'scramble for Africa'*

Until the second half of the nineteenth century, Britain's presence in Africa was strictly limited. The West African settlements (Sierra Leone and the Gold Coast), trading networks further inland (for example along the Niger River) and Cape Colony in the south represented Britain's main assets. However, between 1857 and 1890, Britain extended its influence across African territory as the table below indicates.

Year	Territory acquired	Type of control
1868	Basutoland	Protectorate established by treaty
1873	Griqualand West	**Settlement** established and subsequently absorbed into Cape Colony in 1880
1877	Transvaal	**Occupied**
1879	Zululand	Protectorate established by war (annexed to Natal in 1887)
1882	Egypt (and the Sudan)	Occupation establishing a **client state**
1884	Southern Nigeria	**Chartered company rule**
1884	British Somaliland	Protectorate established by treaty
1885	Bechuanaland	Protectorate established by treaty
1885	Northern Nigeria	Chartered company rule
1888	Gambia	Settlement established
1888	British East Africa	Chartered company rule
1888	Uganda	Chartered company rule

It was not until the 1890s that British expansion in Africa really accelerated. On the whole, in the 1857 to 1890 period, Britain was more reactive to the initiatives of other powers, particularly France, than aggressively seeking

KEY TERM

settlement: a loose term to denote an area containing British settlers and under partial British control

occupied: an area containing British settlers/military forces but not under British control

client state: an area with its own ruler but with strong British influence which restricted that ruler's independence politically, militarily and economically

chartered company rule: an area by a trading company (through native rulers) with a special licence by the British government which gave it political as well as economic rights

CROSS-REFERENCE

The role of the chartered companies is covered in more detail in Chapter 3, pages 28–29.

out new lands for their own sake. As the British tried to match the claims of others, so they sought to define their control of areas where British traders had been operating – often for many years. Thus, companies such as the Royal Niger Company, the Imperial British East Africa Company and the British South Africa Company were chartered to implement British claims and ensure that other Europeans were excluded from lucrative British bases. It was only in Egypt that intervention was more direct and even here, the British still claimed to be acting on the defensive.

The Suez Canal and Egypt

Britain and Egypt

KEY TERM

Khedive: the ruler of Egypt, who exercised authority on behalf of the Ottoman Sultan

KEY PROFILE

Isma'il Pasha (1830–95)

Known to his people as Isma'il the Magnificent, Isma'il Pasha was the Khedive of Egypt and Sudan from 1863 to 1879. He helped to modernise Egypt and Sudan during his reign, investing in industrial and economic development. His policies placed his khedivate in severe debt, leading to the sale of the country's shares in the Suez Canal Company to Britain in 1875. This led to his fall, which came about partly as a result of British pressure.

Fig. 4 *The Suez Canal in the 1870s, shortly after opening*

In 1857, the idea that Egypt would fall under British control would probably have been laughed at. Although British traders had used Egypt for centuries as an important route between Europe and Asia and from the eighteenth century it had become a key route to India, Britain had been largely hostile to the Muslim rulers of Egypt.

A CLOSER LOOK

Britain, France and Egypt in the early nineteenth century

Napoleon had recognised the commercial importance of Egypt and had sent troops in 1798 to undermine the British and protect French trading interests. However, British troops forced him to withdraw in 1801. The British remained in Egypt until 1805 when a new and vigorous Egyptian leader, Muhammad Ali, came to power. Muhammad Ali ruled Egypt until 1848, during which time the British supported the ailing Ottoman/Turkish Empire against the ambitions of Muhammad Ali who wanted to throw off his Turkish overlordship. The French, however, supported him and increased their economic base there. Muhammad Ali was succeeded by members of his dynasty, firstly his son Ibrahim (in 1848), followed by Abbas I (in 1848), Said (in 1854) and Isma'il (in 1863).

British interest in Egypt revived during the American Civil War of 1861 to 1865, when British mills were starved of raw cotton. Egypt, whose cotton was a particularly good quality product, attracted those who were anxious to find new sources of this vital raw material. British companies began investing heavily in the production of Egyptian cotton and in the ambitious modernising programme of the ruling **Khedive**, **Isma'il Pasha**. Trading interactions consequently grew and by the 1870s 40 per cent of Egypt's imports were coming from Britain.

Isma'il Pasha came to power in Egypt in 1863. He was committed to the process of modernisation initiated by the Ottoman ruler from 1805 to 1848, Muhammad Ali Pasha who had established a professional army and extended Egyptian rule through the Sudan. Isma'il embarked on a number of projects – from irrigation and railways to schools, street lighting and, most ambitiously, the cutting of the Suez Canal through Egypt to connect the Mediterranean with the Red Sea and the Arabian Peninsula. The canal helped British seafarers and merchants, not least those trading with India and China. The route to India was 6,000 miles shorter than that via the Cape.

The Suez Canal – new passage to India

Fig. 5 *The Suez Canal, opened in 1869, provided a new and quicker passage to the Far East*

Between 1854 and 1856, a Frenchman, Ferdinand de Lesseps, had obtained a concession from Egypt to create a company to construct a canal for international shipping. This Suez Canal Company, set up in 1858, was to run

KEY TERM

tariff: a duty or tax paid on goods travelling between countries or zones

CROSS-REFERENCE

The role of the British Prime Ministers Disraeli and Gladstone is discussed in Chapter 5, page 43.

the canal for 99 years. Work began in 1859 and was completed ten years later, with shares in the project made available internationally. Outside France there was limited interest, however. The British did not buy a significant number of shares and were rather sceptical about the project, since they thought the canal would be unsuitable for large ships.

However, the canal had an immediate and dramatic effect on world trade, reducing the profits of those British traders in the Cape who operated warehouses for the storing of goods. Consequently when, in 1875, Isma'il Pasha, who faced increasing debts, sought a buyer for his country's share in the canal for £4 million (about £85.9 million in 2014's money), the British Prime Minister, **Benjamin Disraeli,** stepped forward. Although France still held the larger number of shares, this gave the British greater control over its passage to India and an income from shipping **tariffs**. Control of the canal also encouraged further British interest in Egypt.

A CLOSER LOOK

Disraeli and the Suez Canal shares

Benjamin Disraeli wasted no time in privately securing the funds to buy Isma'il's stock in 1875. Disraeli borrowed the necessary £4 million to provide Britain with the controlling stake in the company without even securing parliamentary consent. This caused a political outcry but in the long run Disraeli's move paid off and this investment proved advantageous for Britain.

The establishment of British control in Egypt

Perhaps unsurprisingly, given Ismail's continuing economic mismanagement, he was deposed in 1879 by the Ottoman Sultan, as a result of both domestic and Anglo-French pressure. His son Tewfiq became the new Khedive, but it was British money and support that kept Egypt afloat and the British Commissioner, Lord Dufferin, thus wielded considerable influence. In order to prop up Egypt's ailing economy, taxes were imposed on Egyptian food and goods and its army was reduced by two thirds. Such measures increased unemployment and led to a nationalist rebellion under Colonel Arabi Pasha and fellow army officers. Tewfiq was forced to appoint Arabi's allies to government positions, where their fiercely anti-European stance provoked British concerns over trade and investment, and over the security of the 100,000 Europeans living in Egypt and of the canal route to India.

In June 1882, political tensions spilled out onto the streets of Alexandria, Egypt, where violence claimed the lives of 50 Europeans. A series of further revolts across Egypt convinced the British Prime Minister, **William Gladstone**, to intervene and British naval forces were sent to bombard Alexandria. Arabi Pasha declared war, but despite his success at Kafr el-Dawwar against British forces heading for Cairo, the British Commander-in-Chief, Sir Garnet Wolseley, was able to secure the Suez Canal with the bulk of the British forces before defeating Arabi's forces at Tel el-Kebir, in a battle lasting little over an hour. This enabled the British to re-take Cairo and restore Tewfiq as a **puppet ruler**: the occupation of Egypt had begun, although supposedly temporarily and without clearly defined intentions.

Major **Evelyn Baring** was installed as **Consul-General** and Tewfik was forced to create a government amenable to Britain, employ British military personnel to supervise his army and rely on British advisors. No matter how seemingly informal, Britain's influence over Egypt was confirmed by the 1885 Convention of London, which secured an international loan for the Egyptian government. Behind the thin veil of both Ottoman and local rule, Egypt was firmly under British administrative control. Egypt thus held the position of a

KEY TERM

puppet ruler: a ruler who has to act as directed by his master – in this case Britain

Consul-General: Britain's highest governmental representative in an overseas territory; the Consul-General speaks on behalf of his state in the country in which he is located

veiled protectorate: a state controlled by another in an indirect manner; in this case, while Britain and Egypt officially enjoyed equal sovereignty, in reality, the British Consul-General ruled

client state; this is sometimes referred to as a '**veiled protectorate**' in which Baring effectively ruled from behind a screen of Egyptian ministers, aided by a group of English administrators.

EXTRACT 3

The occupation of Egypt was a spectacular act of imperial expansion. It was sanctioned, very much contrary to its declared principles, by the Liberal government of Gladstone. The British government's explanation for the invasion was that it was engaged in an operation to restore order and create stable government. Much was said, after the invasion had actually been launched, about protecting the Suez Canal. Critics, however, pointed to the large sums of money lent to the Egyptian government and detected a kind of capitalist plot. There is no evidence that Gladstone intervened specifically to protect the bond-holders who had lent money to the Egyptians, but there would have been no invasion of Egypt if so much Western money, and with it so much Western interference, had not been poured into Egypt, creating resentment among Egyptians and the instability which the British feared so greatly. In a situation of world-wide European rivalry, the British were not prepared to leave Egypt alone. Doubts about its stability were resolved by the use of force.

Adapted from 'The Empire under Threat' by P.J. Marshall (1996)

CROSS-REFERENCE

The role and influence of Evelyn Baring is discussed in Chapter 4, pages 28–39.

ACTIVITY

1. Construct a flow chart to demonstrate increasing British involvement in Egypt.
2. With a partner, use the flow chart to compile a hierarchy of reasons for British involvement in Egypt, ranging from the most to the least important.

PRACTICE QUESTION

Evaluating historical extracts

Using your understanding of the historical context, assess how convincing the arguments in Extracts 1, 2 and 3 are, in relation to reasons for the expansion of the British Empire in Africa in the years before 1890.

The Sudan

STUDY TIP

Each extract puts forward a different reason and argument for the expansion of the British Empire. You should evaluate each in turn, identifying the arguments it contains and evaluating that argument in the light of your own knowledge. Try to provide a short summary conclusion with a comment on how convincing the arguments are and, perhaps, how they jointly help explain British imperial expansion across Africa.

Fig. 6 'The Death of General Charles George Gordon at Khartoum', painted in 1885

KEY TERM

Mahdi: an Islamic redeemer – regarded by Shi'ites as the Twelfth Imam (the final successor to the Prophet Muhammad)

KEY TERM

jihadist: a person fighting a holy war

CROSS-REFERENCE

Developments in the Sudan after 1890 are discussed in Chapter 7, pages 66–67.

ACTIVITY

Extension

Find out more about General Gordon and what happened at Khartoum in 1884. You could also explore the reaction to his death in Britain.

Colonel Charles Gordon was sent from Britain to act as Governor-General of Egyptian-administered Sudan, on behalf of their 'puppet' Khedive Isma'il between 1877 and 1880. However, the British administrators faced opposition from the Sudanese Islamic cleric Muhammad Ahmad who, in June 1881, proclaimed himself the **Mahdi** or saviour of mankind.

Drawing on long-term hostility towards Egyptian rule, combined with more recent resentment of British influence, the self-proclaimed Mahdi transformed an emerging political movement into a **jihadist** army. The Mahdists sought to liberate Sudan from outside rule, whether Egyptian or British and by 1882 had taken complete control over the area surrounding Khartoum. In 1883, a joint British-Egyptian military expedition under the command of Colonel William Hicks launched a counter-attack against the Mahdists, in which Hicks was killed. Gladstone, reluctant to get drawn into further conflict, ordered General Gordon to oversee the evacuation of both British and Egyptian troops from Khartoum in 1884 but the British-Egyptian forces defending Khartoum were overrun in January 1885. Virtually the entire garrison was killed, and General Gordon was beheaded during the attack. Nevertheless, Gladstone did not retaliate as he was anxious to avoid further loss of life and money for no obvious gain. It was not until **1896** that another campaign was launched to assert Britain's control over the Mahdists and the Sudan.

Summary

ACTIVITY

Summary

This chapter explored a range of reasons for British involvement in Africa, with particular reference to Egypt and the Sudan. Draw up a table with four headings – Economic, Strategic, Moral, Other – and under these headings gather supporting evidence that exemplifies the reasons behind British interest in the continent.

STUDY TIP

Your summary diagram should help you in planning this answer. You will need to identify as many examples as you can of strategic interests and, of course, Egypt will be important amongst these. However, you will also need to balance this interest against a range of others and draw a conclusion as to which was the most important. Try to decide whether you will agree or disagree with the quotation before you begin to write. In that way, you should be able to sustain a judgement in your answer.

 PRACTICE QUESTION

'British interest in Africa in the years 1857 to 1890 was primarily strategic.' Explain why you agree or disagree with this view.

2 Imperial and colonial policy

EXTRACT 1

At the 'high politics' level of imperial decision-making, strategic and political calculations were dominant. International rivalries and anxieties about prestige were central. However, this is not to say economic considerations had no place. They did. But they operated at a different and secondary level from governments preoccupied with their global perspectives. At the 'private sector' level, the interests of individuals were decidedly limited and selfish. But they created situations that might force statesmen to make decisions, or situations which they could utilise for their own policies. But there was another level of activity in which policies were handed down from the centre. What drove policy was an effective interaction between 'high politics' and the 'private sector'.

Adapted from *Understanding the British Empire* by Ronald Hyam (2010)

LEARNING OBJECTIVES

In this chapter you will learn about:

- India's administration and defence
- international relations
- colonial policy and the scramble for Africa
- informal empire.

ACTIVITY

Evaluating historical extracts

1. According to Extract 1 what were the driving forces of British imperial policy?
2. As you read this chapter, reflect on the importance of the decisions made by the British government and its representatives in shaping the Empire.

KEY QUESTION

As you read this chapter, consider the following key questions:
- What influenced imperial policy?
- How important was the role of key individuals or groups?

Policy decisions concerning the rule of Britain's overseas territories lay with the elected government and, as in other government areas, a separate office had been created to deal specifically with this. This 'Colonial Office' had been formally established by William Pitt the Younger's government in 1801. It was initially combined with the War Office, but it functioned quite separately from 1854 and was divided into five departments: North America; Australia; West Indies; Africa and Mediterranean and, from 1870, General.

The office was headed by a **Cabinet minister** with the title 'Secretary of State for the Colonies', although he was generally known as the 'Colonial Secretary'. Most politicians saw this office as a stepping-stone to greater things and few served longer than a year or two. The longest-serving colonial secretaries of the 1857 to 1890 period were: the Duke of Newcastle (1859–64), the Earl of Kimberley (1870–74), the Earl of Carnarvon (1874–78), the fifteenth Earl of Derby (1882–85) and Lord Knutsford (1887–92).

In the course of the nineteenth century the work undertaken by the Colonial Office increased enormously, although from the middle of the century, the white settler colonies became more self-governing. The Office had to cope with the demands of territorial acquisitions and 'orders in council' were issued on the advice of law officers in London as a means of administering the Crown colonies without local consultation.

The Colonial Office did not have responsibility for all British possessions overseas, however, and responsibilities varied. Some protectorates and other areas (particularly Egypt and the treaty ports in China) were under the authority of the Foreign Office (headed by the Foreign Secretary). Moreover, from 1858, a separate India Office, with its own Secretary of State, handled Indian and Far Eastern Affairs; this reflected the importance of British involvement in India and the impact of the **Indian Mutiny** of 1857 which had shaken British confidence.

KEY TERM

Cabinet minister: one of a committee of senior ministers responsible for controlling government policy

CROSS-REFERENCE

The Indian Mutiny of 1857 is covered in Chapter 6, pages 51–52.

Administration in the white colonies of settlement

Following the 1838 Durham Report, Britain had moved towards a system of 'responsible government' in the white (settler) colonies, whereby British governors ruled with the support of representative assemblies, appointing ministers who could command a majority. This was the system adopted in Canada in the 1840s, in all but one of the Australian colonies in the 1850s and in New Zealand from 1856. Western Australia (which was the poorest of the Australian colonies) was finally included in 1890 and Cape Colony (South Africa) in 1872. The West Indian colonies, however, remained under direct British rule because the number of voters (who had to be white) was small – white people represented only 1,903 of 456,000 Jamaicans, for example, in 1864.

India's administration and defence

The expansion of British influence in India had originally been overseen by the British East India Company. Under its control, millions of subjects had been added to the British Empire by conquest or annexation, adding vastly to Britain's expenditure on administration and defence. When the first census of the Indian population was taken in 1871, it indicated that at least 236 million lived either directly under British rule, or in states protected by treaties with Britain. The cost of government in India was not far short of that of Britain itself and the army stationed there was considerably larger.

The British East India Company

The East India Company had been granted a **monopoly** over English trade with Asia in 1600. By 1750 it had large bases at Madras, Calcutta and Bombay and was a powerful organisation controlling trade through agreements with local nawabs and rajas (princes). After Robert Clive defeated France (Britain's main rival for control) at the Battle of Plassey in 1757, the Company was to rule India until 1858. It became aggressively expansionist, so provoking the Indian Mutiny of 1857.

KEY TERM

monopoly: means an exclusive right to control trade

CROSS-REFERENCE

The reasons behind the Indian Mutiny are discussed in Chapter 6, pages 51–52.

KEY TERM

sepoys: Indian soldiers serving in the East India Company Army

India's administration

The attempt to control a **mutiny** of Indian **sepoys** serving in the British East India Company Army in India in 1857 hit the British hard. It lasted a year and brought thousands of deaths. The dispatch of British troops to support the East India Company Army demonstrated the British resolve to retain India at all costs. It is not surprising, therefore, that the British government determined that, after the Mutiny had been quelled, a change of rule was necessary to prevent any recurrence. Thus, in 1858, the East India Company handed the running and control of India over to the British government and the Company was entirely dissolved. Queen Victoria informed the Indians: 'We desire to show Our Mercy, by pardoning the Offences of those who have been thus misled'.

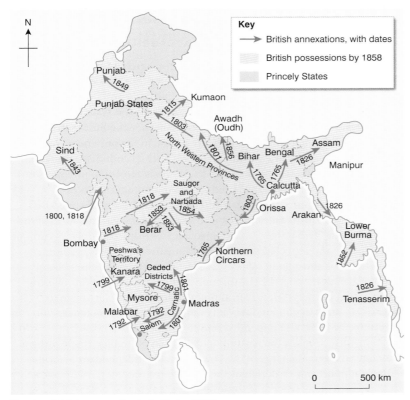

Fig. 1 *British expansion in India by 1858*

The Government of India Act, 1858

By the terms of this Act:
- The East India Company's territories in India were passed to the Queen and the Company ceased to exist.
- The position of Secretary of State for India (a Cabinet post) was created. This Secretary of State received the powers and duties formerly exercised by the East India Company directors.
- A council of 15 members (the India Council), with experience of Indian affairs, was appointed to assist the Secretary of State for India and act as an advisory body in India affairs.
- The Crown appointed a **Viceroy** to replace the Company's Governor-General.
- The Indian Civil Service was placed under the control of the Secretary of State.

Fig. 2 *Queen Victoria is proclaimed Empress of India in 1877*

KEY TERM

Raj: taken from the Hindi term for 'king' or 'rule', formal British rule in India between 1858 and 1947 became known as the British Raj

During the years of the **Raj**, which lasted from 1858 to 1948, the priority for the British government was to maintain its control. On 1 January 1877, Queen Victoria was made Empress of India as a symbol – to both Britain and India – of British domination. Although the Queen never visited India, her title acted as a reminder of Britain's imperial power.

Administration

The Viceroy ruled India with a Legislative Council of five who held responsibility for finance, law, the army, economy and home affairs. In the provinces, the Viceroy was represented by provincial governors (or chief commissioners) with their own legislative councils and on a day-to-day basis across the provinces district officers oversaw local councils and reported on practical issues.

Running the Raj required a vast staff and it was effectively maintained by around a thousand British civil servants who were employed as members of the Indian Civil Service. This professional bureaucracy of British officials was unique within the Empire and attracted some able administrators since a position afforded both status and a good salary. Candidates continued to compete for jobs – as they had done since 1853 – through academic examinations offering open competition for posts. However, although official posts were open to candidates of all races, senior civil servants were virtually all white males.

The running of India also depended on the co-operation, indeed collaboration, of sections of the native population. In particular, the Viceroy relied on native rulers, in charge of the 565 nominally independent Princely States whose support was essential for the smooth running of the subcontinent. Until 1858 a 'doctrine of lapse' had ensured that the Princely States fell under British rule when their rulers' line of descent ended. However, the removal of this doctrine helped ensure the princes' loyalty and although they all accepted the ultimate sovereignty of the British Crown, an elaborate hierarchy of status bolstered the princes' prestige. Within the civil service, bilingual Indians

KEY CHRONOLOGY

Viceroys of India

1858–62	Earl Canning
1862–63	Earl of Elgin
1864–69	Sir John Lawrence
1869–72	Earl of Mayo
1872–76	Lord Northbrook
1880–84	Earl of Dufferin
1884–94	Marquess of Lansdowne

(In 1863 and 1872 there were temporary appointments.)

A CLOSER LOOK

The Viceroy's base was at Government House in Calcutta; however, during the long hot Indian summers the Viceroy's entourage, military attachés, civil servants and British families left the dusty and malarial plains of India and headed for the hills in their thousands. Shimla was declared India's summer capital in 1864 and during the viceroyalty of Lord Lansdowne (1888–94), Viceregal Lodge was built and a narrow-gauged railway was completed to facilitate moving the Raj administration.

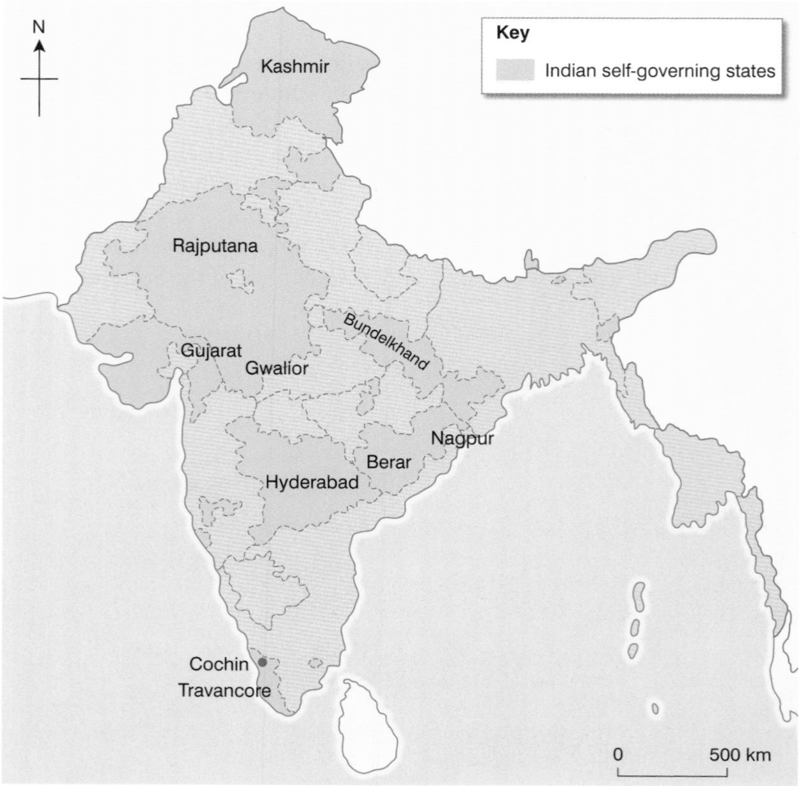

Key
Indian self-governing states

Kashmir
Rajputana
Gujarat
Gwalior
Bundelkhand
Nagpur
Berar
Hyderabad
Cochin
Travancore

0   500 km

Fig. 3 *The make-up of the Indian provinces*

were recruited as low-level clerks across India's 13 provinces. These acted as intermediaries between the British elite and the mass of the population.

India's administration

The eight sizeable provinces of India were Bengal, Bombay, Burma, Central Provinces, Madras, North East Frontier, Punjab and the United Provinces. There was also a number of smaller provinces administered by a Chief Commissioner. The remaining 40 per cent of India was made up of Princely States; these retained native rulers in treaty alliance with Britain which was responsible for their external affairs and defence and also had some influence over general policy. In the major Princely States of Hyderabad, Baroda, Jammu and Kashmir, Mysore and Gwalior, a 'Resident' was installed to oversee affairs on behalf of the Viceroy. In the remaining self-governing states, an 'Agent' represented the Viceroy's interests.

The basic administrative functions performed by this array of officials were the collection of taxes, the maintenance of law and order and the running of the courts. The legal system was developed as the old East India Company courts were merged with Crown Courts and English law prevailed. However, in the years after the Mutiny, greater respect was shown for traditional Indian practices and customs, particularly in relation to marriage and family law. Christian missionaries were actively discouraged but the government accepted responsibility for the promotion of education. British control of India also provided an opportunity for the development of public works' schemes and transport – particularly the building of a great railway network.

From an Indian perspective, the replacement of Company rule by Crown control brought little tangible difference. Englishmen (and often the same ones as under Company rule) still ran the subcontinent, or local princes exercised power on behalf of the Raj.

Some sections of the Indian population, however, showed increasing political awareness and the formation of the Indian National Congress in 1885 reflected this. Its members met to discuss public affairs and although it was not set up to challenge British rule, it offered a forum for debate and criticism in which a demand for a greater role for Indians in government became increasingly strident.

CROSS-REFERENCE

Chapter 6 discusses the development of education, public works and the building of railways in the aftermath of the Indian Mutiny.

ACTIVITY

Extension

To learn more about the Raj and the hierarchy and duties of British administrators, read E.M. Forster's *A Passage to India* which was based on Forster's visit to India in 1912.

ACTIVITY

Copy this diagram and annotate it with details of the role played by each group or individual in Indian administration.

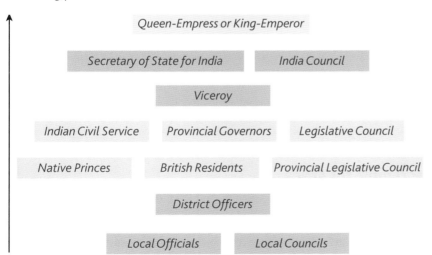

Fig. 4 *This diagram shows the administrative and power hierarchy in the Raj*

A CLOSER LOOK

Being a native member of the Indian Army brought advantages and prestige. Many Hindu families in the Punjab changed their name to Singh which was a name used by members of the Sikh religion. Suggesting an association with the Sikhs helped maximise their sons' chances of being accepted for a military career.

A CLOSER LOOK

Indian troops were sometimes deliberately deployed abroad in order to lessen the risk of rebellion in India. For example, in late 1859, 10,000 Indian troops were sent to Shanghai during the Second Opium War against China. They were also useful as a cheap supply of ready-trained troops and 7000 were sent to Egypt to suppress Colonel Arabi Pasha's Revolt in 1882 (see Chapter 1, page 6).

India's defence

The very evident risk to British lives, interests and investments posed by the 1857 Mutiny showed that Britain's controlling influence over India could not be taken for granted. Consequently, from 1858, efforts were made to strengthen the British Indian Army which, at the outbreak of the Mutiny, had numbered fewer than 40,000 British troops. The East India Company's armies were brought under the control of the Crown and the proportion of British to Indian troops raised to a ratio of roughly 1:2. There was an army of 70,000 Britons and 125,000 native troops by the late 1880s.

The regiments of **native Indian troops** were trained and stationed in their own districts and cut off from one another to prevent any sense of unity. They were also deliberately mixed, by **caste** and religion. The army enlisted greater numbers of Gurkhas and Sikhs (from Nepal and the Punjab respectively), who had been loyal to Britain during the Mutiny, replacing Bengali troops which had not. Indeed, 62 of 74 Bengali regiments were disbanded and the high-caste Brahmin regiments, which had also acted independently, disappeared. To reduce the risk of rebellion further, the number of British officers was increased and all field artillery was placed in British hands. Moreover, Indians were placed under British commanders and denied officer ranking, although the British were ordered to show greater respect to sepoy beliefs and traditions.

A CLOSER LOOK

The caste system

Hindus traditionally have been divided at birth into particular social strata known as castes. There is a hierarchy of castes: the lowest ranks are the Dalits or Untouchables who have traditionally suffered much discrimination, while the Brahmin are the highest or priestly caste. Some historians believe that the caste system was actually intensified by British imperial rule, which institutionalised the treatment of different castes as part of the system of government.

The growth of the railways also helped India's defence: 3000 miles of track were added in the decade following the Mutiny, exaggerating British presence and enabling swifter deployment of troops in the event of trouble. An armoured gun train was introduced for mobile enforcement purposes, while the first Viceroy, Lord Canning, set up an Imperial Police Force as an extra layer of security and, no doubt, to avoid over-reliance on the army.

ACTIVITY

Draw a diagram to show the changes to the Indian Army and defence that took place after the Indian Mutiny. You might like to illustrate this by finding photographs online of Indian soldiers during the Raj.

International relations, colonial policy and the scramble for Africa

By the later nineteenth century, Britain was becoming increasingly concerned about its position in relation to other European powers. Having dominated the seas (and consequently enjoyed considerable world influence) for the past 200 years, it began to face a challenge from other expanding and industrialising powers. In 1871 Germany was united as a single country and became a new powerhouse in Europe. With its huge supply of natural resources and favourable geographical location in the centre of Europe, it soon began to show its industrial potential and German merchant ships made an increasing appearance on the High Seas.

Fig. 5 *Indian soldiers at Portsmouth Dock Yard waiting to be shipped to Egypt in 1882*

Although defeated by Germany in 1871, France transformed its armed forces thereafter and rapidly recovered, with a new determination to assert its 'rightful place' in the world. The Russians, too, although considerably less industrially advanced, started to transform their economy, extending their control into central Asia so that, by 1884, Russia had taken its empire to the borders of Afghanistan. What is more, the Russians began constructing a railway network which, the British feared, could carry an army to challenge the British position in India.

The naval building programmes of France and Russia also caused concern in the 1880s, although the threat from Germany was not to become acute until the last decade of the century. Naval power gave other nations the means with which to explore areas, for example in Asia and Africa, where previously the British had faced no serious competition. In South East Asia, the French established a foothold in Indo-China in the 1860s and began to push north – where they were joined by Germans also seeking commercial concessions. Furthermore, Russia appeared set on imperial expansion in the north of China. Work on the Trans-Siberian Railway would begin in 1891.

The British response to the French activity in Indo-China was to annex territory in Malaya (from 1874) extending British influence beyond its existing base in Singapore (established in 1819). Britain also took Sarawak, North Borneo (1881), Brunei (1885) and Upper Burma (1885), leaving Thailand as a buffer between the rival European powers.

The impact of the Great Depression on the industrialising countries of Europe also encouraged new interest in expansion in Africa, where markets for manufactured goods and new sources of raw materials might be found, quite apart from the prestige of acquiring overseas territories. The French became considerably more active in Africa in the 1880s, expanding beyond their old coastal settlements, while the Germans began making annexations from 1884 in the south-west and western regions.

The scramble for Africa

As a result of international developments, two conferences were held to facilitate Europeans' access to, and control over, African territory: the Brussels Conference of 1876 and the Berlin Conference of 1884 to 1885, which is often regarded as the beginnings of 'the scramble for Africa'.

The Brussels Conference, 1876

In 1876, King Leopold of Belgium hosted a conference of explorers and leaders from geographical societies across Europe. This Brussels Conference was motivated largely by the desire to protect Belgian interests in the Congo; it concluded that:

- Africans were incapable of developing the natural resources to be found in central Africa. European intervention was therefore necessary.
- The routes to Africa's great lakes needed to be developed by building roads or railways.
- An International African Association should be established to coordinate the Europeans' efforts.

The co-operation that the Conference supposedly promoted actually heightened competition as European governments were suspicious of Leopold's intentions. The International African Association hired Henry Morton Stanley (from Britain's Royal Geographical Society) to advise in the Congo region but it soon became apparent that Leopold was intent on establishing his own **Congo empire**. The French hired an Italian-born explorer, Pierre de Brazza, to stake their own claims to the region, while the German government hired the explorer Gustav Nachtigal to assert influence. France extended its control from Senegal into Western Sudan in 1879 and Portugal asserted its claims to control the mouth of the Congo River in 1884.

The Berlin Conference, 1884–85

Fig. 6 *An artist's depiction of the Berlin Conference*

By 1884, a scramble for territory had already begun. Although 80 per cent of Africa was still under local control, with the European powers largely restricted to the coastal areas, the need for some regulation had become apparent. It was the German Chancellor, Otto von Bismarck, who initiated and hosted the Berlin Conference, from 1884 to 1885. This was attended by the foreign ministers of 14 European states as well as the USA but France, Germany, Great Britain, and Portugal were the major players since they controlled most of colonial Africa at the time.

The Conference's initial task involved securing agreement that both the basins and mouths of the Congo and Niger rivers were to remain neutral and open to trade. Thereafter, representatives of the major powers negotiated their respective claims to territory which were formally mapped out into recognised spheres of influence across the whole of Africa. The Conference concluded with the signing of a General Act, which promised:

KEY TERM

Indigenous: native or born in the area

A CLOSER LOOK

Leopold's Congo empire

The explorer H.M. Stanley surveyed the basin of the Upper Congo River in order to establish King Leopold's own imperial enclave in central Africa. In November 1879, Leopold's International African Association was renamed the International Association of the Congo. Stanley signed over 450 treaties with local chiefs to establish Leopold's sovereignty over their territories, which became known as the Congo Free State from May 1885. It remained Leopold's private African kingdom until 1908.

- All nations should be permitted to trade in the basin of the Congo and its outlets.
- There should be **free trade** in these regions.
- The powers with influence in the area should help protect indigenous people and suppress the slave trade.
- The powers should support and protect religious, scientific or charitable undertakings, Christian missionaries, scientists and explorers.
- If any power took possession of further land on the coasts of the Africa it should notify the signatories of the Act, in order to enable them to assert any claims of their own.

The principle established was known as '**effective occupation**'. A European power could assert a claim to land that it 'effectively' occupied and notify other powers. Only if another power could put in a rival claim was its right to colonise questioned. This General Act triggered a further scramble for territory across Africa and, by 1900, 90 per cent of the continent was in European hands.

The Conference was a success in terms of European relations, enabling European countries to expand their empires in an ordered fashion and without the risk of conflict with one another. Africa acted as a safety-valve for Europe; historian A.J.P. Taylor has referred to the continent as a 'safe arena' for competing countries where, thanks to its size, they were unlikely to tread on each other's toes in pursuit of land or prestige. However, the Berlin Conference and General Act did little for the indigenous populations. There was no African representation at the Berlin Conference and European ministers mapped out spheres of influence with little concern for natural borders or ethnic, linguistic or religious division.

Furthermore, despite the apparently good intentions, in the following years there was no concerted effort to combat the African or Arab slave trade, nor was much attention given to indigenous concerns. The well-being and religious customs of locals were frequently overlooked.

KEY TERM

free trade: a market system whereby goods are both imported and exported without restriction or imposition of tariffs

effective occupation: a European power which could demonstrate that it had a local treaty agreement and an active administration and was able to police the territory it claimed, was recognised as the rightful ruler of that territory

EXTRACT 2

The colonial powers superimposed their domains on the African Continent. The African politico-geographical map became a permanent liability that resulted from three months of ignorant, greedy acquisitiveness, during a period when Europe's search for minerals and markets had become insatiable. The European colonial powers shared one objective in their African colonies: exploitation. In the way they governed their dependencies, they reflected their differences. Some colonial powers were themselves democracies (the United Kingdom and France); others were dictatorships (Portugal, Spain). The British established a system of indirect rule over much of their domain, leaving indigenous power structures in place and making local rulers representatives of the British Crown.

Adapted from *Geography: Realms, Regions and Concepts* by H.J. de Blij and Peter O. Muller (2003)

EXTRACT 3

Colonisation was not produced by any blind 'structural forces' but was consciously decided by men; historical human agents working for a variety of motives and reasons. And the men who made the ultimate historical decisions on the partition of Africa were neither industrialists nor other capitalists, nor lobbyists, but holders of state power. They were sovereigns, top ministers and a handful of high officials in the major European countries. The partition of Africa was essentially a state action, not a private venture. If there is one conclusion which emerges from the extensive study of diplomatic correspondence, it is that the men who embodied the official mind were not thinking as much in terms of rates of profit and monetary inputs and outputs, as in terms of power and prestige and, ultimately, war and peace. It is not for nothing that the historians of diplomacy are fond of speaking of the 'chessboard of European power politics'.

Adapted from 'The Partition of Africa – A Scramble for a Mirage?' by Juhani Koponen (1993)

 PRACTICE QUESTION

Evaluating historical extracts

With reference to Extracts 1 and 3 and your understanding of the historical context, which of these two extracts provides the more convincing interpretation of British imperial expansion in the nineteenth century?

 PRACTICE QUESTION

Evaluating historical extracts

Using your understanding of the historical context, assess how convincing the arguments in Extracts 1, 2 and 3 are, in relation to the driving forces shaping British imperial policy in the years 1857 to 1890.

Informal empire

It is more difficult to determine the extent of the British Empire by 1890 than might be thought. This is because, in addition to Britain's Crown colonies and protectorates, there were also areas over which Britain had no legal claim, but which formed part of what is described as its 'informal empire'. The informal empire comprised places influenced by British power, particularly economic power, sealed through free trade agreements or by British investment in the country. Most frequently, British influence derived from commerce, financed by British capital, carried in British ships and providing profits for British companies, bankers and insurance firms. These strong links sometimes led to areas becoming settled by British citizens and adopting English culture or language.

Commercial agreements extended Britain's informal empire into Latin America, in particular Chile and **Argentina**. British public capital in Latin America stood at over £80 million by 1865 and Latin America accounted for 10 per cent of Britain's exports and imports in the second half of the nineteenth century. A British City financer, Charles Morrison, acquired the Mercantile Bank of the River Plate in Argentina in 1881 and invested directly in the country's utilities; this prompted the US consul in Buenos Aires to claim: 'it almost seems that the English have the preference in everything pertaining to the business and business interests of the country. They are "in" everything, except politics, as intimately as though it were a British colony.' British citizens lived an elite lifestyle in Buenos Aires, with their own institutions and way of life.

Sometimes the acquisition of informal empire required threats or the use of force. For example, pressure was put on Mexico in 1861 to keep access open and to uphold free trade treaties, while the threat of the Royal Navy ensured compliance in Peru and Chile in 1857 and 1863 respectively.

In the East, Siam (Thailand) was brought under British influence through trade treaties, as was Iran in the Middle East. The weak **Chinese Empire** was also forced to make concessions to Britain, which used its naval power to

threaten attempts to disrupt its lucrative opium trade from India to China. By the Treaties of Nanking (1842) and Tientsin (1858), the British gained trading bases, for example at Shanghai, as well as other islands, such as Hong Kong. These were settled with British people, governed under British laws and operated outside Chinese control.

In 1863, Robert Hart was appointed as the head of the Chinese Imperial Maritime Customs Office, which acted as a branch of the Chi'ing government, with the purpose of protecting British interests. In such ways, parts of China joined Britain's informal empire, and the British gained unhindered access to Chinese markets. A similar pattern was evident in Afghanistan in 1879; in this case, the threat of full invasion secured the Treaty of Gandamak, which provided Britain with strategic territorial gains and control over Afghanistan's foreign policy.

Elsewhere, territories of vital strategic importance fell under British influence through diplomatic pressure and the appointment of key advisers. So, for example, Britain was able to exercise its influence on the Sultanate of Zanzibar in East Africa, an area which commanded the African coast of the Indian Ocean, through the activities of the trader John Kirk. As a result, in 1891, a government was established which made the Sultan's first minister a British representative.

Of course, the economies of the 'informal empire' did not revolve exclusively around Great Britain and in these areas Britain had no ultimate authority. Indeed, there were times when the British were unable to assert their influence, but, for the most part, informal empire meant that Britain was able to enjoy power around the world without the costs of responsibility.

Summary

British imperial and colonial policy was influenced by a mixture of central government concerns, including the ever-present need to ensure peace and stability within Britain's territories by ensuring effective administration and defence, and local concerns, often of a commercial nature. Increasingly, in the course of the nineteenth century, international pressures also came to play a part, and nowhere was this more the case than in Africa. Alongside the formal establishment and protection of empire went a third strand too. Informal empire was, in some respects, a useful 'halfway house', whereby the British government reaped strategic and commercial advantages at little cost. Informal empire did, however, rely on Britain's ability to command the seas and back up its claims, if necessary, by force.

 PRACTICE QUESTION

To what extent was imperial and colonial policy in the years 1857 to 1890 influenced by international pressures?

A CLOSER LOOK

Britain and China

British informal empire in China was a product of British formal control of India. It originally stemmed from the need to finance the activities of the British East India Company through the sale of opium to the Chinese. This led to two Opium Wars between Britain and China, the second of which resulted in the granting of five cities to the British.

CROSS-REFERENCE

For more on the trading activities of John Kirk, look ahead to Chapter 4, page 32.

STUDY TIP

As in all essays, you will need to provide a balanced answer which weighs up the importance of international pressures and compares these against other factors that were influencing policy at this time. You could look at your findings to the activity on Britain's imperial rivals as a starting point. You will probably want to highlight the changes in international pressures that occurred between 1857 and 1890. Whatever your argument, ensure you provide plenty of precise examples to support your comments.

3 Trade and Commerce

EXTRACT 1

One imperial end was basic to all others: profit. Many nobler and subtler motives played their part and many passionate imperialists did not stand to gain at all, but the deepest impulse of empire was the impulse to be rich. It had always been so. Romantics saw the empire as a **cornucopia** from which good things flowed along the seaways to their islands – gold and furs from the western possessions, gold, skins, diamonds, wine and feathers from the south, silk, rice, tea and precious stones from the east, ivory from Africa and food from all quarters. Wool, wood, rubber, cotton, tin, iron ore, zinc – all these essentials of British prosperity, produced within the Empire, flowed back to Britain in a safe, sure stream. Around a third of all miners and quarrymen in the world worked in imperial soil.

Adapted from *Pax Britannica* by Jan Morris (1968)

ACTIVITY

Evaluating historical extracts

What interpretation of empire is offered in Extract 1? With reference to what you have read so far, would you agree or disagree with this interpretation?

Trade and commerce

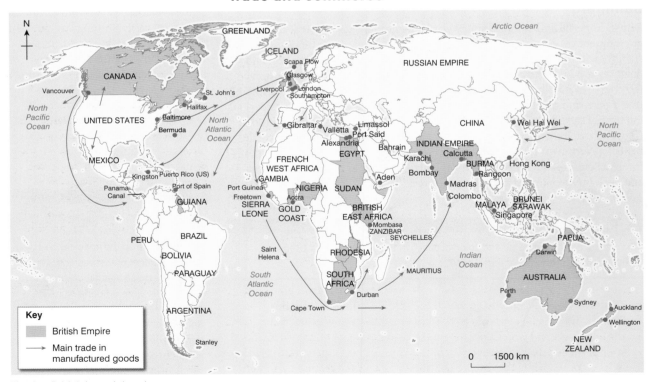

Fig. 1 *British imperial trade routes*

Expanding trade and commerce was one of the defining features of the Empire in the years 1857 to 1890. In the eighteenth century, the trade and commerce of the Empire had been strictly regulated in a system of '**mercantilism**'.

whereby colonies had been obliged to send most of their produce to Britain, to buy British manufactured goods, and use British ships for both their imports and exports. In the first half of the nineteenth century, this highly regulated **protectionist** system had been dismantled, under the influence of new theories of 'free trade', as advocated in Adam Smith's influential book, *The Wealth of Nations*. In this he argued that wealth was indefinitely expandable and freedom from commercial restrictions was the only way to maximise prosperity.

Britain was able to indulge this theory thanks to its position as **the world's foremost trading nation**, and from the middle of the nineteenth century, British trade was left free from government trading restrictions. The government was, however, active in supporting free trade agreements around the world and was ready to resort to threats, and sometimes outright coercion, to achieve them. Sometimes other nations were willing to grant them; where they were reluctant – as in the case of China in the **Opium Wars** – the British Navy could always be relied upon to enforce British terms. Economic dominance was thus sustained by a limited application of force; an approach sometimes referred to as the 'imperialism of free trade'.

Of course, not all British trade was with its colonies, but there was always a concern that non-colonial trade could be restricted – as happened during the American Civil War – whereas colonial markets would remain open. Furthermore, colonies wanted to continue trading with Britain, partly out of a sense of loyalty, or perhaps a feeling of duty to do so, but also because it was easier. Trading patterns had been well established and, at least as far as commerce was concerned, the countries of the Empire used a common language and a common or tied currency and shared a common system of commercial law. Borrowing in the London capital markets was also cheaper because lenders had faith in the reliability of British possessions.

Fig. 2 *Unloading tea at the British East India Docks in London, 1860s*

The coming of free trade saw imperial trade and investment grow enormously, creating an 'industrial empire' in which the colonies supplied both the foodstuffs and the raw materials which British industry converted into finished goods for export and which, very often, the colonies bought back. In the third quarter of the nineteenth century, around 20 per cent of Britain's imports came from its colonies, while the Empire provided a market for around a third of British exports. The City of London became the world's financial capital as British investment overseas increased and sterling became the main currency of international trade. Also supporting this growth in trade were technological improvements in railways, steamships, underwater cables and telegraph lines as well as innovations in banking and company organisation.

KEY TERMS

mercantilism: a system of regulations governing trade

protectionist: using tariffs – particularly duties on imported goods to regulate trade

CROSS-REFERENCE

The pressure applied by Britain to China during the Opium Wars is outlined in Chapter 2, page 21.

A CLOSER LOOK

Britain, the world's foremost trading nation

By 1857, Britain was the most industrially advanced country in the world. Its factories were producing heavy iron goods and textiles for a global market – everything from railway stock to clothing and buckles. Britain's urbanisation, in turn, had increased its reliance on imports from overseas. Britain was the world's largest consumer market for food and raw materials. Tropical goods came to Britain from the plantations of the West Indies, the Malayan Straits settlements and West Africa; minerals and wool were imported from Australia, raw cotton from India and timber and wheat from Canada. Industrial Britain thus lent on its colonies to feed and provide for its workforce.

ACTIVITY

Mount a large map of the British Empire on your classroom wall and, working in pairs or small groups, choose a colonial country or area each. Research your area's main trading products – both imports and exports. Then use threads and notices to show the trading products of the areas investigated on your wall map.

While Britain adopted free trade, there was no internal free trade between colonies and the self-governing 'settler' colonies were permitted to adopt protective tariff systems of their own. The first Colonial Conference of 1887 discussed the issue of whether there should be some special trading preference between colonies – creating a 'free trade empire' – but this was turned down by Britain. Several colonies, beginning with Canada in 1859, and subsequently Australia in the 1860s, chose to impose tariffs against imported manufactures (including those from Britain) from the 1850s in order to protect their own growing industries.

The infrastructure of trade

British capital and technology were used to ensure that the Empire had an adequate infrastructure to facilitate trade and maximise profits. Ever more efficient cargo ships were built for the carriage of goods, while ports and harbours were extended and developed to accept such shipping and enable the loading and unloading of goods to take place with the minimum of delay. The British also developed railway systems wherever they went and they extended river transport and canals where necessary to make the internal transport of goods to the ports both faster and more cost-effective.

Clipper ships

The boom years of clipper ships began c1843 as a result of the Treaty of Nanking (see Chapter 2, page 21) and the growing demand for tea from China. However, their predominance was short-lived and after the opening of the Suez Canal in 1869, they rapidly declined in number.

Ships and shipping

Sailing ships reached their highest state of efficiency in the 1860s, with **clippers** sailing all over the world, and in particular on the route to China and the East. These fast ships were ideally suited to low-volume, high-profit goods, such as tea, opium and spices and they were also used to carry mail and people. Competition among the clippers was fierce, and their times were recorded in newspapers. However, the ships had a short life-expectancy and usually had to be broken up after about 20 years of use.

For bulky and heavy goods needing to be carried across oceans and up rivers, steamships were used. British iron-hulled ocean-going ships were made more efficient by the development of the compound steam engine in the 1850s (which consumed less coal than earlier vessels) and this enabled steam ships to trade economically with distant possessions. From the 1850s, steamship companies reduced the travel time between Great Britain and West Africa to less than three weeks and increased their cargo capacity considerably. The opening of the Suez Canal in 1869 and development of the triple expansion steam engine in the 1870s further stimulated the construction of steam carriers. Steamships were also used in inland regions. By the 1870s, several British companies were sending steam-trading vessels up the Niger, for example.

Railways

Historians sometimes speak of British 'railway imperialism', since the building of railways, which was key to economic development, ensured British control. The British provided the investment, the engineers and the rolling stock and the colonies' resulting dependence on Britain could be used to pressurise governments. For example, Canada was forced to accept British policies on defence in the mid-1860s, as the price of London capital guarantees.

Railways provided the largest single investment of the period in the self-governing colonies of Canada, Australia and New Zealand and South Africa; they opened up the Canadian prairies, enabled Australia to export its wheat and wool and offered South Africa a chance to expand its territories and commercial interests into the interior. In India, whilst railways may have been built with a strategic purpose in mind, they also linked the cotton and jute-growing areas of the north with the mills of Bombay and Calcutta and enabled rice to reach ports for export.

In less developed areas, such as West Africa, railways provided the vital link between the interior areas of production and the sea. In short, railways were themselves a trading commodity, investment in railways provided '**invisible trade**' for Britain and the spread of railways within the Empire facilitated commercial enterprise. Peter Mathias has written:

KEY TERM

invisible trade: the provision of services or investment overseas; money made in this way is referred to as 'invisible earnings'

Fig. 3   *Construction of the Suez railway, 1857*

EXTRACT 2

The greatly increased flow of capital abroad from the 1850s, was dominated by railway-building and the scale of investment in relation to national income reveals its importance. A great surge of foreign investment took place in 1886–1890 when the outflow of money was greater than that into investment at home. A clear link developed between the export of capital and rising British export trades. In the first three-quarters of the nineteenth century, Britain was the only country with a large low-cost iron industry and modernised engineering industry from which the capital equipment associated with the export of capital could be purchased. Although, from the 1870s, loans were not usually tied legally to the purchase of British equipment as they had been earlier, British exporters still profited and were sometimes paid in the shares of the railways they supplied. On the import side, the effects of foreign lending on the pattern of trade were even clearer. Railway-building was instrumental in opening up vast land-masses and developing export sectors in primary produce – foodstuffs, hides, wool and metals – for Britain.

Adapted from *The First Industrial Nation* by Peter Mathias (2001)

ACTIVITY

Evaluating historical extracts

According to Mathias in Extract 2, how did railways contribute to the growth of British trade?

CROSS-REFERENCE

The role of explorers and exploration in the expansion of the Empire is discussed in Chapter 4, pages 31–33.

ACTIVITY

Extension

You might like to collect some pictures and further information about the transport systems that supported the Empire in the middle third of the nineteenth century. You could start with clipper ships – and if possible, visit the *Cutty Sark* in London, which was the last example of these to survive.

Canals and rivers

Internal river systems were an important means of transport for trading products and were often the focus of **explorers**' quests to discover what lay behind the more easily accessible coastal areas of continents such as Africa. To facilitate trade, rivers sometimes had to be straightened, diverted and deepened. Elsewhere canals might be built to avoid hazardous stretches of water or provide waterways where there were none.

In India, for example, new canals were developed on a huge scale after 1857. In Canada, after 1867, canals were deepened around the St Lawrence/ Great Lakes seaway system and the Welland Canal was built to overcome height differences between Lakes Eyrie and Ontario.

The products of trade and commerce
Agriculture

Most colonial economies, with the possible exception of India which had some small-scale industrial development, were naturally agricultural. In Canada,

Australia and New Zealand, for example, there were vast tracts of land permitting the production of cheap foodstuffs and agricultural raw materials such as wool. These colonies produced goods that were available in Europe, but at a cheaper price.

The tropical colonies, such as South Africa, produced goods that were not available in Britain such as sugar, coffee, cocoa, groundnuts, copra (from coconuts) and palm oil. Although the production in these areas was small-scale, often an addition to local subsistence farming, native farmers were generally willing to sell at whatever price they were offered – and sometimes these fell very low.

Elsewhere, products might be grown on plantations, run by the British. For example Indian 'coolies' were transported to work in the West Indian colonies for fixed periods – usually five years – in return for their transport. Some were also taken to South Africa. There were plantations for sisal in Kenya and Tanganyika, for coffee and tea in Ceylon and Kenya, for **tea in India**, for sugar in Mauritius and Natal, for rubber and palm oil in Malaya and North Borneo, for coconuts (copra) in the Solomon Islands, and for sugar in Fiji and in Queensland, Australia. Workers were often paid low wages for hard, unpleasant work.

A CLOSER LOOK

Indian tea

Perhaps the most renowned Indian crop was tea (grown in Darjeeling and Assam) following the plant's importation from China. In the aftermath of the Mutiny, Britons sought to expand the tea trade by extending tea-growing across the subcontinent. New plantations were established at Coonoor in the Nilgiri Hills by Henry Mann and by James Taylor in Ceylon in the 1860s, and by Arthur Hall at Nelliampathy in Kerala in the 1870s. Tea became the cheapest and most popular drink amongst Britons before the close of the nineteenth century.

ACTIVITY

Study the table below which shows the value of British imports from India before and after the establishment of the Raj in 1858. What might you conclude from these figures?

British imports from India	Value in 1854	Value in 1876
Raw cotton	£1,642,000	£5,875,000
Raw jute	£510,000	£2,799,000
Tea	£24,000	£2,429,000
Wheat	£0	£1,647,000

CROSS-REFERENCE

The influx of migrants destabilised the Transvaal, and thus contributed to the outbreak of the Boer War of 1899–1902, which will be covered in Chapter 12, page 115.

The importance of diamond mining in Africa is discussed in Chapter 4.

Mining

One of the motives behind European expansion had been the desire to discover precious metals and these became an important trading commodity. Tin in Nigeria, gold along the Gold Coast and diamonds in Sierra Leone had all helped develop these colonies. The discovery of further mineral deposits in central and south Africa brought further colonial growth. Copper was found in what was to become Northern Rhodesia and coal and gold in Southern Rhodesia.

However, the discovery which captured most attention in Britain was that of gold in South Africa. In 1886, gold deposits were found on the Witwatersrand. This prompted a gold rush to the previously struggling, rather poor, Dutch-**Boer** republic of the Transvaal. At the very time tin mines were closing down in Cornwall, the Transvaal gold mines required skilled labourers and over 30,000 travelled there from Britain. Such an **influx of migrants** encouraged British ambitions in the area. Expectations were fuelled further by the discovery of **diamonds** in the area, which led to the formation of the Kimberley Diamond syndicate in 1890.

Gold was also discovered in New South Wales, Australia in 1851, and by 1866 Victoria was producing £124 million worth of gold – a third of the then total world production. New South Wales produced a further £25 million worth. However, the Australian mines began to run dry in 1860s, after the first Australian gold rush, although there was a later wave of discoveries in the 1880s around Kalgoorlie in Western Australia. More gold deposits were discovered on the west coast of South Island, New Zealand in the 1860s.

KEY TERM

Boers: Dutch population which settled in South Africa in the late 1600s

Fig. 4 *The Kimberley diamond mines, South Africa, in the 1870s*

Industry

There was limited development of industry in the colonies, partly because many had a very small internal market and partly because they could not compete in a world market with British manufacture. In India, for example, where there was a large local demand, native mills could not compete in price with imported British textiles.

Whether the system of trade and commerce established by the British was advantageous or disadvantageous for the peoples of the Empire remains an area for debate. On the one hand, undeveloped areas were propelled to modernise, thanks to British capital and technology but, on the other, their independent economic development was curbed by the way that the British controlled and exploited their economies. Consider the two views below:

EXTRACT 3

Britain in its economic heyday provided benefits which no other imperial power could match and to which the colonists would not have had the same access had they not been part of the Empire. Britain was then the world's leading source of both technology and capital. It was also the most important trading and shipping centre. Britain could provide every economic service that colonies might need. Moreover colonies could buy some of these services in

Britain more cheaply than foreign states could do. Britain was probably even more important as a market than as a lender. For a young colonial economy, whether a colony of settlement or a tropical dependency recently linked to the international trading world, Britain was the key to establishing profitable export staples, which in turn provided the resources that could be used to create an effective infrastructure.

Adapted from 'For Richer, for Poorer?' by David Fieldhouse (1996)

EXTRACT 4

It is sometimes said that the British Empire fostered globalisation, overseas investment and free trade and – in the long run – this raised levels of prosperity all round. Possibly so: but individual human beings do not live by the free market alone and nor do they live in the long run. The immediate impact of British imperial free-trading was often the collapse of local indigenous industries which were in no position to compete, and a consequent destruction of livelihoods and communities. This points to the tension at the heart of empire. Its exponents may seek (as many Britons genuinely did) to make the world a better place, but they also want to dominate. The Victorians wanted to spread the gospel of free trade, but they also wanted to continue being the premier workshop of the world.

Adapted from *Empire* by Niall Ferguson (2008)

 PRACTICE QUESTION

Evaluating historical extracts

With reference to Extracts 3 and 4 and your understanding of the historical context, which of these two extracts provides the more convincing interpretation of the impact of trade and commerce in the British Empire in the years c1857 to c1890?

 PRACTICE QUESTION

Evaluating historical extracts

Using your understanding of the historical context, assess how convincing the arguments in Extracts 1, 2 and 4 are, in relation to the benefits of trade for Britain and the Empire in the years c1857 to c1890.

STUDY TIP

These three extracts offer a variety of views on the importance of trade within the Empire. Apply your own knowledge to assess them and try to comment on whether each is totally convincing, reasonably convincing or unconvincing. You must, of course, provide some precise historical detail to support your views.

The role of the chartered companies

A CLOSER LOOK

Chartered companies before 1857

In the seventeenth century, the world's leading economy had been India, and the royal chartered East India Company had been established to gain access to India's merchandise and markets. Other **chartered companies** followed. Such companies were government-recognised commercial organisations which were granted monopoly rights to a specific territory's resources in return for its administration.

However, by the nineteenth century Britain had become the dominant trading power, and free trade was considered the best means of assuring

Fig. 5 *A British Colonial Rupee used by the British East Africa Company*

Britain's global economic leadership. In that spirit, in 1841, Lord Palmerston had asserted that 'it is the business of the government to open and secure the roads for the merchant, but no more.' The advent of free trade, together with the Indian Mutiny of 1857, brought an end to these chartered companies and to the East India Company in particular.

Chartered companies had been the normal means of organising trade in the colonies until the mid-1850s. The government allowed trading to proceed at its own pace in the 1850s and 1860s, seeing competition between rival companies as a healthy sign of successful capitalism. However, attitudes changed in the 1870s, when Britain's economic supremacy faced challenges in the form of both European and American industrialisation and the onset of the **Great Depression**. The idea of the chartered company was thus revived as a way of extending British trade and control (at no cost to the government).

In 1881, the North Borneo Trading Company received a charter for the purposes of administering the territory. North Borneo benefited from deposits of coal, iron and copper besides the development of tobacco and coffee plantations. It also represented a key strategic site for Britain in the South China Sea at something of a mid-point between India and Hong Kong.

This charter set a precedent which was subsequently followed by the granting of charters to:
- the National African Company, renamed Royal Niger Company (1886). This charter not only permitted trade in the lands alongside the Niger and Benue rivers but also gave permission for expansion northwards and, crucially, for the company to serve as a government of the Niger region.
- the Imperial British East Africa Company (1888)
- the British South Africa Company (1889).

Supporting this development of chartered companies was the Imperial Federation League. This was founded in Britain in 1884 to promote colonial unity and rapidly established branches throughout the country, attracting the support of the business community.

Summary

ACTIVITY

Summary

Make a chart headed with three columns headed Empire, Trade and Comment. List the main colonial territories mentioned in this chapter in the left hand column; give examples of their trade and commerce in the second column and add any comments, for example on how trade led to territorial expansion and/or the benefit of their trade to Britain or the colony itself, in the third.

 PRACTICE QUESTION

'Trade with Britain was of great benefit to those living in the Empire in the years 1857 to 1890'. Explain why you agree or disagree with this view.

KEY TERM

chartered companies: a trading company would gain status, legal rights and privileges on award of a royal charter; among its privileges were 'monopoly' or total rights which would prevent any competitors from challenging its position; such a company would be granted permission to rule indirectly within its territory of operation

KEY TERM

Great Depression: this was a worldwide economic slump beginning in c1873 and lasting until c1896. During this period, prices fell and trade slumped, while manufacturers experienced falling profits and investment

CROSS-REFERENCE

The part played by individual merchant-imperialists in the establishment and expansion of the companies mentioned here will be found in Chapter 4, pages 35–37.

STUDY TIP

Make a plan before you begin this essay; you could create a bullet point list of the benefits of trade to those living in the British Empire in these years and another of the disadvantages of, or even harm caused by, reliance on trade with Britain. The number of points you are able to make should help you to decide which way you will argue. Remember you need to show an awareness of both viewpoints but you should muster sufficient evidence to offer a judgement as to why you agree or disagree with the statement.

4 Attitudes to empire — the role and influence of individuals

LEARNING OBJECTIVES

In this chapter you will learn about:

- the roles of explorers, missionaries, traders and colonial administrators

- how these individuals and groups influenced attitudes to the British Empire.

KEY QUESTION

As you read this chapter, consider the following key questions:
- What influenced imperial policy?
- How important was the role of key individuals and groups and how were they affected by developments?

EXTRACT 1

In the nineteenth century, people had the capacity to get overseas and to do things when they arrived – trade, explore, preach, settle – and so they did. There were serious risks, but enough people considered them acceptable, especially as technology and science combined to increase their chances of surviving sea voyages, disease, and hostile natives and environments. Others were simply desperate enough – for survival or for glory – to try. There was a world out there to be acted upon, fortunes to be won, lands to be conquered, curiosity to be satisfied, souls to be saved. Increasingly, as hazards of climate, distance and resistance were mastered, it became a British world, and to be a Briton abroad within the Empire's bounds became an exalted status.

From *The British Empire, A Very Short Introduction* by Ashley Jackson (2013)

ACTIVITY

Evaluating historical extracts

According to Jackson, in Extract 1, why did the British engage in imperial expansion?

The British Empire expanded from 1857 in a piecemeal fashion, as individuals sought out the opportunities it had to offer. Such individuals might venture overseas for a variety of reasons: scientific impulse and the pure thrill of exploration; moral compunction and a belief in a Christian duty to 'spread the word to the heathen'; desire for wealth and profits or maybe for the power and status that accompanied lucrative imperial administrative posts. So, for example, a small settlement first established for strategic purposes increasingly attracted traders, in the wake of which explorers or missionaries might arrive and, as the settlement grew, independent and ambitious administrators. There was no central plan for empire and it has even been suggested that it was acquired almost by accident. This may be over-stating the position but there is no doubt that individuals played a major role in Britain's incessant imperial growth.

The role and influence of explorers

Those early Victorian adventurers who departed Britain's shores had to be prepared to face the unfamiliar, even the perilous. Whether they sought fame, fortune or a fresh start – or perhaps had some deeper educational or scientific purpose in mind – such pioneers thrived on the excitement and challenge of empire and their exploits shaped and inspired attitudes towards the Empire at home.

David Livingstone, John Kirk, Richard Burton and John Hanning Speke became household names; their tales of discovery and exoticism attracted the interest of Victorian society. More than that, however, such explorers opened up the interior of Africa both by lecturing and publishing their findings and, not least, by producing maps. Their exploits lent traders and Christian missionaries alike the opportunity for action and gain.

Case study: David Livingstone

Fig. 1 *Livingstone delivers his message to African natives, c1870*

The most famous early Victorian explorer, David Livingstone, provided an inspiration to the public – and to other explorers. He began his travels as a missionary doctor in South Africa in 1841, but he was soon exploring the hinterland. After returning to Britain to huge acclaim in 1856 to 1857, he conducted a series of celebrated lectures at Cambridge University, recounting the geography, mineralogy, diseases, languages and cultures he had encountered in Africa. Announcing that, 'I go back to Africa to try to open up a path for commerce and Christianity', he received government funding for a return in 1858. With the official title of Consul for the East Coast of Africa, he began an exploration along the Zambezi River from whence his 2000 letters back to Britain thrilled the public imagination. Innumerable accounts of this and Livingstone's subsequent journey to find the source of the Nile were published with illustrations to exemplify Livingstone's supposed saintliness. His dramatic disappearance and rediscovery by Henry Stanley in 1871 was just what the Victorian public needed to cement their picture of Livingstone as a martyr who sacrificed his life for Africa and the Empire.

KEY PROFILE

David Livingstone (1813–73) was a Scot, who first travelled to South Africa in 1841. Lured by adventure, he explored the Kalahari Desert, discovered Lake Ngami (1849) and the Zambezi River (1851) and travelled westwards to Luanda (1853), discovering the Zambezi falls (1855), which he renamed the Victoria Falls. He crossed the continent from west to east before returning to Britain and publishing *Missionary Travels and Researches in South Africa* (1857). In 1858, he attempted a difficult expedition along the Zambezi and in 1866, he went missing while trying to locate the source of the Nile. The *London Daily Telegraph* and *New York Herald* sent the journalist Henry Stanley to Africa to find him. In 1871, Stanley located him in a small village; he is said to have greeted him, 'Dr. Livingstone, I presume?' Livingstone died in Africa from dysentery and malaria in 1873.

Case study: John Kirk

John Kirk (1832–1922) was another Scottish physician whose career embraced the spirit of adventure, science, Christian duty and desire for a respectable colonial position. He had a keen interest in botany and was appointed chief medical officer and economic botanist for Livingstone's Zambezi expedition on the recommendation of the Royal Botanical Gardens at Kew. During this expedition, he not only explored waterways with Livingstone, nearly drowning in rapids in 1860, but also collected many aquatic specimens, notably mussels which he both sent back to Britain and wrote about.

He returned to Africa in 1868 as medical officer and Vice-Consul in the Sultanate of Zanzibar and lived out the rest of his career until 1886 as a diplomat. Zanzibar was of commercial interest to the British because of its clove and ivory exports. It was also a wealthy state and home to East Africa's first steam railway. Kirk ensured that Zanzibar operated as a British client state. British-initiated treaties ensured the Sultan outlawed Zanzibar's slave trade and, with British aid, its commerce grew. Kirk's efforts thus gave Britain the toe-hold on Africa's east coast which was to grow into British East Africa in 1895.

CROSS-REFERENCE

Refer to the map in Chapter 1, page 2 to identify the places mentioned in this section.

Case study: Sir Richard Burton

Sir Richard Burton (1821–90) was a linguistic scholar, explorer and adventurer who had become famous in the 1850s for his stories of Muslim life and manners, based on his daring visits to sacred Islamic cities such as Mecca, where no Western Christian had gone before. Although wounded in the jaw by a native's javelin, on an exploration of Somaliland in 1855, he was undeterred and undertook another expedition inland from the island of Zanzibar in 1857 to 1858. However, he was forced by malaria to abandon this, thus allowing his companion, John Speke, the glory of discovering Lake Victoria, which Speke believed to be the Nile's source. Burton's unwillingness to accept this theory led to quarrels with Speke and in 1864 the British Association for the Advancement of Science invited Burton and Speke to debate their theories. Unfortunately, Speke's death prevented this and Burton spent his final years travelling and publishing. In all, he produced 43 volumes on his explorations, including five books on West Africa describing tribal rituals concerning birth, marriage and death, as well as fetishism, ritual murder, cannibalism and bizarre sexual practices. He also produced 30 volumes of translations, including the *Kama Sutra* (1883) and a 16-volume edition of the *Arabian Nights* (1885–88). He acquired a wild and dangerous reputation for his daring essays on pornography, homosexuality and the sexual education of women.

ACTIVITY

Extension

Try to find out more about these and other Victorian explorers. You could divide into groups for research and produce short illustrative PowerPoints looking not only at their careers but at their writings and impact in Britain. You could also watch *Mountains of the Moon* (director Bob Rafelson, 1990) to get a sense of the time and the tribulations of Burton and Speke's African expeditions.

Case study: John Hanning Speke

John Hanning Speke (1827–64) joined Richard Burton's Somaliland exploration in 1855. Although he suffered a wound at the hand of the natives, he re-joined Burton in the quest to find the origin of the Nile in 1857. After exploring the East African coast for six months to find the best route inland, the two men became the first Europeans to reach Lake Tanganyika, in February 1858. On the return trip, Speke left Burton and struck out northward alone. In July 1858, he reached a great lake, which he named 'Victoria' in honour of the Queen.

However, his conclusion about the lake as the source of the Nile was not only rejected by Burton, it was disputed by many in England. On a second expedition (with James Grant) in 1860 Speke mapped parts of Lake Victoria and found the Nile's exit from the lake at what he called Ripon Falls. The explorers attempted to follow the course of the river and reached southern Sudan, where they met further Nile explorers, Samuel Baker and Florence von Sass, who later became Baker's wife. Speke and Grant told them of another lake said to lie west of Lake Victoria, thus enabling Baker's group to locate another Nile source – Lake Albert. Accounts of these explorations were published in 1863 and 1864 but although Speke's claims were to have been tested in a public debate with Burton in 1864, Speke was killed by his own gun (probably suicide) while hunting before this could take place.

The role and influence of missionaries: Christian imperialism

Missionaries were extremely active overseas in the nineteenth century. **Anglicans**, **Roman Catholics** and particularly **non-conformist** groups such as **Presbyterians** and **Methodists** all sought to spread the Christian faith among the non-Europeans. Indeed, it is sometimes suggested that the missionary movement represented a distinct form of cultural and 'Christian imperialism'.

Missionary societies had existed since the end of the eighteenth century and shared a common conviction that world-wide conversion was both possible and a duty. Indeed, missionaries, buoyed by their absolute adherence to Christianity and belief in the worthlessness of other faiths, could sometimes be quite aggressive in their claims for influence, although this was certainly not universally the case. Nevertheless, missionaries sometimes helped to open up territories to British rule by penetrating beyond colonial frontiers (for example, into the Congo in Africa or inland China in the 1880s), establishing links with indigenous communities and seeking imperial protection – perhaps sharing their geographic and strategic knowledge with the **secular** authorities. Elsewhere, as in the Punjab in the 1850s, the missionaries followed imperial conquest.

EXTRACT 2

Non-conformist societies in particular tried to steer clear of any political involvement in their work; but the manner in which missionary attitudes merged with support for colonialism or the extension of powerful British influences goes far beyond such a superficial neutrality. As white settlers maltreated non-Europeans or obstructed missionary preaching, so missions turned inevitably to the imperial authorities to defend their rights. This often involved an expansion of colonial power. In Africa from the second wave of missionary expansion in the 1840s to the conclusion of colonial partition c1900, missions grew steadily more prepared to request colonial or imperial protection and began in the 1880s to force the break-up of tribal groups (such as the Ijebu in Nigeria) that were resistant to their message.

Adapted from 'Empires in the Mind' by Andrew Porter (2001)

Methodist missionaries were particularly active. By the middle of the century, Wesleyan missionaries had set up 'Conferences' to oversee missions in Canada, New Zealand and Australia and it was Methodist missionaries from Australia who prepared the ground for the establishment of British rule in Fiji in 1874. A 'South African Conference' was similarly established in 1882; and in 1883, the missionary John Mackenzie put pressure on the British government to establish a protectorate over Bechuanaland. When the government did so, Mackenzie was duly appointed Deputy Commissioner.

KEY TERM

Anglicans: members of the Protestant (non-Catholic) Church of England; the established Christian Church of Great Britain with the monarch, Queen Victoria, at its head

Roman Catholics: those who believed the Pope to be the Head of the Christian Church and did not accept Anglicanism

non-conformist: a member of a Protestant Church which acts independently from the established Church of England

Presbyterians: a Protestant non-conformist denomination deriving from Calvinist ideas of a Church which preferred simple services and has no bishops, Presbyterianism was particularly strong in Scotland

Methodists: a Protestant non-conformist group with ideas based on those of Charles and John Wesley; Methodists share some of the views of the Presbyterians; this movement had grown strongly in some of England's industrial working class communities in the early nineteenth century

KEY TERM

secular: means without religious basis; secular authorities here include police, military powers and governments

ACTIVITY

Evaluating historical extracts

According to Extract 2, what links were there between the missionary societies and the growth of the British Empire?

Methodist missions were also established from China from the 1850s, with a new station at Fat-shan in 1860 and a mission for North China at Han-kau in 1862. A West Indies Conference was established in 1885, and missions in India expanded rapidly from the 1850s. Such was the enthusiasm for spreading the word abroad that a 'Ladies' Committee for the Amelioration of the Condition of Women in Heathen Countries' was founded as an auxiliary to the Wesleyan Missionary Society in 1858.

A CLOSER LOOK

Female missionaries and social reformers

A number of women felt called to undertake missionary work. They were particularly concerned about the rights of women and children and many learned local languages and assimilated the local culture, so winning the respect of native peoples. Among the most prominent was Mary Slessor (1848–1915), a Victorian mill girl who left the slums of Dundee to live among the tribes of Calabar, Nigeria. Slessor fought hard to end the local practice of killing twins (and often their mother too), which the local tribes attributed to the work of the devil. Another was Amy Carmichael (1867–1951) who came from a devout Presbyterian family in Northern Ireland and worked for 55 years in India, producing 35 books about her experiences. Carmichael tried to rescue the 'temple children' – mostly young girls who were forced into prostitution. She dressed in Indian clothes, and dyed her skin with dark coffee so that she would blend in with the indigenous people. Mary Carpenter (1807–77) was another British Christian who travelled to India in 1866 and tried to improve female education there. She encouraged both Indian and British colonial administrators to improve the provision of schools, hospitals and gaols and won funding to set up a training college for female Indian teachers in 1868.

Missionary groups generally established compounds, set up churches and typically provided housing and farm work in return for native conversions to Christianity. In this way, missionaries offered native peoples material gains (food, jobs and houses), as well as education, answers to moral questions (about death, for example), and the opportunity for personal advancement by embracing the 'white man's faith'. Furthermore, missionaries advanced imperialism not only by staking a claim to (or consolidating) territorial control but by extending Britain's commercial reach.

Fig. 2 *Mary Slessor, a Scottish missionary, pictured here with Nigerian children*

ACTIVITY

Extension

Find out more about missionary groups and their work in different parts of the Empire. You might begin with the work of the London Missionary Society, the Universities Mission to central Africa and the Livingstone Inland Mission.

Nevertheless, while missionaries hoped to create Christian bases that would become self-financing, self-governing and expansionist in their own right, in practice this was difficult to achieve. Conflicts could arise between the missions and the indigenous peoples, between the missions and the colonial rulers and even between one mission and another. In the 1880s, the Anglican Church Missionary Society clashed with the first Anglican African bishop in the Niger region – Samuel Crowther, a former slave who had been ordained into the Church of England in London. Crowther was forced to resign in 1891 amidst accusations that he was too lax towards heathen practices.

Although British missionary enterprise could provide the means for imperial expansion, it must also be noted that, at times, it delayed annexation and colonisation and challenged imperial authority. Sometimes Christian missions provided a focus for local resistance and opposition to colonial rule, so the connection between religious expansion and the British Empire overseas is not a straightforward one. Whilst religion and empire frequently mingled, they were as likely to undermine each other as they were to provide mutual support.

The role and influence of traders

It is sometimes difficult to separate business and trading interests from strategic or even moral concerns, but traders seeking new markets or materials clearly had an important role to play in the development of attitudes to empire. Once commercial enterprises had established a foothold somewhere, British administration often followed; in this way, the East India Company led the way towards British control of India and the commercial exploits of Cecil Rhodes, William Mackinnon and George Goldie helped ensure that the British flag followed British trade in Africa in the nineteenth century. The establishment of British protectorates was not only a means to shore up friendly governments or to consolidate adjacent British colonies, but also a way of protecting commercial interests.

CROSS-REFERENCE

The expansion in Africa that took place as a result of the activities of the traders discussed in this section is shown on the map in Chapter 1, page 2.

Case study: Cecil Rhodes

One of the prime movers behind British expansion in South Africa was the diamond magnate and Cape Colony politician, Cecil Rhodes. Owning all South Africa's diamond mines (some 90 per cent of global diamond production), Rhodes had the wealth to pursue his distinct ambition, namely: 'the furtherance of the British Empire and the bringing of the whole of the uncivilised world under British rule'.

CROSS-REFERENCE

Chartered companies, including Rhodes' British South Africa Company, are discussed in Chapter 3, page 29.

KEY PROFILE

Cecil Rhodes (1853–1902)

Rhodes was a sickly boy and was sent, for the sake of his health, to South Africa, to join his brother Herbert on his cotton farm in Natal. The farm failed but in 1871, 18-year-old Rhodes and his brother set out for the diamond fields of Kimberley. Rhodes succeeded over the next 17 years in borrowing money from N M Rothschild & Sons and buying up all the smaller diamond mining operations in the Kimberley area. His amassed an enormous personal fortune and created the De Beers Consolidated Mines Company in 1888. In 1890, he went into partnership with the London-based Diamond Syndicate and so gained a monopoly of the world's diamond supply. In the 1880s, Rhodes invested in fruit-growing, after the Cape vineyards were wiped out in an epidemic. This began the modern-day Cape fruit industry. He also formed his own company, the British South Africa Company, which received a **royal charter** in 1889. Rhodes became Prime Minister of the Cape Colony from 1890 to 1896 and tried to avoid the interference of bureaucrats in the Colonial Office in London. He forced indigenous tribes from their lands to make way for industrial development, but also introduced educational reform. By his will, he endowed the Rhodes Scholarships, for young people to study at the University of Oxford.

CROSS-REFERENCE

The role played by Cecil Rhodes between 1890 and 1914 is discussed in Chapter 10, page 93.

Rhodes' British South Africa Company of 1889 came, through concessions and treaties, to control a large area of land in the interior of Africa. This territory, initially known as 'Zambesia' after the Zambezi River, had its name changed, in 1895, to 'Rhodesia', in honour of its founder. Rhodes' only disappointment was a failure to annex Bechuanaland Protectorate (now Botswana).

Rhodes framed his imperial ambitions in moral terms which reflect something of the confidence and arrogance of the Victorian age. In 1877, in his *Confession of Faith*, Rhodes wrote: 'I contend that we are the finest race in the world and the more we inhabit, the better it is for the human race.'

Case study: Sir William Mackinnon

Sir William Mackinnon (1823–93) was a 'self-made' Scottish ship-owner and businessman who built up substantial commercial interests. He began in the coasting trade around the Bay of Bengal and in 1856 he founded the Calcutta and Burma Steam Navigation Company. This became the British India Steam Navigation Company. This grew into a huge business organisation, trading through the Indian Ocean, Burma and the Persian Gulf and extending its reach to Zanzibar and along the coast of East Africa.

Mackinnon then founded the Imperial British East Africa Company. This received a charter in 1888 and was supported by the British government as a means of establishing influence in the region. However, despite its official privileges, the company was rapidly bankrupted.

Mackinnon combined his business enterprise and religious principles by helping to found the Free Church of Scotland East African Scottish Mission in Kibwezi, now in Kenya, in 1891.

Case study: George Goldie

The family of **George Goldie (1846–1925)** bought a palm oil business in the Niger basin in 1875. Palm oil proved a particularly adaptable product: not only did it serve as an industrial lubricant, it could be used as the main constituent in both candles and soap. Goldie formed the Central African Trading Company in 1876 and visited West Africa for the first time in 1877. In 1879 he persuaded all the British trading firms on the Niger River to join forces with his family firm to create a single company, the United African

Company, which **controlled 30 trading posts**. However, his application for a royal charter in 1881 was refused because of competing French interests in the Niger region.

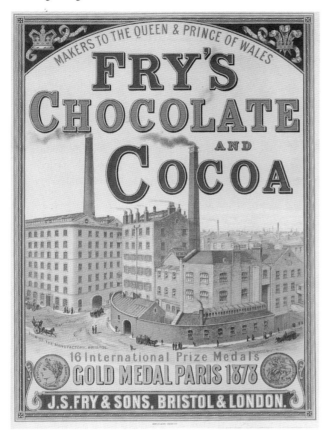

Fig. 3 *Fry's Chocolate Cream bar was launched in 1866*

Besides exporting palm oil, Goldie greatly benefited from Englishman F.W. Loder's discovery that the previously unused palm kernels could be used to manufacture margarine. As a consequence, palm kernel exports came to exceed palm oil in value. Goldie secured concessions from tribal chiefs, with whom he signed treaties obliging them to trade solely with the company's agents in return for a commitment to buy up all the local exportable products (such as shea butter and ivory). His efforts meant that he won the trade war with rival French companies and bought them out too. He also established coffee and cocoa plantations – reflecting a growing trend in drinking chocolate and the emergence of the chocolate bar. Goldie's success was largely a result of his agents having secured over 450 local treaty arrangements which transferred territory and jurisdiction to the United African Company. In return tribal chiefs were promised protection and provided with compensation and an annual subsidy, besides being offered a range of weapons, ammunition, rum, gin and smaller gifts of tobacco, salt and Manchester cotton goods.

As a result of Goldie's efforts, Britain successfully asserted its right to proclaim a protectorate over both northern and southern Niger at the **Berlin Conference** (1884–85). Consequently Goldie's firm was chartered as the Royal Niger Company in 1886 and Goldie was knighted in 1887.

In later years, Goldie became a British colonial administrator, using a mixture of force and persuasion to bring the peoples living in the hinterland of the Niger under the British sphere of influence. He was thus responsible for

CROSS-REFERENCE

To recap on the Berlin Conference, look back to Chapter 2, pages 18–19.

Northern Nigeria became an official British Protectorate in 1900.

the development of **Northern Nigeria** into a prosperous British protectorate. He was, however, a very different character from Cecil Rhodes. He preferred a quiet life and ordered that all his papers be destroyed on his death.

The role and influence of colonial administrators

Fig. 4   *Evelyn Baring, British statesman and colonial administrator*

Men on the spot

Professor John Galbraith presented the idea that it was often the 'man on the spot' who played a crucial role in extending British control and so expanding the Empire. The man on the spot, he suggested, was certainly as important as, and sometimes more important than, imperial or company policy, which often opposed control of further territory because of the expense.

Britain's empire was typically run by 'men on the spot', those company directors, governors, high commissioners and consuls who found themselves in positions of control within the colonies. Such administrators were sometimes tempted by opportunities to acquire more influence and so bring more lands under the British flag and many took independent decisions about the way territories should be administered and developed. Although formal governors were appointed by the Colonial Office in London to serve as British representatives, they often had considerable discretion to interpret instructions as they saw fit.

Some 'men on the spot' started out as explorers or traders. William Mackinnon, Cecil Rhodes and George Goldie all finished up as powerful colonial administrators. John Kirk in Zanzibar left his days of exploration behind when he became Vice-Consul in Zanzibar, where he developed such an influence over Sultan Barghash that he was effectively the ruler of the island. He even negotiated the handover of the Sultan's Mombasa coastal strip to the Imperial British East Africa Company, run by Mackinnon.

Sir Evelyn Baring, on the other hand, was a professional administrator; but he too took his appointment as Consul in Egypt to mean that he had the right to supervise and reform the Egyptian government.

Case study: Sir Evelyn Baring

Evelyn Baring (1841–1917), who became Earl of Cromer in 1901, began his career as a colonial administrator, serving in India as private secretary to his cousin, Lord Northbrook, Viceroy from 1872 to 1876. He was an able administrator, although his high levels of efficiency coupled with his arrogant and rather patronising manner led his colleagues to nickname him 'Over-Baring'. He was, in many respects, the 'typical' Victorian colonial administrator: hard-working, fair and a believer in liberal reform, but also inflexible and with a sense of British superiority which made him condescending towards his inferiors – colleagues and natives alike.

Baring's second posting was in Egypt in 1877, when he was sent to help Isma'il Pasha out of his financial difficulties. Since his advice was ignored, he returned to Britain and it was not until 1882 that he again went to Egypt, this time as Consul-General. He approved the Dufferin Report of 1883, which established an Egyptian puppet parliament with no power, and asserted the need for British supervision of reforms in what was then a bankrupt country. This established a 'veiled protectorate', whereby he ruled the rulers of Egypt, with the assistance of a group of English administrators trained in India, who were placed in key positions as advisers to the Egyptian government. He remained the real ruler of Egypt until his resignation in 1907.

CROSS-REFERENCE

Baring's role in Egypt from 1877 is discussed in Chapter 1, pages 6–9.

Case study: Bartle Frere

Fig. 5 *Frere was educated at the East India Company College, which trained colonial administrators*

Bartle Frere (1815–84) began his career in the Indian Civil Service. His support in the crushing of the Indian Mutiny in 1857 won him a knighthood and a place on the Viceroy's Council at Calcutta. He subsequently became Governor of Bombay, a member of the India Council (in Britain) between 1867 and 1877 and a baronet. His experience led to his appointment, in 1877, as High Commissioner and Governor of Cape Colony.

The Conservative Colonial Secretary, Lord Carnarvon, had chosen him to carry out a **planned confederation** in the area, merging British South

A CLOSER LOOK

Moves to confederation

The discovery of diamonds in Griqualand West, north of the Cape Colony in 1867, drew the attention of both the Transvaal Boers and the British. The Griqua sought British protection and were duly incorporated into the Cape Colony in 1880. This encouraged British administrators to push for a British-led federation of South Africa, which they claimed was the best means of preserving regional stability.

KEY TERM

federation: a confederation is a union of states with some or most political power vested in a central authority; an act of federation involves the merging of several states into a single 'confederation', leaving them with some independence in internal affairs; this type of government is sometimes referred to as a 'federal government'

CROSS-REFERENCE

The Zulu War is covered in more detail in Chapter 6, pages 55–57.

Africa with the Dutch Boer republic of the Transvaal. However, Frere found the South African colonists hostile to Carnarvon's plans, while the Transvaal Boers wanted their independence. Frere was left in quite a weak position when Carnarvon resigned in 1878, but he decided to take action, nevertheless. He deliberately provoked a **war with the Zulus**, whom he considered an obstacle to **federation**, in December 1878. Although this war ended in a British victory, the shocking defeat of British forces by the Zulus at Isandhlwana in January 1879 and the high cost of the war led to an official reprimand. Frere was hastily withdrawn from South Africa by Gladstone's Liberal government in 1880 and denounced for acting recklessly. Frere's example nevertheless exemplifies the power of the 'men on the spot' in influencing British imperial policy.

There were many more colonial administrators who, in their various ways shaped the development of the British Empire. Jan Morris has written this, of them:

EXTRACT 3

To a really ambitious man, the highest posts of empire could bring most of the satisfaction of politics without the degradation of hustings or debate. Great splendours of position attended the successful imperial administrator. The chance of a truly regal status in life, such as a Colonial Governor enjoyed, with his own court and etiquette, his palace on the hill, a subject people at his feet and the Union Jack at his flagstaff – the mere possibility of such an elevation was enough to make a susceptible bureaucrat become imperialist. Ambitions were compelling enough to create an interested lobby for the extension of empire. Sir George Campbell, Lieutenant-Governor of Bengal (1871–74), thought the existence of a large and increasing class of people wanting to fulfil themselves abroad 'reason and justification for foreign extensions where they can legitimately be made'.

Adapted from *Pax Britannica* by Jan Morris (1968)

STUDY TIP

Using the knowledge you have acquired in this chapter, you should be in a position to evaluate each suggested factor relating to the way individuals and groups promoted the growth of empire, and provide a reasoned judgement on each. Look both at the broad interpretation put forward in each extract and at any subsidiary views.

 PRACTICE QUESTION

Evaluating historical extracts

Using your understanding of the historical context, assess how convincing the arguments in Extracts 1, 2 and 3 are, in relation to the growth of empire in the years 1857 to 1890.

Summary

Much empire building was the result of the activities of individuals and groups who, although they had differing motives for involving themselves in empire, shared a similar outlook. These explorers, missionaries, traders and administrators exuded, in varying degrees, the same British confidence that was a feature of mid-Victorian society. They believed they knew what was best and they were convinced that, whatever misfortunes befell them on the way, they were going to succeed. For the most part they showed a happy contempt for those peoples whose lands they explored, pilfered or attempted to convert and rule. To the individuals behind the Empire, they were serving God and making the world a better place.

ACTIVITY

Extension

Find out more about the Indian viceroys – from Canning to Lytton. In what ways did these colonial administrators influence the development of the British Empire?

PRACTICE QUESTION

How significant a role did men on the spot play in promoting Britain's empire?

This question invites you both to identify what you understand by 'men on the spot' and to provide examples of the way they promoted the British Empire. It will probably be helpful to think thematically here, looking, for example, at the extension of territory, the growth of trade and wealth, and the extension of political and perhaps military control. For each theme try to produce at least two examples from different areas of the Empire.

EXTRACT 1

Before c1875, the Empire was entirely outside the experience and even knowledge of most Britons. A tiny number of people worked for the Empire directly; but few of those who could be said to have worked for it indirectly — in cotton factories, for example — can have realised they were doing so. It had a minimal obvious effect on their ordinary material lives — work, shelter, food — until shortage of these forced some of them to emigrate to the colonies. Once there, such people were generally lost to those who had stayed at home. Neither emigration nor soldiering — the other main reason for people to visit the Empire in substantial numbers — was likely to make them feel particularly fond or proud of it. The only exception was the small and closed group of men who administered the Empire, or officered the poor soldiers sent out there. The rest of the population had no need to be enthusiastic about the Empire, or even particularly aware of it.

Adapted from *The Absent-Minded Imperialists* by Bernard Porter (2006)

Attitudes to empire: the British government

Fig. 1 *Britannia forces imperial rule on reluctant leaders*

The British government did not pursue a very active or interventionist role in empire before the mid-nineteenth century. This was partly because of the distances involved in an age of slow communications, partly because of a lack of institutions to deal with the Empire and partly from a general lack of commitment to intervention itself. It was not that politicians totally lacked interest – the Empire was bound up with a sense of national prestige and identity; but it was the freedom to trade and access to markets that concerned the country the most.

Benjamin Disraeli (twice Prime Minister and regarded in the 1870s as a great supporter of empire) had asserted in 1852: 'Those wretched colonies will all be independent in a few years and they are a mill-stone around our necks.' His Liberal rival, **William Gladstone**, went as far as to promise 'to abstain from any territorial acquisitions and from contracting any new obligations.'

Benjamin Disraeli (1804–81)

Fig. 2   *Disraeli was an influential voice in world affairs*

A Jew by birth, Disraeli became a Christian and both Conservative Party leader and short-lived Prime Minister in 1868. He served a second, full term of office as Prime Minister between 1874 and 1880. Disraeli maintained a friendship with Queen Victoria. He flattered her with the Empress of India title in 1876 and she bestowed upon him the Earldom of Beaconsfield in the very same year.

William Ewart Gladstone (1809–98)

Fig. 3   *Gladstone brought a firm moral perspective to his politics*

Gladstone served as both Prime Minister and Chancellor of the Exchequer on four separate occasions. He attended Oxford University before being elected to Parliament in 1832. Gladstone served as Colonial Secretary (1845–46) in a Conservative government before becoming leader of the newly formed Liberal Party from 1868. Gladstone was influenced by his mother's commitment to Scottish non-conformism.

In the first half of the nineteenth century, successive governments had resisted calls to secure new territories; for example, they withheld **charters** from commercial colonising companies which they did not feel were viable. In 1865, a Parliamentary Select Committee even recommended withdrawal from Britain's West African settlements on the grounds of cost.

The 1870s, however, saw a shift in attitude and a new intensity of debate about empire. Central to this was concern about the ambitions of other European powers. As other nations grew stronger industrially, Britain found itself facing greater economic competition. Furthermore, European and American protective tariffs made it harder to flood the Western hemisphere with British manufactured goods.

CROSS-REFERENCE

To recap on the charters for commercial companies, look back to Chapter 3, page 28–29.

Party political conflict

Disraeli and the Conservatives

The Empire became a hot political topic. Whereas the dominant Conservative and Liberal parties had previously been united in their 'acceptance' of empire, in the 1870s, Disraeli began to assert that the Conservatives were the 'party of empire' and that their Liberal opponents would allow the Empire to crumble. Disraeli presented this new perspective in his Crystal Palace speech of 1872: 'in my opinion no minister in this country will do his duty who neglects any opportunity of reconstructing as much as possible our colonial empire, and of responding to those distant sympathies which may become the source of incalculable strength and happiness to this land. Therefore, gentlemen, with respect to the second great object of the Tory party also – the maintenance of the empire – public opinion appears to be in favour of our principles.'

Disraeli's new-found enthusiasm for empire was partly a way of winning support from an electorate that had been much enlarged by the **1867 Reform Act**. The Conservative Party had not won an election since 1841 and 'playing the imperialist card' seemed to pay off when the party secured an electoral victory in 1874. This 'imperial card' was again to be played by Disraeli's successor, Lord Salisbury (Prime Minister 1886–92 and 1895–1902) although both were sceptical about unlimited acquisitions or a restructuring of the Empire.

A CLOSER LOOK

Until 1867 only 650,000 adult males in England and Wales had the vote, which was based on property and income. The **1867 Reform Act** extended this to part of the urban male working class, extending the franchise to 1.5 million men.

KEY TERM

jingoism: Empire-related patriotism, encouraging and celebrating British imperial gains, boasting about Britain's power

CROSS-REFERENCE

Disraeli's purchase of shares in the Suez Canal in 1875 is outlined in Chapter 1, page 8.

A CLOSER LOOK

A College of Arms was established by the British in Calcutta, and various ranks, titles and crests were given to Indian princely families during the durbar. This mirrored the medieval practice of ennobling those who served the Crown. There was an attempt to link the Indian past with England's past glories and suggest that the British were destined to rule India and had a legitimate right to be there.

A CLOSER LOOK

A group of committed 'imperialists' emerged in the last quarter of the nineteenth century. They were a powerful pressure group and some wanted to go much further in restructuring the Empire than even the Conservative Party was ever prepared to commit itself to.

Attitudes to empire produced intense party rivalry from the 1870s – although the Liberal leader, Gladstone, never tried to disassociate the Liberals from empire, so differences were not as great as Disraeli tried to make out. According to Gladstone, Britain needed to avoid new acquisitions and concentrate on developing the existing colonies, helping them towards self-government. He distinguished between 'imperialism', which he opposed and 'empire' which he supported. In the eyes of the Liberals, Disraeli's 'imperialist' talk was dangerous and he was accused of stirring up '**jingoism**'.

As Prime Minister, Disraeli lived up to his imperialist stance, for example, buying £4 million' worth of Suez Canal shares in 1875. This established the Conservative Party's imperial attitudes and agenda for the late nineteenth century.

Disraeli also steered the Royal Titles Act through the House of Commons in order to bestow the title 'Empress of India' on Queen Victoria in 1877. The Act was a means to embed British rule over India and Disraeli took this further by appointing Robert Lytton as Viceroy and backing his 'coronation durbar' (or reception), a massive display of pomp in Delhi in 1877.

Disraeli and his Viceroy additionally sought to consolidate, if not expand, the Raj by attempting to turn India's northern neighbour, Afghanistan, into a client state. Such were their fears of the incursion of Afghan tribes into India and, even more so, of Russian aspirations in that area, that Lytton launched an invasion of Afghanistan in November 1878. A protracted conflict followed which saw British-Indian troops suffer a series of setbacks, and almost 10,000 losses, before eventual victory secured British control over **Afghanistan** and the strategically significant north-west frontier. (This became the North-West Frontier Province in 1901.)

Disraeli's government embarked on a similar statement of intent in South Africa by annexing the Boer republic of the **Transvaal** in 1877 and launching war on the **Zulu** and Pedi tribes in the hope of establishing a British confederation over Southern Africa.

Regardless of imperial ambitions, the initial invasion of Zululand proved a failure, with British troops humiliated at Isandlwana in January 1879 before belatedly securing victory at Ulundi, six months later. The setbacks in the Afghan and Zulu campaigns contributed to the Conservatives' resounding defeat in April 1880's general election and the return of a Liberal government under Gladstone.

Gladstone and the Liberals

Gladstone had been highly critical of Disraeli's foreign and imperial policies but he was forced to pick up the pieces of Conservative adventurism when the Transvaal Boers mobilised to throw off British control and declared their independence in December 1880. The Boers' civilian militia besieged British garrisons across the Transvaal – thus starting the **First Boer War of 1880–81**, which was more like a series of half-hearted skirmishes. Following the British forces' defeat at Majuba Hill, in February 1881, Gladstone declined to commit further troops, time or money to uphold Disraeli's ambition for British **hegemony** over South Africa.

The same was true during the **Mahdist Rebellion** in the Sudan in 1884: Gladstone urged the withdrawal of Anglo-Egyptian troops and reflected that the Sudanese are 'rightly struggling to be free'. In this way, Gladstone clearly showed the difference between Liberal and Conservative colonial policy.

However, despite his principles, Gladstone became embroiled in **Egypt**, not for its own sake but for the sake of a safe passage to India and also as a result of public pressure as exemplified in the press. Arabi Pasha's uprising of 1881 threatened the security of the Suez Canal, European lives and British investments in Egypt. Once order was restored, in 1882, Khedive Tewfiq was installed as ruler in Britain's newest occupied territory.

Gladstone's hand was further forced by the **Berlin Conference** of 1884–85 which officially started formal land-grabbing across Africa. This resulted in the conversion of Somaliland and Bechuanaland (north of the Cape Colony) into British protectorates. However, the local Tswana rulers were left in power in British Bechuanaland, which suggests that Gladstone was reluctant to take on either further management or the costs associated with empire. The same hesitancy was evident when Germany claimed the Pacific island of New Guinea in 1884, renaming it Kaiser Wilhelmsland: Gladstone resisted intervention and the prospect of direct confrontation with Germany. Instead, Thomas MacIlwraith, the Premier of Queensland, ordered the occupation of the island's south-eastern zone to establish British control there. Australia subsequently financed the development of British New Guinea.

Gladstone resigned as Prime Minister in June 1885 having overseen the 1884 Parliamentary Reform Act which further extended the vote to 5.5 million men. This meant that the trend of using or promoting imperialism for popular support returned under the Conservative governments of Lord Salisbury.

An off-shoot of Gladstone's support for colonial self-government was his sympathy for the cause of the Irish nationalists, who had long campaigned for Irish independence from Great Britain. When he returned as Prime Minister in 1886, he introduced a **Home Rule Bill for Ireland**, confirming his reluctant imperialist status and igniting further debate in Parliament and across Britain.

A CLOSER LOOK

Irish Home Rule

An Act of Union in 1801 had formally incorporated Ireland into the United Kingdom. Although Irish voters could select MPs, it was the Westminster Parliament which governed Ireland. The idea of 'Home Rule' grew strongly from the 1860s: it promoted the idea of a separate Irish legislature to decide

CROSS-REFERENCE

The situation in the Transvaal and the Afghan and Zulu campaigns are discussed in more detail in Chapter 6, pages 55–57.

KEY TERM

hegemony: dominance by one state over others in the region

CROSS-REFERENCE

For more on the First Boer War of 1880–81, look ahead to Chapter 7, page 69.

The Mahdist Rebellion in the Sudan is outlined in Chapter 1, page 10.

CROSS-REFERENCE

Gladstone's reluctant intervention into Egypt in 1882 to suppress Arabi Pasha's uprising is discussed in Chapter 1 page 8.

CROSS-REFERENCE

To recap on the Berlin Conference, which allocated African territories among the European powers, look back to Chapter 2, pages 18–19.

upon its domestic affairs, while Ireland still remained part of the United Kingdom. Gladstone's Liberal government failed in its attempt to pass the Irish Government Bill through Parliament in 1886 and on a second attempt in 1893 also.

Attitudes to empire: the British public

From the 1860s and 1870s, the Empire began to fire the public imagination in a way that it had never done in the earlier years of the century. This was, at least in part, the result of the reporting in the growing popular press which saw the value of stories of the exotic, of heroism and of national one-upmanship. The Education Act of 1870 had increased national literacy rates and the extension of the vote in the 1867 and 1884 Reform Acts made the public more politically aware. It was against this background that Disraeli chose to use the cry of empire for political gain.

As early as 1857, the press had shown its power to influence public attitudes to empire in its reporting of the Indian Mutiny. The British were horrified by stories of massacres and tortures such as at **Cawnpore**, and thrilled by tales of brave soldiers, not least Major-General Henry Havelock who recaptured Cawnpore in July and Lucknow in September 1857. The press turned Havelock into a national hero so that, when he died of dysentery in November 1857, the public paid for a statue of him to be erected in Trafalgar Square.

In 1882, it was Arabi Pasha's revolt in Egypt that occupied the reporters, who told the tale in such florid tones that Gladstone was well supported in his decision to intervene.

A CLOSER LOOK

Cawnpore

Typical of media reporting on the Indian Mutiny was the Well of Cawnpore incident. As British troops approached the rebel-held town of Cawnpore in July 1857, the decision was taken to kill 200 captive British women and children. Most were hacked to death by hired butchers and then stripped before their bodies were thrown down a nearby dry well.

A CLOSER LOOK

She

H. Rider Haggard's novel *She* was first serialised in *The Graphic* magazine between 1886 and 1887. The story traces the journey of Horace Holly and Leo Vincey into the Africa interior where they encounter a lost kingdom ruled over by Queen Ayesha – 'She who must be obeyed'.

A CLOSER LOOK

Reporting of Arabi Pasha's revolt in Egypt, 1882

While *The Pall Mall Gazette* wrote of 'the Moslem mob' (13 March 1882), the *Daily Telegraph* sensationally recounted that rebels had killed 'all the Christians they could find' in Alexandria and had left the ancient city in ruins (14 July 1882). The *Evening News* reported that more Europeans had been murdered with 'further massacres imminent' (21 July 1882), while the *Economist* predicted that 'very great losses must be incurred and great disturbances to business' (17 June 1882). By incensing the public against the 'wickedness' of the rebels, the press thus made Gladstone's government's decision to intervene decisively in Egypt easier.

Imperialist literature, such as H. Rider Haggard's *King Solomon's Mines* (1885) and *She* (1887), also made an appearance in bookshops, whilst younger Victorians were regaled with tales of adventure in the new comic genre. *The Boy's Own Paper* first appeared in 1879 and featured stories portraying soldiery and bravery across the globe. It included contributions from Colonel Baden-Powell (founder of the Scout Movement) who urged readers to lead 'manly and Christian lives'.

School books reflected similar themes, while clubs and associations such as the Boys' Brigade (1883) sprang up, reinforcing imperialist values by offering military training and by reminding young men of what it meant to be part of the 'glorious' British Empire.

ACTIVITY

Create a page for *The Boy's Own Paper* either featuring a true episode in imperial history in comic form or creating your own tale of adventure based on your own knowledge of imperial explorers and adventurers.

The impact of empire at home

By the 1870s, stories of explorers and missionaries were being avidly read in British newspapers and magazines and heroic tales helped to reinforce the Victorian idea of British benevolence and superiority. Nineteenth-century British – like white men everywhere – held attitudes which we would today condemn as racist, but which were then considered perfectly acceptable. The British saw their empire as an 'empire of races' and believed themselves infinitely superior to other indigenous peoples in everything from their religion and morals to their laws and political institutions. This was accompanied by a belief that bringing these peoples into the Empire could somehow 'civilise' indigenous peoples, leading them away from their heathen, savage existence and turning them into hard-working and law-abiding citizens.

Imperial exhibitions

Fig. 5 *A Pears soap advert from the 1880s; the original caption said: 'Even if our invasion of the Soudan has done nothing else it has at any rate left the Arab something to puzzle his fuzzy head over'*

A CLOSER LOOK

Missionaries reported back on their evangelical work (converting heathens)and their dispatches were used for missionary pamphlets, newspapers and Sunday School stories. On their return to Britain they lectured at meetings and not only gained coverage for their civilising mission but, in some cases, even achieved celebrity status, as in the case of David Livingstone.

Britons' moral right or 'imperial duty' to control overseas territories was reinforced by the view that the white races were naturally superior. This attitude was encouraged by the publication of Charles Darwin's *Origin of Species* in 1859. Although Darwin himself never suggested it, his theories of natural selection, whereby certain species had advantages over their competitors, were soon applied to human races. Quasi-scientists justified their views by pointing to the disappearance of the 'weak' North American Indians, Maoris and Aborigines, while anthropologists seized on the theory to define racial attributes and categorise different racial groups.

Evaluating primary sources

In pairs, discuss the advertisement for Pears soap (Fig. 5). How does the advert depict the people of the Sudan? What does it suggest is the effect of empire on the lives of these people?

The sense of British Victorian society's physical and social superiority was reinforced by a series of popular exhibitions. Following the success of the Great Exhibition of 1851, the 1862 International Exhibition held in South Kensington featured over 28,000 exhibitors from 36 countries. It represented a wide range of industry, technology and the arts and displayed 7000 exhibits from India alone.

In 1877, a Nubian Village, featuring both animals and humans collected in the Sudan, was put on display at London's Alexandra Palace and in 1886, the Colonial and Indian Exhibition was held in South Kensington to 'give to the inhabitants of the British Isles, to foreigners and to others, practical demonstration of the wealth and industrial development of the outlying portions of the British Empire.'

A CLOSER LOOK

The 1886 exhibition

The buildings that housed the 1886 exhibition were built in Indian style. A huge princely gateway and innumerable artefacts were displayed, from ceremonial swords to fly-swatters. Reflecting Victorian attitudes, native Indians were brought to Britain as 'living exhibits'; they were described as Indian craftsmen in the exhibition catalogue although it later turned out that they were probably prisoners who had been trained as part of a project to 'reform the criminal castes'.

London also hosted an Africa Exhibition in 1890. This was the work of traders, government officials, missionaries and scientific groups who wanted to showcase **Stanley's African travels**. It celebrated explorers and colonisation and provided a display of photographs, maps showing European colonial expansion in Africa and the routes of famous British explorers. There were also trophy displays of shields, spears, axes and throwing knives, an African hut and two boys from Bechuanaland. The exhibition stimulated scientific and anthropological interests and appeared to justify the British presence in Africa, bringing the word of the Christian God to the natives.

A CLOSER LOOK

Darwin's *Origin of Species* was used as a basis for a theory that individuals, groups and peoples are subject to the same laws of natural selection as plants and animals. 'Social Darwinism' was advocated by Herbert Spencer and others in the late nineteenth and early twentieth centuries to justify imperialism and racism.

CROSS-REFERENCE

Stanley's African travels are described in Chapter 4, page 31.

ACTIVITY

Drawing on the information in this chapter, produce a pamphlet on behalf of a missionary society, encouraging volunteers to join a mission to either Africa or India.

EXTRACT 2

It was the Indian Mutiny that helped to generate the atmosphere of hero-worship so characteristic of late nineteenth century imperialism. The military leaders of its suppression, figures such as Sir Henry Havelock, became evangelical knights, defenders of the faith as well as of the Empire. Religion, heroism, and empire were joined in a potent mix. Nineteenth-century heroes, most notably Livingstone and **General Gordon**, were essentially religious figures, portrayed as moral giants facing dark forces which martyred them in a Christ-like sacrifice. The churches and missionary societies were important sources of the popular culture of empire. The myths of the Mutiny fed into the visual, theatrical, and fictional representations of imperial action in the later part of the century. They also contributed to the tradition of Christian militarism, which helped enhance the reputation of both army and navy and was reflected in the founding of youth organisations with their military forms and an imperial patriotism as part of their moral training.

Adapted from 'Empire and Metropolitan Cultures' by John M. Mackenzie (1999)

CROSS-REFERENCE

General Gordon and his role in the Sudan are discussed in Chapter 1, page 10.

EXTRACT 3

From the mid-nineteenth century, opportunities across the Empire for men seeking their fortune – as settlers, soldiers, servants, traders, farmers, medical men, clerks or colonial officials – and for women – as wives, teachers and missionaries – increased greatly. The experiences of these varied colonists were shaped by the places they went to and the kind of colonial project on which they were engaged. Their families and friends heard about their lives through letters or listened to the tales of those who returned. Their listeners told their stories to others. At the same time, peoples of the Empire came to Britain: African sailors, Indian servants, traders and colonial politicians all passed through and some, especially sailors and dockers, settled in Britain, establishing mixed communities in London, Cardiff, Bristol, Liverpool and Glasgow. Most Britons had seen people of colour by the mid-nineteenth century. This spread the word about the imperial world.

Adapted from 'Culture and Identity in Imperial Britain' by Catherine Hall (2008)

 PRACTICE QUESTION

Evaluating historical extracts

With reference to Extracts 2 and 3 and your understanding of the historical context, which of the two extracts provides the more convincing interpretation of why public interest in the Empire grew in the years 1857 to 1890?

STUDY TIP

Consider each view in the light of your own knowledge and comment on whether you find it convincing. You will then have to decide which view you find most convincing and give your reasons for this.

Summary

British interest in, and attitudes towards empire, in the years 1857 to 1890, reflected a combination of factors – from greater literacy and party politics to popular culture and the press. Drawing on the benefits of Christianity, commerce and liberal reform, an imperial ideology was established and effectively used to justify British imperial gains. The exploits of figures such as Livingstone and Rhodes were used to show that Britain had something beneficial to offer native peoples. It was their efforts, and the influence of hundreds of others, which fashioned Victorian imperial attitudes.

 PRACTICE QUESTION

'The British view of empire in the years 1857 to 1890 was primarily shaped by what people read in the newspapers.' Explain why you agree or disagree with this view.

 PRACTICE QUESTION

'Attitudes towards imperialism in Britain in the years 1857 to 1890 were unduly triumphalist, reflecting a one-sided and narrow-minded outlook.' Assess the validity of this view.

STUDY TIP

Whether you attempt the AS or A Level essay, you will need to set up a debate in your answer. For AS you will need to balance the effect of media reporting against other ways in which the Empire shaped British culture. For A Level you will need to balance the negative aspects of attitudes to imperialism against more positive ones. At both levels you should aim to make full use of the words of the quotation. AS students should aim to judge 'primarily' while A Level answers should address 'triumphalist', 'one-sided' and 'narrow-minded' as three separate stimuli for debate.

6 Relations with indigenous peoples

LEARNING OBJECTIVES

In this chapter you will learn about:

- the Indian Mutiny and its impact
- relations with Boers and Bantu peoples in southern Africa.

EXTRACT 1

The Empire was nearly destroyed by the great rebellion of 1857, described inaccurately as the Indian Mutiny. The result of complex and multiple causes, the rising expressed the accumulated anger of many sections of the population in north and central India – dispossessed princes, disgruntled soldiers and a harassed peasantry from whom the East India Company's army was largely recruited. The rebels committed acts of great brutality and were repressed in equally brutal ways. The British in India bayed for even more bloody revenge. The rebellion created a legacy of racial hatred which permeated all aspects of the relationship between the ruler and the ruled. The leaders of the rebellion feature prominently in the demonology of British imperial history. It is significant that they were, and are, viewed very differently in India. Leaders like Rani of Jhansi and Kunwar Singh are revered heroes in Indian folk memory and nationalist myth has elevated the rising to the status of the 'First War of Independence'.

Adapted from 'British Rule in India: an assessment' by Tapan Raychaudhuri (1996)

KEY QUESTION

As you read this chapter, consider the following key question:
How did the indigenous peoples respond to British rule?

ACTIVITY

Evaluating historical extracts

1. Can you explain the author's references in Extract 1 to 'the great rebellion of 1857' and the 'First War of Independence' (rather than the Indian Mutiny)?
2. What impression of the events of 1857 is given in Extract 1?

The Indian Mutiny and its impact

The Mutiny

Fig. 1 *Indian mutineers attack the Redan Battery at Lucknow*

The Mutiny had begun among sepoys serving in the Bengal Army. They were mainly peasant-soldiers from north India and proud of their military status which set them above the ordinary labourers. However, in 1857, grievances about pay and changes to their condition of service exploded.

The traditional explanation for the outbreak of the Mutiny was that that cartridges in the new Enfield rifles they had been issued with had been greased in animal fat, which offended their religious sensibilities: for both Muslims and Hindus, contact with impure cow or pork fat was religiously unacceptable. However, the real trigger was the anger felt by landlords and nobles who had been deprived of their lands by Governor-General Dalhousie.

The sepoys in Bengal refused to obey orders in February 1857. Other battalions followed suit. At Meerut, outside Delhi, sepoys turned on their British officers and a mob set upon local Europeans. Sepoys seized control in most of the northern cities (including Agra, Lucknow and Cawnpore) and there was a short-lived attempt to resurrect the old Mughal Emperor as a figurehead. The sepoys were joined not only by sections of the urban population but also by rural populations. Some rebels were discontented landowners who had lost out under British rule, others were peasants who resented taxation or joined the rebellion to get back at feuding neighbours.

CROSS-REFERENCE

The Indian Mutiny, along with its impact on British colonial policy, is introduced in Chapter 2, page 11.

CROSS-REFERENCE

For a map of the provinces of India, look back to Chapter 2, page 13.

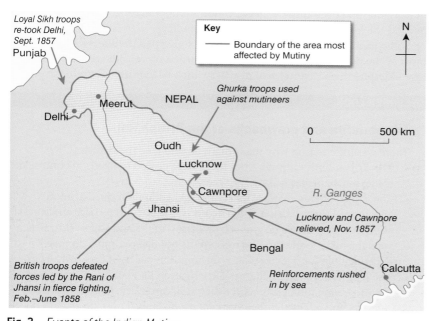

Fig. 2 *Events of the Indian Mutiny*

Although large areas of India were untouched by the Mutiny, the cost of the rebellion in terms of human suffering was immense. The Emperor's sons were swiftly executed so that remaining rebels lost any hope of restoring the Mughal dynasty to rule over India. Delhi and Lucknow were devastated; villages burnt; mutineers tortured and British officers, their wives and children murdered. British rule was not entirely reasserted until June 1858 following a final battle at Gwalior, some 180 miles south of Delhi.

If the Mutiny had been precipitated by the increasing British presence and control, if not interference, in India, the post-Mutiny period produced more of the same. The post-Mutiny era saw Britain use India in a way that provided compensation for the costs of suppressing the revolt – hence its rapid extension of the rail network and, for instance, of the tea trade.

A CLOSER LOOK

The outbreak of mutiny

The trouble began at the headquarters of the Bengal Army in Meerut. Discipline was notoriously slack here; many of the troops came from the recently annexed Oudh and included high-caste Hindus with strict beliefs, while many of the officers were elderly. Among their concerns there were rumours that the regiments were about to be sent by sea to Burma – offending caste laws about crossing water. The British did not understand the sepoys' conflict of loyalties and their announcement that any disobedience would be severely punished merely inflamed the situation.

ACTIVITY

Extension

In groups undertake some further research into the causes and events of the Indian Mutiny and prepare an illustrated presentation for your class. Each group could examine a different episode or area and should try to include some historians' interpretations of the Mutiny.

The impact of the Mutiny

In 1858, India passed into the direct rule of the British Crown and the internal wars that had been a constant feature of life in many parts of the subcontinent during the time of East India Company rule came to an end. India had a single, centralised government.

Government and society in India

The relationship between the ruler and ruled had been soured by the experience of rebellion – and by the reporting it received within Britain, which emphasised the savagery of the Indians, whilst ignoring much of the brutality of the British. Belief that the East could be 'Westernised' was questioned and this fuelled the arrogance of white men buoyed up by Social-Darwinist theories of superiority. Although the British tried to act in a more religiously sensitive way in the wake of the Mutiny, they also grew more aloof. Whereas the earlier years of the century had seen some degree of curiosity about and even 'admiration' for the exotic and unfamiliar Indian culture, after 1858 a greater degree of separation set in.

Although the Indian Raj was administered under British notions of 'fairness', the legal systems imposed favoured the white man and were far too complex and expensive to help the poor, particularly in matters of land tenure. Similarly the supposed 'equality of opportunity' offered by British rule may have provided more educational opportunities for some of the wealthier Indians who formed the new professional classes, but it did little for the mass of peasants; and even those with education found it hard to obtain promotions beyond the lower ranks of the colonial bureaucracy.

Some Indian princes and large landlords supported the Raj. However, for most of the population, British rule was regarded more with indifference than love – despite the pageantry and displays which tried to suggest otherwise.

CROSS-REFERENCE

The government and administration of India following the Mutiny is described in Chapter 2, pages 12–15.

A CLOSER LOOK

After the 1857 Mutiny there was a growing recognition that imposing Western Christian values on the Indians could be counter-productive. Missionary activity was discouraged and religious sensitivities acknowledged.

A CLOSER LOOK

The benefits and drawbacks of the British Raj

There was little reason why the Indians should love the British.
- The British built railways – but these were geared to needs of control and trade; most villages lacked even mud roads.
- The British offered markets for Indian agricultural produce – but this encouraged specialisation in the higher-value cash-crops (rice and wheat) at the cost of lower value grains (rye, barley, millet and coarse rice) which were the main food staple for most of the population. India became dependent on food imports and consumption per head declined.
- The British developed schemes for irrigation and land improvements – but these only took place where they supported British commercial interests and affected only 6 per cent of the land.
- The British provided Indians with cheap British manufactures – but India was unable to develop viable industries of its own (such as had once existed) and its economy was skewed.
- The British provided schools and universities – but only the privileged few could benefit; illiteracy remained widespread.
- The British provided jobs for Indians – on the railways, in the army, police and civil service and as clerks. However, only a minority of Indians could obtain such employment.
- Poverty continued; death rates from famine were high.

KEY TERM

Star of India medal: this was an order of chivalry founded by Queen Victoria in 1861 with three classes: Knight Grand Commander (GCSI), Knight Commander (KCSI), Companion (CSI); the motto of the order was 'Heaven's light our guide' and the emblem of the order, the 'Star of India', also appeared on the flag of the Viceroy of India

Between 1859 and 1861, Viceroy Canning made an exhaustive tour of India designed to win back those who had been dispossessed or felt alienated by British rule. As a result of his efforts:

- Some land and titles were returned to native Indians.
- **Star of India medals** were introduced.
- Positions in either the Imperial Assembly or Statutory Civil Service posts were shared amongst the Indian nobility.
- More educational establishments, teaching in English, were opened.

The extension of education

Universities were established in Bombay, Madras and Calcutta in 1857 while elite schools such Rajkumar College, Mayo College and Bombay's Cathedral School were set up in order to produce 'Westernised Oriental Gentlemen' (pejoratively known by the acronym 'wogs'). In the 30 years following 1857, some 60,000 Indians entered the universities, overwhelmingly in Arts, but some 2000 in Law. Of the 1712 Calcutta students to graduate by 1882, over a third entered government service and slightly more went into the legal profession. Graduates of the three universities by 1882 accounted for some 1100 appointments to government service.

Fig. 3 *Mayo college, Rajasthan*

Social reformer **Mary Carpenter** visited India four times between 1866 and 1875: she helped establish a corps of British teachers for India as well as girls' schools in Bombay and Ahmedabad, besides opening a college to train female Indian teachers.

Economic change

The greatest change to the Indian economy following the changes of 1858 was a growth investment – particularly in the **railways**, which were built more for strategic than economic purposes but which certainly helped stimulate trade and the development of previously inaccessible areas. Some European-style factories were built although, since the bulk of manufactured goods came from Britain, there was virtually no heavy industry. Subsistence farming prevailed, although the number of tea plantations increased from just one in 1851 to 295 by 1871; and there was an increase in the domestic production of raw cotton for export to Britain in the 1880s and 1890s.

Overall attitudes

Many British believed their 'benign rule' in India was a genuinely liberating experience for the Indians. The Whig reformist T.B. Macauley believed that educating that Indians to ensure they became 'English in taste, in opinions, in morals', was sufficient to justify the British domination of the subcontinent.

Mary Carpenter (1807–77)

Fig. 4 *Carpenter was an educational and social reformer*

Primarily concerned with the state of girls' education and women's prisons in India, Carpenter set up the National Indian Association in 1870 in order to promote reforms in British India.

Railways

Railways developed across India at an astounding rate of some two miles a day in the aftermath of the Mutiny. Trains were used to lend a higher profile to British rule and to help affirm control, not least by transporting personnel and soldiers more quickly. The British relied on Indians to run the railways and those employed included a disproportionately high number of (mixed race) Anglo-Indians and Christian Indians since they were regarded as likely to be more loyal to the Raj. Such workers were accommodated in new 'railway colonies' to form a community separate from the population at large.

The following extract from a book written in 1930 – 17 years before India achieved independence – reflects some of that same belief:

EXTRACT 2

For the welfare of India, the responsibility of the British government is still direct; and a terrible responsibility it is. Here, in an area about as large as Western Europe, are a fifth of the whole human race. It is no exaggeration to say that about a fifth of them owe their existence to British rule, for it is the law and order, the science and the enterprise introduced by the British, that has enabled the Indian peoples to double their population in the last 100 years or so. The British in India have exercised so profound an influence on the country that it is hard to realise the smallness of their numbers. India is anything but a White Man's home. It is an alien tropical country to which picked and specialised white men – soldiers, civil servants, merchants, planters, doctors and teachers – have gone to pursue their special callings, returning when their work is done to their homes in England and Scotland.

Adapted from *The British Empire* by D.C. Somervell (1934; originally published 1930)

STUDY TIP

These two sources present clearly contrasting pictures of the British Raj. Identify the main points of contrast and comment on these with reference to your own contextual knowledge. You must justify which you find the more convincing.

 PRACTICE QUESTION

Evaluating historical extracts

With reference to Extracts 1 and 2 and your understanding of the historical context, which of these two extracts provides the more convincing interpretation of British rule in India in the later nineteenth century, after the Indian Mutiny?

Relations with the Boers and Bantu peoples in southern Africa

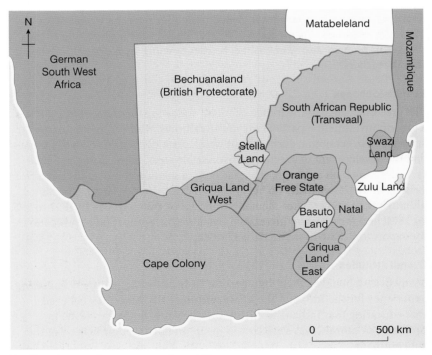

Fig. 5 *Nineteenth-century southern Africa*

Fig. 6 *Painting depicting the Anglo-Zulu War, 1879*

The British Cape Colony at the tip of Africa neighboured the republics of the Orange Free State and Transvaal. These republics were in the hands of the Boers: descendants of the original Dutch settlers from the Cape area, some of whom had moved north from 1833 – at first to Natal, which the British annexed in 1845, and subsequently further into the interior to create their own states. Relations between the British and Boers had been reasonably peaceable until the middle of the nineteenth century and the British had recognised the Boer states in the 1850s, although they still claimed some control over their affairs. However, in the second half of the nineteenth century, circumstances changed and the British came into conflict with both the Boers and the native Bantu tribes of southern Africa.

Relations with Boers and Bantu, 1867–80

It was the discovery of diamonds in 1867 near Kimberley on the Vaal River in **West Griqualand**, bordering the Orange Free State, that opened the path towards greater friction. The discovery triggered a 'diamond rush' attracting both white settlers and native Bantu-speaking peoples to the area.

In 1868, the British annexed Basutoland (land of the Khoi Khoi and Sotho people), claiming that the indigenous Africans were seeking British protection against the Boers, and in 1871 the British also took West Griqualand. Following the annexation, 2000 Griqua trekked eastwards, to establish Griqualand East in 1873. However, this too was annexed by Britain the following year. The British went on to propose a federation of the British and Boer territories in 1875, but the Boers gave a firm rejection.

CROSS-REFERENCE

The annexation of West Griqualand and the role of Lord Carnarvon and Sir Bartle Frere in trying to bring about a federation with the Boers are outlined in Chapter 4, pages 39–40.

ACTIVITY

Evaluating historical extracts

According to Extract 3, what were:
a) the successful aspects and
b) the unsuccessful aspects of the British development of a colony in the south of Africa?

ACTIVITY

Create a large map of the south of Africa for the classroom wall. Identify the places mentioned in the text and use strings to connect them notices giving details of developments in each.

The area suffered from extreme instability as both the British and the Boers tried to exert greater control over an area which was had become of great value for traders. In the Xhosa War of 1877–78, the British easily disarmed neighbouring tribesmen and annexed their communities to the Cape, but the Boers were rather less successful in their conflict with the Pedi tribe, which had successfully maintained its independence in the eastern Transvaal. Seizing on this failure, the British announced the annexation of the Transvaal in 1877, claiming that they needed to defend the white European settlers against not only the Pedi but also the Zulus, the most powerful African tribe in the area. The Boers reluctantly accepted British aid and the British launched an invasion of Zululand in January 1879.

The British army decisively defeated the Zulus at Ulundi in 1879 and Zululand was duly incorporated into Natal. The campaign was rounded off with an attack on the Pedi who were similarly defeated. However, once the Zulus had been defeated, the Boers declared their total independence from Britain, in 1880.

EXTRACT 3

In the 1870s, the British could take some satisfaction from the growth and development of their colony in the south of Africa. The economy was transformed by gold and diamonds, so its value as a trading partner with Britain and as a home for British investment was set to grow enormously. There was, however, a blot on the record of success. The protection of vulnerable non-European peoples was part of the Victorian civilising mission. By and large Britain abandoned this. The Bantu of the south of Africa had featured prominently in the concerns of British humanitarians but in the end Britain was not prepared to go very far in using its authority on their behalf against the wishes of the dominant white community. Instead, it provided the military power through which these wishes could be enforced. The Xhosa of the Eastern Cape lost their lands as a result of defeat by British forces.

Adapted from '1783–1870: An Expanding Empire' by P.J. Marshall (1996)

Relations with Boers and Bantu, 1880–90

From 1880, the Boers turned on the British, attacking British army garrisons across the Transvaal and winning a series of victories that culminated in a humiliating British failure at Majuba Hill in February 1881, where over 150 Britons were killed. The British were thus forced to sign the Convention of Pretoria, which recognised Boer self-government in the Transvaal, although the British still claimed a right to control over external affairs.

Further problems arose with the arrival of the Germans in south-west Africa in 1884. The German presence raised British fears that the Boers might form an alliance with Germany. Consequently, in 1885, the British annexed a section of territory between German South-West Africa and the Transvaal – **Bechuanaland** – as a strategic attempt to prevent the combining of the German and Boer colonies.

A CLOSER LOOK

Bechuanaland

A British military expedition of 4000 British and local troops was sent from Cape Town under the leadership of Major-General Charles Warren in late 1884 in order to assert British sovereignty in an area that was home to the Tsawana tribes. Warren met the Boer leader, Paul Kruger, in January 1885 and was given assurances that the Boers could maintain order in Bechuanaland. Warren ignored these promises and forced the annexation. Northern Bechuanaland became a Protectorate and the south, a **Crown Colony**.

KEY TERM

Crown Colony: a colony ruled directly by an appointee of the British crown and accountable to the Colonial Office

In 1886, new gold discoveries at Witwatersrand near the Transvaal capital of Pretoria produced further instability. This gold was eagerly sought by trading companies and brought a mass of non-Boer Europeans (known as Uitlanders) into the Transvaal. Among the traders was Cecil Rhodes, who received a charter for his 'British South Africa Company' in October 1889 and sought not only to enrich himself but to extend the British Empire. His ultimate aim was to create a continuous British land route from Cape Town to Egypt, which had come under the control of the British in 1882. In September 1890, Rhodes' company established a fort at Salisbury in Mashonaland, home to the Shona people, bringing yet another area under British control. However, by 1890, British dominance in South Africa was still far from assured.

CROSS-REFERENCE

The role and influence of Cecil Rhodes are discussed in Chapter 4, pages 35–36.

Treatment of the Bantu

In all of this constant expansion and empire-building, little thought was given to the local Bantu tribes whose land was increasingly eroded by the white settlers. The discovery of diamonds and gold, did, of course, increase the wealth of the region but the profits remained firmly in the hands of the settlers. Laws were passed at the insistence of the mining companies that limited the right of black Africans to have any claims over the mines or to trade in their products. Black Africans were therefore relegated to performing manual labour, while white people got the skilled jobs and reaped the profits. In addition, black workers were forbidden by law from living wherever they wanted, and were forced to stay in segregated neighbourhoods or mining compounds.

ACTIVITY

In pairs, discuss the ways in which both Boers and Bantu tribes were affected by the British presence in southern Africa and create a chart or diagram to illustrate your ideas.

Summary

ACTIVITY

Summary

British interference can be seen to have promoted conflict in both India and across southern Africa. Were British relations with indigenous peoples in these regions similar or different?
Create a summary chart and record evidence on both sides. This activity should help you answer the A Level and AS questions below.

 PRACTICE QUESTION

Evaluating primary sources

Using your understanding of the historical context, assess how convincing the arguments in Extracts 1, 2 and 3 are, in relation to British rule in the Empire in the years 1857 to 1890.

STUDY TIP

Evaluate each extract in turn, commenting on the arguments it employs and the evidence it presents about British rule. You will need to use your own knowledge to comment on those arguments, using factual evidence to support or criticise them.

STUDY TIP

You might start by jotting down the ways in which British rule was 'disastrous' for each group. Try to balance these points with evidence that would suggest otherwise. After this, you should be able to decide whether you wish to agree or disagree with the quotation. You can of course only agree in part, but you should put forward a view – and offer a balanced response.

PRACTICE QUESTION

'British rule was disastrous for both the Indians and the Bantu of South Africa in the years 1857 to 1890'. Assess the validity of this view.

Fig. 7 *The British Empire c1890*

2 Imperial consolidation and Liberal rule, c1890–1914

7 Consolidation and expansion of the British Empire in Africa

From c1890, the Victorians saw an almost unbelievable revolution in their political relations with Africa. Against all the trends of previous expansion, the British occupied Egypt and staked out a huge tropical African empire. At the centre of this lies an apparent paradox. The main streams of British trade, investment and migration continued to leave tropical Africa practically untouched; yet it was tropical Africa that was bundled into empire. The flag was not following trade and capital; nor were trade and capital as yet following the flag. The late Victorians seemed to be concentrating their imperial effort in the continent of least importance to their prosperity. The collapse of African governments under the strain of earlier Western influences may have played a part, even a predominant part in the process. It is also quite possible that they did not acquire a new empire for its intrinsic value, but because Africa's relationship to their total strategy in Europe, the Mediterranean or the East had altered.

Adapted from *Africa and the Victorians* by Ronald Robinson, John Gallagher and Alice Denny (1961)

ACTIVITY

Evaluating historical extracts

1. With reference to Extract 1, explain what is meant by: a) 'an almost unbelievable revolution' and b) 'an apparent paradox'.
2. Identify the reasons given in Extract 1 for British expansionism in Africa. As you read this chapter, look for evidence that would support these views and for other reasons behind the consolidation and expansion of the British African empire.

LEARNING OBJECTIVES

In this chapter you will learn about:

- the consolidation and expansion of the British Empire in Africa.

KEY QUESTION

As you read this chapter, consider the following key question:
Why did the British Empire grow?

A new African empire

From the 1890s, British policy in Africa became more assertive. Until the 1880s, the British had largely established bases for their strategic value or for the purposes of trade. This sometimes involved reacting to the initiatives of other powers – matching settlement by the French or Germans in particular by claiming the area where British traders had already established themselves. On the whole, private chartered companies had been used to occupy and administer territory and although there was some direct intervention, as seen in Egypt and South Africa, British policy had been generally cautious. This changed as imperial attitudes within Britain had their effect on British expansionism in Africa. The Conservative government, elected in 1895, was determined to uphold Britain's position in every part of the world and this brought wars, and threats of wars, over Africa and ambitious programmes to consolidate the Empire. British imperialism took on a less haphazard appearance. British protectorates were expanded in order to provide better security to pre-existing ports, markets or resources and new territories were taken in order to limit the advance of fellow European imperialists. Either way, the British found themselves expanding their interests and possessions in a form of domino effect.

THE RHODES COLOSSUS
STRIDING FROM CAPE TOWN TO CAIRO.

Fig. 1 *This cartoon featuring Cecil Rhodes was published in 1892*

CROSS-REFERENCE

For the allocation of land among the European powers at the Berlin Conference of 1884–85, look back to Chapter 2, pages 18–19.

The ground rules agreed upon at the **Berlin Conference** of 1884–85 meant that imperial powers had to show evidence of their 'effective occupation' of African territories – encompassing both their administration and defence – in order to claim them as a formal colony. Britain and its rival colonising powers proceeded to do this with vigour. Whereas 80 per cent of the African continent had been under native or traditional forms of control at the time of the conference, only 10 per cent remained outside European control 20 years later.

EXTRACT 2

In 1870 barely one tenth of Africa was under European control. By 1914 only about one tenth – Abyssinia (Ethiopia) and Liberia – was not. Most of the partition of Africa, colloquially but accurately described as the 'scramble' or 'grab' for Africa, had taken place during a period of only ten years between the Berlin West African Conference of 1884–85 and a series of 'tidying-up' agreements in 1895–96. To the Victorians, this seemed not only natural but inevitable. One explanation is obvious. Europe had undergone an industrial revolution and Africa had not. For the first time in History there was an enormous gap, economic, technological and military, between the two continents with the balance entirely in Europe's favour. The second explanation is less obvious but equally important – the mindset of the Europeans. Europeans were at the forefront of progress and civilisation; Africans, 'primitive' and 'backward'. Naturally the Europeans would take over. This was sometimes justified by a debased form of '**Social Darwinism**' which had little to do with what Charles Darwin had really argued about 'natural selection' in the animal world.

CROSS-REFERENCE

To recap on Social Darwinism, look back to Chapter 5, page 66.

Adapted from *The Scramble for Africa,* by M.E. Chamberlain (2010)

ACTIVITY

Evaluating historical extracts

Identify Chamberlain's views in Extract 2. Create a spider diagram to show reasons for British consolidation and expansion in Africa, using the information you have read so far.

The extent of British expansion in Africa, 1890–1914

The table below indicates how and when British occupied territory was converted into British protectorates or colonies in the years 1890 to 1914.

Initial acquisition of territory	Expansion and consolidation of British rule 1890–1914
Sierra Leone 1808	Protectorate established 1896
Gold Coast 1867	Incorporation of Ashantiland into Gold Coast Colony in 1902
Transvaal 1877 (until December 1880)	Integrated into British Union of South Africa 1902
Egypt (and Sudan) 1882	From 1899, Sudan was a **condominium** of Britain and Egypt Egyptian Protectorate established 1914
Southern Nigeria 1884	Royal Niger Company (RNC) rule converted into British Colony 1906, before establishment of united Nigeria in 1914
Northern Nigeria 1885	RNC rule converted into British Colony 1900, before establishment of united Nigeria 1914
British East Africa 1888	Imperial British East Africa Company (BEAC) rule replaced by formal Protectorate in 1895
Uganda 1888	BEAC rule replaced by formal Protectorate in 1894
Zanzibar 1890	Formal Protectorate established, albeit maintaining the rule of the Sultan of Oman
Nyasaland 1891	British South Africa Company (BSAC) rule replaced by formal Protectorate in 1907
Matabeleland 1893	Territory incorporated into Rhodesia 1895
Rhodesia 1895	Southern Rhodesia Protectorate established 1901 and Northern Rhodesia in 1911, both under BSAC administration

KEY TERM

condominium: the joint control of a state's affairs by other states

CROSS-REFERENCE

Relations between the British and indigenous peoples are covered in more detail in Chapter 12.

As can be seen in this chart, the occupation of territories by chartered companies – which had produced evidence of 'effective occupation' on behalf

In *Africa and the Victorians: The Official Mind of Imperialism* (1961), Gallagher, Robinson and Denny presented the idea that Britain was pulled into Africa by local crises or events which threatened its interests and credibility. This idea is known as the 'peripheral theory' of imperialism.

of Britain – gave way to formal control from the 1890s. This was partly because the costs for companies were financially unsustainable.

British expansionism came through a mixture of treaties, intimidation and aggression and was, at least in part, driven by regional disorder or perceived threats. The British needed to feel the boundaries of their possessions were secure – no matter how arbitrary these were in ethnic terms. If borders were threatened by local crises or resistance, the British felt they had every right to take action, using force and coercion.

Expansion in Tropical Africa

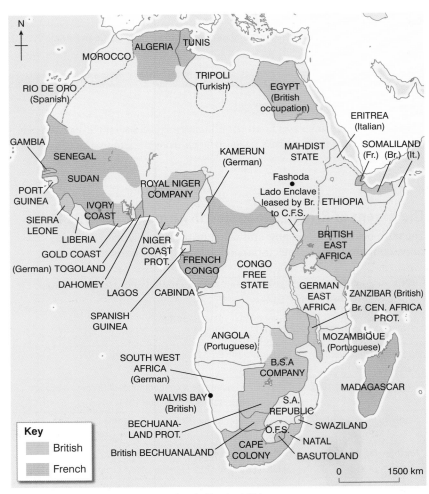

Fig. 2 *British and French expansion in Tropical Africa*

The **Ashanti** were an ethnic group which had once possessed a large empire along the Gulf of Guinea. They strongly resisted attempts by Europeans, mainly the British, to conquer them. Britain fought four wars against the Ashanti kings between 1823 and 1896.

British West Africa

To the old British colonies of Gambia, Sierra Leone and the Gold Coast, were added Ashantiland (an extension to the original coastal strip that made up the Gold Coast) and Nigeria (the area penetrated by Goldie's Royal Niger Company).

Ashantiland

British actions towards the **Ashanti** around the Gold Coast are typical of the way the British acted to protect their territories. Tired of the skirmishes and wars that characterised British–Ashanti relations throughout the nineteenth century, in the early 1890s, the British demanded that their King, Prempeh, should turn over the remainder of his empire to the British as a protectorate; he refused. This produced a fourth Anglo-Ashanti War in which Britain conquered the Ashanti territories and forced Prempeh from his throne in 1896. A further and final Ashanti uprising in 1900 led to Britain's formal annexation of the kingdom. Ashantiland was incorporated into the Gold Coast Colony in 1902.

Nigeria

The British were able to establish their claim to Nigeria by virtue of their occupation and by an 1890 agreement with the French, who agreed to recognise Britain's domination of the area in return for Britain's recognition of the French claim to Madagascar. The British government took over the responsibilities of the Royal Niger Company and established direct British control in the North in 1900, and in the South in 1906. Nigeria was eventually unified in 1914.

British East Africa

The British East African empire was much expanded in the years after 1890 during which Rhodesia, Zanzibar, Uganda, Kenya, the Sudan and Somaliland were developed to form a formidable British holding.

Zanzibar

In 1890 Britain and Germany signed a treaty establishing spheres of influence in East Africa. Zanzibar was ceded to British influence, whilst Germany was given control over mainland Tanzania. Britain duly declared Zanzibar a Protectorate of the British Empire (1890) and installed its own 'puppet' Sultan, Hamad bin Thuwaini. However, following the mysterious death of Sultan Hamad at his palace in 1896 (amidst rumours of poison) and the accession of his cousin Khalid, without Britain's blessing, there was a confrontation. The British ordered Khalid to stand down and when he refused mounted a naval bombardment of the Sultan's palace. This is sometimes recorded as the shortest war in history. After just 38 minutes, Khalid was overthrown and the pro-British Sultan Hamud placed on the throne of Zanzibar, which he ruled under British protection for the next six years.

Fig. 3 *The bombing of Zanzibar by the British army, 1896*

Buganda: The ethnic group of the Bugandan people formed one of the largest and most powerful states in East Africa during the eighteenth and nineteenth centuries – Buganda. The name Uganda is the Swahili term for Buganda, and was adopted by British officials after they annexed the Bugandan territories

CROSS-REFERENCE

Lord Lugard is profiled in Chapter 8, page 79.

Uganda

In the course of the nineteenth century, Anglican and French Catholic missionaries as well as Zanzibari Muslims had all permeated **Buganda** and achieved significant success in converting the Bugandan peoples. In 1886, King Mwanga had attempted to assert his authority – executing around 30 Catholics and Protestants and provoking a civil war, during which **Mwanga fled**.

He promised to hand over some of his sovereignty to the Imperial British East Africa Company, in return for British backing and was duly was restored to power in 1889. In 1890 he signed a treaty with **Lord Lugard** on behalf of the Imperial British East Africa Company, ceding powers over revenue, trade and the administration of justice to the Imperial British East Africa Company. These powers were transferred to the Crown in 1894 and Buganda became a Protectorate – as part of Uganda.

A CLOSER LOOK

Mwanga made two further attempts to regain his lost territories, one in 1897 and another in 1898, following which he was captured and exiled to the Seychelles where he spent the rest of his life.

To make the best of their new colonial possession, the British constructed the Uganda Railway from Mombasa from 1896 in order to connect the coast with the fertile and temperate highlands bordering Lake Victoria. The Uganda Railway consolidated Britain's formal takeover of both the East Africa Protectorate and Uganda; it linked the respective colonies with each other and, crucially, with the Indian Ocean.

CROSS-REFERENCE

The Colonial Secretary, Joseph Chamberlain, is profiled in Chapter 10, page 91.

A CLOSER LOOK

The Uganda Railway

The 660 miles of rail track took five years and £5 million to build, and took the lives of some 2500 labourers owing to accidents, disease and wildlife. The project and its expense to the British tax payer were supported by Colonial Secretary Chamberlain and the Conservative government. They could, and did, justify the railway as it:

- enabled access to new markets
- encouraged colonial settlement
- facilitated the export of both tea and coffee
- stopped the need for slave porters to access the interior
- protected the source of the River Nile against Britain's (potential) enemies
- promoted British tourism, particularly safari tours.

The railway soon became known as the 'Lunatic Line' owing not only to its engineering ingenuity but because of the difficulties encountered during construction. The most notorious episodes include the Kedong massacre (in which almost 500 labourers were killed by Masai tribesmen) and the Tsavo incident, which saw somewhere between 35 and 100 rail workers attacked and eaten by two lions. The Uganda Railway consolidated Britain's formal takeover of both the East Africa Protectorate and Uganda. It linked the respective colonies with each other and, crucially, with the Indian Ocean.

ACTIVITY

Extension

What can you find out about the Lunatic Line? Imagine it is 1895 and you want to petition the House of Commons. Prepare a persuasive leaflet or speech either supporting or opposing the Uganda Railway.

Kenya

The British interest in the area to be called Kenya dated back to the Berlin Conference of 1884–85, when this fell into Britain's sphere of influence in East Africa. It was seen as useful territory because it offered a route from the coast to Uganda. The British made use of a succession dispute between the native Mazrui and the Muslim majority to try to force their control. Sheikh Mbaruk bin Rashid took up arms against the British, obtaining weapons from the Germans, and it took the British nine months to crush the opposition. However Sheikh Mbaruk fled and this territory became part of Britain's East Africa Protectorate of 1895 (although it was not officially declared a British Colony until 1920).

ACTIVITY

Create a large classroom wall map of Africa in the years 1890 to 1914. Identify the places mentioned in this chapter and attach brief details of British consolidation and expansion.

Sudan

The **Mahdist revolt** against Egyptian government in the Sudan, which had broken out in 1881 and brought about the death of General Gordon at Khartoum in 1885, had left the area in a weakened state. Khalifa Abdullah, who had succeeded the Mahdi on his death the same year, had tried to bring the peoples of the Sudan together under his leadership but his state was plagued by war from internal resistance fighters, disease and famine. Gladstone had always intended that British troops should be withdrawn from Egypt as soon as it was safe to do this, but Salisbury, who became Conservative Prime Minister in 1885, believed that Egypt was vital to the security of Britain's sea-route to India, hence Salisbury's concern to reconquer at least parts of the Sudan.

Salisbury was also worried by the interest which other European nations were showing in Africa. The British were concerned about French and German expansion inland in East Africa, fearing they might try to gain control of the headwaters of the Nile which were vital for the welfare of Egypt. Determined to keep Britain's rivals out, Salisbury signed a treaty with the Germans in 1890 whereby they agreed to take Tanganyika while the British took Kenya and Uganda. The French were persuaded to concentrate on West Africa, although they were not entirely appeased. Italian expansion on the Red Sea coast at Massawa was regarded as beneficial by the British, since it diverted the Khalifa's attention from the Egyptian borders, but when Italian forces were defeated at Adowa in 1896, whilst trying to seize Abyssinia, this diversionary help was lost. Nevertheless, this gave Salisbury the excuse he needed for a British **campaign in the Sudan**. It could be sold to the public as a campaign to aid Italy and uphold European civilisation against African barbarianism. Such a campaign was also welcomed as an opportunity to avenge the death of General Gordon.

CROSS-REFERENCE

To recap on the Mahdist revolt up to 1890, look back to Chapter 1, page 6.

Fig. 4 *Area affected by the Sudan campaign*

The Sudan campaign

The initial Egyptian expeditionary force of 10,000 was transported up the Nile by a fleet of pleasure-steamers supplied by Thomas Cook & Son to Wadi Halfa. A railway was then constructed into the heart of the Dervish territory and the men and supplies carried forward as stretches of line were completed. All this took place amidst sandstorms, torrential rain, a bad outbreak of cholera and a number of **Dervish** attacks.

Dervish: a member of a Muslim order committed to the defence of their faith through frenzied attack

Developments in the Sudan 1890–99

1890   Treaty between Britain and Germany

1896   Italian forces defeated at Adowa; Salisbury launches campaign in the Sudan under Kitchener

1898   Battle of Omdurman

1898   Fashoda incident

1899   Agreements between Britain and France and between Britain and Egypt; Kitchener appointed Governor-General of Sudan

General Sir Herbert Kitchener, appointed Commander-in-Chief of the Egyptian Army in 1896, was given orders to penetrate Sudanese territory as far as Dongola; but Kitchener was determined to go further, take Khartoum and conquer the whole region. Having recruited additional volunteer forces imbued with imperialist fervour, he won a resounding success at the Battle of Omdurman in 1898.

This was not quite the end of the campaign. Kitchener had been given sealed orders by Salisbury to open after defeating the Sudanese. These ordered him to go to Fashoda on the headwaters of the Nile – where a French expedition under Major Marchand had arrived. Kitchener and Marchand both pressed their nation's claims to the area (accusing the other of trespassing) but the meeting was not particularly fiery. The British press, however, reacted strongly to the 'Fashoda incident', suggesting that Britain and France were on the brink of war. Fortunately for Salisbury, the French government, facing internal problems and aware of the British army in the Sudan, chose to back down. By an agreement of 1899, the French promised to stay out of the Nile Valley in return for territory further west.

1899 also brought an agreement between Britain and Egypt, whereby Anglo-Egyptian Sudan was established. This would be administered in an arrangement known as a condominium. In practice, this meant that the Sudan would be run by the British, with Egyptian support. The British appointed Lord Kitchener as the first Governor-General (officially ruling in the name of the Khedive of Egypt); he was followed by General Reginald Wingate from 1902. Kitchener set up 'Gordon College' to train young Sudanese to run their own country and, despite Egyptian expectations, Britain frustrated ambitions for the unification of the two countries.

EXTRACT 3

As so often in the history of the Empire, one thing led to another. By taking control of Egypt, the British had also assumed responsibility for Sudan, the biggest country in Africa. Ministers were worried that if they did not take control of that region, then the French might and with it the headwaters of the Nile. There was the usual worry – in this case certainly nonsensical – about the risk to the Suez Canal and there was the death of General Gordon to avenge. Britain's involvement in Egypt and the Sudan shows that not all empire was acquired by design. There was, of course, a large element of racial prejudice in the self-appointed responsibility of the British which could not sit back when other races were getting out of hand. Businessmen who believed their money was at risk roared on demands for military action. The jingoism was shared by public opinion and whipped up by the press. Succumbing to that pressure put the Sudan mission in the hands of the **zealot**, Kitchener who, like many empire-builders, presented the task he had been given as a moral mission.

Adapted from *Empire* by Jeremy Paxman (2012)

KEY TERM

zealot: a person who is fanatical and uncompromising in pursuit of their ideals

ACTIVITY

What reasons does Jeremy Paxman give for Britain's involvement in the Sudan?

Somaliland

Britain reinforced its Somaliland protectorate (established in 1888) with both administrative and military personnel in 1898 as a means of limiting both French and Italian ambitions in that area. Although the region had few resources, its location was important since it commanded Britain's crucial access to the Indian Ocean and its colonies in the East.

Expansion in British South Africa

British expansion in Rhodesia and Nyasaland in the 1890s was followed by a drive to strengthen and extend their control of Cape Colony.

Rhodesia

Rhodes had established a British presence in '**South Zambesia**', (after the Zambezi River). This became known as 'Southern Rhodesia' from 1895 after Rhodes had used force to establish British settlers in the area. In wars with the native Ndebele (1893–94 and 1896–97), nearly half of those settlers died, but the territory was eventually taken and that north of the Zambesi River followed as a result of separate treaties with African chiefs.

CROSS-REFERENCE

Cecil Rhodes' establishment of a British presence in South Zambesia is outlined in Chapter 4, page 36.

Nyasaland

The British also sought control over Nyasaland, a small territory on the shores of Lake Nyasa, that had been opened up by Livingstone and settled by Scottish missionaries. However, they faced Portuguese-backed Arab attacks and it was not until 1891 that they were able to establish control there. **Guerrilla warfare** continued on and off until 1897, however, with the area operating under the control of Rhodes' British South Africa Company until 1907, when it became a Protectorate.

KEY TERM

guerrilla war: war pursued by civilian forces rather than conventional armies

CROSS-REFERENCE

The concept of a confederation of South Africa had been discussed before 1890 – look back to Chapter 5, page 44 for the background.

The role of Cecil Rhodes c1857–90 is covered in Chapter 4, pages 35–36. His involvement c1890–1914 is explored in more detail in Chapter 10, page 111.

The role of Joseph Chamberlain is explored in Chapter 10, page 91.

CROSS-REFERENCE

Gold discoveries at Witwatersrand in 1886 and the resulting influx of non-Boer Europeans, or Uitlanders, are outlined in Chapter 6, page 57.

KEY TERM

Afrikaner: this term gradually replaced the use of 'Boer' to denote an Afrikaans-speaking person in South Africa, descended from the predominantly Dutch settlers there

KEY PROFILE

Leander Starr Jameson (1853–1917)

Following his failed raid on the Transvaal, Dr Jameson became Prime Minister of the Cape Colony between 1904 and 1908. His qualities and character were the inspiration for Rudyard Kipling's celebrated poem *If*.

Cape Colony

The quest for a British confederation of South Africa, as advocated by the Cape Prime Minister, Cecil Rhodes, and Joseph Chamberlain (Colonial Secretary 1895–1903) was taken up with vigour in the 1890s – largely to counter German territorial gains and Boer confidence derived from the Transvaal's gold wealth.

In 1895, the gold-seeking Uitlanders of the Transvaal, who were being denied citizenship and voting rights by the Boer government under Paul Kruger sought the help of Cecil Rhodes, who was one of the leading financial magnates of the Rand goldfield. This also provided an excuse for British intervention.

A **raid** was launched on the Transvaal from neighbouring British Rhodesia by Dr Jameson, Rhodes' agent there. The whole affair was a fiasco and even though no official support had been given to this, it brought discredit on the British government and stiffened the Boers' determination to resist British intrusions. Kruger became a people's hero and the Boers still living in Cape Colony formed an anti-British '**Afrikaner** Bond' to show their solidarity with their fellow-Boers in the Transvaal.

Fig. 5 *Leander Starr Jameson returning home after his 'raid' on the Transvaal*

A CLOSER LOOK

The Jameson raid

Although the Uitlanders pulled back from a planned rising against the Boer government, Rhodes still instructed Dr Jameson (his agent in Rhodesia) to invade the Transvaal. Jameson's 'raid' – with just 500 mounted police – was easily defeated and he was forced to surrender after four days. Jameson and 12 companions were sentenced to imprisonment by a British court. Rhodes was forced to resign from the Cape premiership but was not put on trial.

Joseph Chamberlain, who had undoubtedly given covert support to the Jameson raid, wanted to avoid war if at all possible, but he was not prepared to accept any weakening of British influence. Negotiations with the Boers broke down in 1899 when the Boers, anxious to strike a blow before the British Army of South Africa could be reinforced, invaded British territory and besieged Ladysmith in Natal. Initially, the Boers had some striking successes in the **'Second' Boer War** (1899–1902); but the British poured in nearly 400,000 imperial troops at a cost of £250 million and under the Generals Kitchener and Roberts took the ascendant from 1900. Even then it took until 1902 before the Boers were defeated.

A CLOSER LOOK

Terminology of South African Wars

The 'Transvaal' or 'South African War' of 1880–81 between Britain and the Transvaal is sometimes referred to as the First Boer War. However, it is the war between Britain and the Transvaal and Orange Free State of 1899–1902 that is commonly known as 'the Boer War' (rather than the Second Boer War, although this terminology is sometimes used).

CROSS-REFERENCE

For details of the Boer War of 1899–1902, look ahead to Chapter 8, page 79.

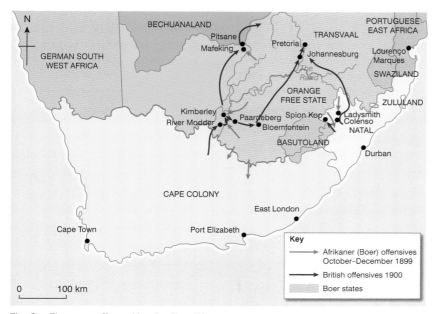

Fig. 6   *The area affected by the Boer War*

By the Peace of Vereeniging of May 1902 which ended the war, the Boers acknowledged themselves as British subjects and the Boer republics became British colonies with a promise of responsible self-government (as in the other white settler colonies). This was finally granted in 1905 and in 1908 the Prime Ministers of the Transvaal, Orange Free State, Cape Colony and Natal drew up a constitution for the 'Union of South Africa'. An Act of Union established a single parliament and the Union of South Africa became a single British Dominion territory in 1910.

Fig. 7   *The flag of Union of South Africa from 1910–1928*

Summary

STUDY TIP

Identify the different reasons given in these extracts for British consolidation and expansion in Africa after 1890 and evaluate them with reference to what you have learnt from Part One of this book (particularly Chapter 1) as well as this chapter. For the AS question you must make a judgement between the two extracts. For the A Level question you should provide a supported judgement on each extract.

 PRACTICE QUESTION

Evaluating historical extracts

With reference to Extracts 1 and 2 and your understanding of the historical context, which of these two extracts provides the more convincing interpretation of the reasons for British consolidation and expansion in Africa in the years 1890 to 1914?

 PRACTICE QUESTION

Evaluating historical extracts

Using your understanding of the historical context, assess how convincing the arguments in Extracts 1, 2 and 3 are, in relation to British consolidation and expansion in Africa in the years 1890 to 1914.

ACTIVITY

Summary

Copy the left hand column of the table of British acquisitions in Africa given on page 61. Create two further columns to the right and record in the first when and in what ways Britain added this area to its empire and in the second the significance of the acquisition. You may need to consult a map to help you.

STUDY TIP

There is much evidence in this chapter for the importance of strategic considerations – protecting one colony by acquiring another and ensuring British control at the expense of that of other powers. However, strategic motives clearly do not explain all British expansion and you should assemble a list of alternative influences and consider their importance as well. Remember that 'to what extent' demands some analysis of *relative* importance.

 PRACTICE QUESTION

'British expansion in Africa in the years 1890 to 1914 was driven primarily by strategic motives.' Assess the validity of this view.

Imperial and colonial policy

It is easy to see why the **Colonial Office**, whose empire included the settler colonies like Canada and Australia, a turbulent South Africa, the old West Indian colonies, new acquisitions in tropical Africa, Gibraltar, Malta, Cyprus, Ceylon, Malaya, Singapore and Hong Kong, as well as a long tail of lesser possessions, preferred reaction to action. Its resources were tiny: some thirty senior staff by 1914. With the onset of free trade, it had abandoned any attempt to control the colonial economies. Its prime concern lay in the selection of governors, drawing up their instructions (to discourage too much individual initiative) and watching them carefully in case of infringements. Governors could be rebuked or even dismissed if they exceeded their powers. Governors' requests for new laws, more money, fresh troops or a frontier advance could be approved or (more likely) rejected. But a governor with friends in high places was hard to control and still harder to remove.

Adapted from *Unfinished Empire* by John Darwin (2013)

LEARNING OBJECTIVES

In this chapter you will learn about:

- the administration of India and Egypt
- 'native policy'
- international relations and colonial policy.

ACTIVITY

Evaluating historical extracts

1. According to John Darwin in Extract 1, what was the relative importance of the Colonial Office and the colonial Governor?
2. What view does Darwin advance in Extract 1?

CROSS-REFERENCE

To recap on the establishment of the Colonial Office and its functions, look back to Chapter 2, page 11.

The Colonial Office continued to have overall responsibility for the Empire, although the Foreign Office found that its responsibilities grew as the newly acquired African protectorates were placed under its jurisdiction, while the remit of the India Office also expanded. This mixture of authorities could cause problems, particularly since the Admiralty and War Office were responsible for external defence while the Treasury controlled the purse strings. If there were disputes between these departments, the Cabinet had to be consulted, making decision-making difficult if not impossible at times.

So, while governors and colonial officials certainly had to take note of their London masters, and could face a loss of career should they fail to keep the confidence of the ministers, they were generally left alone provided they did what was expected and kept their colony in order. The worst that could happen to them was an outbreak of disorder or rebellion, or for a media storm to blow up over an incident in their area. It was therefore usually safer for administrators to lie low, take cautious decisions and avoid controversy.

KEY QUESTION

As you read this chapter, consider the following key questions:
- What influenced imperial policy?
- How important was the role of key individuals or groups?

Administration of India and Egypt

British rule in India and Egypt shared one characteristic – in both, the right to self-rule was explicitly denied. This is not to say that the British did not seek to work with the native peoples, nor even hold back moves to some political representation; but there was never any doubt about the need to maintain overall British control. In other respects, however, the difference between the rule of the Raj and that of Egypt was marked.

India

Fig. 1 *Viceregal Lodge at Shimla – India's summer capital from 1864*

British officials appointed by London continued to enjoy unrestrained power in the Indian Raj – at least until 1909 when an element of representative government was introduced at provincial level. At their head was the Viceroy, backed by the Indian Civil Service (almost all white British and recruited from Oxford or Cambridge). It was their job was to ensure the regime was secure, the native peoples acquiescent (if not content) and India profitable to Britain. This administrative elite remained comparatively small. There were strict limitations on the size of the civil service because its pay and pensions were costly, so there were often no more than three to four officers per district.

Rule continued, therefore, to require the collaboration of the native population – and all the more so as India began to modernise, with the extension of the railways and spread of education which enabled more Indians to read English. Economic and social development also required more British intervention into Indian life, both physically as the economy developed and cities grew and also in terms of raising more money through taxation. The Indian Civil Service accomplished this, to some extent, through a policy of 'divide and rule'. They emphasised the divisions within India (by race, language, religion, caste, occupation and region) and asserted Britain's moral authority to bring enlightened reform to such a diverse nation. They acknowledged some degree of educated Indian representation on provincial councils in reforms in 1892 and 1909. However they both managed the change in such a way as to preserve British executive influence and also exploited the division between the educated Indians and the illiterate rural masses to create an 'Anglo-Indian' administrative elite. Despite stirrings of nationalism, many educated Indians still saw British rule as the best road to the future and accepted British values.

Viceroy Curzon (1899–1905) was particularly energetic in the cause of reform – partly in response to Indian demands. He was mindful of the growing criticisms of British rule which emanated from professional 'middle class' Indians and their representative body, the **Indian National Congress,** which had been established in 1885 to campaign for home rule. Although members of the Congress were cautious (they opened their proceedings by singing the British National Anthem) they criticised British trading arrangements, restraints on Indian industry and the heavy taxation to

KEY CHRONOLOGY

Viceroys of India

1888–94	Marquess of Lansdowne
1894–99	Earl of Elgin
1899–1905	Viceroy Curzon
1905–10	Earl of Minto
1910–16	Lord Hardinge

CROSS-REFERENCE

The role and influence of Lord Curzon is further explored in Chapter 10, pages 93–94.

The Indian National Congress and its motivations are discussed in Chapter 12, page 112.

which the Indians were subjected in order to pay the high-earning British civil servants of the Raj. Pressure also came from social and humanitarian groups such as 'The Servants of India Society' which was active among the 'Untouchable' community at the bottom of the caste system and wanted to see the reform of old restrictive laws and practices.

Curzon made some changes in the civil service to improve efficiency and founded the Imperial Cadet Corps, in 1901, to give native princes and elite figures military training and 'special' officer commissions. He also reformed the universities and the police, lowered taxes and adopted the **gold standard** to ensure a stable currency. However, for all his reforming impulses, he is best known for his ill-fated attempt to divide the province of Bengal in 1905.

KEY TERM

gold standard: a system by which the value of the currency was defined in terms of gold, for which the currency could be exchanged (see Chapter 9, page 87)

A CLOSER LOOK

The defence of India

The **defence of India** was another of Curzon's concerns and in 1901 the North-West Frontier Province (NWFP) was created to protect the border from feared Russian incursions. This merged the north-westerly areas of the Pashtun lands of the Afghan people with the Punjab and a Chief Commissioner was put in place there. Curzon also mounted a temporary invasion of Tibet from 1903 to 1904 to counter Russia's perceived ambitions in the area and the two counties also clashed over influence in Persia. Their disputes were only resolved after Curzon left office. An 'entente' or agreement in 1907 established spheres of influence in Persia and both countries agreed to respect the independence of Tibet.

A CLOSER LOOK

Curzon's other reforms

Curzon set up a new Commerce and Industry Department, promoting industry, and an Agricultural Department, sponsoring research and overseeing the establishment of agricultural banks. His many projects ranged from the preservation of ancient monuments to railway expansion and irrigation.

CROSS-REFERENCE

The defence of India from 1858 to 1890 is discussed in Chapter 2, page 16.

The partition of Bengal

In July 1905, Curzon decided that Bengal should be divided into two separate provinces: a Muslim-majority province of East Bengal and Assam and a Hindu-majority province of West Bengal. When this was carried out in October, it produced an uproar among the Hindu elite of West Bengal, many of whom owned land in East Bengal that they leased to Muslim peasants.

The Hindus saw the partition as a pay-back for their criticisms of British rule and there were strikes, protests and boycotts of British-made goods. Surendranath Banerjee, who had twice been president of the Indian National Congress, led the campaigns and a new strand of strident nationalism began to develop. The event split the Congress between the extremists and continuing moderates and helped bring about Curzon's resignation in 1905.

CROSS-REFERENCE

The impact of Curzon's partition of Bengal on the relationship between the British and the Indians is discussed in Chapter 12, page 112.

The development of the All India Muslim League is the subject of Chapter 13, page 128.

A CLOSER LOOK

The consequences of the partition of Bengal

The Muslim elite, which supported the partition of Bengal, formed the All India Muslim League in 1906 to safeguard the rights of Indian Muslims. This was generally favourable to British rule. However, the Hindu/Muslim division was used to justify British control as the only means of avoiding serious religious conflict. Following further political protests, the two parts of Bengal were reunited in 1911 and in 1913 the **All India Muslim League** adopted self-government for India as its goal.

ACTIVITY

Extension

Find out more about the protests of 1905–06 and create an illustrated wall poster.

The Morley-Minto reforms

Viceroy Minto (1905–10) was left to deal with the fall-out of Curzon's plans. With the encouragement of the new Liberal government in Britain from 1906, and the help of John Morley, Secretary of State for India, he introduced a limited programme of reforms in 1909 in an attempt to appease the Bengalis.

The Indian Councils Act of 1909 enabled 27 Indians to be elected from provincial constituencies to the Viceroy's Council, which advised the Viceroy and assisted in the making of laws. Although these elections were held on a very narrow franchise and, in some cases, representatives were chosen by the British, the reform provided for greater Indian participation in government. Further democratic reform in 1910 meant that in elections for enlarged provincial councils, 135 Indians were able to secure seats across the subcontinent and thus play a greater part in government at provincial level.

Viceroy Hardinge (1910–16), appreciating the damage done by Curzon's partition of Bengal, used the visit of King-Emperor George V to India in 1911 as an opportunity to reunite Bengal in 1911. He also moved the Indian capital from Calcutta to Delhi (a Muslim stronghold) as a means of undermining the revolutionary Hindu groups, and the monarch laid the foundation stone of the capital, New Delhi.

George V was the first and only British monarch to visit the Raj. He was crowned Emperor of India and a grand celebratory durbar was held in 1911, in a display of both power and pageantry designed to shore up the loyalty of Indian princely rulers.

When Viceroy Hardinge declared war on India's behalf in August 1914, it was to be a test of India's commitment to British rule, particularly as he did so without consulting India's population or its elected representatives. For the most part, the Indian population accepted and supported Britain's efforts; but Indian service during that war raised hopes of a 'new deal' for India once the war was over.

A CLOSER LOOK

George V's durbar, 1911

The durbar covered an area upwards of 20 square miles and the viceroy's camp alone cost the equivalent of £2 million in today's terms. Enormous reception tents hosted formal dinners and entertainment for Indian nobles.

ACTIVITY

Evaluating historical extracts

With reference to Extract 2, explain:
a) 'a Frankenstein's monster' and
b) 'the servants were busy turning the floor boards into firewood'.
What is Fergusson's view of British rule by 1900?

EXTRACT 2

The British had set out to create Indians in their own image. However, when they alienated the Indian Anglicised elite, they produced a Frankenstein's monster. In the late nineteenth century the British had called into being an English-speaking, English-educated elite of Indians; a class of civil service auxiliaries on whom their system of administration had come to depend. In time, these people naturally aspired to have some share in the government of the country, just as some Victorians had predicted. But, in the age of Curzon, they were spurned in favour of decorative but largely defunct Maharajas. The result was that by the Empress-Queen Victoria's twilight years, around the turn of the century, British rule in India was like one of those palaces Curzon so adored. It looked simply splendid on the outside. But downstairs the servants were busy turning the floorboards into firewood.

Adapted from *Empire* by Niall Ferguson (2008)

Egypt

Fig. 2 *The Aswan Dam, southern Egypt, c1902*

While India was entirely under British control, Egypt was a more complex case and it was not until the onset of the First World War in December 1914 that Britain assumed direct rule, turning Egypt into a formal Protectorate. Before then it was a 'veiled protectorate', with the British running Egyptian affairs and British advisers keeping watch over every aspect of government. Despite this strong British presence, Egypt was not regarded as a Colony – only under military occupation, which had originally been intended as **temporary**. In this strange administrative arrangement, Egypt still belonged (strictly speaking) to Turkey – with **the Sultan** as the Khedive's overlord.

There were further hindrances to the British freedom of action:

- The Capitulations. All foreigners in Egypt came under regulations known as the Capitulations – privileges once granted by the Sultan to protect Europeans from Muslim laws against Christians. So, for example, a foreigner could claim the right to be tried in his own country's law courts and any new Egyptian law affecting Europeans had to be approved by the governments of all countries represented in Egypt, which slowed down law-making.
- The Caisse de la Dette (which included Austria-Hungary, France, Germany, Russia, Italy as well as Britain). This controlled Egypt's finances. About half the country's revenue went to paying European bond-holders. The members of the Caisse could prevent the British Consul-General from spending Egypt's money on matters they disapproved of. (Cromer's plans to use Egyptian money to finance the re-conquest of the Sudan were, for example, thwarted by Russia and France.)
- The Mixed Courts. These had been set up to deal with cases involving both Egyptians and Europeans and were presided over by European and Egyptian judges who were not always supportive of the British.

The French, with their strong interest in Egypt, posed a particular challenge to British supremacy. However, after the **1898 Fashoda incident**, Britain and France grew closer together and in 1904 signed an Entente Cordiale, by which the French agreed to respect Britain's special rights in Egypt, in return for British recognition of the French take-over of Morocco. With this agreement, the Caisse de la Dette ceased to control Egyptian finances and became only a debt-collection agency for foreign bondholders.

CROSS-REFERENCE

For the manner in which the British 'temporarily' occupied Egypt, look back to Chapter 1, page 6.

A CLOSER LOOK

The British had tried to reach an agreement with **the Sultan** in 1887 by which they would withdraw their troops after three years. When this came to nothing in 1890, the British largely ignored Turkish rights – and the Sultan did not interfere.

CROSS-REFERENCE

The 1898 Fashoda incident is outlined in Chapter 7, page 66.

CROSS-REFERENCE

Evelyn Baring is discussed in case studies in Chapter 4, pages 38–39 and Chapter 10, pages 95–96.

Evelyn Baring (Lord Cromer), the British Consul-General, acted as 'adviser' to the Khedive between 1883 and 1907. Egypt had a partially-elected parliament, consisting of an Advisory Council of Laws and a General Assembly – but all Egyptian government ministers had the 'support' of a British adviser. If they resisted British advice or interference, they could be dismissed. The number of Britons working in government in Egypt steadily increased. In 1885 there were only about 100 – by 1905, there were over 1,000.

Baring's main task was to try to regularise Egyptian financial affairs. Khedive Isma'il had accrued £70 million debt – mostly to European bondholders. In order to balance Egypt's account books, Baring made cutbacks to Egypt's military and bureaucracy. At the same time he revitalised the economy by improving communications and investing in irrigation schemes (carried out by British engineers, some of whom had worked on similar schemes in India). He also improved conditions for Egyptian labourers and introduced better sanitation and health services in towns. Within ten years, exports of cotton and sugar had trebled and the population had risen from seven to ten million. Egypt thus enjoyed a new-found prosperity.

CROSS-REFERENCE

This dam was added to by the creation of the Aswan High Dam between 1960 and 1970. This was a project of the government of Colonel Nasser, who came to power in Egypt in 1952 – see Chapter 20, page 195.

A CLOSER LOOK

The Aswan Dam

Under the direction of Sir John Aird, a wall, 18 metres high and a quarter of a mile long was built to hold back the waters of the Nile. This Aswan Dam took six years to build and cost £2 million (raised by the friends of Lord Cromer). It opened in 1902 and enabled half a million acres of former desert to be irrigated with water from its reservoir, thus enabling year-round cultivation.

Baring also reformed Egypt's army, not least by placing 6000 British troops within it to ensure that British interests were not jeopardised by either military or popular disturbances. This army was placed under the command of **Kitchener**. Britain simply could not risk a threat to its Egypt-based investments or to the Suez Canal as the preferred passage to India. Other changes were made to the law courts, police and education, although Baring was wary of extending educational opportunities to the Egyptians, since he had seen the effects of raised expectations in India, where they had led to a growth of nationalist protest. Egyptians were therefore rarely offered more than a few years of elementary schooling and it was not until 1909 that a new university was founded (to supplement the University of Cairo which only offered religious education) to teach modern subjects and train men for the professions.

CROSS-REFERENCE

For the part played by Kitchener and the Egyptian Army in the Sudan campaign of 1896–98, re-read Chapter 7, pages 66–67.

A CLOSER LOOK

Egypt and tourism

Baring oversaw the rapid expansion of modern tourism, to the extent that Thomas Cook & Son became Egypt's largest employer – providing jobs in hotels, houseboats and excursions. By 1900 it had become very popular for wealthy Britons to 'winter' in Egypt. Tourists enjoyed both the climate and Egypt's ancient treasures, most notably the pyramids, biblical sites and Cairo's citadel, built by Saladin during the Crusades. Some took a steamer up the Nile; others enjoyed the city bazaars – but few ventured into the surrounding countryside and guidebooks discouraged Europeans from mixing with local people.

The Egyptian upper classes generally benefited from the British occupation but by the late 1890s there was a growing middle-class nationalist movement, fuelled by newspapers, which attacked the British for failing to deal with the corruption of the Khedive's government and for doing little to help Egypt's poor. It was said, with some justification, that the British failed to promote the Egyptian cloth-making industry, which would have provided jobs for the unemployed, because they were only interested in the production of raw cotton to keep the spinners of Lancashire employed. The nationalists also complained of the lack of opportunities for educated Egyptians who, after years of British rule, seemed even less likely to be able to run their own government than they had been before.

A National Party (al-Ḥizb al-Waṭanī), first formed in 1881 but revived in 1893 as a secret society, attracted Egyptian lawyers and professionals, many educated in Egyptian and European (particularly French) establishments. They sought the end of British occupation and their own representative government. Cromer largely ignored these demands, although he did appoint a nationalist, Saad Zaghluls Pasha, as Minister for Education.

In 1906, a clash between British officers and Egyptian villagers at **Denshawai** was related with horror in the nationalist press. A series of misunderstandings and high-handed British action led to the arrest of 52 villagers, four of whom were convicted of murder and sentenced to death. One was given a life sentence of penal servitude and 26 were given various terms of hard labour and ordered to be flogged. An Egyptian policeman who had testified on behalf of the villagers was given two years imprisonment and 50 lashes. This provoked a further questioning of British rule in Egypt.

Fig. 3 *An advert for Thomas Cook's Nile cruises from 1908*

A CLOSER LOOK

The Denshawai incident

In June 1906, a group of British officers angered the residents of Denshawai by pigeon-shooting for sport near their village. The pigeons were bred by the villagers for food and in the ensuing confusion – with neither side understanding the other – an officer's gun went off and wounded the wife of a Muslim prayer leader. The soldiers were set upon and an officer fleeing the scene collapsed and died in the intense heat. Other soldiers, discovering his body, killed a villager whom they falsely took to be his assassin.

KEY CHRONOLOGY

Consul-Generals of Egypt

1883–1907	Sir Evelyn Baring
1907–11	Sir Eldon Gorst
1911–14	Viscount Herbert Kitchener

Baring was succeeded as Consul-General by Eldon Gorst. Gorst brought more Egyptians into responsible government positions in an attempt to weaken the Egyptian National Party. He also tried to impose a tighter censorship of the press in 1909 and used various penal measures to attempt to quell the growing nationalism within Egypt, but to little avail. The German government provided funds to fuel anti-British sentiment.

CROSS-REFERENCE

Kitchener's role as Army Commander-in-Chief in Egypt is outlined in Chapter 7, pages 66–67.

Viscount Herbert Kitchener, hero of the Boer War and former Army Commander-in-Chief, also tried to curb Nationalist sentiment and uncover those groups who were stirring up trouble. Under his consulship from 1911, British dominance increased rather than diminished. In 1913, a new Legislative Assembly replaced the Advisory Council of Laws and General Assembly, consisting of 66 elected members and 17 appointed nominees. This represented rich landowners rather than the ordinary people of Egypt.

With the coming of the First World War, which placed the Ottoman Empire on the side of the Central Powers (Germany and Austria-Hungary), Britain unilaterally declared a protectorate over Egypt in November 1914. Since control of the Suez Canal was crucial for the British, the ruling Khedive (an ally of the Ottoman Sultan) was deposed and his successor, Hussein Kamel, was compelled to declare himself as an independent Sultan of Egypt, under British protection.

ACTIVITY

Complete the chart below to compare British rule in India and Egypt.

	Main means of British control	Degree of native involvement in government	Native opposition to British control	Degree of British control in 1914
India				
Egypt				

Native policy

It could be argued that Britain never had a distinct 'native policy', but rather reacted according to time and circumstances.

The most successful form of 'native rule' was that deployed in the **white, settler colonies** such as Canada and Australia. These self-governing colonies had exercised some form of self-government since the mid-nineteenth century – as did South Africa's Cape Colony from 1872 – albeit with British control over defence, international commerce and foreign affairs. Canada became a semi-independent 'Dominion' from 1867, Australia from 1901 and Newfoundland and New Zealand from 1907. The South African states were united in 1910. Since Britain was responsible for neither the administration nor the costs of government in these Dominions, any control was largely symbolic. Britain relied on such countries as a means to preserve its global power. Dominion status actually meant a shift away from British 'domination'.

Elsewhere in the Empire, local elites were typically used to facilitate British rule and those who were prepared to uphold British interests and participate in administration might expect material rewards or positions of influence. Sometimes these elites were actually appointed to leadership by the British, as was the case for the rulers of Zanzibar (Sultan Hamad, 1893 and Hamoud, 1896); sometimes they already held positions of considerable power in their own right and were allowed to keep these, as in the case of the Indian princes. Often, large landholders or hereditary notables gained titles or privileges while co-operative middle classes were also favoured with positions in administration; many Indians, for example, served in the administration of the Raj. However, although full civil service positions were theoretically open to all Indians, applicants had to travel to England to sit the examinations for entry. In 1890 there were just 30 Indian Civil Service officers and the figure barely doubled by 1914.

Sometimes 'native policy' involved befriending one group against another, as happened in so much of the British expansion in Africa. In British East

CROSS-REFERENCE

To recap on administration in the white, settler colonies before 1890, look back to Chapter 2, page 12.

CROSS-REFERENCE

To recap on the Royal Niger Company, look back to Chapter 3, page 29.

Africa, for example, the Masai were favoured and rewarded with cattle and tokens of office such as badges or caps in preference to the Kikuyu. In large areas, conventional methods of control were unworkable. **Lord Lugard**, working for the Royal Niger Company, relied on trusted chiefs (the Fulani emirs) to exercise governance and within the Uganda Protectorate, Buganda's Kabaka (King) maintained autonomy and his chiefs were given land as a reward for their loyalty. Such an approach was cheap to implement, supported existing power structures and helped to legitimise British authority.

ACTIVITY

Native policy can also refer to the ways in which governors and consuls improved the position of the native people under their control through welfare and other reforms. Look back through this chapter and make a list of all such policies in both India and Egypt.

EXTRACT 3

Both sides came to rely on a form of political bargain, or what has sometimes been called 'collaborative politics'. Collaboration allowed local elites to protect their own social privileges and helped them to control the vertical links binding their districts to imperial rule. Many communities, tribes and individuals were well placed to offer their services – as soldiers, clerks, policemen and teachers – to the colonial regime and reap the reward. The limits on their manpower meant the British had to rely on collaboration with indigenous teachers, clerics and law-givers. This was all the more necessary because the British were obsessed with the need to codify. They wanted fixed schedules of rights and claims so that their men on the spot should not be too much in the dark. They consulted learned men and turned to chiefs, scholars, and native lawyers for help. Thus, far from assaulting local traditions, the British more often allied with interested parties to fabricate a 'traditional' order, in which the past was re-invented to suit the mutual convenience of both parties.

Adapted from *Unfinished Empire* by John Darwin (2013)

KEY PROFILE

Sir Frederick Lugard (1858–1945)

Fig. 4 *Lugard was a soldier, explorer and colonial administrator*

Lugard fought in colonial wars in Afghanistan, Sudan and Burma, and became a leading colonial administrator. He was Governor of Hong Kong (1907–12) and Governor of Nigeria (1914–19). He became known as an authority on the principles and methods of British colonial rule, as explained in his book of 1922, *The Dual Mandate*. He was the British representative on the League's Permanent Mandate Commission (see Chapter 13, page 122) from 1919 to 1936.

 PRACTICE QUESTION

Evaluating historical extracts

Using your understanding of the historical context, assess how convincing the arguments in Extracts 1, 2 and 3 are, in relation to the problems of British administration in the colonies.

STUDY TIP

Look for the overall argument in each extract and comment on this first, but don't forget to examine any subsidiary arguments or views also. Use your own knowledge of colonial administration to draw a conclusion as to how convincing each is.

International relations and colonial policy

Britain had maintained a policy of 'splendid isolation' since the end of the Napoleonic Wars in 1815, trusting to its dominant navy to maintain its status and empire. The Navy was assumed capable of defeating any naval force that challenged it, so the Empire was considered safe. The Army, however, was regarded as of secondary importance. It was the Boer War of 1899–1902 that forced a drastic review of strategy, since it was felt that the need to concentrate military power in South Africa had left India vulnerable.

Two alliance systems had emerged in Europe in the late nineteenth century. Germany made an alliance with Austria-Hungary in 1870, which was joined by Italy in 1882. This alliance was promptly countered by military agreements between France and Russia in 1892, followed by an alliance between them in 1894.

CROSS-REFERENCE

For the 1898 Fashoda incident, look back to Chapter 7, page 66.

Britain was left in an uneasy position. Whilst isolation might have been the preferred strategy, it could leave Britain vulnerable to the ambitions of both alliances. Britain had conflicted with Russia, France and Germany over colonies, although disputes in Africa, had been largely resolved peaceably. Britain's clashes with France in North Africa, which had culminated in the 1898 **Fashoda incident**, had been peacefully resolved, but Britain continued to have grave concerns about Russian ambitions, particularly in Afghanistan (a buffer state between Russia and India), but also in the Middle East.

A CLOSER LOOK

Britain and Russia before 1907

Afghanistan provided a constant source of conflict between Russia and Britain in the nineteenth and early twentieth centuries – sometimes known as the 'Great Game'. The expansion of Russia and the establishment of a Russian railway to Tashkent (within striking distance of Afghanistan) caused concern for the British. The movement of 300,000 Russian troops in manoeuvres near Afghanistan in February 1900, at a time when Britain was stretched by war in South Africa and had fewer than 100,000 soldiers in the Indian Army to defend northern India, added to Britain's worries. Britain's concerns about Russia's ambitions in the Middle East were also aggravated by a Russian naval presence in Toulon on the Mediterranean, following the military agreements with France in 1892. This appeared a potential threat to the Suez Canal and, therefore, to British India.

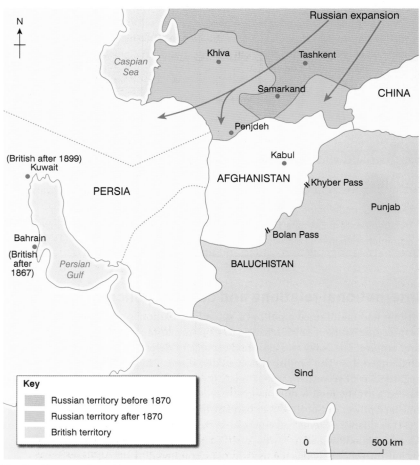

Fig. 5 *Reasons for British anxiety over Russian expansionism by 1907*

Look back through this book and make a table to show Britain's colonial conflicts between 1857 and 1907.

	Where and when clash occurred	Outcome
Russia		
France		
Germany		

Fig. 6 *Haydarpasha train station, Constantinople, c1910*

Germany, under its new and ambitious Kaiser, Wilhelm II (1888–1918), also challenged Britain in the colonies. For example, the Kaiser sent a telegram of support to the Transvaal following the **Jameson raid** and supplied the Boers with weapons during the 1899–1902 war. He also established warm relations with the Ottoman Empire, as a means to better access Africa, the Persian Gulf and India's trade markets without depending on the British-controlled Suez. It was German money that financed railway construction from Constantinople to Baghdad and huge sums were spent to build up the German Navy in what appeared to the British to be a deliberately provocative move to counter Britain's dominance of the High Seas, so essential for the maintenance of empire.

Britain tentatively abandoned splendid isolation by signing an Entente Cordiale (friendly alliance) with the French in 1904. This did not, however, provide much security, since it ranged Britain against the Triple Alliance and left its relationship with Russia open. The cost of defending its naval supremacy was a furious naval race with Germany which intensified from 1906. However, after Russia had suffered a humiliating defeat in war with Japan in 1905 (which shattered Russian naval power), and Tsarist power had been shaken by internal troubles, Britain, Russia and France came together in a 'Triple Entente' in 1907. This settled Britain's main imperial concerns by declaring the Persian Gulf a neutral zone and recognising Afghanistan as a British sphere of influence.

CROSS-REFERENCE

The Jameson raid in the Transvaal in 1895 is covered in Chapter 7, pages 68–69.

The Moroccan crises, 1905 and 1911

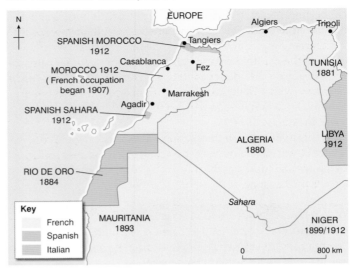

Fig. 7 *Areas affected by the Moroccan crises with European takeover dates*

The strength of Britain's support for France was tested when the Kaiser threatened French interests in Morocco on a visit in 1905. After several weeks of tense discussion, the matter was resolved at the Algeçiras Conference (1906) when Britain stood by the French. A further crisis erupted when, in 1911, the French sent 20,000 soldiers to disperse Moroccan rebels who had attacked Fez. The Kaiser sent a warship (the *Panther*) to the port of Agadir 'to prevent a French invasion'. The British, fearful that Wilhelm was planning to seize Agadir (near British Gibraltar) as a base, prepared the Royal Navy for war. Wilhelm gave way and ordered the *Panther* home.

The Imperial Conference, 1911

Against a background of concern over German ambitions, an Imperial Conference was called in 1911 to forge closer ties between Britain and the Dominions. Foreign Secretary Edward Grey successfully conveyed the vulnerability of the Dominions if Britain lost its maritime supremacy. The South African government promised to commit 40,000 men to attack German South-West Africa in the event of European conflict, while Australia and New Zealand agreed to take action against German colonies in the Pacific.

Britain: strategies and war

Agitation in Britain over the naval race with Germany spread to the colonies. A special **Imperial Conference** on defence was held in 1909 and the formation of a Dominion fleet considered. Britain accepted that it was no longer in a position to maintain a 'two power standard', whereby it could match the two next strongest naval powers; instead it settled for a 60 per cent margin over Germany. However, even this looked ambitious by 1912. All attempts to come to an agreement with the Germans failed and in July 1912, Britain withdrew the Navy from the Mediterranean, in order to redeploy it in the North Sea. The Army was also remodelled for deployment on the European mainland. Britain was thus reduced to relying on the support of France (with whom secret military conversations had taken place since 1905) to protect its Mediterranean interests and the naval approaches to Egypt. By 1914 Britain appeared to be refocusing away from empire to the defence of Britain in Europe.

Britain's change of strategy might appear dramatic. British industrial power was entering a period of relative economic decline and the strain of upholding its world-wide pre-eminence in the face of the ambitions of the other European powers seemed to be telling. However, it would be wrong to exaggerate the degree of pre-war change away from empire, since strength in Europe was also vital for Britain's imperial interests.

The outbreak of war in 1914 was more the result of other nations' quest for empire than of British ambitions. Russia, Germany and Italy all had hopes of extending their empires in the Balkan area, where the Turkish Ottoman Empire was in decline. Meanwhile Austria-Hungary, which bordered the Balkan states, wanted to crush the Slavs – who were stirring up trouble within the Austro-Hungarian Empire and in Serbia. A series of Balkan Wars and the assassination of the heir to the Austrian throne in July 1914 by a Bosnian Serb Slav led these powers into direct conflict with one another. The German invasion of Belgium (whose neutrality the British had promised to protect since 1839) and the Kaiser's failure to reply to the British ultimatum **led Britain into war in August 1914**.

Not only was this to become an international war, involving the colonies of the warring states, it was also to be a war that challenged the very legitimacy of European empires and hinted at the urgent desire for national self-determination across the globe.

A CLOSER LOOK

Britain declared war in August 1914 in support of France and Russia against Germany and Austria-Hungary. Italy did not commit itself and only entered war in 1915 on the British/French side.

Summary

Between 1890 and 1914 Britain experienced what has sometimes been referred to as the 'high noon' of empire. The late Victorians and **Edwardians** had absolute faith in the permanence of the Empire and even though some changes occurred in the administration of countries such as India and Egypt, and 'native policy' saw reforms introduced for the benefit of the indigenous peoples, both were administered with self-confidence and attempts at moral justification. However, there were anxieties just below the surface and the abandonment of 'splendid isolation' and the strategic withdrawal from the Mediterranean may be viewed as a sign of impending trouble as British affairs became more intimately entwined with those of the other European powers.

AS LEVEL — PRACTICE QUESTION

'British colonial policy in the years 1890 to 1914 was changed by the activities of other European powers.' Explain why you agree or disagree with this view.

ACTIVITY

Draw a flow chart to show how international relations developed between 1890 and 1914. Indicate the points at which international affairs impinged on British colonial policies.

KEY TERM

Edwardian: Queen Victoria died in 1901 and was succeeded by Edward VII (ruled 1901–1910); the Edwardian era denotes this period (and is sometimes extended to refer to the period up to 1914)

STUDY TIP

In this question you will need to consider Britain's colonial policies and comment on the ways in which the activities of other European powers affected Britain's actions. You could start by looking back at Chapter 7 for the ways in which other powers affected Britain's expansion and consolidation in Africa. You might also find the flow chart you made in the activity above helpful in considering developments in international relations outlined in this chapter.

9 Trade and commerce

EXTRACT 1

The union of commercial and imperial muscle was the foundation of the British world system. The vast scale of British trade, the fleets of merchant shipping, the treasure chest of overseas investment and the resources it commanded were widely seen as the real embodiment of British world power. They supplied the economic energy to sustain the show of empire and pay for its defence. They formed the invisible chains that bound the visible empire of dependencies and settler states to their far-off **metropole**. They provided the means to expand the sphere of British influence and turn the undeveloped estates of Empire into imperial assets. In a world in which a handful of imperial superstars was expected to hold sway, they were the guarantee of premier status, and of independence.

Adapted from *The Empire Project* by Ian Darwin (2009)

Trade and commerce

With the exception of a few dissenting voices, there was a general assumption, in 1890, that the Empire made Britain wealthy – and more empire would make the country wealthier still. This was, in fact, a fallacy. Britain did, of course, have plentiful trade with the Empire. Even under free trade – which meant that it made no economic difference to a colony to trade within the Empire – Britain had a disproportionate amount of trade and investment in its own colonies. India, for example, represented a particularly large market since it took about 20 per cent of Britain's total exports, worth almost £150 million, to businesses by 1914. In return, India exported huge quantities of goods to Britain, not least raw cotton and tea. These items were both consumed in Britain and exported on from Britain to other countries.

Other territories played their part too, in terms of both clothing and feeding Britons. There was wool and sugar from South Africa and Australia, dairy produce and lamb from New Zealand, and beef and wheat from Canada. Indeed, Canada supplied upwards of 10 per cent of Britain's beef and 15 per cent of its wheat flour by 1914. Between 1900 and 1914, there was a six-fold increase (to over 45 thousand square miles) in Canadian land set aside for wheat production. Britain also imported West African timber, cocoa, rubber, peanuts and palm oil.

A CLOSER LOOK

The ocean steamship remained the major bulk carrier and railways continued as a major means for facilitating trade and offering investment opportunities. A line was built, for example, from Uganda to the sea at Mombasa c1900, and the Indian network continued to expand.

A CLOSER LOOK

A pale ale for export had been devised for Britons in India and elsewhere. British Breweries competed for the colonial market, including Hodgson's of Essex, Phipps of Northampton, Shepherd Neame of Kent and both Bass and Allsopp of Burton-on-Trent. English beer was exported to India, partly to keep officials away from potent local brews. The beer had extra hops and alcohol (for better preservation).

However, the benefits of trade with the Empire were less significant than is often imagined. Indeed, the **Imperial Federation League** which had been established in 1884 to promote closer colonial ties was disbanded in 1893 (less than a decade after its inception) partially reflecting a waning interest in the Empire's commercial importance. Fig. 2 indicates Britain's trade with the Empire just before the outbreak of the First World War.

CROSS-REFERENCE

The establishment of the Imperial Federation League is covered in Chapter 3, page 29.

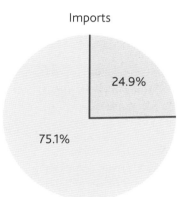

Fig. 1 *An advert for John Smith's IPA beer from 1893*

Instead of reliance on empire, Britain's trade was growing with the non-imperial world – particularly with the USA. In 1894, Britain had imported 64 million hundredweight of wheat – 30.7 million from the USA, 17.2 million from Russia and only 3.6 million from Canada. Only in cheese, apples, potatoes and fresh mutton was the Empire Britain's main food supplier. Other foodstuffs came from elsewhere, with the Empire providing less than 10 per cent. The Empire's total trade in 1896 was worth £745 million, but trade between

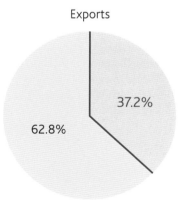

Fig. 2 *The proportion of British imports and exports from Empire countries and other countries in 1913*

the countries of the Empire only £183 million. Furthermore, while trade between Britain and foreign countries was increasing, that with the Empire was almost static. So, despite the expansion of the Empire, there had been no corresponding expansion of trade. In 1897, the whole of Tropical Africa took only 1.2 per cent of British exports and over the ensuing years the colonies bought increasing amounts from foreign nations, rather than from Britain.

Given these circumstances, anti-imperialists argued that the Empire cost middle-class people more than it benefited them. They were supporting the cost of imperial defence in their taxes. The Empire was also blamed for Britain's failure to modernise its industry. Anti-imperialists believed that it was holding back developments that would have helped raise living standards for workers.

Certainly Britain lagged behind in chemical and electrical engineering as a result of poor investment and productivity. So, for example, while Britain was relying on rubber imports from Africa or Asia, the French, Russians and Germans had successfully started their own synthetic rubber production by 1910.

Anti-imperialists argued that the colonies blunted British commercial enterprise and that the import of colonial food produce into Britain undermined domestic food production and served to depopulate the countryside. It was also suggested that cheaper foreign labour in the colonies was depressing wages within Britain.

Added to this were the costs of empire; not least the cost of maintaining a huge navy. Although India was self-financing and white colonies only relied on Britain for defence, others had to be subsidised and the costs of acquiring some of this empire far outweighed any returns from it.

Investment in empire

Fig. 3 *An 1882 cartoon depicting imperialism*

KEY PROFILE

John A. Hobson (1858–1940) was an economist who wrote *Problems of Poverty* (1891), *Evolution of Modern Capitalism* (1894) and *Problem of the Unemployed* (1896), but is best known for *Imperialism* (1902). His ideas in *Imperialism* were formulated when he worked as a correspondent for the *Manchester Guardian* in South Africa during the Boer War. He believed the mine owners had tricked the British into fighting the Boers in order to preserve their own profits. He was a critic of empire, which he thought benefited capitalists only.

It is not too much to say that the modern foreign policy of Great Britain has been primarily a struggle for profitable markets of investment. To a larger extent every year Great Britain has been becoming a nation living upon tribute from abroad. The classes who enjoy this tribute have had an ever-increasing incentive to employ public policy, the public purse, and the public force to extend the field of their private investment, and to safeguard and improve their existing investments. It is this economic condition of affairs that forms the taproot of imperialism. If the consuming public in this country raised its living standards to keep pace with the rise of productive powers, there would be no excess of goods or capital nor a clamour for Imperialism in order to find markets.

Adapted from *Imperialism: A Study* by John Atkinson Hobson (1902)

Even the immense overseas investments of the British were no longer primarily imperial investments. Although British investment doubled from £2 billion to £4 billion between 1900 and 1913, not all of this was with the Empire. Far more British capital went to the USA and India, and the disparity increased. While loans within the Empire were regarded as safe, loans to foreign nations might provide bigger returns. Added to this, loans within the Empire might be used to develop rival manufactures to Britain; for example building up Indian cotton and jute mills, and this was seen as dangerous.

Nevertheless, London remained the world's financial capital and capital for imperial projects was raised there. Shares were sold in ventures from minerals, tobacco and timber to transport and public utilities. The Colonial Loans and Colonial Stocks Acts of 1899 and 1900 facilitated a number of infrastructure projects, including rail links into the African interior from the ports of Lagos and Mombasa.

A CLOSER LOOK

By 1914 Britain had invested twice the amount of the French and three times that of the Germans overseas. The immense amounts of capital invested in Latin America maintained the 'informal empire' and commercial treaties were made with Latin American countries, Turkey, Morocco, Siam, Japan and the South Sea Islands. Free trade with the developing world suited Britain. With its huge earnings from overseas investment, not forgetting other '**invisibles**' such as insurance and shipping, Britain could afford to import vastly more than it exported. Moreover, the terms of trade (the relationship between export and import prices) moved by around 10 per cent in Britain's favour between 1870 and 1914.

Britain also set the standard for the international monetary system, forcing other nations to mirror Britain by adopting the **gold standard**. By 1908, only China, Persia and a handful of Central American countries still used a 'silver standard'. The gold standard had thus become the basis for a global monetary system – and was effectively a 'sterling standard'.

EXTRACT 2

The later years of the nineteenth century witnessed the relative decline of the British economy, caused by the slow growth of manufacturing output. Manufactured exports grew much more slowly after 1870 than before and Britain's share of world visible trade fell. Invisibles, on the other hand, increased rapidly until 1914 with profits being made from the growing service sector, led by the

Evaluating primary sources

1. What do you understand by Hobson's phrase 'this economic condition of affairs that forms the the taproot of imperialism'?
2. What do you think Hobson's personal perspective is on British imperialism?

KEY TERM

'**invisibles**': this refers to any export that provides income but does not have a physical presence. Examples include insurance, banking services and return on overseas investments

A CLOSER LOOK

The gold standard had been adopted by the Bank of England in 1821. In theory, every pound sterling in circulation was backed by a fixed amount of gold, held in the reserves of the Bank of England. In practice, currencies on the gold standard were fixed in value against each other, aiding international commerce. The gold standard become a symbol of Britain's economic strength.

global extension of the sterling standard and credit from the City of London. The influence of industry on central government and on economic policy continued to be limited by its relative lack of access to the major sources of power and influence. Manufacturers were still largely outside the circle of gentlemanly culture and did not 'speak the same language' as the aristocratic elite.

Adapted from 'Gentlemanly Capitalism and British Expansion Overseas: New Imperialism, 1850–1945' by P.J. Cain and A.G. Hopkins (1987)

ACTIVITY

Evaluating historical extracts

What view of the British economy in the later years of the nineteenth century is advanced by Cain and Hopkins in Extract 2?

ACTIVITY

Create a 'scales' diagram on which you weigh up the costs of empire against the benefits. You should reflect on what you have learnt before you begin and decide which way your scales will tip.

CROSS-REFERENCE

The role and influence of Joseph Chamberlain and the issue of 'imperial preference' are discussed in Chapter 15, pages 147–148.

Debates over trade and commerce within the Empire

The early years of the twentieth century saw some fierce debate between those who saw the colonies as an expensive encumbrance and those who believed they were a valuable asset that should be made more of. One such pro-imperialist was **Joseph Chamberlain**, the Conservative Colonial Secretary (1895–1903), who convened the 1902 London Colonial Conference for leaders from Britain and the self-governing white settler colonies (or 'Dominions') of Australia, Canada, New Zealand, Cape Colony, Natal and Newfoundland. This Conference discussed creating closer economic ties in the form of an imperial customs union. This would have given a boost to imperial trade through mutual customs agreements and protective tariffs against imports from non-imperial powers. Chamberlain believed that imperial trade was preferable because it would be strategically reliable in times of emergency. He also believed the colonies and commerce between them had the potential for much greater productivity and growth. Such as arrangement is known as 'imperial preference'.

Fig. 4 *A poster highlighting colonies as valuable assets; although produced in the 1920s, this poster presents views that were already strong before the turn of the century*

However, Chamberlain's ideas met with resistance from the manufacturing, shipping and banking industries; their interests were with free trade and the wider international community rather than with a specifically imperial economy. They argued that Britain's wealth had come from free trade and the old economic meaning of empire (as had existed in the days of **mercantilism**) had long since disappeared. The Empire was not an economic unity and far from self-sufficient.

CROSS-REFERENCE

The former system of mercantilism is introduced in Chapter 3, pages 22–23.

ACTIVITY

Look back at Chapter 3 to help you to complete this diagram about types of trade:

	Mercantilism (eighteenth/ early nineteenth centuries)	Free trade (mid-nineteenth/ early twentieth centuries)	Chamberlain's proposed 'imperial preference' programme
Advantages for Britain			
Disadvantages for Britain			
Effect on the colonies			
Overall comments/ conclusions			

The death knell of imperial preference came in the form of the 1906 general election when the public roundly rejected Chamberlain's proposals, not least because it would have put up food prices. Voters overwhelmingly favoured the Liberal Party's commitment to free trade.

Before the outbreak of war in 1914, Australia, New Zealand and South Africa had all imposed import tariffs as a means of asserting their national interests over any loyalties or ties to Britain. Canada had made its own trading agreements with Germany, France, Italy and Japan and a separate commercial union with America was regarded as a distinct possibility. Worse still, in India, British textiles and goods were boycotted and burned in the streets as the *swadeshi* (self-sufficiency) movement sought to undermine the Raj in the years after 1905.

CROSS-REFERENCE

The *swadeshi* movement is outlined in Chapter 12, page 112.

EXTRACT 3

The mere fact that Britain ruled a particular market as a colony did not necessarily mean that she only traded with it because it was a colony. The ideological free traders in the first half of the nineteenth century argued that she might have done even more business with the country if it had not been. They offered the example of the United States – with whom Britain's trade actually rose after the War of Independence (1775–1783) – to prove their case. Furthermore, in the late nineteenth century, the anti-imperialist economist J. A. Hobson argued that, in addition, imperialism depressed wages in Britain. Others claimed that it also cost middle-class people more than it benefited them, through the taxes they were forced to pay for imperial defence. By the early twentieth century it became fashionable to blame the Empire for cushioning Britain from the need to 'modernise' her industry in a way that (it was implied) would have benefited its employees even more.

Adapted from *The Absent-Minded Imperialists* by Bernard Porter (2006)

ACTIVITY

Evaluating historical extracts

Identify the various anti-imperialist views put forward by Porter in Extract 3.

Both questions are concerned with the economic benefits of the Empire to Britain in the years 1890 to 1914. For both you will need to identify the arguments put forward in the extracts, supporting your comments with reference to the passages. For the AS question you need to show which you feel is the more convincing by applying your own knowledge. For the A Level question you should use your contextual knowledge to evaluate and judge each extract in turn, but you are not required to compare them directly.

 PRACTICE QUESTION

Evaluating historical extracts

With reference to Extracts 1 and 3 and your understanding of the historical context, which of these two extracts provides the more convincing interpretation of the economic benefits of the Empire to Britain in the years 1890 to 1914?

 PRACTICE QUESTION

Evaluating historical extracts

Using your understanding of the historical context, assess how convincing Extracts 1, 2 and 3 are, in relation to the economic benefits of the Empire to Britain in the years 1890 to 1914.

Summary

The years 1890 to 1914 saw a shift in Britain's economic relationship with its empire. Imperial commerce undoubtedly sheltered Britain during the Great Depression – perhaps overly so, lulling the British into a sense of false security as other countries caught up with Britain in industry and science. Nevertheless, investment in colonial projects made a powerful contribution to British wealth, although the costs of empire continued to grow. The First World War was to lead to a further examination of the costs of empire.

STUDY TIP

This question presents a statement that is open to challenge. Before beginning to write, make a list of points which both support and challenge the statement. You can use these to reflect on the view you will adopt in your answer. Remember to back your comments with plenty of precise evidence.

 PRACTICE QUESTION

'Britain's wealth rested heavily on the growth and maintenance of its empire in the years 1890 to 1914.' Assess the validity of this view.

10 Attitudes to empire – the role and influence of individuals

EXTRACT 1

There can be little doubt that, as British acquaintance with the non-European world grew in the nineteenth century, so did a readiness to be highly critical and even totally dismissive of alien cultures, as well as a view that Britain had a mission or national duty to spread the benefits of its civilisation, economy, and religion as widely as possible overseas. Critical stereotypes and assumptions of British superiority were used for at least 100 years to justify colonial rule in various forms. Between 1890 and 1914, for example, both Evelyn Baring and Sir Alfred Milner defended at length a continued British presence in Egypt on grounds of the inability of Egypt's own ruling classes to maintain a stable and prosperous state. In east and central Africa only the combination of colonial rule and white-settler farming was thought capable of attaining similar goals.

Adapted from 'Empires in the Mind' by Andrew Porter (1996)

LEARNING OBJECTIVES

In this chapter you will learn about:

- the role and influence of Joseph Chamberlain
- the role and influence of Cecil Rhodes after 1890
- colonial administration.

KEY QUESTION

As you read this chapter, consider the following key questions:
- What influenced imperial policy?
- How important was the role of key individuals and how were they affected by developments?

The role and influence of Joseph Chamberlain

Joseph Chamberlain was 'a man with a mission' and the most committed Colonial Secretary of the Victorian era. He turned down the office of both the Chancellor of the Exchequer and Home Secretary in 1895, in order to become Secretary of State for the Colonies. Although he acknowledged Britain's relative decline in both the industrial and military spheres towards the end of the century, as other nations (particularly Germany) posed a challenge to British dominance, he believed that effective use of the Empire could sustain British prosperity and prestige.

ACTIVITY

Evaluating historical extracts

1. What view of British attitudes to empire is advanced in Extract 1?
2. In this chapter you will read about a number of individuals who helped shape the British Empire. Consider how far the views of each of these reflects the argument of Extract 1.

KEY PROFILE

Fig. 1 *Chamberlain resigned as Colonial Secretary to promote the Tariff Reform League in 1903*

Joseph Chamberlain (1836–1914) had served as Mayor of Birmingham before becoming its Liberal Member of Parliament in 1876. However, he opposed Gladstone's proposal for **Irish independence** (Home Rule) and joined a Conservative-led coalition government as Colonial Secretary between 1895 and 1903. Chamberlain was nicknamed 'Joseph Africanus' by the press because of his interest in African expansion. He initiated the **Uganda Railway** connecting the East African coast with the interior, sanctioned the conquest and **annexation of Ashantiland** into the Gold Coast of West Africa and, in 1900, supervised the acquisition of the territories of the **Royal Niger Company** which became formal British colonies. Although a parliamentary inquiry exonerated him of any responsibility for the **'Jameson raid'** of 1895–96, he supported Rhodes' ambitions in South Africa. He presided over success in the **Boer War** (1899–1902) and having added South Africa to Britain's dominions, tried to develop closer imperial ties at the 1902 Colonial Conference – albeit without success. His subsequent fight for imperial preference failed in 1905.

CROSS-REFERENCE

Gladstone's proposal for Irish independence is outlined in Chapter 5, pages 45–46.

The building of the Uganda Railway is discussed in Chapter 7, page 64.

The annexation of Ashantiland is covered in Chapter 7, pages 62–63.

The acquisition of the Royal Niger Company in 1900 is set out in Chapter 3, page 29.

The Jameson raid of 1895–96 is discussed in Chapter 7, pages 68–69.

The Boer War of 1899–1902 is outlined in Chapter 12, pages 115–117.

ACTIVITY

Find out more about Chamberlain and the tariff reform campaign, then divide your group into two and prepare a speech each. This should resemble a speech delivered at one of the Tariff Reform League's public meetings – one group should nominate a representative to speak in favour and the other a representative to speak against. The rest of the group can ask questions and perhaps even heckle the speakers!

ACTIVITY

Evaluating historical extracts

1. What is A.J.P. Taylor's view of Chamberlain in Extract 2?
2. Use the extract and key profile of Chamberlain to create a timeline of Chamberlain's career, noting key events and details.

Chamberlain was a powerful influence on attitudes to empire. He believed that the imperial bonds needed reinforcing if the Empire was to be preserved or if, indeed, Britain wanted to maintain its status as a world power. Following the failure of the first Colonial Council in 1887 to get agreement for an Imperial Council (or parliament) to serve the Empire, Chamberlain summoned and chaired two further Colonial Conferences, in 1897 and 1902. At these, he proposed an imperial defence and customs union. These conferences involved only the self-governing, white settler colonies and they rejected Chamberlain's ideas.

Despite such setbacks, as a strong advocate of 'colonial development', Chamberlain promoted government investment in the less profitable areas of empire. Not only did he want to promote tropical trade, he believed in a sense of imperial duty. His convictions very much reflected the spirit of high imperialism: 'I believe that the British race is the greatest of the governing races that the world has ever seen.'

When the Boer War broke out in 1899, Chamberlain was viewed as a national hero. However, the war dragged on and Chamberlain lost some of his glory. When Salisbury retired in 1902, he was passed over as Prime Minister in favour of Balfour and in 1903, he resigned his post as Colonial Secretary. He fought back by conducting a campaign of 'tariff reform' in an attempt to convince the British public of the need for duties on all foreign goods (including food) so as to give the colonies 'imperial preference' and access to a duty-free British market. A Tariff Reform League was formed which organised the distribution of large numbers of leaflets and played Chamberlain's recorded messages to crowded public meetings on a gramophone. Chamberlain was convinced that favourable trade between Britain and the colonies would benefit Britain and reduce unemployment. However, although he campaigned with great zeal and energy, he failed to carry the Conservatives with him, split the party and brought about Balfour's resignation. In the 1906 election, he also failed to convince the public, who feared rises in the cost of living. The electorate gave the Liberals their greatest majority since the 1830s. Shortly after the election, Chamberlain suffered a stroke and his political career was over.

EXTRACT 2

Joseph Chamberlain was certainly a surprising leader for British imperialism. Imperialism evoked traditional British glories. Chamberlain rejected many of those traditions, including the predominance of the aristocracy and the Established Church. Imperialism was aggressive and nationalistic. Chamberlain was at first a radical opponent of wars. Perhaps he stumbled on his true nature by surprise. Or perhaps his imperialism was more altruistic than it appeared. But Chamberlain's great energies and great gifts were successful only in destruction. He ruined first the Liberal and then the Unionist (Conservative) party. He defeated Irish Home Rule and left Ireland with an almost insoluble problem for the future. He estranged the Boers and ultimately lost South Africa for the British Empire. He was unscrupulous in his means. He was almost certainly privy to Jameson's raid on Johannesburg in 1895, which outraged the Boers. Chamberlain brought a new bitterness into British politics. He was unsparing in victory and savage in defeat. Joseph Chamberlain was not a good advert for the imperial cause.

Adapted from 'Joseph Chamberlain' by A.J.P. Taylor (1972)

The role and influence of Cecil Rhodes

Fig. 2 *Cecil Rhodes (1852–1902)*

Cecil Rhodes, who had risen from the rank of trader to secure the prime ministership of Cape Colony in 1890, was driven by a strong conviction that British civilisation and control were key to the betterment of the world. Using his vast fortune, political power and control of Cape newspapers, Rhodes impressed upon audiences at home and abroad both the right and duty of Anglo-Saxons to dominate **Africa** and beyond.

His hope was to establish British rule from the north to the south of Africa, linking the Cape to British-dominated Sudan and Egypt. It was to this end that, in 1890, he had sent settlers to establish Fort Salisbury in Matabeleland, opening up territories that from c1899 were to be known as the Rhodesias in his honour. One of Rhodes' projects to outflank the Boer republic of the Transvaal and the Germans in the rush to central Africa was the railway line north from the Cape through Bechuanaland. Rhodes intended the railway to continue along the spine of the mountain system, hoping that it would eventually reach the Nile and so ensure British domination of all east-central Africa. However the dream of a Cape to Cairo route was blocked by the German occupation of East Africa from 1891 and never completed.

Rhodes resigned from his post as Prime Minister in 1896 after the **Jameson raid** and died only six years later. He had, however, made a great fortune out of empire and his funds helped to promote the British Empire after his death, for example in the publicity work of the Round Table, an imperial pressure group established in 1910 by a like-minded ally of Rhodes, Alfred Milner.

Colonial administration

There was a wide variety of forms of colonial government – and consequently a variety of colonial administrators emerged. Among the most prominent in the years 1890 to 1914 were the Viceroy of India, Lord Curzon, the Consul-General of Egypt, Evelyn Baring, and Britain's High Commissioner for South Africa from 1897, Sir Alfred Milner.

CROSS-REFERENCE

The role and influence of Cecil Rhodes up to 1890 is discussed in Chapter 4, pages 35–36.

British expansion in Africa from 1890 is the subject of Chapter 7.

CROSS-REFERENCE

To recap on the Jameson raid of 1895, turn back to Chapter 7, pages 68–69.

ACTIVITY

Look back at the detail of Rhodes' earlier career in Chapter 4 and create a display for your classroom wall identifying the various stages of Rhodes' life: Rhodes the trader; Rhodes and the expansion of the British Empire; Rhodes the administrator and Prime Minister; Rhodes' political views, influence and legacy.

CROSS-REFERENCE

For more detail on Conservative support for imperialism, including a profile of Lord Salisbury, look ahead to Chapter 11, page 99.

Curzon's creation of the North-West Frontier Province and expedition to Tibet are outlined in Chapter 8, page 73.

British colonial policy in India, including decisions taken under Curzon, is discussed in Chapter 8, pages 72—74.

Case study: Viceroy Curzon

At the height of **Conservative imperialism** in 1899, the Prime Minister, Lord Salisbury, appointed George Curzon as Viceroy of India. Curzon was a great traveller. He had travelled around the world, exploring and producing several books, most notably on Russia and Persia. It was concern about Russian expansion that led him to create the **North-West Frontier Province** in 1901 and to dispatch a military expedition into Tibet.

Curzon, like other colonial figures believed in a moral imperial duty, certain of 'the hand of Divine Providence behind the creation and expansion of an empire which is a supreme force for good in the world.' He took great pride in representing Britain and its imperial mission and, as Viceroy, worked to strengthen **British India**. He established both commissions and legislation to improve India's administration and agriculture – making provision for famine relief and irrigation projects. Curzon oversaw the re-arming of native regiments, the expansion of provincial police, the promotion of scientific and medical education and, crucially, construction of a further 6,000 miles of railway track to consolidate British control of India. He also founded the Imperial Cadet Corps to give Indian nobles a military role and the prospect of officer commissions. He lavished hospitality and rewards on its members at his elaborate Delhi durbar of 1903 and both the durbar and Curzon's costly restoration of the Taj Mahal were his way of honouring colonial India.

However, administrators like Curzon were wary of giving Indians too much responsibility. Curzon had a rather low opinion of the abilities of Indians. A Hindu, for example, would be distrusted by the Muslim community and a Bengali found it difficult to assert himself outside Bengal. Even in his own province, an Indian lacked an Englishman's authority and self-confidence and Curzon refused to appoint more to senior posts for fear that they were unequal to emergencies and 'rather inclined to abdicate or to run away'.

So, he took it upon himself to uphold the Raj and believed that by dividing the troublesome province of Bengal in 1905 he would weaken the Raj's internal enemies. Instead, the partition backfired, forcing Curzon to resign in the same year.

Fig. 3 *The Taj Mahal was restored by Viceroy Curzon under his Ancient Monuments Preservation Act of 1904*

The subcontinent had excited Curzon's imagination ever since, as a boy at Eton, he heard a talk which inspired him with a vision of India, imperial glory and British greatness. When he became Viceroy in 1899, he was naturally imperious towards the Indians, whatever their rank. He treated the princes as a pack of ignorant, unruly schoolboys who had to be disciplined for their own good. They were to be awed by assertions of power. Yet although Curzon was the shadow-sovereign of what he hoped would be a thousand-year Raj, he nursed doubts. He recognised the growth of national feeling and repeated that Indians would rather rule themselves badly than be well ruled by the British. He determined to kill Congress by kindness – giving India the best government it had ever enjoyed – and his administration lived up to his exalted aspirations. He laboured with indefatigable zeal (and self-pitying complaint) to give India measures of justice, reform and public welfare. Curzon – unbending and condescending – virtually reconstructed the Raj.

Adapted from *The Decline and Fall of the British Empire* by Piers Brendon (1998)

Case study: Evelyn Baring

Evelyn Baring was Consul-General in Egypt between 1883 and 1907. He saw himself as a moral reformer just as much as an administrator and like, other opinion-makers, Baring was certain that 'the code of Christian morality is the only sure foundation on which the whole of our vast Imperial fabric can be built if it is to be durable'.

Baring believed that a long occupation of Egypt was essential and he established a new guiding principle – the 'Granville Doctrine' (named after the Foreign Secretary, Lord Granville). This doctrine allowed Baring to dismiss Egyptian ministers who refused to accept British directives.

Baring placed British officials in key ministries and created the veiled protectorate in which British officials held the actual power. Baring thus effectively controlled Egypt until 1907, and this arrangement worked well for the first ten years of British control because Tewfiq was weak and happy to abdicate governmental responsibility. Baring considered the Egyptian army to be untrustworthy, due to its previous mutinies against the Khedive, so it was disbanded and a new army organised similar to that created by the British in India. Baring dealt with the budget, promoted irrigation projects and helped to bring economic prosperity to Egypt. He believed that British control would have to end at some point in the future, but only after the Egyptian people had learned proper self-governance.

However, when, in 1892, Tewfiq died and was succeeded by Abbas Hilmi II, the new, young and ambitious Khedive wanted to throw off British rule. He encouraged a nationalist movement, but Baring bullied him into submission.

Baring regarded Egypt as something of a battleground between civilised Christianity and Islam, which he viewed as a set of outdated Arabian customs detrimental to modern Egypt. Baring was particularly concerned with Islamic society's acceptance of slavery, its antiquated justice system and its treatment of women. Baring's moral mission in Egypt would have both echoed and informed public opinion back in Britain. Baring took action to:

- stop the slave supply into Egypt
- discourage slave-ownership in Egypt
- abolish forced labour
- outlaw punishment by use of the *kurbash* (leather whip)
- halt the import of hashish by establishing a Camel Corps to patrol Egypt's borders
- regulate alcohol sale licences

ACTIVITY

Evaluating historical extracts

What view of Lord Curzon is given in Extract 3?

CROSS-REFERENCE

For the role and influence of Evelyn Baring before 1890, look back to Chapter 4, pages 38–39.

KEY PROFILE

Fig. 4 *Milner was influential in foreign and domestic policy*

Alfred Milner (1854–1925)

Viscount Milner was of mixed German/British ancestry. He was an able but inflexible British administrator whose pursuit of British **suzerainty** over the Boer States while he was High Commissioner in South Africa and Governor of the Cape Colony helped to bring about the Boer War (1899–1902).

KEY TERM

suzerainty: control over another state, particularly in foreign affairs while allowing the subservient nation internal autonomy

- close gambling houses
- stop local money-lending and extortion by establishing the National Bank and Post Office Savings Bank.

However, he was forced to resign his post after the controversy following the flogging and hanging of locals at **Denshawai** in 1906.

The new Liberal government which came to power the same year under Sir Henry Campbell-Bannerman favoured a more lenient policy towards Egypt but, nevertheless, Parliament awarded Baring £50,000 in 1907 in recognition of his 'eminent services' in Egypt. Baring returned to Britain and devoted himself to preventing women's political rights as President of the Men's League for Opposing Women's Suffrage.

He published a two-volume set of books on *Modern Egypt* in 1908, narrating the events in Egypt and the Sudan since 1876. In 1910, he also published *Ancient and Modern Imperialism*, a comparison of the British and Roman empires.

Case study: Alfred Milner

Milner was an administrator who had served in Egypt (1889–92) and as chairman of the Board of Inland Revenue (1892–97). He was an ardent imperialist and was hand-picked by Chamberlain to become Britain's High Commissioner for Southern Africa from 1897. Milner, like Chamberlain, was convinced of British superiority over both Africans and Boers and of the need for British regional supremacy. With Britain and the Transvaal close to conflict, he took on the most critical post in the Empire.

When Kruger was re-elected as President of the **Transvaal** in February 1898, Milner concluded that 'there is no way out of the political troubles of South Africa except for reform in the Transvaal, or war.' While Milner founded a series of English-speaking 'Milner Schools' in Pretoria and Johannesburg, he is mostly remembered for taking Britain into the Boer War.

Milner demanded full citizenship rights for the Uitlanders after five years' residence; and by the time of the Bloemfontein Conference (May–June 1899), he had already decided to use force to get his way, although it was actually Kruger who declared war in October 1899.

When Britain annexed the former Boer territories of the Orange Free State and the Transvaal in 1901, Milner left his post as Governor of the Cape and took over the administration of these areas. As High Commissioner, he, negotiated the Peace of Vereeniging (31 May 1902) alongside Lord Kitchener, the military commander, and he was made a baron (1901) and a viscount (1902) for his services.

After the war, he and a group of promising young administrators and lawyers known as 'Milner's Kindergarten' worked to resettle the Boers and promote economic growth, particularly in the gold-mining industry. Milner had hoped to attract British settlers and introduced a vigorous English language education programme to try to anglicise the area. However, more British residents left than arrived during the years of depression that followed the Boer War and Milner and the British government decided to use Chinese labourers (known as coolies) on three-year contracts to make up the shortfall in workers in the gold-mining industry. The first batch of Chinese reached the Rand in June 1904, but public opinion in Britain was soon outraged to learn that these coolies were being badly treated and even flogged in breach of the law.

In March 1906, there was a move to censure Milner, but this backfired and produced a counter-campaign, led by Sir Bartle Frere, which expressed high appreciation of the services rendered by Milner in Africa. However, the issue of the Chinese coolies probably contributed to the Conservative election defeat in January 1906 and the new Liberal government rejected Milner's plans for the future of the Transvaal.

CROSS-REFERENCE

The incident at Denshawai in 1906 is outlined in Chapter 8, page 77.

CROSS-REFERENCE

The tensions in the Transvaal, the issue of the Uitlanders and the Second Boer War (1899–1902) are covered in Chapter 12, pages 115–117.

ACTIVITY

Extension

In pairs, investigate some other key individuals who played an important role in the Empire during the years 1890 to 1914. Some suggestions include:
- Sir Henry 'Harry' Johnston, British Consul of Nyasaland
- Frederick Lugard, African explorer and colonial administrator and Governor of Hong Kong (1907–12)
- Lord Kitchener, commander in Mahdist War (1884–99) and Boer War (1900–02) and Commander-in-Chief, India (1902–09)
- Mary Kingsley, female explorer

Milner resigned his Southern African posts and returned to England, where he wrote *The Nation and the Empire* in 1913.

Summary

The development of the British Empire was partly moulded by the individuals who played key roles in its administration. These included two men who were highly controversial figures, both in their own times and since. The first, one of Britain's most committed colonial secretaries, Joseph Chamberlain, was driven by his devotion to the imperial idea; the second, Cape Prime Minister Cecil Rhodes, developed 'big ideas' on British expansion in Africa (and elsewhere) which had a profound effect on British policy-making. Curzon, Baring and Milner are three other powerful imperial administrators who viewed their positions from a patriotic British standpoint. They never doubted the enormity, nor the importance, of the work they did and they carried out their duties in the manner of the 'superior' but benevolent upper class British aristocrats that they were.

 PRACTICE QUESTION

Evaluating historical extracts

Using your understanding of the historical context, assess how convincing the arguments in Extracts 1, 2 and 3 are, in relation to the influence of individuals on attitudes to empire in the years 1890 to 1914.

> **STUDY TIP**
>
> You should evaluate the arguments put forward in each extract and look for both broad and specific views. Remember that you must consider how individuals influenced 'attitudes to empire' and not simply look at what the individuals mentioned did. Use your own knowledge to provide a supported judgement on each extract.

 PRACTICE QUESTION

'British administrators were driven more by a sense of superiority than by concern for native peoples in the years 1890 to 1914.' Explain why you agree or disagree with this view.

> **STUDY TIP**
>
> You will probably want to look back at Chapter 8 before planning your answer to this question. Try to find specific evidence which would support the influence of 'a sense of superiority' in the behaviour of administrators (which would include viceroys and consul-generals as well as lesser officials) and also look for examples of genuinely altruistic behaviour where concern for native peoples was shown.

11 Attitudes towards imperialism in Britain

LEARNING OBJECTIVES

In this chapter you will learn about:

- supporters and critics of imperialism

- national efficiency

- the British Empire and popular culture

- representations of empire.

KEY TERM

bellicosity: an aggressive attitude suggesting an eagerness to fight

KEY QUESTION

As you read this chapter, consider the following key questions:
- What influenced imperial policy?
- How did the Empire influence British attitudes and culture?

EXTRACT 1

The later nineteenth century witnessed the elevation of the monarchy into an institution endowed with patriotic and imperial symbolism, enjoying a world-wide significance. With the great climax of the Diamond Jubilee in 1897, Queen Victoria came to almost represent an 'Imperial Britannia' herself. An imperial ideology; a powerful mixture of patriotism, excitement about adventure and colonial warfare; reverence for the monarchy; the application of British cultural values to other peoples; admiration for military virtues and an almost religious approach to the obligations of world-wide power came to dominate many aspects of popular culture. Throughout society, sporadic excitement about imperial affairs turned patriotism into jingoism, attitudes to other peoples often shaded into outright racism and imperial self-righteousness was capable of being transformed into extreme **bellicosity**.

Adapted from *Empire and Metropolitan Cultures* by John M. Mackenzie (1999)

ACTIVITY

Evaluating historical extracts

1. What view is given in Extract 1 about British attitudes to empire in the later nineteenth century?
2. As you read this chapter, look for evidence that would support this view and evidence that would challenge it.

Queen Victoria's Diamond Jubilee, in 1897, was celebrated with much pomp and grandeur. It was a tremendous spectacle that encapsulated some of the imperialistic fervour that prevailed in the 1890s. However, in the subsequent years up to 1914, challenges to the earlier Victorian triumphalism began to be heard. The international economic and political situation had undermined Britain's complete faith in its supremacy, and strident imperialists put forward a programme to preserve Britain's status through the development of the Empire. This became a topic of fierce political debate, intensified by the Boer War. Nevertheless, the Empire and the imperial attitudes associated with it survived.

Fig. 1 *Queen Victoria's Diamond Jubilee procession, London, 1897*

Imperialism – supporters and critics

Supporters

'Empire' was widely accepted among the ruling elites of the late nineteenth and early twentieth centuries. Indeed, it was widely supported at all levels of society, with varying degrees of ardour, and the public displays of support for empire which greeted the Boer War in 1899 and helped the Conservatives win an impressive victory in the 1900 '**khaki election**' might be taken as evidence of this. The Empire was sometimes justified on authoritarian/moral grounds as a 'responsibility', even a 'burden' that God had placed on the British in order to bring stability and order to the world; and sometimes on more liberal premises such as 'civilising' the colonial peoples, freeing them from local oppression and providing welfare and the rule of law.

The main political parties had different conceptions of empire, however. The Liberals looked beyond the Conservative support for good government and 'white rule' for its own sake. They aimed at the 'education' and improvement of the colonies and their peoples – with the objective of ultimate self-rule. Nevertheless, even they were reluctant to bring an 'end' to empire. Both the Liberals and the growing Labour party at the beginning of the twentieth century generally preferred freedom 'through' empire to freedom 'from' empire.

The real 'imperialists' – those who were enthusiasts for empire rather than simply accepting it – were mostly, although not exclusively, Conservatives, and on the radical right of the party. During the years of Conservative ascendancy between 1895 and 1905, the supporters of the Prime Minister, **Lord Salisbury** (himself a more moderate imperialist), embraced the imperialist cause. They argued in favour of the creation of a stronger and more closely united empire. This not only meant support for territorial expansion, for example in Africa and northern India, but support for schemes that would bind the empire together in trade and government. It was believed that the correct policies could benefit British society and turn the Empire into an economic superpower.

KEY PROFILE

Robert Gascoyne-Cecil, the third Marquess of Salisbury (1830–1903), was the last aristocratic statesman to lead a British government from the House of Lords, rather than the Commons. He served three times as Conservative Prime Minister (1885–86; 1886–92; 1895–1902) and four times as Foreign Secretary (1878; 1885–86; 1886–92; 1895–1900). Salisbury was an imperialist and believed European, preferably British, rule to be indispensable for the advancement of the 'backward' races. He had no hesitation in imposing this rule by force, as he did in the Sudan from 1896 to 1899. He opposed Gladstone on the question of Home Rule for Ireland and his years in office were preoccupied by the partition of Africa and managing the international situation. Salisbury opposed alliance commitments which he believed unnecessary and dangerous for Britain and his foreign policy was dictated by the defence and enlargement of the Empire. His years in office also encompassed the Boer War.

The most fervent imperialists viewed the Empire as a sort of racial duty. Lord Curzon proclaimed that, 'there has never been anything so great in the world's history than the British Empire, so great an instrument for the good of humanity' and Lord Alfred Milner, High Commissioner for South Africa (1897–1905), argued that every white man of British birth should feel equally at home in every state of the Empire. These 'high imperialists' wanted a stronger empire, but an empire ruled by white people. They believed that

A CLOSER LOOK

Khaki election

During the Boer War (1899–1902), the British forces became known as 'khakis' because of their uniforms which were a dull brownish-yellow colour, designed to merge with the terrain. The idea of such 'camouflage' wear was relatively new. After victory in the war the government called an election to exploit public approval. This has given rise to the term 'khaki election' for subsequent elections in similar circumstances.

service in the colonies made men stronger. This attitude relegated the non-white peoples of the Empire to the rank of 'subjects'; citizens with rights but not capable of controlling their own destinies.

Joseph Chamberlain, the Colonial Secretary, was another high imperialist. He believed there was a 'national crisis' (because of the industrial and military development of other powers) which only the Empire could solve. A reorganised empire would enable industrial recovery and provide employment. It would generate wealth to fund social reforms such as pensions and strengthen the moral fibre of the British people. He believed in educating the public about the values of empire as he saw its promised benefits as a way of winning the loyalty of the working class. Chamberlain tried to forward the imperialists' desire for a union between Britain and the colonies of settlement for the purposes of defence and trade but his ideas (involving a **pooling of sovereignty** and an imperial parliament) proved too idealistic to win widespread support.

Most imperialists also argued for the economic benefits of empire. Some (including Chamberlain) sought 'colonial development' beyond the white colonies and India and favoured the policy of '**imperial preference**' (tariff reform). Others such as Lord Meath (1841–1929), a diplomat, spoke in more social terms and argued that state-organised emigration and colonisation were essential to check the expansion of British cities and simultaneously strengthen the Empire.

Many imperial activists were members of societies like the Royal Colonial Institute, founded in 1870 to provide a meeting place for those interested in colonial and Indian affairs. Such societies proliferated in the early twentieth century. The Victoria League, founded in 1901, was a non-political organisation founded by women to promote a closer union between different parts of the then British Empire through 'hospitality, fundraising, friendship and education'. The **Round Table movement** was founded in 1909 on an idea of **Lord Milner**, to promote a closer union between Britain and its self-governing colonies and in 1910 to 1911 Round Table groups were formed in South Africa, Australia, New Zealand and Canada.

KEY TERM

pooling of sovereignty: shared authority, so that Britain no longer had supreme power over the Empire

CROSS-REFERENCE

Chamberlain's support of 'imperial preference' is discussed in Chapter 9, pages 88–89.

CROSS-REFERENCE

The role and influence of Lord Milner are discussed in Chapter 10, page 96.

A CLOSER LOOK

It has been suggested the Round Table movement grew out of a secret society inaugurated by Cecil Rhodes, namely the Society of the Elect in 1889, which had an impressive following of aristocratic members.

KEY PROFILE

Leo Amery (1873–1955) was born in India (speaking Hindi at the age of three) and was educated at Harrow and Oxford, after which he became a barrister. He became a great admirer of Alfred Milner and during the Boer War, gained a public profile as a correspondent for *The Times*. He later edited and largely wrote *The Times History of the South African War* (seven volumes; 1899–1909). He also supported tariff reform. In 1911, he was elected as a Conservative MP and served until 1945, becoming Colonial Secretary (1924–29), Secretary of State for Dominion Affairs (1925–29) and Secretary of State for India and Burma (1940–45). He was a strong advocate of imperial unity and supported the Empire's gradual transition to the Commonwealth.

Another pro-imperial group was the Empire Day movement, which followed the lead of Lord Meath in 1896, although an Empire Day was not celebrated until 1902 and only officially recognised by Parliament in 1916. The idea of a day of festivities was intended to reinforce imperial unity and celebrate the image of a motherly Queen Victoria, Empress of India. The movement was part of the imperialists' drive to educate the British public about empire. Journalists such as **Leopold (Leo) Amery** and the Anglo-Canadian **Lord Beaverbrook**, who was to become the chief proprietor of the *Daily Express* in 1916, also helped represent the Empire to the British people, emphasising the 'imperial family' and propagating imperialist values.

CROSS-REFERENCE

Lord Beaverbrook is profiled in Chapter 15, page 148.

EXTRACT 2

Despite the ever-greater polarisation of international politics between 1902 and 1904, there was no reordering of the Empire. The wish of the settler colonies to preserve control of their own affairs, the attractions of free trade to the British electorate in 1906 and the weight of the United Kingdom's non-imperial interests, were sufficient to defeat the imperial consolidationists' onslaught. This was perhaps just as well. Attempts at a stronger subordination of the tropical colonies to British needs might have overwhelmed more constructive approaches to their administration. The evidence of local political mobilisation in India and Egypt after 1900 suggests that it would also have provoked serious indigenous protest. Centralisation at the expense of the Dominions before 1914 could have jeopardised those compromises which subsequently enabled cooperation to continue and the Dominions to make vital contributions to Imperial defence and welfare during the First World War.

Adapted from *The Oxford History of the British Empire: the Nineteenth Century* by Andrew Porter (1999)

ACTIVITY

Evaluating historical extracts

What is Porter's explanation for the imperialists' failure to win support for their ideas in the years before 1914?

KEY TERM

rhetoric: effective or persuasive speaking or writing

Critics

The **rhetoric** of the high imperialists, which was at its strongest between 1890 and 1906, did not go totally unchallenged. One of the strongest critics of empire was **John A. Hobson**, an economist who wrote *Imperialism* in 1902. His view, catalysed by the Boer War, was that imperial expansion had been driven by a search for new markets and new opportunities for the rich capitalists of Britain to make profits through investment. These capitalists, he argued, were a small and powerful elite, whose political power and connections had enabled them to shape imperial policy. The Boer War had, he contested, been fought to secure the gold resources of South Africa for rich entrepreneurs and the mining interests. Thus, he concluded, imperial expansion was a 'capitalist plot'.

Hobson's views did not signal the total rejection of empire but they did provoke debate and fed into socialist anti-imperialism, although they had little immediate impact on policies.

Other critics of empire emerged in the aftermath of the Boer War, although initial concerns were more to do with the conduct of war than a direct challenge to the concept of empire. Reports from the welfare campaigner **Emily Hobhouse**, which led to a government enquiry into the conditions in the British concentration camps during the **Boer War**, helped tarnish the allure of imperialism and its supposed civilising mission.

CROSS-REFERENCE

A passage from Hobson's *Imperialism* is quoted in Chapter 9, page 87, where you will also find a key profile.

A CLOSER LOOK

In 1901, Emily Hobhouse produced a detailed report of conditions in the concentration camps deployed by the British during the Boer War. Her claims were corroborated by the 1901 Fawcett Commission and British conduct was subjected to considerable criticism from Liberal and Irish MPs, Church figures and continental Europe.

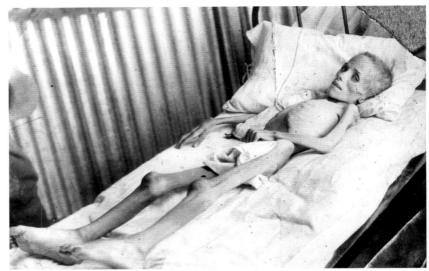

Fig. 2 *A child who died in a concentration camp during the Boer War; scenes like this enflamed anti-imperialist feeling*

CROSS-REFERENCE

For the Boer War, look ahead to Chapter 12, pages 115–117.

Rudyard Kipling is profiled later in this chapter, on page 105.

ACTIVITY

Extension

Find out more about these anti-imperialists and their friends and associates. You could create an anti-imperial poster incorporating some of their names and views.

Lesser known figures to challenge the imperialist ideal included:
- Wilfrid Scawen Blunt (1840–1922,) a diplomat and poet who (in imitation of the pro-imperialist poet **Kipling**) penned the line in 1899 'The white man's burden, Lord, is the burden of his cash'
- Herbert Spencer (1820–1903), an influential philosopher who criticised the Victorian enthusiasm for colonial acquisitions of colonies
- Frederic Harrison (1831–1923), a radical left-wing lawyer and historian who believed imperialism to be unethical
- William Digby (1849–1904), a writer and propagandist who had served in India and set up the Indian Political and General Agency in London in order to raise awareness about Indian grievances in the British Parliament and press in 1888
- Walter Crane (1845–1915), an Arts and Crafts designer, children's book writer and socialist who used his design skills to produce anti-war illustrations in order to encourage those on the left to embrace anti-imperialism.

However, for the most part the voice of the anti-imperialists was hidden beneath a broad swathe of imperial support, if not exuberance. While the Liberals were in power in the years from 1906 to 1914, imperialism declined as a political topic. The Liberals preferred to disassociate themselves from colonial conflict and the excessive imperialism of the right-wing Conservatives, but the continuation of empire was not questioned.

A CLOSER LOOK

In 1900 statistics showed that 56 per cent of men measured in army recruitment medicals were less than 5'6" in height, compared with only 10 per cent in records from 1845.

National efficiency

As well as the horrors of the concentration camps, another national concern was exposed in the aftermath of the Boer War – Britain's 'national efficiency'. 30,000 Boers had held out against British forces for two and a half years in South Africa and although the British had been able to use troops from India, Australia and Canada, 'home-grown' soldiers had proved hard to come by. Up to 40 per cent of the British recruits in Britain had been tested and found unfit for military service and, in Manchester, 8000 out of 11,000 would-be volunteers were turned away. Poor diet and living conditions had weakened Britain's manpower. This was a threat to Britain's imperial supremacy just as it was to Britain's industrial strength.

British concerns were all the greater given the decline in British industrial production relative to that of both the USA and Germany. Across the media and political spectrum, there was concern that the nation needed to be both better educated and healthier. In 1902, it became common for journalists and political commentators to speak of the need for 'national efficiency' as the only way of preventing Britain's decline. They referred to Britain as a nation of amateurs and argued that government needed to be better organised: leadership made stronger and waste and muddle replaced by scientific planning. Without 'national efficiency' the country would be eclipsed by growing powers such as Germany.

Measures taken to improve national efficiency included:

- the 1902 Education Act (Conservative) which sought to raise school standards and led to the opening of 1000 secondary schools over the following decade
- the modernisation of the Royal Navy by committing to a new class of battleship – the Dreadnought, first launched in 1906 (in the wake of the German naval laws and the **expansion of the German fleet**)
- a new centre of technological, medical and scientific excellence, established in London in 1907 and entitled 'Imperial College'
- a spate of Liberal social reforms including free school meals (1906), school medical inspections (1907), a children's welfare charter (1908), old age pensions (1908), a trade boards act (1909), and unemployment and health insurance (1911) giving the right to free medical treatment. The leading exponents of the 'New Liberal' philosophy were **David Lloyd-George** (Chancellor of the Exchequer 1908–15), and **Winston Churchill** (President of the Board of Trade 1908–10 and Home Secretary 1910–11); they worked with the Prime Minister, **Herbert Asquith**.

CROSS-REFERENCE

The growing naval threat from Germany is explored in Chapter 8, pages 81–82.

CROSS-REFERENCE

Winston Churchill is profiled in Chapter 13, page 126.

KEY PROFILE

Fig. 3   *Lloyd George was the last Liberal politician*

David Lloyd George (1863–1945) was a leading Liberal politician who served as Chancellor of the Exchequer from 1906 to 1915. He was made Minister of Munitions in 1915 when there was a 'shell crisis' in Britain and vigorous action was needed. Lloyd George's drive led to his becoming Prime Minister at the end of 1916 where he remained until 1922. His government brought together politicians of all parties to provide national solidarity in war.

KEY PROFILE

Herbert Asquith (1852–1928) had served under Gladstone, but was out of office from 1895 until the new Liberal Prime Minister of 1906, Henry Campbell-Bannerman, appointed him as Chancellor of the Exchequer. When Campbell-Bannerman resigned through ill-health in 1908, Asquith became Prime Minister. His government passed important social welfare reforms and developed the Royal Navy to counter a perceived German threat. He tried to introduce Home Rule in Ireland, although this was shelved with the advent of war. He formed a coalition government in 1915, but the pressures of war and the 1916 Easter Rising in Dublin (see Chapter 18, page 169) forced his resignation and he was replaced by Lloyd George.

The campaign and reforms to improve national efficiency were collectively a means, not only of addressing internal shortcomings but, crucially, of showing that the ideas of the high imperialists were unnecessary for the successful continuation of empire and strengthening Britain to improve its capability to both run and defend the Empire.

ACTIVITY

Write down the main concerns of the high imperialists and alongside each point indicate how the measures undertaken to strengthen national efficiency would address concerns.

The British Empire and popular culture

A vibrant popular culture emerged in Britain in the later nineteenth century, celebrating Britain's 'imperial glory'. Popular enthusiasm for empire was the product of a range of factors from the spread of education and greater literacy to the emergence of mass politics (and in particular the Conservatives' decision to vaunt the imperialist cause), following the widening of the franchise in 1867 and 1884. Organised entertainment, particularly in the flourishing music halls, and the spread of advertising aimed at mass markets were also responsible, while magazines and the popular press found that 'imperialism sold'.

Popular press

The years between 1890 and 1914 were something of a 'golden age' of newspaper publication as technical advances in printing and the emergence of the professional journalist with a political agenda enabled print to respond to demand and reach out to a new mass audience.

Alfred Harmsworth, Lord Northcliffe (1865–1922)

Alfred Harmsworth worked his way up from working as a freelance journalist to becoming as a press magnate, gaining a peerage as Lord Northcliffe in 1905. He established the *Daily Mail* (1896) and *Daily Mirror* (1903). He helped create 'tabloid journalism' which appealed to popular tastes; the *Daily Mail* held the world record for daily circulation until his death. He went on to rescue the financially desperate *Observer* and *The Times* in 1905 and 1908, respectively, and in 1908 also acquired *The Sunday Times*.

Fig. 4 *An 1899 front page of the* Illustrated Mail *showing three of London's top regiments*

Alfred Harmsworth (from 1905 Lord Northcliffe), pioneered the production of an entirely new form of cheap, populist newspaper in 1896 with the *Daily Mail*. The paper was deliberately aimed at the 'lower-middle class' market and sold at a low retail price. During the Boer War of 1899–1902, it was selling over a million copies a day, filling its pages with stories of the war and unashamedly damning the Boers and Kruger whilst praising the heroism of the British troops. J.A. Hobson, writing in 1902, criticised its 'crude sensationalism'.

In the early twentieth century, the *Mail* turned its vitriol against the Germans, who were portrayed as posing a military threat to the Empire. The *Mail* serialised a number of patriotic books including: Headon Hill's *The Spies of Wight* (1899), Erskine Childers' *The Riddle of the Sands* (1903), Walter Wood's *The Enemy in Our Midst* (1906) and Captain Curties' *When England Slept* (1909).

Literature and music

The celebrated and popular writer Rudyard Kipling did much to shape the attitudes of the British public towards empire in the years before 1914. Contemptuous of politicians, intellectuals and stuffy civil servants, he could often be critical of imperial administrators, but he had an almost religious belief in empire and filled his works with references to Britain's 'higher goals'. Consider this poem by **Rudyard Kipling**, entitled, 'The White Man's Burden':

SOURCE 1

Take up the white man's burden,
Send forth the best ye breed,
Go bind your sons to exile
To serve your captives' need;
To wait in heavy harness,
On fluttered folk and wild –
Your new caught sullen peoples,
Half devil and half child.

KEY PROFILE

Rudyard Kipling (1865–1936) came from a Methodist family and was born in Bombay. He became a celebrated poet and writer, penning imperial, military and patriotic verses as well as *The Jungle Book* and *Kim* among other novels. He won the Nobel Prize for Literature in 1907. He was a great believer in empire and Britain's greatness.

ACTIVITY

Extension

Try to read some more of poetry and identify some of his key themes. You could choose a poem to share with the rest of your class. Some suggestions include: 'The Ladies'; 'The Supplication of Kerr Cross'; 'Missionary'; 'Chant-Pagan'; 'English Irregular Discharged'; 'Recessional'.

The works of Kipling, the books of Samuel Baker and G.A. Henty's tales of military campaigns (*The Dash for Khartoum* and *With Clive in India* amongst others) proved to be Victorian bestsellers. More subtle encouragement for imperialism featured in women's writing, particularly in romantic fiction. Gertrude Page emigrated to Rhodesia in 1900 and produced over 20 novels

A CLOSER LOOK

The media and the Boer War

The Boer War produced an outpouring of jingoistic media coverage. A film, *The Dispatch Rider*, included a scene showing a British soldier giving a Boer a drink of water and then being shot in the back. The novelist Fox Russell penned *The Boer's Blunder* (1900) based on the story of an English girl abducted by a Boer.

ACTIVITY

Discuss the meaning of this poem with a partner; see if you can rewrite it, in prose, in accessible modern English.

based on the lives and loves of fellow settlers. Similar romantic tales were presented by Mary Gaunt whose novels focused on committed colonialists such as missionaries, civil servants and scientists. British India proved perhaps the most popular setting: Anglo-Indian love stories proliferated from the 1890s, not least those of Maud Diver who wrote many accounts of British romance and heroism in the subcontinent.

Nationalist and imperialist themes were also to be found in music and could be heard up and down the country in music halls, concert halls and churches. Such music was played at coronations, jubilees, pageants and exhibitions. 'Imperial' ballads, patriotic hymns, stirring choral works and military marches were performed by brass bands, church choirs and town choral societies and could be heard in town music halls. Sir Arthur Sullivan, for example, worked with the librettist Sir William S. Gilbert, to create a series of 'Gilbert and Sullivan' operas which often conveyed a patriotic and imperialist message in a humorous way.

The best-known and most popular 'imperial' composer was **Edward Elgar** (1857–1934) who deliberately sought to stimulate his listeners' emotions and create mental images, which captured 'the nobility of empire'. Elgar became a widely popular composer, writing an 'Imperial March' for Queen Victoria's Diamond Jubilee (1897), 'Caractacus', a cantata containing dazzling military march music (1898) and five 'Pomp and Circumstance Marches' (from 1901). Having received a copy of a poem by Cardinal Newman (which he had found in Gordon's residence in the Sudan) as a wedding gift in 1889, he was inspired by Gordon's 'last stand' to write the choral work 'The Dream of Gerontius'. He also wrote a 'Coronation Ode' (1902) for Edward VII on his accession as the new King and Emperor and composed 'The Crown of India' for the Delhi durbar of 1911. He continued to compose and conduct imperial works until his death.

There was also an interchange of musicians within the Empire which served to strengthen imperialist ties. Sir Henry Coward, for example, took his Sheffield choir on a musical tour of the Dominions in 1911, while the popular British contralto, Clara Butt, whose repertoire included many Elgar songs, performed in Australia, New Zealand and Canada. The Australian operatic soprano Nellie Melba and Australian baritone Peter Dawson in turn achieved great popularity in Britain.

Youth and the Empire

CROSS-REFERENCE

The continuing influence of Elgar's music after 1914 is discussed in Chapter 16, page 164.

ACTIVITY

Extension

Try to listen to some of the British patriotic music of Gilbert and Sullivan (available on YouTube) and some 'imperial' music by Elgar. How does Elgar seek to stimulate an emotional reaction?

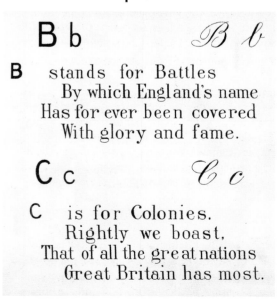

Fig. 5 *An extract from* An ABC for Baby Patriots *(1899)*

It was hard for children (except for the most deprived) to escape the imperialist messages spread through books, organisations and schools. Increased literacy had produced a new market for books and comics and the young were fed a diet of adventure stories with imperial themes. Tales of the exotic and illustrations from British outposts were presented in E.J. Brett's *Boys of the Empire* (produced from 1888 to 1900) besides his other, shorter-lived, comics such as *Boys of England* and *Young Men of Great Britain*. The Religious Tract Society produced both the *Boy's Own Paper* and the *Girl's Own Paper*, which secured a readership of between a quarter and half a million in the years 1890 to 1914. These comics were read in schools and church halls across the country; their popularity was based on their promotion and celebration of both military and missionary activity.

KEY PROFILE

Howard Handley Spicer (1872–1926) was the founder of the Empire League and editor of the League's magazine, *Boys of the Empire*. He also edited books on sport for both boys and girls. The published aim of his magazine was 'to promote and strengthen a worthy imperial spirit in British-born boys'. The League provided lectures, sermons and cultural visits on imperial themes.

Howard Handley Spicer published an alternative *Boys of the Empire* and a separate *Boys of Our Empire* magazine. He also set up the Boys' Empire League which boasted 7000 members in 1900, as well as an annual book focusing on the colonies. Each year an exam was set with a first prize of £25, and the offer of a free passage to one of the colonies.

Robert Baden-Powell, himself a 'hero' of the Boer War, in imitation of the earlier Boys' Brigade of 1883, established the Boy Scout movement in 1908, followed by the Girl Guides in 1912. The movement was organised almost like a military cadet force (although Baden-Powell disliked conventional military training) and was designed to train defenders of empire through competitive challenges bringing the chance to earn badges. Its handbook *Scouting for Boys* exhorted members to 'be a friend to all the world'. It proved the most successful of all the attempts to mobilise young people behind imperial themes and was extended to other countries of the Empire.

Other youth organisations had a Christian dimension: for example the Nonconformist Boys' Life Brigade and Anglican Church Lads' Brigade established in the 1890s. An older Church organisation, The Girls' Friendly Society, boasted over 200,000 members by 1914 as well as its own colonial emigration secretary, Ellen Joyce, who encouraged girls to consider emigration to improve themselves.

The History and Geography books used in the state elementary schools also tended to emphasise the glories of empire and presented the explorers and missionaries who had helped create it as heroes. Even simple reading books contained imperial themes seen, for example, in Mary Frances Ames' *ABC for Baby Patriots*, produced in 1899. Children of all classes enjoyed the pageantry of Empire Day, while those in the public schools took part in cadet corps and continued to be reminded of their imperial mission and duty.

ACTIVITY

For a closer look at Empire Day, have a look at the film footage of *Preston's Empire Day 1909* via the Colonial Film Database at *www.colonialfilm.org.uk*

Representations of empire

British culture was permeated by imperial themes on many levels and images and motifs, exhibitions and advertisements all helped spread awareness of empire. Advertisers frequently used imperial connotations to sell their

ACTIVITY

Choose any episode, person or event from your knowledge of the Empire and write a page for a primary school History or Geography textbook, making the imperial theme exciting for young readers.

goods, which would suggest that the British public felt favourably disposed to empire.

THE BLACK BABY.

Mr. Bull. "WHAT, ANOTHER!!—WELL, I SUPPOSE I MUST TAKE IT IN!!!"

Fig. 6   *Uganda, portrayed as a baby, on John Bull's doorstep, 1894*

ACTIVITY

What messages about imperialism are conveyed by the *Punch* cartoon in Fig. 6?

The Empire was also represented in architecture and the imperial creations of Herbert Baker and Edwin Lutyens. Lutyens designed both in Britain and in the Empire itself. He was responsible for the Johannesburg Art Gallery from 1911 and the British Pavilion at the international exhibition in Rome the same year. In 1912 he was invited to help design New Delhi, as a home for the Government of India which was to move from Calcutta. Lutyens travelled to India and mapped out his vast city plan developing buildings which fused Mughal and neo-classical elements. Lutyens and his fellow architect Herbert Baker made annual winter visits to India until 1914 to supervise this work.

One of the greatest representations of empire was Queen Victoria's Diamond Jubilee celebration of 1897. Here is Jan Morris' view of the occasion:

EXTRACT 3

It was not a sophisticated occasion, the Diamond Jubilee. It was full of sentiment and extravagance, indulgent tears and thumping brass bands, strung about with flags and lavishly illuminated. The procession itself was a superb display of boastful arrogance. With its 50,000 troops, it was thought to constitute the largest military force ever assembled in London, and as it marched in two separate columns through the streets of the capital, to converge upon St Paul's for the thanksgiving service, even the exuberant reporters of the 1890s sometimes found themselves struggling to produce sufficient embellishment. 'How many millions of years has the sun stood in heaven?' inquired the *Daily Mail*. 'But the sun never looked down until yesterday upon the embodiment of so much energy and power.'

Adapted from *Pax Britannica* by Jan Morris (1968)

King George V's coronation was also celebrated with a Festival of Empire at the Crystal Palace in London in 1911. Three-quarter-size models of the parliamentary buildings around the Empire were erected and used to display exhibitions of imperial products. The festival was accompanied by a pageant dramatising the history of London, England and the Empire, for which music was composed by Ralph Vaughan Williams and Gustav Holst, among others, and performed by a military band and a 500-voice chorus. An intra-Empire sports championship was held as part of the festival which became the forerunner of the British Empire Games (later the Commonwealth) Games. Souvenir books and postcards as well as the media reports all helped convey the value of empire to the general public.

Summary

ACTIVITY

Summary

Create a chart to record the key information in this chapter as follows

	Key Points
Supporters of imperialism and their arguments	
Opponents of imperialism and their arguments	
The impact of the 'national efficiency' debate	
Popular culture	
Ways in which representations of empire reinforced imperialist attitudes	

 PRACTICE QUESTION

Evaluating historical extracts

Using your understanding of the historical context, assess how convincing the arguments are in Extracts 1, 2 and 3 in relation to British attitudes to empire in the years 1890 to 1914.

STUDY TIP

To answer this question you need to think about what each author has to say about British attitudes to empire. In the case of Extract 3 in particular, you may find it helpful to reflect on the tone of the extract. Try to evaluate the arguments with reference to your own knowledge and produce judgements that are supported by reference to the extracts themselves.

You will find this question easier to answer if you break down 'imperialism' to consider the 'high imperialism' of men like Chamberlain and Milner separately from the broader imperialistic attitudes seen in the media and the popular representations of empire. This division should help you to organise points for and against the quotation and enable you to offer a judgement.

 PRACTICE QUESTION

'Imperialism had widespread popular appeal in the years 1890 to 1914.' Explain why you agree or disagree with this view.

12 Relations with indigenous peoples

Empire depended on a belief in superiority. The most powerful notions were cultural, civilisational and racial. The superiority of the British, and thus their right to rule others, was established by their allegedly 'higher capacities'. In future times, under proper tutelage, non-Europeans might match or emulate their achievements. The justification of empire was to create such conditions: it was essentially an educational or civilising enterprise. This belief was widely voiced around 1900. The turn of the century was also the apex of the belief that differences in culture or technological achievement reflected biological ones; 'scientific racism'. Closely linked to the role of racial beliefs in imperial ideology was that of violence, repression and atrocity; the seemingly standard assumption that quite different rules applied when fighting 'savages' than in warfare between European powers. The idea of colonialism as a modernising force also accords with the self-image of the empire builders. But the notion of the colonial relationship coming from a rational drive by the expansionary power simply does not fit with much of what we know about the British.

Adapted from 'Empire and Ideology' by Stephen Howe (2008)

Challenges to British rule

Fig. 1 *The assassination of Curzon Wyllie, 1909*

LEARNING OBJECTIVES

In this chapter you will learn about:

- challenges to British rule
- the Sudan
- the causes and consequences of the Boer War.

KEY QUESTION

As you read this chapter, consider the following key question:
How did the indigenous peoples respond to British rule?

ACTIVITY

Evaluating historical extracts

1. According to Howe, in Extract 1, what factors influenced the British relationship with the indigenous peoples in the Empire?
2. As you read this chapter, look for examples of these influences at work.

A number of British administrators, including the Governor of Bengal, were targeted in attacks organised by nationalists, although the British initially thought the activity was uncoordinated and represented desperate attempts by low-bred Indians. However, in April 1908, when two British women were killed by a bomb intended for a district judge, an intensive police investigation was mounted. It revealed this attack to be the work of a terrorist organisation, known as the Anushilan Samiti. This was led by Pramathanath Mitra P. Mitra, a Calcutta High Court barrister.

CROSS-REFERENCE

Viceroy Curzon's proposal to partition Bengal is outlined in Chapter 8, page 73.

The role and influence of Mohandas Gandhi is discussed in detail in Chapter 16, page 153.

ACTIVITY

Create a poster for the *swadeshi* movement. Refer to specific British goods to emphasise support for Indian self-sufficiency and hostility to British imports. You might want to look back to Chapter 9 to help with this.

ACTIVITY

With the help of some on-line research, create a cartoon strip of the activities of the 'Mad Mullah'.

British rule met with some challenges from the indigenous peoples of the Empire. Sometimes the resistance came in the form of political action and protest; this was most prevalent in India, where a nationalist campaign took hold and grew in the years to 1914. Elsewhere, challenges were more overt as the British were forced to fight to consolidate their dominance; this was particularly the case in various parts of Africa during and after the era of expansion. All these challenges to empire came at a cost to Britain – in terms of money, time, attention and, of course, pride.

Challenges in India

There were some varied and complex challenges to British rule on the Indian subcontinent. In the 1890s, political opposition to British rule grew amongst the educated Indian professional classes and an outlet for protest was found in the emergence and growth of nationalist newspapers. Both Bal Tilak, editor of *Kesari*, and Shivram Paranjape who founded a weekly called *Kaal* in 1898, were sentenced to imprisonment for stirring up hostility. Tilak was accused of inciting the murder of a medical officer, while the popularity of *Kaal* (which can be translated as both 'Times' and 'Terminator') led to Paranjape's arrest for sedition in 1908. He served 19 months of imprisonment with hard labour and after his release in 1910, the British authorities banned the publication of *Kaal* and also confiscated his writings.

The Abhinav Bharat (Young India) organisation, founded by two brothers, Vinayak Damodar Savarkar and Ganesh Damodar Savarkar in 1903, became the home for several hundred revolutionaries and political activists. It established branches in various parts of India and carried out assassinations of British officials, including a district magistrate, Arthur Jackson, and a London-based military advisor, Lieutenant-Colonel Curzon-Wyllie, in 1909.

It was Viceroy Curzon's controversial **partition of Bengal**, however, that prompted the most vociferous opposition to the Raj. Tilak was at the forefront of a *swadeshi* or self-sufficiency campaign designed to undermine British rule. Besides petitions and protests, a public boycott of British goods took place. This six-year campaign was successful in as much as Bengal was reunited in 1911; however, its methods and principles also greatly influenced the later campaigns of **Mohandas Gandhi**.

Challenges in Africa

There were a number of challenges to British rule in Africa. Some were the result of the competition of other European powers and settlers, while others emanated from local peoples who sought to resist British influence. Among the latter were the challenges in:

- **British Somaliland**
  Sayyid Hassan, a self-styled Somali religious warrior known to the British as the 'Mad Mullah', was typical of those who saw it as their duty to resist British authority. Sayyid Hassan built up a force of c20,000 Dervish forces, armed with weapons from the Ottoman Empire. His aim was to halt Ethiopian, Italian and British gains in Somalia with the declared intention of driving all Christians into the sea. From c1900, his forces mounted raids on British Somaliland, antagonising the local communities. To counter Hassan and his Dervishes, the British conducted joint military action with Ethiopia's Emperor Menelik, although without conclusive success. The Dervishes secured a somewhat hollow victory over the outnumbered British 'Camel Constabulary' at the Battle of Dul Madoba in August 1913 but were never fully suppressed until after the First World War.

Fig. 2 *The Mad Mullah's rising, as depicted in the* Illustrated London News, *1901*

- **Zanzibar**
  On the island of **Zanzibar**, Britain's control was challenged briefly by Khalid bin Barghash who assumed power in August 1896 following the suspicious death of the pro-British Sultan Hamoud. Although Khalid commanded 3000 men, he quickly fled following heavy bombardment from British ships anchored nearby. This challenge lasted less than two days.
- **West Africa**
  In 1898, the British Governor of Sierra Leone, Colonel Cardew, introduced a new, severe tax on dwellings, known as the 'hut tax' and also insisted that local chiefs organise their followers to maintain roads. His demands were met with resistance. Cardew responded militarily and eventually deployed a '**scorched earth**' approach, which involved setting fire to entire villages, farms and crops. This tactic secured surrender from Cardew's primary adversary, Chief Bai Bureh, in November 1898, although hundreds had been killed in the process. Despite the British government's plea for leniency, Cardew had 96 of the chief's warriors hanged.

However, the greatest challenges to British rule in Africa arose in the Sudan and the Transvaal, where the crises were not easily addressed.

The Sudan

Kitchener's conquest of the Egyptian Sudan, culminating in the Battle of Omdurman and the fall of Khartoum in 1898, was reported in the *Daily Mail* as having secured the 'downfall of the worst tyranny in the world'. Although

CROSS-REFERENCE

The challenge to British contol in Zanzibar is described in more detail in Chapter 7, page 63.

KEY TERM

scorched earth policy: this is a military strategy that involves destroying anything that might be useful to the enemy while advancing through (or withdrawing from) an area

A CLOSER LOOK

In 1899, a joint Anglo-Egyptian government over the Sudan was declared. The military and civil government of the Sudan was invested in a Governor-General appointed by the Khedive of Egypt, but nominated by the British government. In reality, Britain ruled the Sudan and Egypt paid; the wishes of the peoples of the Sudan were ignored.

many Sudanese did welcome the downfall of the Mahdist regime, which had all but destroyed the Sudanese economy and seen a decline of 50 per cent in the population through famine, disease, persecution, and warfare, the arrival of the British (who effectively took control in the Sudan) meant little more than exchanging one oppressor for another.

It took the British more than 30 years to subdue the tribes in the south of Sudan. British attempts to create a modern government, introduce new penal codes, establish land tenure rules and establish a system of taxation for the first time in Sudan's history incensed the Sudanese peoples. Tribes refused to renounce their customs and pay taxation; inter-tribal feuds persisted, bringing down the heavy-hand of British law. A total of 33 punitive expeditions were mounted to force tribesmen to accept the new order and rebellious natives were often brutally treated. There were even Mahdist uprisings in 1900, 1902–03, 1904 and 1908. A series of swift public hangings accompanied the last as the British sought to make an example of the rebels – not even affording them a trial.

Set against this, the region experienced considerable economic development at the hands of the British, particularly in the Nile Valley. Telegraph and railway lines were extended to link key areas in northern Sudan and Port Sudan opened in 1906, as the country's principal outlet to the sea. In 1911 a joint government/private initiative set up the Gezira Scheme to provide high-quality cotton for Britain's textile industry and there were improvements in irrigation systems.

CROSS-REFERENCE

For more detail for British conquest and rule in the Sudan after 1890, look back to Chapter 7, pages 66–67.

ACTIVITY

Write a short imperialist article on Sudan for an edition of the *Daily Mail* in 1911.

Fig. 3 *The charge of the 21st Lancers at Omdurman*

KEY TERM

Pax Britannica: Latin for 'British Peace'; the term was used to mirror the Romans' use of 'Pax Romana' meaning a period of peace brought about by the dominant power – in this case, Britain, which acted as a 'global policeman'

EXTRACT 2

British racial attitudes were not all arrogance and condescension. Even in the glaring noon of empire, much generosity and respect still gave nobility to the **Pax Britannica**. The higher motives of the imperialists were not all humbug. The Colonial Office in London consistently stood for fair play towards the subject races, often against bitter criticism from white men on the spot. There were countless acts of individual kindness. It was not viciousness, nor even conceit, that fostered the general aloofness of the British. It was partly a sense of ordained separateness, partly the natural reserve of islanders and partly, no doubt, the awkwardness people feel when they do not understand a foreigner, or more especially do not speak the language. Many a British official learnt to love his charges with a passionate sincerity. Even Alfred Milner, writing from Cairo in 1893, regarded the Sudanese with half-amused, half-admiring and inoffensively patronising affection.

Adapted from Pax Britannica by Jan Morris (1968)

 PRACTICE QUESTION

Evaluating historical extracts

With reference to Extracts 1 and 2 and your understanding of the historical context, which of these two extracts provides the more convincing interpretation of British attitudes towards indigenous peoples in the years 1890 to 1914?

The causes and consequences of the Boer War

Causes

Once **Cecil Rhodes** became Prime Minister of the Cape in 1890, the British and Boers seemed set on a collision course. Rhodes' overriding aim in South African politics was to bring the Boer republics (the Transvaal and the Orange Free State) into a South African federation, in which the British at the Cape would be the dominant partner. His ambition stemmed partly from irritation at the damage which the high tariffs imposed by the Boers were causing to trade and partly from his personal hostility to Paul Kruger, the leading Boer politician.

The Transvaal's prestige and power had grown with the discovery of gold on the Rand in 1886 and it had extended its control over Swaziland by establishing its own independent rail network to the Portuguese-controlled port of Lourenco Marques. Both Rhodes and the Colonial Secretary **Chamberlain** were worried that Britain's dominance in southern Africa was threatened. This resulted in their support for the ill-fated **Jameson raid** of 1895 which attempted to topple Paul Kruger's government; and in continuing clashes over the **voting rights of the Uitlanders**.

Alfred Milner, the South African High Commissioner from 1897, encouraged the British to pursue a vigorous policy, while Kruger's success in securing a fourth term as Transvaal President in 1898 reflected the Boers' strong nationalist sentiment and resentment of British interference. To make matters worse, an Englishman, Tom Edgar, was shot by a Transvaal policeman in December 1898. This prompted Uitlander outrage and pressure on the British government from the Uitlanders for firm action.

ACTIVITY

Write a speech, such as might have been given by Alfred Milner in 1889, encouraging British action against the Boers. Some members of your group could present their speeches and respond to questions; others could prepare arguments to counteract and question Milner's stance.

At the Bloemfontein Conference of May–June 1899, Milner demanded that the Transvaal grant voting rights to the Uitlanders; Kruger refused. Despite some half-hearted attempts at compromise, both sides began to mobilise their troops. In October 1899, Kruger issued an ultimatum demanding a British withdrawal from the borders of the Boer republics. War broke out when the British stood firm.

STUDY TIP

Read each extract carefully and identify the interpretation it puts forward. You should explain this interpretation with reference to the detail in the extracts and your own knowledge. Decide which of these two contrasting views you feel is the more convincing and explain why. Again, ensure you substantiate your judgement with historical detail.

CROSS-REFERENCE

Expansion in Africa from 1890 to 1914 is covered in Chapter 7.

The roles and influence of Cecil Rhodes and Joseph Chamberlain are explored in Chapter 10, pages 92–93.

To recap on events in the Transvaal including the Jameson raid, look back to Chapter 7, pages 67–69.

There is a case study of Alfred Milner in Chapter 10, page 96.

A CLOSER LOOK

Uitlanders' voting rights

The Uitlanders were the British settlers who had flocked into the Transvaal in search of gold. Although they paid taxes, they were effectively denied the vote; they had to secure 14 years' residency in the Transvaal and be over 40 years of age to qualify. This meant 50,000 Britons were excluded from political rights, despite the fact that Boer residents living in the British-run Cape Colony were given voting rights.

Using the information in this chapter as well as Chapters 7, 10 and any other research materials you have, complete the following chart to categorise the causes of the Boer War thematically and consider their relative importance.

Causes of the Boer War

Factors	Examples and importance
Political	
Economic	
Social	
Influence of individuals	

Consequences

Fig. 4 *Boer prisoners in a camp at Bloemfontein*

Britain's eventual military victory in 1902 came at an incredible cost. Commander-in-Chief General Kitchener deployed a 'scorched earth' policy which involved incinerating Boer farms and livestock. Boer families and black Africans were interned in concentration camps and suffered horrendous conditions. Interned Boer civilians and black Africans perished in them as a result of both malnutrition and disease.

Concentration camps

By the end of the war, about 115,000 people were living in these camps and many more – primarily women and children – had died in them.

Epidemics spread easily within the camps, although this was not a consequence of deliberate British policy but the result of contemporary medical and sanitary ignorance. Indeed, more than 16,000 British soldiers were also killed by disease, nearly three times as many as died from enemy action. Humanitarians, left-wing liberals and socialists in Britain refused to believe that 'the ends justified the means' and described the use of camps as 'methods of barbarism'.

CROSS-REFERENCE

For the impact of the Boer War on attitudes to imperialism in Britain, look back to Chapter 11, page 101.

The lasting effect of the war was not so much the Boers' surrender in May 1902 or that the Transvaal and Orange Free State had to accept British sovereignty (with a promise of future self-rule) but, rather, the moral and military shortcomings displayed by Britain in the name of empire.

The war shook Britain's confidence as an imperial power. It had been anticipated that the conflict would last three to four months, involving 75,000 troops, and cost no more than £10 million. Instead, it dragged on for the best part of three years, involved 400,000 troops and cost £230 million. The war also saw 22,000 British military killed, to just 6000 Boer troops.

The war showed the vulnerability of Britain's imperial control and, perhaps, made it more aware of its inability to inflict its will on other peoples without a cost. Britain had to call on troops from other parts of the Empire (notably India) to maintain the fight and the danger of leaving other dependencies without adequate armed back-up was grave. In South Africa, the British had not been able to rely on their long-vaunted sea power. The war's shortcomings dictated the drive for national efficiency and dampened the jingoism that had characterised the 1890s. Thereafter, only the Conservatives still spoke out politically for imperialism, although the sentiment was far from dead.

ACTIVITY

Write a letter to *The Times* that might have appeared in the wake of the Boer War and the revelations about the concentration camps.

ACTIVITY

Look back at the chart you constructed on the causes of the Boer War and create another like it on the consequences of the war.

A CLOSER LOOK

Defeat in the war prompted the Boers to develop a more distinctive 'Afrikaner' culture. The Taalbond ('language union') was formed in 1903 to promote the use of the colloquial version of Dutch spoken by the Boers, rather than English, and the writing of Afrikaans poetry and prose was promoted. Political organisations committed to Afrikaner self-government were formed: Het Volk ('The People') was established in the Transvaal in 1905, and Orangia Unie ('Orange Union') in the Orange River Colony in 1906.

The concluding Treaty of Vereeniging of May 1902 granted the Boers £3 million compensation in order to restore and restock their farms. Milner also worked to integrate the economies of the British and Boer colonies, bringing them into a single customs union and amalgamating their railway systems. As promised, the Transvaal was granted self-governing status in 1906, and the Orange River Colony in 1907, but the integration of the states was such that, in 1910 the parliaments of the Cape Colony, the Transvaal and the Orange River Colony, as well as the people of Natal who voted in a referendum, agreed to the establishment of the Union of South Africa, as an independent **Dominion** within the British Empire. However, the constitution allowed the states to retain their own voting policies: a compromise that was to store up trouble for the future.

A CLOSER LOOK

Dominion status had been given to Australia in 1901 and New Zealand in 1907, setting a precedent for a South African Union. However, the mixture of black and white peoples in South Africa set it apart from the other 'settler' Dominions and while the Cape Colony permitted all races to vote in its parliament, the other three colonies retained a 'whites' vote.

Summary

British rule in the Empire often seemed to show scant regard for the indigenous peoples. They were intimidated, bullied and sometimes physically coerced into an acceptance of British rule. Nevertheless, the imperialists were always ready to claim that these actions were in the best interests of the native peoples. When the British fought, it was against injustice or because others stood in the way of a rule that would ultimately improve the well-being of those under their care. The British genuinely believed themselves to be a civilising influence, no matter how different things might look to those who were on the receiving end.

STUDY TIP

You should try to show that you understand what the British ideas of racial superiority were and give some examples that would suggest that racialism affected British attitudes towards indigenous peoples. You should also consider the many other factors which influenced relationships, and before beginning to write it would be advisable to make a list of these. Try to use some specific historical examples (drawn from this chapter or elsewhere) to support your arguments.

 PRACTICE QUESTION

To what extent was the British relationship with indigenous peoples in the colonies in the years 1890 to 1914 damaged by British notions of racial superiority?

Fig. 5 *The British Empire c1914*

ACTIVITY

Summary

Look back at the map on page xvii of the Introduction, which shows the British Empire in 1857, and compare this with Fig. 5 in this chapter. Make a list of the changes you can see. Using the text and/or additional research, explain how these changes came about.

3 Imperialism challenged

13 Expansion and contraction of empire

The impact of the First World War

The crucial watershed in the British conduct of World War I came, both at home and in the Empire, with Asquith's replacement by Lloyd George in December 1916. While Asquith clung to the normal peace-time ways of running government, Lloyd George enjoyed addressing the emergency of war. It has been said that the new Prime Minister regarded the Dominions with a sympathetic eye; it might also be described as the hard, envious gaze of the recruiting sergeant. The Empire, in short, was to provide the resources for the more aggressive policy followed by the Lloyd George government. Before December 1916, Britain was at war, assisted by her Empire; after December 1916, the Empire was at war, arranged by Britain as the agreed leader among equal partners. In short, the Empire came to play a much more important role in the war effort.

Adapted from 'The British Empire and the Great War, 1914–1918' by Robert Holland *The Oxford History of the British Empire: The Twentieth Century*, Judith M. Brown and Wm Roger Louis (eds.) (Oxford University Press 1999).

ACTIVITY

Evaluating historical extracts

1. With reference to Extract 1, why might December 1916 be seen as a 'turning point'?
2. As you read through the next section, find evidence which supports Holland's argument about the importance of Empire in the First World War from 1916.

LEARNING OBJECTIVES

In this chapter you will learn about:

- the impact of the First World War on the British Empire
- how Britain expanded its imperial power through mandates
- the impact of the Second World War on the British Empire
- the British withdrawal from India and the Middle East

KEY QUESTION

As you read this chapter, consider the following key questions:
- Why did the British Empire grow and contract?
- What influenced imperial policy?

In 1914, world peace was shattered by the outbreak of war between the two alliance systems: Britain, France, Russia and (from 1915) Italy, against Germany, Austria- Hungary and Turkey. Britain declared war on behalf of the whole Empire – but most British leaders believed that the war would be short and would end with rapid victory or a negotiated settlement. The anticipated that the fighting would be done by the British themselves, with limited help from the Empire.

In practice, the colonies sent approximately 1.4 million men to fight for the Empire between 1914 and 1918, supporting the 5 million men from the British Isles. Britain not only called upon Indian and African troops, which were at British disposal, but was also supported by troops from the white Dominions which controlled their own armed forces. The Empire also supplied Britain with vital raw materials and food, which played a major part in ultimate British victory in 1918.

This brought a move towards joint decision-making, to meet pressure from colonial leaders who wanted some say in the direction Britain was taking their troops. The Presidents of the Dominions and nominated Indian representatives joined the war cabinet in London in 1917. This 'Imperial war cabinet' seemed to symbolise the union of the British Empire in war; but it held only two sessions and the British still dominated proceedings.

A CLOSER LOOK

In 1917, Lloyd George created an Imperial War Cabinet to coordinate imperial military policy. Meeting during 1917 and 1918, it included Lloyd George; Sir Robert Borden (Prime Minster of Canada); Louis Botha and General Jan Smuts (successive prime ministers of South Africa); Billy Hughes (Prime Minister of Australia); Bill Massey (Prime Minister of New Zealand); Edward Morris (Prime Minister of Newfoundland); and Sir James Meston (Governor of Agra and Oudh).

Coalition government: a government combining a number of different political parties.

For the issue of free trade versus imperial preference, which caused much political debate before the First World War, look back to Chapter 9, pages 88–89.

Before reading further, discuss with a partner the ways in which the Empire might be able to aid Britain in fighting the war. Consider the practical, moral and strategic advantages of having the Empire fighting alongside Great Britain.

Gallipoli and Vimy Ridge

Australian and New Zealand forces (known as Anzacs) played an important role in the 1915 Gallipoli campaign – an attempted invasion of Turkey. Canadian forces fought strongly at Vimy Ridge in Northern France in April 1917.

Find out more about the contribution of the 'Anzacs' – who they were, where they went and what they achieved. Look at these different aspects in pairs or small groups and present short illustrated presentations of your findings to the rest of the group.

The Indian National Congress Party (the main political party campaigning for independence in India) is introduced in Chapter 2, page 16.

The role and influence of Edwin Montagu is discussed in Chapter 16, page 157.

Imperial preference

In 1916, Asquith was replaced as Prime Minister by David Lloyd George at the head of a wartime **coalition government**. Under Lloyd George a far greater effort was put into the use of the resources of manpower and materials from the Empire. 'Imperial preference' was introduced for suppliers and schemes for future imperial self-sufficiency discussed.

Colonial involvement in the war and its impact

The White Dominions

The peoples and governments of the White Dominions were mostly keen to help Britain. Large numbers of volunteers in the Dominions rushed to join the armed forces, although the Canadian, Australian and New Zealand leaders insisted that their forces maintain their distinct national identities. Conscription was even introduced in New Zealand in 1916 and Canada in 1917.

The Australians and New Zealanders (known as Anzacs) were applauded for their bravery in the **Gallipoli** campaign (April–December 1915) and the Canadians for their part at the battle for **Vimy Ridge** in April 1917. Canada also supplied Britain with munitions (a third of the munitions used by the British Army in France from 1917 to 1918) and wheat.

In South Africa, General Smuts, who had once fought against the British in the Boer War, formed the South African Defence Force, which fought successfully against the Germans in its colonies. Smuts was a member of Lloyd George's Imperial War Cabinet and attended the London Imperial War Conference and even advised on military strategy in Europe. 136,000 South African troops fought in the Middle East and on the Western Front.

However, whilst the war demonstrated the overall loyalty of the White Dominions to Britain and Empire, it also triggered debate about the Dominions' relationship to Britain and their long-term future. The war was not popular everywhere. French Canadians in Quebec regarded the war as a pro-British affair, and in March 1918 there were protest riots against conscription in Quebec City. Similarly, the Australians rejected conscription in two referendums, in October 1916 and again in December 1917. In South Africa, a republican movement led by J.B.M. Hertzog grew and the Afrikaner movement questioned the imperial connection.

The overall impact of the war on the participating Dominions was to boost confidence and strengthen self-worth. In many ways, this was just as dangerous for the future of the Empire since it ultimately promoted a desire for independence from imperial control.

India

Around a third of the troops in France in the autumn of 1914 were either Indians or British soldiers who had formerly served in India. Indian troops also made major contributions to the fighting in the Middle East (in the campaign against the Turks in Palestine, Syria and Iraq) and in Africa, although their record was less successful than that of the Dominion forces. Furthermore, in 1917 the Indian government contributed £100 million to Britain's war effort.

In acknowledgement of India's contribution, and in response to growing support for Indian independence as put forward by the **Congress Party**, in August 1917 the Secretary of State for India, **Edwin Montagu**, promised more 'responsible' self-government for India. This included a measure of democratic representation for ordinary Indians: a logical continuation of earlier policy, but one that made it necessary to review India's status once war had ended.

Africa

Africans also participated in the war. Egypt was turned into a Protectorate in 1914 and 1.2 million Egyptians were recruited to defend Egypt and the Middle East (Saudi Arabia, Iraq, Jordan and Palestine). 100,000 Egyptian soldiers fought in Europe, of whom 50 per cent were killed. Black people from the tropical colonies and black South Africans did not fight but were recruited to work in France as labourers and carriers. Some joined the million 'human porters', from British East Africa who were forced to serve in the fight against the Germans in Tanganyika (Tanzania) where nearly 100,000 died. This experience of war was also to prove formative in the development of independence movements. It is no coincidence that the first Pan-African Congress was held in France in 1919 or that a delegation from South Africa attended the post-war Versailles Peace Conference of 1919 to present the African case.

The League of Nations mandates

Following the end of war in November 1918, the allies drew up a series of post-war peace treaties. The Treaty of Versailles of 1919 stripped Germany of its former colonies, which were, in future, to be '**mandates**' administered for the League of Nations by specified allied powers. The colonial territories of the Ottoman Empire were subject to the same ruling by the Treaty of Sèvres (1920) and the Treaty of Lausanne (1923), and distributed among the allied powers by the Treaty of San Remo (1920).

> **ACTIVITY**
>
> Write a patriotic newspaper account headed 'fighting in the colonies'. You may wish to undertake some further research into a specific campaign for this.

A CLOSER LOOK

The growth of British control, 1919–20

As a result of the post-war peace treaties, the British Empire reached its greatest extent with the addition of 1,800,000 square miles and 13 million new subjects. The colonies of Germany and the Ottoman Empire were distributed to the allied powers as League of Nations mandates. Britain gained control of Palestine, Transjordan, Iraq (formerly Mesopotamia), parts of Cameroon and Togo, and Tanganyika. The Dominions themselves also acquired mandates of their own: the Union of South Africa gained South-West Africa (modern-day Namibia), Australia gained German New Guinea, and New Zealand gained Western Samoa. Nauru was made a combined mandate of Britain and the two Pacific Dominions.

> **KEY TERM**
>
> **mandate:** a territory allocated by the League of Nations to a particular country to be governed by that country on the League's behalf; such territories were referred to as mandates, but the word mandate can also be used as a verb to describe the act of passing on the authority (to mandate)

A CLOSER LOOK

The League of Nations

The League was an international organisation set up by the post-war peace treaties. It aimed to prevent war by settling international disputes by negotiation. The League tried hard to keep the peace in the 1920s and 1930s, but the refusal of the USA to join, the lack of an international army, and the subsequent rise of Fascism and Nazism helped to undermine it.

A guiding principle of the Treaty of Versailles was **self-determination**. This ideal was especially advocated by the US President Woodrow Wilson, but was

KEY TERM

self-determination: the right of a distinct national or ethnic group of people to determine their own nation-state and form of government

at odds with the attitude of countries like Britain and France who possessed global empires.

The British and French argued that the German and Turkish colonies in Africa, the Middle East and the Pacific were politically and economically undeveloped, with uneducated populations. They were therefore not yet ready to govern themselves, and needed the guiding hand of countries like Britain and France, which had experience of governing less developed territories. Thus the mandate arrangements were supposed to be about helping these territories in becoming independent nations. However, in practice, the principal mandated powers, Britain and France, secured virtually imperial control over their new mandates.

Under the terms of the mandate system, although the allied powers were given control over the former imperial possessions of the defeated powers, they were obliged to fulfil certain obligations. The territories were defined according to a system of categories reflecting the extent to which these territories were considered 'developed'. These were:

- 'A' category (Palestine and Mesopotamia mandated to Britain; Syria and Lebanon mandated to France) – territories seen as quite developed, so independence might be a viable possibility in the relatively near future
- 'B' category (the former German colonies of Tanganyika mandated to Britain; Togoland and Cameroon split between Britain and France; Ruanda-Urundi mandated to Belgium) – territories which required a much longer period of guidance before independence could be contemplated
- 'C' category (German territories in New Guinea and Samoa mandated to Britain and to Britain in collaboration with Australia and New Zealand; German islands in the South Pacific mandated to Japan; German South-West Africa to the Union of South Africa) – territories where independence was not considered feasible.

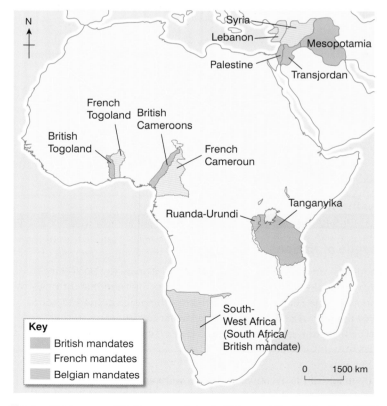

Fig. 1   *The League of Nations mandates in Africa and the Middle East, 1920*

The Palestinian mandate

Britain had been particularly anxious to acquire the Palestinian mandate for economic and strategic reasons. The Middle East was crucial to the British, since it incorporated the main overland route to Britain's Indian and Asian empire and because of its proximity to the Suez Canal. Mesopotamia (modern day Iraq) was also increasingly valued because it was oil-rich.

A CLOSER LOOK

At the end of the First World War, Palestine was highly unstable. There had been heavy fighting between British and Turkish forces, and the Turks had enforced conscription on the Palestinian Arabs, as well as seizing crops, thus increasing Arab determination to control their own future.

In 1915, the British and French had secretly plotted to divide up the Middle East between them. The British and French diplomats Sir Mark Sykes and Georges Picot had made an agreement whereby France would take south-eastern Turkey, northern Iraq, Syria and Lebanon and Britain would acquire Jordan, southern Iraq and Palestine. During the war, both the British and French encouraged Arab rebellions against the Turkish Empire and **T.E. Lawrence** ('Lawrence of Arabia') played an especially important role in helping these revolts.

KEY PROFILE

T.E. Lawrence (1888–1935) was an archaeologist who became a British officer. He played an important role in promoting rebellion by Arab tribes against Turkish rule, especially from 1917 to 1918.

ACTIVITY

Extension

Lawrence of Arabia is the subject of a famous film produced by David Lean in 1962. Try to watch this. You might like to investigate its historical accuracy.

The Balfour Declaration

In 1917, the Foreign Secretary, **Arthur Balfour**, sent a letter to Walter Rothschild, a member of the prominent banking family and leader of the British Jewish community. This 'Balfour Declaration', which expressed sympathy with Jewish **Zionist** aspirations, was released to the press. It promised British support for a 'national homeland' for the Jews in Palestine. However it did so on the understanding that this would not constitute a separate Jewish state and that it did not undermine the rights of the Arab Palestinian population to continue living as they had always done.

The Declaration came partly out of genuine sympathy for the plight of the Jews, but also out of an attempt to win the support of the anti-imperialist American public to an acceptance of British influence in this area.

KEY TERM

Zionist: Zionism was a political belief and movement advocating the creation of a national Jewish homeland based on the historic kingdom of Israel in the Middle East; it arose as a result of the persecution of Jewish people in many parts of Europe, especially in the east.

KEY PROFILE

Arthur Balfour (1848–1930) was Conservative Prime Minister from 1902 to 1905, and Foreign Secretary from 1916 to 1919 in Lloyd George's coalition government. He was a strong supporter of British ambitions to control Palestine.

The Balfour Declaration and Palestinian mandate were to prove troublesome for the British. When a Zionist Commission was set up in Palestine in 1918 to campaign for Jewish rights, Muslims and Arabs formed the Muslim-Christian Association in response and between 1918 and 1920, there were violent clashes between Arabs and Jews, with deaths on each side. Increasing Jewish immigration into Palestine brought the total Jewish population of Palestine to 60,000, or about 6.8 per cent of the total population by 1918. By 1931, it was 175,000 (17.7 per cent of the population), which was to make it difficult for the British to fulfil their declaration promises.

CROSS-REFERENCE

Developing relations in Palestine are discussed in Chapter 14, page 132.

Leo Amery is profiled in Chapter 11, page 100.

Lord Milner's role before 1914 is discussed in Chapter 10, page 46 and Chapter 11, page 115.

A CLOSER LOOK

Several leading British politicians, including **Leo Amery** and **Lord Alfred Milner**, argued in favour of supporting the Jews. This was not entirely out of sympathy for their plight. They also believed support for the Jews would win the sympathy of influential Jewish interests in USA and so enable Britain to extend its influence in the Middle East without American opposition.

The expansion and contraction of empire

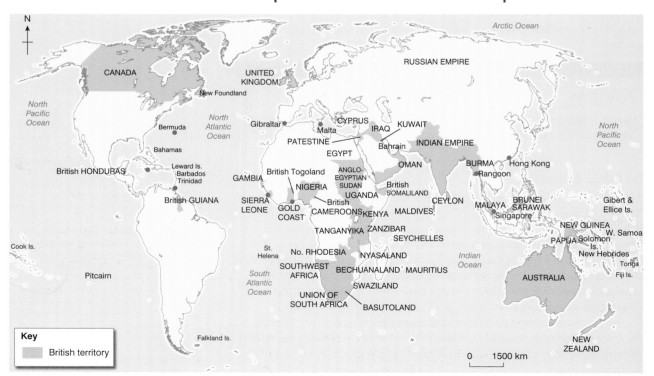

Fig. 2 *The British Empire c1919*

Although the British Empire had reached its greatest extent by 1920, there was, nevertheless, one significant casualty of war: Britain's oldest colony, Ireland, was lost.

Ireland had been joined to the United Kingdom in 1801 and had experienced a vociferous Home Rule (independence) movement throughout much of the nineteenth century. Gladstone had failed to carry Irish independence and although Asquith had come close, his Third Home Rule Bill, which had been given royal assent in 1913, had provoked a tide of opposition in Ulster, which wanted to remain united with the rest of Britain. It was never implemented because of the outbreak of war. During that war, the Irish Volunteers prepared an armed rising against the British.

The April 1916 Dublin Easter Rising was quickly put down but was followed by a period of guerrilla warfare that only ended in 1921 when the Anglo-Irish Treaty was signed. A new Catholic Irish Free state was set up and given 'Dominion' status. However, its existence was contested by the six northern Protestant counties, which opted out and chose to remain under British sovereignty. The Irish Free State took the name of Eire and achieved full independence in the 1937 Statute of Westminster.

There were two further losses in the aftermath of war. In 1922, Egypt, which had been declared a British Protectorate at the outbreak of the First World War, was granted formal independence, although it continued to be a British client state until 1954. British troops remained stationed in Egypt until the signing of the Anglo-Egyptian Treaty in 1936, under which it was agreed that the troops would withdraw but continue to occupy and defend the Suez Canal Zone. In return, Egypt was assisted to join the League of Nations.

Britain's other loss was Iraq (Mesopotamia) in 1932. Britain ruled Iraq as a mandated territory for 12 years after 1920, providing British protection for a monarchical rule by the royal family of Hejaz (the Hashemites). However, the country was never entirely stable and conflicting nationalist movements caused problems. In October 1932, the Kingdom of Iraq was granted its independence under King Faisal I, although the new government maintained close economic and military ties with Britain, which retained air bases in the country.

CROSS-REFERENCE

Gladstone's support for Home Rule for Ireland is outlined in Chapter 5, page 45.

CROSS-REFERENCE

The 1937 Statute of Westminster is discussed in Chapter 14, pages 139–140.

For more on the Easter Rising of April 1916, look ahead to Chapter 18, page 169.

ACTIVITY

Did the First World War strengthen or weaken the British Empire? In pairs, design a poster outlining on one side the factors which strengthened the Empire, and on the other side the ones that weakened it.

The impact of the Second World War

EXTRACT 2

For **Churchill**, the thought of abandoning the Victorian legacy of world power was not acceptable. While his ideas on colonial government were not inflexible, he believed it was essential to keep some ultimate British control over the various elements of the imperial system. Above all, Churchill insisted that Britain must preserve her authority over India which he saw, with an unchanging conviction, as the second centre of British world power. If Britain lost the Indian Empire, he once declared, she would sink in two generations to the rank of a minor power. Churchill's wartime colleagues may have cringed sometimes at the bluntness of his imperial patriotism. But his fierce defence of British rights and status commanded their general support. He checked any

ACTIVITY

Evaluating historical extracts

According to Extract 2, what is Darwin's view of Churchill, the British Prime Minister, in wartime?

Fig. 3   *As a young army officer Churchill saw action in India and Africa*

Winston Churchill (1874–1965) came from an aristocratic background and was a vigorous supporter of empire. As a part-time journalist, he covered the Boer War, but from 1900, his career was in politics, first as a Conservative, from 1904 as a Liberal Party member, and from 1925 as a Conservative again. In the 1930s, he opposed Indian independence. In 1940, Churchill became Prime Minister of an all-party coalition government and led Britain through war. He lost office in 1945, was re-elected as Prime Minister in 1951, but resigned in 1955.

tendency towards anything that smacked of international interference in the British Empire. 'Hands off the British Empire' is our maxim' – so said the Prime Minister in December 1944.

Adapted from *Britain and Decolonisation* by John Darwin (1988)

Colonial involvement in the war and its impact

Conflict in the Empire itself had been limited during the First World War. However, in the Second World War of 1939–45, fought by the British, Americans and their allies against the Germans, Italians and Japanese, the Empire was a major theatre of war. Key areas of conflict included South East Asia and Northern Africa and again the involvement of the colonies led to new demands for greater autonomy in the aftermath of war.

South East Asia

In early 1942, Japan seized the major European imperial possessions in South East Asia. Most devastating for Britain was the loss of Singapore in February 1942. This was Britain's main military naval base in the region and its loss brought the largest surrender of British troops in history. The Japanese seized Hong Kong, overran Malaya and Burma, and by the summer of 1942 seemed poised to attack India itself. An attempted Japanese invasion of India in 1944 was, however, narrowly averted and thereafter British and allied forces were able to roll back the Japanese conquests in the region.

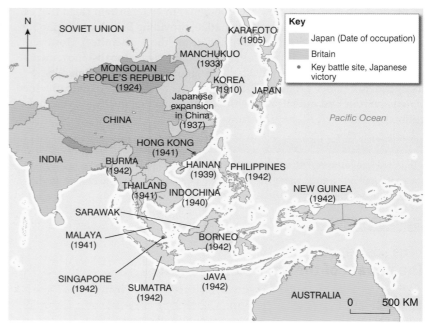

Fig. 4   *Japanese conquests in south-east Asia*

Subhas Chandra Bose is profiled in Chapter 18, page 174 and Aung San later in this chapter, on pages 131–132.

However, the success of the Japanese ended the myth of 'white invincibility' and gave new confidence to independence movements across South East Asia. Some even sided with the Japanese:

- 30,000 Indian troops that had been captured by the Japanese in Singapore joined the Indian National Army (INA) which aimed to rid India and Asia of the British. The INA, led from 1943 by **Subhas Chandra Bose**, fought against the British in Burma and elsewhere.

- In Burma, the independence leader **Aung San**, under the guidance of the Japanese, formed the Burma Independence Army. This also fought against the British.

North Africa

North Africa became an important battleground between Britain and its enemies, the Italians and Germans. Britain was desperate to preserve its influence in Egypt and access to Suez and oil in the Middle East but the Germans came close to dislodging the British and were only driven back at the **Battle of El Alamein** in November 1942. Both the Egyptians and Palestinians saw the opportunity for exploiting British weakness.

CROSS-REFERENCE

Aung San is profiled in this chapter, page 131.

A CLOSER LOOK

The Battle of El Alamein

This was a battle in Egypt in October–November 1942 in which the British defeated the German army, and began the process of sweeping Germany out of North Africa and securing British control of Egypt and British interests in the Middle East.

ACTIVITY

1. Draw a spider diagram to show: a) the ways in which the Second World War strengthened Britain's imperial position and b) the ways in which it weakened it.
2. Compare this with the poster you created on the impact of the First World War. Which war had the greater effect and why?

British withdrawal from India and the Middle East

Although Britain emerged from war victorious, in 1945, circumstances had changed.

- **Britain's economic position** had been severely weakened.
- The first majority **Labour government** was elected to power in 1945 under **Clement Attlee**. Traditionally Labour politicians had always been more sceptical than the Conservatives about empire, particularly questioning the morality of conquering other countries.
- Independence movements had grown stronger, particularly in India and the Middle East.

A CLOSER LOOK

The post-war Labour government, 1945–51

In the post-war elections of July 1945 the Labour Party under Clement Attlee won a landslide victory with a majority of 145. The result was a shock to the Conservatives under Winston Churchill; particularly after Churchill's popularity as a war leader. The result reflected the voters' belief that Labour would be more successful rebuilding Britain and carrying through much-needed social reform.

KEY PROFILE

Clement Attlee (1883–1967) was a Labour politician and leader of the Labour Party from 1935 to 1955. He was Deputy Prime Minister during the wartime coalition government (1942–1945) and became Prime Minister between 1945 and 1951 following Labour's victories at the general elections of 1945 and 1950. His governments were renowned for major economic and social reforms in Britain, and for the first moves to grant independence to parts of the British Empire.

CROSS-REFERENCE

The economic impact of the war is discussed in Chapter 15, pages 149–151.

ACTIVITY

As you read this section on India create a flow chart of the key steps leading to Indian independence.

CROSS-REFERENCE

The Government of India Act and the shared power agreement (known as the dyarchy) are discussed in Chapter 14, page 134.

The Amritsar massacre of April 1919 is described in Chapter 18, page 170.

Growing nationalism is discussed in detail in Chapter 18.

The Round Table Conferences of the 1930s are discussed in Chapter 14, page 135.

The Government of India Act of 1935 is outlined in Chapter 14, page 135.

The Muslim League and the Congress Party and their aims are discussed in Chapter 18.

Jinnah is profiled in Chapter 18, page 175.

Gandhi's role and influence are discussed in Chapter 16, pages 153–155.

CROSS-REFERENCE

The emergence of the Indian National Army under Subhas Bose is discussed on page 126.

The nationalist response to Cripps' offer of Dominion status in 1942 is outlined in Chapter 18, page 171.

India

The inter-war years

India had become an increasing worry to the British in the 1920s and 1930s. Nationalist demands for self-government after the First World War had resulted in the **Government of India Act, 1919**, which allowed a limited system of self-government for India, based on the **sharing of powers** between Indian ministers and the British Viceroy.

This arrangement had been intended to satisfy the demands for greater Indian representation among the more 'moderate' nationalists, by presenting the reforms as a step towards full Dominion status for India. However, the British were deeply concerned that these reforms might strengthen nationalist aspirations for faster change. As a result, they adopted what was effectively a 'twin track' strategy: a combination of reforms and a determination to make them work, combined with a clear signal that any resort by the nationalists to create mass resistance would be dealt with ruthlessly. This second, tougher strand was enshrined in the passage of the Rowlatt Act of 1919, which gave the authorities harsh powers to arrest and imprison anyone who protested against British rule. These two measures formed a 'carrot and stick' approach to containing demands for Indian representation.

In the short term, the Rowlatt Act proved to be counterproductive, producing much resistance and tragic results, including the **Amritsar massacre** of April 1919. **Nationalism grew** but negotiations on moves towards Dominion status for India, at the **Round Table Conferences** in London in the early 1930s, failed. Even when the British increased the numbers of Indians eligible to vote and strengthened the elected provincial assemblies in the **Government of India Act, 1935**, the weight of nationalist opinion still favoured complete Indian independence.

During the 1930s, the British increasingly retreated to their former policy of 'divide and rule', playing on the growing divisions within the nationalist movement:

- The **All India Muslim League**, led by **Muhammad Ali Jinnah**, wanted a separate, independent Muslim state: Pakistan.
- The Hindu **Congress** movement, led by **Mahatma Gandhi** wanted a united Indian state.

Although Gandhi preached Hindu–Muslim unity, the Muslims viewed Hindu leaders with suspicion. The British favoured the Muslim League, arguing that there was a case for a Muslim 'homeland' within a federal India. They suggested that the divisions between Hindus and Muslims proved the necessity of continued British rule, since the alternative was likely to be a bloody Hindu–Muslim civil war.

India and the Second World War

The nationalists suspended their protests in 1939 and supported the British war effort. However, British defeats in South East Asia in 1942 emboldened the Hindu Congress, which demanded immediate reforms. British anxieties were multiplied by the emergence of the **Indian National Army** (INA). The British therefore adopted a policy of repression, imprisoning Congress leaders and blatantly leaning in favour of the Muslim League.

In March 1942 the British Prime Minister, Winston Churchill, aware of the vulnerability of the British Empire in Asia, sent Sir Stafford Cripps, a Labour member of the wartime coalition government, to promise the Indians **full Dominion status**. However, this was not enough. In August 1942, Gandhi and the other Congress leaders launched a 'Quit India' Campaign, calling for the British to leave India entirely. Gandhi and others were arrested and spent the rest of the war in prison.

Fig. 5 *The human costs of quitting India: cartoon from the* Daily Mail *17 December 1946*

Post-war withdrawal from India

The Labour government of 1945 concluded that it was no longer feasible or desirable to keep India and decided to grant India independence as soon as possible. This was for a number of reasons.

- They feared that if they tried to keep India, there would be widespread violent resistance, which would stretch military resources to the limit.
- The activities of the INA and the strength of pro-independence feeling meant that the Indian Army might not be reliable and large numbers of British troops might have to be deployed: a move that would be expensive and unpopular, at a time when the country was in deep economic trouble.
- India was no longer the great market for British cotton exports it had once been, so the cost of holding onto it would massively outstrip any economic benefits.

In 1947 the government sent a new Viceroy, **Lord Louis Mountbatten**, with instructions to bring about Indian independence as soon as possible, and no later than June 1948. In April–May 1947 it was decided that India would be partitioned: independence for Pakistan as well as India would be granted by 15 August 1947.

This deadline was met, but violence between Muslims and Hindus escalated as millions of people of both faiths fled their homeland for the security of the country in which their own co-religionists would dominate. At least a million people died in the violence, leaving a legacy of bitterness between Pakistan and India. Thus British attempts to keep India in the Empire by a mixture of limited concessions of democracy and repression, had failed, and even the grant of independence proved messy.

KEY PROFILE

Lord Louis Mountbatten (1900–79) was a British naval officer (and second cousin of Queen Elizabeth II). He was Supreme Allied Commander Southeast Asia Command, Viceroy of India in 1947, and Governor-General of the Independent Dominion of India in 1947. He guided India and Pakistan to independence. He was assassinated by the IRA in 1979.

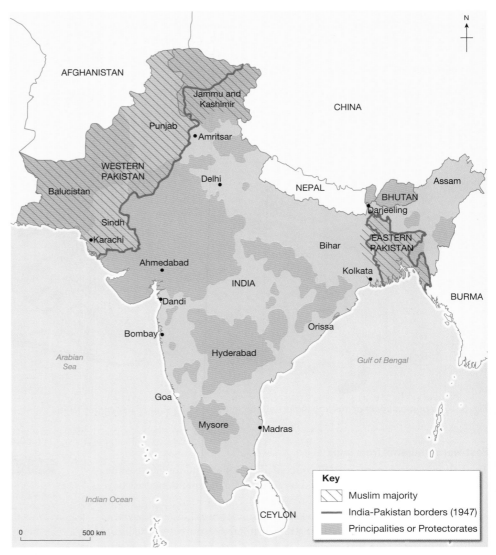

Fig. 6 *The partition of India*

CROSS-REFERENCE

The concept of the British Commonwealth is covered in Chapter 14, page 139.

ACTIVITY

Evaluating historical extracts

Read Extract 3 above. How accurate is the view that British chose to leave India rather than being forced to do so? Find some evidence to support each viewpoint and discuss with a partner.

EXTRACT 3

The post-war Labour government would not contemplate the Raj's re-establishment in the face of Indian opposition, as it believed this to be impossible in terms of manpower, expenditure, and both British and international politics. Always practical imperialists, the British weighed the ideological and material costs (in India and in Britain) of the Indian Raj against its benefits. After the war had ended in 1945, the British calculated that alliance with a free India in the Commonwealth was preferable to continued dominion. Indeed, an independent India was the only viable option open to the British, given their diminished resources and changed interest in South Asia. This was no failure of British commitment to empire, no recoil from harsh measures in principle. In other parts of the Empire they would show themselves prepared to use force to secure imperial priorities. In 1945–46 the British recognized, however reluctantly, that in the particular and unique circumstances of post-war India an Imperial Raj no longer achieved the goals they sought.

Adapted from 'India' by Judith Brown Single (1999)

In groups of three consider the strategies used by the British between 1914 and 1947 to try to keep India in the British Empire. List examples of these strategies in action, and the problems which they encountered.

Strategies for keeping India in the British Empire	Examples of these strategies in action	Problems with these strategies
Negotiating with the nationalists		
Divide and rule		
Violent repression		
Giving political concessions		
Others (please specify)		

AS LEVEL PRACTICE QUESTION

Evaluating historical extracts

Using your understanding of the historical context, assess how convincing the arguments in Extracts 1, 2 and 3 are, in relation to the impact of war on British imperialism in the years 1914 to 1947.

Burma

The years up to 1947 also saw the first steps towards decolonisation in Burma, a region occupied by the Japanese during the Second World War. The forces of the Anti-Fascist Organisation (AFO) had initially supported the Japanese against the British during the war. Nevertheless, they had belatedly come to accept, in 1944, that a British/allied victory would be more likely to win Burmese independence, and switched sides. However, the restoration of the British Governor, Sir Reginald Dorman-Smith, who believed that the physical reconstruction of Burma should precede any political change, turned the AFO into a resistance force, under the new name, the Anti-Fascist People's Freedom League (AFPFL).

A CLOSER LOOK

The Anti-Fascist Organisation (AFO) and Anti-Fascist People's Freedom League (AFPFL)

Burma was liberated from Japanese control in 1944–45, by a combination of British forces and the Anti-Fascist Organisation (AFO) – a coalition of Burmese forces, including the Burmese National Army led by **Aung San**, the Burmese Communist Party and the People's Revolutionary Party. In 1945, the AFO was renamed as the Anti-Fascist People's Freedom League (AFPFL), and resisted the re-establishment of British imperial rule.

Lord Mountbatten, Allied Commander in Southeast Asia, recognised the strength of support for Aung San. In September 1945, he agreed that the

STUDY TIP

In answering this question, you need to think about how wars affected attitudes to imperialism and you should exemplify this with reference to your own knowledge. This should be the starting point for assessing the fairness and accuracy of the three extracts.

CROSS-REFERENCE

Independence in Burma in 1948 is covered in Chapter 19, pages 185–186.

KEY PROFILE

Aung San (1915–47) was a Burmese nationalist who resisted British rule in Burma. Fearing arrest in 1940 he fled to Japan where he founded the Burmese Independence Army (BIA) in 1941. However, he became disillusioned with the Japanese and led the BIA in revolt against them. In 1947, he was rewarded by the British with an agreement that Burma would become independent within a year. He was assassinated in July 1947.

Burma National Army would be incorporated into a new army for the country, thereby effectively recognising Aung San as a legitimate leader in the post-war politics of Burma.

In September 1946, mounting civil disobedience and the increasing ungovernability of the country prompted the replacement of Sir Reginald Dorman-Smith with the more liberal Sir Hubert Rance, who not only admitted Aung San onto the ruling Executive Council, but virtually placed him in charge of it. By December 1946 Clement Attlee, the British Prime Minister, confirmed that his government was not able, nor willing, to commit sufficient troops to impose British authority. Burma would finally **become independent** in 1948.

Middle East

The war left the British under acute pressure in Palestine. Since the 1930s Nazi repression of European Jews, culminating in the **holocaust**, had led to massive increases in the numbers of Jewish people wanting to migrate to Palestine. By 1945, Arab–Jewish relations were deteriorating so rapidly that the British were keen to limit the scale of Jewish immigration into Palestine, in an effort to dampen down the conflict.

There were two major problems for Britain.

- President Truman and the weight of American and international opinion favoured Jewish settlement in Palestine, because of the way the Jews had been treated by the Nazis. However, while Britain needed American economic aid and international support, it also wanted to retain allies (among the Arabs) in the Middle East because of its need for oil from the region.
- There were outbreaks of Jewish terrorism inside Palestine against British troops. The British faced the prospect of having to police a country in violent turmoil at a time when their resources were stretched to the limit.

Britain sought a solution by negotiation between Arab and Jewish leaders. There were three possible solutions:

- a **unitary state** – as favoured by the Arabs who, as the majority, wanted to be able to dominate; this was unacceptable to the Jewish leadership
- **provincial autonomy** in which Palestine would be divided into smaller provincial areas, each with a measure of self-control, but ultimately led by a nationally elected government. The Jews rejected this also, as it would still lead to Arab rule
- the partition of Palestine into separate Jewish and Arab states; this was the only solution the Jews would support, but it was not acceptable to the Arabs.

Faced with deadlock, in February 1947 the British government referred the question to the **United Nations**. The UN favoured partition, largely because of pressure from the USA. So as not to alienate the Arab world, the British decided, in September 1947, that they would **withdraw from Palestine** by May 1948, and hand over control to a UN commission.

Summary

The First World War was largely followed by the expansion of the Empire, despite the loss of Ireland during the war, Egypt shortly afterwards and Iraq in 1932. However the Second World War saw some major contraction, particularly the granting of independence to India and Pakistan in 1947 and the announcement of British withdrawal from Palestine, which would take place in 1948, together with the recognition that Burma would soon follow. Nevertheless, in 1947, the concept of empire remained strong. Britain still regarded the rest of the Empire in Africa and Malaya as essential for the national interest and tried to develop these remaining imperial possessions, so that they could become more valuable to Britain.

KEY TERM

holocaust: The policy of murdering all of the Jewish population of Europe, which was pursued by the Nazis between 1941 and 1945

KEY TERM

unitary state: a nation state governed by a single centre of power (government), and where that government only devolves as much power as it chooses to do

provincial autonomy: a nation state where there is a central government, but in which the different provinces are constitutionally given a measure of control of their own affairs

United Nations: established at the end of the Second World War, this was the successor organisation to the League of Nations: its aim was to maintain world peace and settling international disputes by negotiation

A CLOSER LOOK

The British withdrawal from Palestine

Britain had little room for manoeuvre in September 1947. In the spring of that year, a Sterling Crisis had severely weakened the economy (see Chapter 15, page 150). Britain had spent in excess of £100 million on governing Palestine since January 1945, and over 330 British soldiers had died in fighting there. This level of commitment could not be maintained.

ACTIVITY

Summary

Consider the impact of the two wars on the British Empire. In the left column, give some examples of how the war and its aftermath saw an expansion of the British Empire. In the second column, show how the same war brought a contraction to the British Empire.

War	Examples of war and the expansion of the Empire during and after the war	Examples of war and the contraction of the Empire during and after the war
First World War 1914–18		
Second World War 1939–45		

 PRACTICE QUESTION

The contraction of the British Empire was started by the First World War, but accelerated by the Second.' Assess the validity of this view with reference to the years 1914 to 1947.

STUDY TIP

You could use your summary activity chart to reflect on the ways in which the First World War brought about a contraction of the Empire and compare the degree of contraction with what happened after the Second World War. Decide whether such points agree with the premise of the quotation, but before you begin to write, also think about the counter-claim that war also helped expand the Empire. It will be useful to take this into account in arguing the validity of this quotation.

14 Colonial policy and administration

LEARNING OBJECTIVES

In this chapter you will learn about:

- colonial policy and administration in India, Africa and the Middle East
- relations with the Dominions
- the Statute of Westminster of 1931
- British imperial defence policy.

Colonial policy and administration in India, Africa and the Middle East

EXTRACT 1

It would be easy to infer from the catalogue of economic set-backs and disappointed expectations during the inter-war years that Britain was in irreversible decline as an imperial power. Standard interpretations of the period emphasise Britain's economic weakness, her faltering will-power and her diminishing ability to maintain political control inside the Empire and influence beyond it. However, there are grounds for thinking that these judgements are not as robust as their frequent repetition might suggest. The resources at Britain's disposal were less plentiful after 1914 than before, but relatively she still remained a long way ahead of her European rivals, while the United States was only just beginning to emerge as a world power. Britain's position in relation to her various satellites and dependencies remained strong.

Adapted from *British Imperialism* by P.J. Cain and A.G. Hopkins (2001)

ACTIVITY

As you read through the chapter, consider Cain and Hopkins' assertion that in the inter-war period (1918–39) Britain's relations with the Empire remained strong. At the end of the chapter you will be asked to evaluate this interpretation.

KEY QUESTION

As you read this chapter, consider the following key questions:
- What influenced imperial policy?
- How important was the role of key individuals and groups and how were they affected by developments?
- What part did economic factors play in the development of the British Empire?

Colonial policy and administration in India

British colonial policy for much of the period between 1919 and 1947 was concerned with granting concessions in order to keep the Empire together and resist the rise of nationalism. This was particularly true of India, where the Secretary of State for India, Edwin Montagu, and the Viceroy, Lord Chelmsford, designed an act to create a system of limited self-government (or 'responsible government'), establishing a '**dyarchy**'.

KEY TERM

dyarchy: a system of rule where power is divided between two centres of authority

The Government of India Act, 1919

Under this Act:
- The Viceroy retained control of major areas, such as defence and foreign affairs, and his council remained a purely appointed body, but it was required to defend its actions before the Legislative Council.
- The Legislative Council was split into:
  - a lower house (the Legislative Assembly), of which 104 of its 144 members were to be elected
  - an upper house (the Council of State), of which 34 of its 60 members were to be elected.
- Provincial councils run by elected Indian ministers took responsibility for local government, health, education and agriculture.

The British regarded the reforms as a concession to critics of British rule in the **Indian Congress** and hoped that the reforms – which the British viewed as a first step towards a system of Dominion self-government – would weaken popular support for them.

CROSS-REFERENCE

For increasing demands for greater power for Indians over their own affairs, and the role of the Congress Party, look ahead to Chapter 18.

The Simon Commission, 1929–30

The Simon Commission (which did not include Indian representation), under **Sir John Simon**, reviewed the India Act and recommended that:

KEY PROFILE

Sir John Simon MP (1873–1954) was a Liberal politician who briefly served as Home Secretary during the First World War, but resigned in opposition to conscription. As an experienced lawyer, he was appointed as head of the 1929 Indian commission because of his intelligence and integrity.

- a federal system of government be created across India, incorporating both provinces under direct British rule and the Princely States
- the provinces be given more power
- defence, internal security and foreign affairs should remain in the hands of a British Viceroy, ensuring overall British control.

The Round Table Conferences, 1930 and 1931

Opposition from the independence movement in India led to two special **'Round Table Conferences'** in London in 1930 and 1931. **Gandhi**, the independence leader, was unable to attend the first as he had been imprisoned, but he represented the Congress Party at the second. However, no agreement was reached. The British rejected self-governing Dominion status for India because of doubts about the competence of non-white leaders and peoples as well as concern for India's strategic and economic importance to Britain.

KEY TERM

Round Table Conference: a meeting between all the political groups interested in a controversial question with a view to working out a commonly agreed way forward

CROSS-REFERENCE

The role and influence of Gandhi are discussed in detail in Chapter 16, pages 153–155.

Fig. 1 *The Second Round Table Conference, 1931; notice that Gandhi and some of the Indian representatives chose to wear Indian dress at the conference*

The Government of India Act, 1935

This Act created a Federation of India by:
- making the provinces completely self-governing (although provincial governors were still to be appointed by the British, and the Viceroy could suspend self-government in emergencies)
- expanding the franchise from 7 to 35 million people.

The Act was opposed by the Congress Party because it fell short of the independence enjoyed by the White Dominions and because of a desire to be completely free of British rule. The Princely States also rejected a federal India, as they wanted to maintain their independence from the rest of India.

In 1939, members of Congress-controlled ministries in the provinces resigned from office, in opposition to Indian participation in the war. The British therefore imposed direct rule, and dealt with independence protests against the war with repression – especially the arrest of independence leaders.

By 1947, it was clear that British colonial policy had failed and **India became an independent state**.

CROSS-REFERENCE

To recap on independence for India in 1947, look back to Chapter 8, pages 72–73.

Colonial policy and administration in Africa

Britain's African colonies fell into two categories:

- colonies which were ruled 'indirectly' by the British through existing local rulers. This included most colonies in West Africa, as well as Tanganyika, Uganda, Nyasaland and Northern Rhodesia. From 1919 the strategy of indirect rule was extended to the **League of Nations mandates**, notably British Togoland, British Cameroon, Tanganyika and South West Africa
- colonies where substantial numbers of Europeans had settled, and where the British ruled directly through their own officials, with some representation for the white settler population. These included Southern Rhodesia and Kenya. The Union of South Africa was the strongest example of a white settler colony and had enjoyed Dominion status since 1910.

Between 1919 and 1939, British policy and administration in these colonies developed as follows:

Colonies under 'indirect' British rule

British colonial policy stressed the promotion of the colonies' economic and social development, both to increase their economic value to the Empire and to improve the living standards of the local populations. There were several notable initiatives in East and West Africa:

- In the Sudan, in 1920, the British government allotted £3 million for the Gezira Cotton Scheme to increase cotton production. It comprised a major dam building and irrigation project.
- In East Africa, in 1925, the British government allocated £10 million for improving rail and dock facilities.
- In West Africa, there was investment in schools and educational facilities.
- Numerous agricultural research stations were set up in colonies across the continent.

But the initiatives were much more limited than it might appear. All of the African colonies were expected to be self-financing, which meant that major projects had to be mainly funded by taxes collected locally from the African people themselves.

The Colonial Development Act of 1929, which earmarked £1 million of British Treasury funds for development projects across the Empire, helped several of the British colonies in Africa. However, like many other parts of the British Empire, the African colonies suffered from the global impact of the **Great Depression** of the 1930s. African dissatisfaction with this, and with the limited nature of imperial development policy, was expressed in a wave of strikes by African workers, notably in the copper mines of Northern Rhodesia.

The white settler colonies

White settlers in Kenya put pressure on the British government to give Kenya a degree of self-government in 1920. Power was given to the 20–30,000-strong white settler community, who dominated the Legislative Council and used their influence to exclude from the Northern Highlands both Indian settlers and the Kikuyu tribe, for whom this was a traditional homeland. The white settler farmers in the region became wealthy through growing tea and coffee, and squeezed the Kikuyu out by taxing them heavily and banning them from growing these commercial products. Many migrated to the major cities such as Nairobi and Mombasa.

This produced the first stirrings of African nationalism among the Kikuyu and alarmed the Colonial Office in London which issued the 'Devonshire

CROSS-REFERENCE

The League of Nations mandates are outlined in Chapter 13, pages 121–123.

CROSS-REFERENCE

The Great Depression is the name given to the worldwide economic crisis that affected most of the world in the 1930s. It is discussed in Chapter 15, page 145.

Declaration' in 1923. This stressed that the interests of the Africans had to be respected. However, despite the colonial authorities' efforts to improve African agriculture and education, momentum built up behind the political movements among both Africans and Indian settlers.

ACTIVITY

Using a blank map of Africa, mark on the colonies of 'indirect rule' and the 'settler' colonies and use arrows to indicate the main developments in colonial government in Africa in the years 1914 to 1947.

In Southern Rhodesia, the white population was similarly dominant. It took political power and won what was effectively self-government in 1923.

In the Union of South Africa, the promises made to protect the rights of ethnic minorities that had been built into the grant of Dominion status in 1910 were also eroded. The white minority had established its control over South Africa's internal affairs by the 1930s and the **Statute of Westminster** of 1931 which gave the Dominions legislative autonomy enabled this white dominance to continue.

Colonial policy and administration in the Middle East

The administration of the British Mandate in Palestine

The task of the British colonial administration was to ensure that Palestine's strategic importance as a buffer against potential threats to the Suez Canal was maintained with a British military presence, and that the internal stability of the country was maintained. This was no easy task given the financial strains imposed on the British and colonial governments by the First World War and its aftermath. A civil government under a British-appointed High Commissioner, Herbert Samuel, was set up in 1920 but reconciling the growing Jewish community with the established Palestinian Arab population, many of whom resented and feared the newcomers, was not easy. A complicating factor was disagreement between the government in London, which tended to be pro-Jewish, and the British authorities in Palestine, who were more sympathetic to the Arabs.

Samuel tried to bring both Arabs and Jews into elected representative bodies with influence over government policy, but his efforts were plagued by eruptions of ethnic tension which prevented co-operation.

As well as religious division, there were problems over landholding. Most Palestinian Arabs were poor farmers, renting land from absentee landowners. When wealthier Jewish settlers began to buy up land, often with the help of the **Jewish National Fund**, growing numbers of Palestinian Arabs were evicted from their farms.

An enquiry in 1929 called for the Jewish policy of land acquisition to be curbed and another, in 1931, recommended restrictions on Jewish land acquisition. However, pro-Jewish feeling in Britain and the USA forced the government to back down.

From 1933, Nazi persecution in Germany accelerated Jewish immigration into Palestine, creating further problems for the British administrators:

- 1936 – The British sent 20,000 troops to Palestine to deal with Arab rioting and attacks on Jews.
- 1937 – The Peel Report recommended that Palestine should be partitioned into separate Arab and Jewish areas, with the British retaining authority over Jerusalem and a small number of holy places. These proposals were opposed by the Arabs.

CROSS-REFERENCE

The Statute of Westminster of 1931 is discussed later in this chapter, on pages 139–140.

CROSS-REFERENCE

The steps leading to the British withdrawal from Palestine are discussed in Chapter 13, page 132.

A CLOSER LOOK

Ethnic tensions

In 1928 to 1929, Arab-Jewish conflict focused on access for worshippers to the Wailing Wall in Jerusalem, a religious shrine holy to both Jews and Muslims. Muslim building works near the Wall were obstructing access, leading to Jewish accusations that this was deliberate. Riots in August 1929 resulted in the deaths of several hundred people on both sides.

KEY TERM

The Jewish National Fund: an international organisation founded in 1901 in Switzerland at the Fifth Zionist Congress; its role was to buy land in Palestine for Jewish settlement, and it played a major role in the Jewish acquisition of land in the inter-war period

CROSS-REFERENCE

For the British withdrawal from Palestine and the formation of the Jewish state of Israel in 1948, turn back to Chapter 13, page 123.

ACTIVITY

Form two groups. Group 1 should write a short speech supporting the change of policy towards Jewish Palestine in 1939. Group 2 should write one opposing it. Having delivered the speeches, discuss the reasons for Britain's change of policy and decide whether it was justified.

- 1937–39 – The British adopted a policy of repression to deal with escalating violence: over 100 Arab terrorists were hanged.
- 1939 – with war imminent and fears of an Italian attack on Egypt, Britain changed its policy. It called instead for a Palestinian state in which Jews currently living in the country would enjoy the right to a 'national homeland'.
- 1939 – Jewish immigration was restricted to 15,000 per year for five years. (The plan was for Palestine to be declared an independent state in ten years, so that restrictions on Jewish immigration would ensure that the Arabs were in the majority.)

Fig. 2 *A British armoured police car during the Arab revolt, late 1930s*

Under pressure from Nazi aggression in Europe, Jewish organisations were forced to accept the British position. Britain entered the Second World War aware that its policy reversal had outraged the Jews without satisfying the Arabs. However, it saw this as the price of temporary stability in its military and strategic positions in Palestine and the Arab world. It was a short term strategy of expediency.

The administration of the British mandate in Iraq (Mesopotamia)

In Mesopotamia (modern-day Iraq), the same issues of curbing the costs of administration by managing internal conflicts between ethnic groups shaped colonial policy.

In 1920, the British were forced to intervene militarily (largely through air power) when widespread Muslim demonstrations against British rule in Baghdad turned into a full-scale revolt. The Kurds, in the north of Iraq, who wanted independence from Iraq, also rebelled.

At the Cairo Conference of 1921, the British, meeting with a limited Arab representation, decided to allow for some local self-government, whilst retaining full British control of military and foreign affairs. The Anglo-Iraqi Treaty of 1922 confirmed **Faisal I**, of the Hashemite dynasty which had ruled Syria, as King. As a renowned Muslim and Arab leader who enjoyed good relations with the British, Faisal was regarded as an ideal compromise candidate. Senior British advisers were nevertheless appointed to most government departments to ensure continuing British control over Iraqi affairs, while Britain controlled major military bases and had much influence over the Iraqi army, which it trained.

CROSS-REFERENCE

Independence for Iraq is covered in Chapter 13, page 125.

A further Anglo-Iraqi Treaty in 1930 promised full consultation between the two powers on matters of foreign policy. From these treaties it was only a small step towards the granting of full independence to Iraq in 1932. However, the British still retained their influence in the area, not least in their control of the oil industry.

EXTRACT 2

The war seemed to have revived Britain's appetite for territorial acquisitions and the redistribution of German colonies and Turkish provinces gave abundant opportunities for indulging that appetite. The British Empire seemed to be much more secure in 1920 than it had been in 1900. The distinction between mandates and colonies did not seem very real to many contemporaries; Britain had made sizeable gains. But the Indian summer of old-style imperialism did not last long. The careers in office of Lloyd George, Curzon and Milner all effectively ended in the 1920s. They were replaced by men who were totally convinced of the need to maintain Britain's standing as an imperial power, but were wary of over-extending Britain's commitments and of ambitious schemes for imperial co-operation. From the 1920s, a rough consensus about imperial policy began to emerge; the Empire must be maintained but overt coercion should be kept to the minimum and dreams of formal structures for imperial unity had little relevance.

Adapted from '1918 to the 1960s: Keeping Afloat' by P.J. Marshall (1996)

ACTIVITY

Evaluating historical extracts

1. What do you think Marshall means by: 'The careers in office of Lloyd George, Curzon and Milner all effectively ended in the 1920s'?
2. According to Marshall in Extract 2, what attitude did the British adopt towards the colonies from the 1920s?

British relations with the Dominions and the Statute of Westminster

The important role played by the Dominions in the First World War led to their aspirations for control over their own affairs. The British authorities in London realised that this could not be ignored, and were especially concerned about the strength of feeling in Canada and South Africa. The bitter history of the **Boer War** led the British to worry that South Africa might be tempted to desert the British Empire altogether, resulting in a huge loss of British influence.

Out of these concerns emerged the concept of the **Commonwealth**. By joining a British 'Commonwealth of nations', the Dominions and other colonies could gradually become fully independent nations, but still retain a 'special relationship' with Britain. The concept was based on the free association of equal nations, involving economic and political co-operation through a range of international institutions and loyalty to the British monarch. The idea was given substance in the Balfour Declaration of 1926 – the result of a meeting of the British and Dominion prime ministers at a special Imperial Conference.

The Statute of Westminster of 1931 recognised that:

- Certain of the Dominions should become independent nations.
- Laws passed in Britain could not be enforced in those countries without the permission of their own parliaments.

A CLOSER LOOK

Oil

An important aspect of the British interest in Iraq was the oil fields in Mosul. The British had negotiated a concession with the Turkish Ottoman Empire before the First World War, for the British-controlled Turkish Petroleum Company to extract oil. The Turkish government had a 20 per cent share in the company. After the war, Mosul became part of the Iraq mandate. The Iraqis were initially promised a 20 per cent share, but the British did not honour this, and the Iraqis had to accept British terms for the newly named Iraq Petroleum Company.

A CLOSER LOOK

King Faisal's full title was Faisal I bin Hussein bin Ali al-Hashimi.

ACTIVITY

Divide into two groups. One group should consider Palestine and the other Iraq. Each should create a PowerPoint presentation to respond to the question: 'How effectively did the British govern their mandated territories in the Middle East?'

CROSS-REFERENCE

The Boer War is discussed in Chapter 7, page 69 and Chapter 12, pages 115–117.

KEY TERM

Commonwealth: an association consisting of the UK together with states that were previously part of the British Empire and its dependencies

- the Dominion countries were to be free to pass their own laws without interference from, or the approval of, Britain.

The Act came into immediate effect in Canada, South Africa and the Irish Free State. It had to be ratified by the parliaments of Australia and New Zealand, and so became law in Australia in 1942 and New Zealand in 1947. Newfoundland never ratified it, and reverted to Crown Colony status; it eventually became a province of Canada in 1949.

Fig. 3 *King George V and Dominion prime ministers at the 1926 Imperial Conference*

At the time, the Statute and the emergence of the Commonwealth were portrayed by politicians and the media as evidence of the civilised nature of the British Empire; however these developments can also be regarded as ways of ensuring British global influence, without the heavy costs of imperial rule. Consider the following extract:

EXTRACT 3

The Balfour Report of 1926 gave birth to, and the Statute of Westminster in 1931 legally enshrined, the concept of equality of status between Britain and the major settlement colonies. But in many ways the notion of equality was no more than a polite fiction. All the White Dominions, save Canada, relied ultimately on the power of Britain and her ability to defend them; Canada escaped this dependence only because she was ultimately protected by proximity to the United States. In matters economic, the Dominions were similarly placed. Between the wars all of them were highly dependent for their prosperity on trade. Britain remained easily the most important trading partner of the Dominions throughout the period, the only exception being Canada, whose trade with the United States was of great importance. Behind trade lay finance: if anything, Dominion dependence on Britain was greater than in trade."

Adapted from *British Imperialism* by P.J. Cain and A.G. Hopkins (2001)

PRACTICE QUESTION

Evaluating historical extracts

Using your understanding of the historical context, assess how convincing the arguments in Extracts 1, 2 and 3 are, in relation to Britain's colonial policies and administration in the inter-war years.

Imperial defence

There were three key problems relating to imperial defence.

- Britain was in severe **economic difficulties** during the inter-war years. Key industries lost out in international markets, and Britain was badly hit by the **Great Depression** of the 1930s. As a result the costs of defending the Empire became a much greater burden.
- In the 1930s, new aggressive regimes emerged in Europe and Asia, posing a direct threat to the Empire, and potentially to Britain itself. Imperial Japan was seen as a danger in Asia; Fascist Italy in Africa, where its attempted conquest of Abyssinia in 1935 posed a threat to British interests in Egypt; and Nazi Germany in Europe.
- The rise of **nationalist independence movements**, especially in India, made the need for military resources in case of trouble more urgent.

The British had to take a **geopolitical** view. They had to prioritise, balancing the costs and military demands of defending an extensive global empire against needs in Europe and at home. In the 1920s and early 1930s there was a mistaken faith that the **League of Nations** could provide the security in international affairs that the British needed; but by the mid-1930s it was clear that this was not so.

British governments therefore adopted a policy of **appeasement** in some parts of the world, in order to allow the deployment of resources to other areas. This meant seeking to diffuse tensions with Nazi Germany and Fascist Italy by allowing them to get much of what they wanted in terms of territorial demands in Europe, thereby allowing British forces to be strengthened against a possible attack on the Empire in Asia from Japan. Thus Britain modernised the Indian army, and continued with a longstanding project to build up Singapore as a formidable naval base. Britain spent £25 million on this in the inter-war years, believing it would deter the Japanese from aggression against the British Empire.

A CLOSER LOOK

Appeasement

Appeasement was a policy associated with British governments in the 1930s, and their efforts to prevent another major European war. It meant surrendering to some of the territorial demands made by Nazi Germany and Fascist Italy in the mistaken belief that Adolf Hitler and Benito Mussolini (the Italian Fascist dictator) were reasonable politicians who could be satisfied by such concessions.

However, Neville Chamberlain (British Prime Minister, 1937–40) badly underestimated the scale of ambition in Nazi Germany and Fascist Italy. As a result, Britain eventually went to war against Germany when it invaded Poland in September 1939. Once this happened British policy in Asia also unravelled. The Japanese attacked Singapore in February 1942, when Britain was at war

STUDY TIP

You should read each extract in turn. You could begin your answer by identifying the main argument in Extract 1 and follow this with comments on any subsidiary arguments. Don't forget to apply your own contextual knowledge to assess how convincing these arguments are. Repeat the same exercise for Extracts 2 and 3. At the end of your answer you should offer a brief summary conclusion.

CROSS-REFERENCE

Britain's economic difficulties, including the impact of the Great Depression, are discussed in Chapter 15, page 145.

For the rise of nationalist movements in various parts of the Empire, look ahead to Chapter 18.

KEY TERM

geopolitical: The effects of geography on the politics of a nation; especially how that nation's concerns and interests around the world influence its foreign, economic and defence policies

CROSS-REFERENCE

The League of Nations is introduced in Chapter 18, page 173.

in Europe and too overstretched to reinforce Singapore adequately. Britain's imperial defence policy thus proved a failure.

Fig. 4 *The fall of Singapore; British, Australian, Indian and Chinese forces are captured by Japanese forces*

Summary

ACTIVITY

Summary

1. Create a chart, showing which events and developments suggest that Britain remained strong in its control of the Empire, and which events and developments suggest that British control was weakening.
2. List the problems and challenges facing British colonial policy in the years 1919 to 1947. For each challenge or problem, give the British a mark out of 10 for how well or badly they did (10 = policy was a complete success; 0 = policy = a complete failure). What overall impression do your marks suggest about British policy?

Events and developments which suggest Britain remained strong in its control of the Empire in the years 1919 to 1939	Events and developments which suggest that British control over the Empire was weakening in the years 1919 to 1939

Discussion

As a class, consider whether Cain and Hopkins' assessment in Extract 1 on page 134 is correct.

 PRACTICE QUESTION

'To what extent did British policies towards its colonies, mandates and Dominions strengthen the British Empire in the inter-war years?

STUDY TIP

To answer this question, you need to do several things. Firstly, ask yourself what were the main features of British policy towards its various colonies, mandates and Dominions. You then need to think about whether these strengthened or weakened the British Empire, and your summary activity chart could help here. You may come to different conclusions about how effective British policy was in the different parts of the Empire.

15 Trade, commerce and the economic impact of war

EXTRACT 1

The British had to ask themselves: what advantages did they desire or expect to obtain from their Empire? What devices would they adopt to ensure such benefits? During the twentieth century the British had to make a choice between economic systems: one based on free trade between all countries, and the other concentrating on its trade with the Empire. Before 1914 the dominant view was that the Empire was a particularly valuable part of the international economy, but that no attempt must be made to increase its value artificially. The First World War weakened this consensus, largely because of the huge economic and military contribution the Empire made to the British war effort. But after 1919, the old pre-1914 attitudes returned. It was not until after 1929, in the crisis of the Depression, that the Empire was again seriously treated as an essential prop to the British economy. Finally, the much greater crisis of the Second World War and its aftermath raised imperial expectations to their highest level.

Adapted from 'The Metropolitan Economics of Empire' by David Fieldhouse (1999)

KEY QUESTION

As you read this chapter, consider the following key question:

What part did economic factors play in the development of the British Empire?

ACTIVITY

Evaluating historical extracts

Read Extract 1. What argument does it advance about the changing attitudes in Britain to trade with the Empire in the years 1914 to 1947?

Britain emerged victorious, and apparently strong, from the two world wars. However, the economic reality was that both conflicts severely weakened Britain, reducing the country's ability to pay for the Empire. The wars also profoundly changed parts of the Empire itself, and the relationship between Britain and its colonies; this brought economic consequences.

Economic impact of the First World War

A CLOSER LOOK

The cost of war

It is estimated that the war cost about £35,000 million. This figure is over 13 times as much as the Boer War of 1899–1902, which was regarded at that time as being an enormously expensive war. Over $4 billion had to be borrowed from the USA, as the country's reserves ran so dangerously low.

Economic impact of war on Britain

The First World War lasted four years and was economically exhausting for Britain. As well as costing the lives of almost a million Britons, the war was extremely **expensive**, requiring the whole economy to be placed on a war footing. Huge amounts of public finances were directed towards the war effort, leaving Britain in severe debt.

- Much of Britain's capital investment overseas had been wiped out.
- The pound sterling (£) had to be removed from the **gold standard** for the duration, because gold reserves ran so low.

A CLOSER LOOK

The gold standard

Since its foundation in 1694 the Bank of England had issued notes promising to pay the bearer a sum of money. For much of its history the promise could be made good by the Bank paying out gold in exchange for its notes. The link with gold helped to maintain the value of the notes and its suspension of this 'gold standard' in wartime was considered a measure of last resort.

CROSS-REFERENCE

The gold standard is introduced in Chapter 9, page 87.

Fig. 1 *The Bank of England, late 1920s*

In addition, the war effort had severe consequences for some of Britain's most important export industries. Production for the war was prioritised over making goods for export to traditional overseas markets, and this meant that Britain's competitors were able to win markets traditionally dominated by British exports. Not all of these overseas markets were won back after the First World War. Britain's traditional industries, such as textiles, shipbuilding, coal, iron and steel, which created income to pay for running and defending the Empire, experienced great difficulties between the wars as they faced new overseas competition, for example from the Japanese in textile production.

The same was also true of Britain's financial sector: the banks and financial institutions, which generated profits from lending money overseas. The result was that the economic burden of the Empire grew, as Britain's ability to pay for it diminished.

This problem was intensified in the 1930s by the **Great Depression**, which saw a collapse of international trade and markets for British industrial exports. A financial crisis in 1931 forced the country off the gold standard again. This in turn reduced earnings from overseas investments. However, the Empire offered economic compensations as well as problems.

CROSS-REFERENCE

The Great Depression is explained in Chapter 14, page 136.

Economic impact of war on the Empire

The British Empire was diverse; war did not affect all parts of it in the same way.

- **India** contributed almost £146 million to the war effort, and the country experienced inflation and shortages during the war as a result. War, however, also brought longer term changes which were not entirely damaging. In 1914 two thirds of India's imports came from Britain, but this started to fall – initially because of wartime disruption to trade, but in the longer term because of the growing strength of foreign competition. India's own economy partly benefited from this; Indian manufacturers began to capture more of the domestic market. After the war, desperate for revenue to help bolster their control in the face of the rising nationalist movement, the British placed high taxes on Indian imports, rising from 11 per cent in 1917 to 25 per cent in 1931. The effect was to give Indian industry protection against its competitors, and it grew accordingly.
- **Canada** benefited from the war, emerging as an industrial power. As in India, British manufactures lost ground here. Indeed, increasingly Canada looked to its southern neighbour, the USA, for investment and markets as the inter-war period progressed.

- **Australia and New Zealand**, as exporters of food, relied heavily on the British market, and consequently were hit hard by the disruption of trade caused by the war.

Trade and commerce between the wars

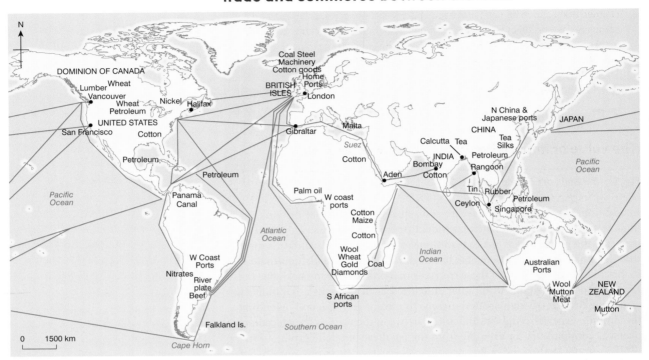

Fig. 2 *British sea trade routes, 1923*

Sterling Area: countries (mostly although not all in the Empire and Commonwealth) that either pegged their currencies to the pound sterling, or used the pound as their own currency; the arrangement was formalised under the Exchange Control Act of 1947 and lasted even after the devaluation of the £ against the US dollar in 1967 precipitated its end

ACTIVITY

Evaluating historical extracts

Explain Cain's view of the changes in British economic policy towards the Empire in the 1930s in Extract 2.

British policy towards imperial trade went through two distinct phases in the inter-war period:

- In the 1920s, Britain tried to recreate the economic system which had existed before 1914 (in which the Empire had no special preference). Thus Britain returned to the gold standard in 1925, in order to stabilise its international trade. One exception to this policy was the Colonial Development Act of 1929, which provided Treasury funds to support colonial development projects.
- In the aftermath of the Great Depression a much greater emphasis was placed on the importance of the Empire for British commerce and imports from the Empire increased (although exports to it did not do so well). Britain was again forced to abandon the gold standard in 1931 but trade with the Empire in sterling proved a great asset.

Most of the countries of the Empire fixed the value of their currencies to sterling and some kept their national reserves in sterling, reflecting their close ties with Britain. This gave access to the British market for countries in the **Sterling Area**, while ensuring a profitable outlet for British overseas investment, at a time when most other international opportunities were closed down. In this way, Britain was able to use the Empire to soften the impact of the damaging effects of the collapse of the international economy in the wake of the Great Depression.

EXTRACT 2

By 1933, the sterling area was central to Britain's international economic policy. The Treasury and the Bank of England saw it as the best means of restoring Britain's international trade position and salvaging a world role for sterling and the City of London from the wreckage of 1931. The sterling area was far more than an emergency arrangement in a crisis. It appeared to offer the chance to reclaim some of the global power lost to Britain during and since the war. Optimism about the sterling area was widespread. Officials at the Bank of England anticipated that the gold bloc centred on France would disintegrate and provide new recruits for the sterling area. One leading financial journalist claimed that London had already recovered her old financial supremacy, and the complete restoration of her role as the world's leading banking centre was only a question of time. Many in London believed in the early 1930s that the sterling area would enable Britain to recover its former financial glory.

Adapted from 'Gentlemanly Imperialism at Work: the Bank of England, Canada and the Sterling Area 1932–36' by P.J. Cain (1996)

The value of imperial trade and commerce for Britain

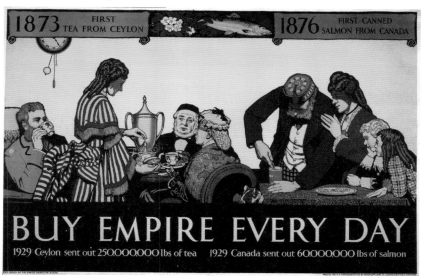

Fig. 3   *Empire Marketing Board Poster, 1930*

It was the promotion of imperial trade, rather than its total volume, that marked the British change in policy, as can be seen from the statistics below:

British exports	1913	1934
Total value of British exports to the world (£m)	£525m	£378m
Total value of British exports to the Empire (£m)	£195m	£166m
Imperial exports as a per cent of total British exports	37.2%	44%

Table 1   *The Empire's share of British exports in 1913 and 1934*

Percentage of certain exports going to the Empire (from Britain)	1913	1934
Cotton goods exports	51.7%	53.2%
Locomotive exports	58.6%	65.3%
Railway carriage exports	58.4%	68.3%
Motor vehicle exports	62.4%	71.7%
Electrical engineering exports	61.6%	61.1%

Table 2   *The importance of the Empire as a market for specific British exports 1913–34*

Lord Beaverbrook (1879–1964)
(William Maxwell Aitken) was a Canadian who had an undistinguished school career and worked as an insurance agent before he grew rich by dealing on the stock market. In 1909 he moved to London where his wealth and friendship with the Conservative politician Andrew Bonar Law enabled him to win a parliamentary seat in 1910. He began buying newspapers from 1911 and purchased a controlling interest in the *Daily Express* in 1916. After the war Beaverbrook concentrated on his newspaper business and turned the *Daily Express* into the most widely read newspaper in the world. Beaverbrook also founded the *Sunday Express* (1921) and in 1929 purchased the *Evening Standard*. He became a member of the war cabinet during the Second World War and throughout his career supported ideas of imperial unity and freedom from foreign entanglements.

CROSS-REFERENCE

The concept of 'imperial preference' is introduced in Chapter 9.

ACTIVITY

Using the information in this section, write a report for the government from the viewpoint of a managing director of a major British company of your choice. You should explain the position of your business and indicate the ways in which the government policies, particularly in relation to the Empire, could help you.

ACTIVITY

In pairs, consider what can be learned from the above table about the value of the British Empire to the British economy between 1909 and 1938.

Exports to the Empire included a wide variety of commodities, but historically cotton textiles had always figured prominently, especially to the markets of Asia and India. Significantly, in the inter-war period, these began to fall as tough competition from Japan and other emerging industrial economies began to be encountered. Nonetheless, at least until the 1930s, the Empire remained important for cotton textile exports, as it did for a range of other industrial products at a time of tough competition, particularly from the USA. As world trade shrank, imperialists, such as **Lord Beaverbrook**, the newspaper magnate, again argued for a return of the idea of '**imperial preference**', ending Britain's historic policy of free trade. This met with opposition from the Dominions which wished to protect their own growing industries and eventually a compromise was reached at the Ottawa Conference of 1932:

- The British introduced a general 10 per cent tax on all imports but the Crown Colonies were exempted.
- Britain and the Dominions gave each other's exports preferential treatment in their own markets.

This reinforced the important role of the Empire in supplying foodstuffs and raw materials to Britain. The following tables convey the importance of the Empire as a source of crucial imports between 1913 and 1934:

British imports	1913	1934
Total value of British imports from the world (£m)	£769m	£727m
Total value of British imports from the Empire (£m)	£191m	£257
Imperial imports as a percentage of total British imports	24.9%	35.3%

Table 3 *The Empire's share of British imports in 1913 and 1934*

Percentage of certain imports coming from the Empire to Britain	1913	1934
Tea imports	87.3%	88.9%
Wheat imports	48.5%	63.3%
Cocoa imports	50.9%	90.7%
Raw cotton imports	3%	17.1%
Raw rubber imports	57.2%	79.7%
Oilseed imports	53.3%	60.5%
Wool imports	80.2%	83.4%
Jute imports	99.4%	98.8%

Table 4 *The importance of the Empire as a source of specific British imports 1913–34*

ACTIVITY

Examine the tables in this section with a partner and comment on what can be learnt from these statistics. What is your conclusion about the importance of the Empire for the British economy in the years 1913 to 34?

Imperial trade was not uniform – certain parts of the Empire increased their commercial links more than others. The Dominions became both an increasingly important market for British exports and a more significant supplier of imports. However, while India largely remained an important supplier of tea and jute, and grew in importance in supplying raw cotton, it absorbed fewer British exports, as key Indian and Asian markets such as cotton textiles were won first by the Japanese and subsequently by emergent Indian cotton textile producers.

Regional shares in British exports and imports, 1909–38%			
British exports to:	**1909–13**	**1925–29**	**1934–38**
Dominions	17.5	20.6	25.9
India and Burma	11.9	11.6	8.0
Rest of British Empire	5.6	5.0	7.4
TOTAL for British Empire	35.0	37.2	41.3
British imports from:	**1909–13**	**1925–29**	**1934–38**
Dominions	14.3	16.9	24.3
India and Burma	7.3	6.1	6.5
Rest of British Empire	5.3	9.9	11.4
TOTAL for British Empire	26.9	32.9	41.2

Table 5 *British trade with the Empire 1909–38*

The value of imperial trade and commerce for the Empire

Some Dominions, particularly Australia and New Zealand, experienced serious economic problems in the inter-war period. The cost of their (largely manufactured) imports from Britain outstripped the income from their (largely foodstuffs/raw material) exports. Both countries ran up debts with Britain although, as the smaller country, developing more slowly than its neighbour, New Zealand suffered less than Australia. Imperial preference became especially important for these countries when international trade turned down sharply in the 1930s.

A CLOSER LOOK

Australia's indebtedness became even more marked in the wake of the Great Depression of 1929–32, because the prices of its main exports (wheat, dairy produce and other food) fell faster than the manufactured commodities that Australia imported. The debts were viewed by the British as evidence of Australian mismanagement of their financial affairs, but to some Australians they seemed to be colonial exploitation by financiers in London. This sense of resentment gave rise to a desire for independence in the Australian Labour Party.

Other British colonies in Asia and Africa also suffered as a result of the collapse of world trade in the 1930s. Burma and Malaya were especially hard hit. Malaya relied on exports of tin and rubber; Burma on exports of rice. African colonies too, which produced food or raw materials, saw tumbling prices in the 1930s. Incomes fell bringing poverty and even starvation and fuelling dissatisfaction with colonial rule.

 PRACTICE QUESTION

To what extent was trade and commerce between Britain and the Empire in the years 1919 to 1939 affected by the legacy of the First World War?

STUDY TIP

This question really hinges on the word 'legacy' which means the long term effects of something; a changed state of affairs. In this sense the question is asking how far the patterns of trade between Britain and its Empire were shaped by the effects of the First World War – as opposed to other factors which affected trade and commerce.

Economic impact of the Second World War

The Second World War hit Britain even harder than the first. The British economy, which had to be geared entirely to war in the years 1939 to 1945, entered the war in a far weaker condition than it had done in 1914 and major defeats in the West and the Far East in the first three years of war proved cripplingly expensive.

The war of 1939–45 had a severe and dramatic impact upon British trade.

- German U boat attacks on British sea traffic were devastating especially in the early years of war. Overall Britain lost 11.7 million tons of shipping in the war, or about 54 per cent of the country's merchant fleet strength at the beginning of the war.
- The loss of major colonies in South East Asia to the Japanese from 1942 disrupted trade and cut off supplies of vital raw materials such as rubber from Malaya.
- The diversion of industrial production to producing weapons of war meant that less was produced for export. The British tried to reduce imports, by campaigns to increase home production and food rationing, but Britain's balance of trade was heavily in deficit during the war.
- A third of Britain's overseas assets (investments in businesses) were sold to pay for the war. Britain borrowed from the USA from 1941 in the form of **Lend-Lease**, and emerged from war with massive debts.
- Britain increased its dependence on the Empire for imports. There was considerable investment by colonial governments, for example in Africa, to help increase the supply of foodstuffs and raw materials.
- Colonial reserves held in Britain (the so called 'sterling balances') were used to help Britain pay for the war effort.

Britain's post-war position was made worse when, in late August 1945, the USA ended Lend-Lease, largely because it was not prepared to support a revived British Empire financially. **John Maynard Keynes** negotiated a massive US loan (approximately £900 million) in 1945, but the conditions were tough; the pound sterling had to be made freely convertible to dollars by the spring of 1947.

Fig. 4   *Keynes was a very influential economist*

John Maynard Keynes (1883–1946) was an eminent British economist of the inter-war period, who argued that government should play an active role in managing the economy to achieve full employment, higher rates of economic growth and control over inflation. He was a major adviser to the wartime coalition and the post-war Labour governments.

A CLOSER LOOK

Sterling Crisis of spring 1947

Free convertibility would require the Bank of England to be able to exchange sterling for dollars, at a fixed rate. The US dollar loan was supposed to enable Britain to build sufficient reserves to do this by 1947. However, Britain almost ran out of its dollar reserves within six weeks (largely because of imperial demands) and had to suspend free convertibility. It revealed how weak the British economy had become.

Britain faced a dilemma. The costs of re-establishing its world power, which had been challenged by the wartime Japanese occupation in the East and emergent nationalism in countries such as India, threatened to exceed the potential economic or political benefits. Consequently a dual approach emerged. Where the costs of controlling a colony massively outstripped its actual or potential value (as in India, Burma and Palestine in 1947 to 1948), imperial control was abandoned. However, where colonies were regarded as of economic benefit to Britain, a new emphasis was placed on colonial economic development. The rubber and tin industry of Malaya which could command major international markets, for example, received heavy government investment since it was hoped that this would earn large amounts of foreign currency (especially dollars) and benefit Britain's international trading position.

Fig. 5 *A young boy collects rubber from a tree near Singapore; a wartime shortage in the USA gave the British in Malaya an opportunity to earn dollars through rubber exports*

The Colonial Development and Welfare Act of 1940 formed the foundation for the new approach. This:
- wrote off some colonial debts
- provided colonial grants or loans of up to £5 million per year.

A further Colonial Development and Welfare Act of 1945:
- increased the aid available to colonies to £120 million over ten years
- required each colony to produce a ten-year development plan showing how it would use such funds.

CROSS-REFERENCE

In 1948 a Colonial Development Corporation was set up to administer colonial development projects in the Empire. More detail on this can be found in Chapter 21, page 203.

ACTIVITY

Work in pairs. Imagine you are members of an independence movement in a colony which has received funding under the Colonial Development Acts. What would be your attitude to the investment in your colony? Would you welcome it or not? When you have discussed your ideas, explain your position to the rest of the group.

EXTRACT 3

Until the 1930s, the basic principle of imperial rule was that the colonies must pay their own way. There was a good reason for this: However rich, Britain could never have afforded to support the economic development of so large an empire from its own resources. If a colony wanted to build a railway or a port it had to borrow money and pay interest on the debt. The result was that the poor colonies stayed poor, unless they struck lucky with gold, diamonds or some other mineral bonanza. It was only after 1940, with the Colonial Development and Welfare Acts, that Britain seriously began to provide unrequited aid to its colonies, and even then, it was not until the 1950s that its own economy, weakened by the Second World War, was capable of putting much capital into the colonies. Meanwhile, between 1939 and 1947, the Empire was milked of its foreign earnings and exploited by the bulk buying of its exports at below world prices.

Adapted from 'For Richer, for Poorer?' by David Fieldhouse (1996)

PRACTICE QUESTION

Evaluating historical extracts

Using your understanding of the historical context, assess how convincing the arguments in Extracts 1, 2 and 3 are, in relation to British attitudes to trade and commerce with the Empire between 1914 and 1947.

Summary

As a result of the First World War, Britain lost ground in many of its international markets, including some within the Empire such as India and Canada. Not all of these were recovered after the war. However, British imperial trade began to pick up in the 1920s. The Great Depression after 1929 saw a major collapse in international trade and from 1932, the Empire became more important as a result of new taxes on overseas imports and the establishment of imperial preference. The Sterling Area arrangements also tended to guide British overseas investment towards the Empire. The Second World War had very damaging effects upon Britain's trading and financial position and the Colonial Development and Welfare Acts of 1940 and 1945 were intended to strengthen the Empire as a trading partner.

 PRACTICE QUESTION

'Trade with the Empire became of increasing importance to Britain as a result of the two world wars of 1914–18 and 1939–45.' Assess the validity of this view with reference to the years 1914 to 1947.

16 Attitudes to empire – the role and influence of individuals

EXTRACT 1

As early as 1909 Gandhi stated his principles: 'I bear no emnity towards the English but I do towards their civilisation'. Gandhi remained true to these principles throughout his life. He was, first and foremost, a moralist and a religious and social reformer. Politics was a means to the religious and moral transformation of India. It was never an end in itself. To oppose the British with violence would be to commit a crime. They must be opposed with love and truth. Even if politics was only a secondary activity for him, Gandhi had great talents as a political organiser and as a director of mass campaigns. For him, the campaigns were probably more important than any objective they might attain. He was vague about the goals – he sought truth not political settlements, and truth was hard to find. Had he lived beyond his assassination in 1948, he would not have had much taste for the modern industrial India that the Congress governments tried to bring about after independence.

Adapted from 'Gandhi' by P.J. Marshall (1996)

ACTIVITY

Evaluating historical extracts

What view of Gandhi as a leader is given in Extract 1? As you read the following section, find evidence which both supports and questions this view.

Individuals continued to play a key role in the running of the Empire after 1914 and whilst the days of the 'high imperialists' had passed, the years between 1914 and 1947 saw a number of intelligent and resourceful administrators attempt to combine the idea of empire with the needs of economic and social progress. Alongside these a group of new, influential 'nationalist' leaders also began to emerge. The foremost of these was Mohandas **'Mahatma'** Gandhi, whose example was to inspire many other nationalists in later years.

The role and influence of Gandhi

Indian nationalism had established itself before the First World War and to secure Indian support in that war, the British had made ambiguous promises of constitutional change. The Indian National Congress had headed the movement for self-government, but had struggled to turn the campaign into a mass movement. It was Gandhi's emergence from c1919 that was to inject the movement with new life – extending its appeal across a diverse society and bringing together many differing demands.

Gandhi's campaigns

Gandhi began his career practising in South Africa for 20 years from 1893. He campaigned against racism and segregation, championing the civil rights of Indians who had settled in the area and challenging both the British, and from 1910, the dominant Afrikaners (the descendants of the Boers).

LEARNING OBJECTIVES

In this chapter you will learn about:

- the role and influence of Gandhi
- the role and influence of colonial administrators.

KEY PROFILE

Mohandas 'Mahatma' Gandhi (1869–1948)

Gandhi was born in western India, but trained as a lawyer in England. He became the leader of the movement for Indian independence. His followers gave him the name 'Mahatma'; it means Great Soul or Great Teacher.

KEY QUESTION

As you read this chapter consider the following key question:
- What influenced imperial policy?
- How important was the role of key individuals and groups and how were they affected by developments?

ACTIVITY

Extension

Try to view the 1982 biographical-drama film *Gandhi* directed by Richard Attenborough.

CROSS-REFERENCE

The 1919 Amritsar massacre is outlined in Chapter 18, page 170. Chapter 18 will also discuss the nationalist movements which are referred to below, and their role in bringing about Indian independence.

In 1915, he returned to India, where he became President of the Indian National Congress and began to immerse himself in political affairs. He travelled the country, supporting popular protests against British rule, wearing Indian dress as a symbol his commitment to Indian culture. In 1917 to 1918 he championed the downtrodden indigo workers of the state of Bihar, and mediated in a textile industry dispute in Ahmedabad as well as a dispute over land taxes in Gujarat. Such activity established Gandhi as a national figure. However, it was only after the 1919 **Amritsar massacre** that his national campaigns for full Indian independence began.

He helped organise the Non-Co-operation Movement of 1920, the Civil Disobedience Movement of 1930–31 and 1932–34 and the Quit India Movement of 1942. He was clear about the importance of political non-violence, but vague about his goals (other than his desire to remove the British so that India could control its own future development). He was imprisoned by the British on several occasions, including almost two years during the Second World War. Although his goal of independence was achieved in 1947, he strongly opposed the partition of India and offended some Hindu and Muslim nationalists who felt his attitude was too moderate and idealistic. He was assassinated in 1948 by a militant Hindu nationalist who accused him (unjustly) of showing a bias for Muslims.

Fig. 1   *Gandhi, the Western lawyer*

Fig. 2   *Gandhi, the Indian nationalist*

ACTIVITY

Can you account for the transformation in Gandhi's appearance between Fig. 1 and Fig. 2?

A CLOSER LOOK

Gandhi's fasts

On several occasions Gandhi fasted in protest against violence between Indians, especially between Hindus and Muslims; fasts which brought fighting to a halt. For example, in 1924, he fasted for three weeks to promote Hindu–Muslim unity; he fasted again for several weeks in 1947 and 1948, when Hindu–Muslin violence following independence was at its height. His reputation for saintliness was reinforced by his assassination in 1948 and the national mourning which followed.

Gandhi's beliefs

Gandhi had expressed his basic principles in '*Hind Swaraj*' (Home Rule for India) in 1909 and he remained true to them throughout his life.

- In accordance with his strong Hindu religious convictions, Gandhi favoured peaceful resistance to British rule, based on the principles of *satyagraha*.
- Gandhi preached harmonious relations between Hindus and Muslims, arguing that tolerance between the two communities should be cemented with equal rights for both religions in an independent India. Gandhi rejected divisions among Hindus based on the **caste system**. In particular he argued fiercely against discrimination against 'Untouchables', and campaigned for equality for all.
- Gandhi wanted an independent India which built on its spiritual and social traditions. He wanted India to remain predominantly agricultural and rural, and to reject the industrialisation and urbanisation which characterised Western development.

Gandhi's importance

Gandhi's reputation was as a moral as well as a political leader. He reconciled western ideas about democracy with the notion of a distinctive Indian culture and national identity, based on the principles of Hinduism, religious tolerance and a vision of a traditional rural India. This offered the benefits of Western liberalism without endangering the character of Indian society and values.

His methods made it difficult for the British to respond. The British saw themselves as a liberal, peaceful, democratic and fair-minded people, committed to the well-being of the colonial peoples they ruled. Non-violent resistance proved effective in hurting British economic interests, and forced the British to use violent repression to break up demonstrations and imprison nationalist leaders. This was difficult for many British imperial administrators, who believed in the 'civilising' mission of the Empire. It was also embarrassing for the British internationally, as it demonstrated that imperial rule ultimately rested not on peaceful and **benign** methods, but on the exercise of ruthless might.

EXTRACT 2

Rather than being ignorant of the need to wield political power, Gandhi sought to exercise it in ways which maximised Indian strength and weakened that of the British. By withdrawing the cooperation and obedience of the subjects, Gandhi sought to cut off important sources of the ruler's power. At the same time the non-cooperation and disobedience created severe enforcement problems. In this situation, severe repression against non-violent people would be likely not to strengthen the government, but to alienate still more Indians from the British Raj and at the same time create not unity in face of an enemy, but dissent and opposition at home. This was a kind of political judo which generated the maximum Indian strength while using British strength to their own disadvantage. The view that Gandhi was ignorant of the realities of political power and that his methods of resistance were ineffective would have been vigorously denied by every British government and Viceroy that had to deal with him and his movement.

Adapted from 'Gandhi's Political Significance Today' by Gene Sharp

KEY TERM

satyagraha: the word means 'insistence on the truth'. It means rejecting violence to combat evil, relying instead upon peaceful protest: the aim is to win by appealing to the moral conscience and compassion of one's opponents; actions include strikes (*hartals*), boycotts (*swadeshi*), protests, peaceful disobedience of unjust laws; but conducted to minimise aggression on both sides; it involves mass mobilisation of people, but to peaceful ends

CROSS-REFERENCE

To recap on the Hindu caste system, in which the Harijans are the lowest class, look back to Chapter 2, page 16.

KEY TERM

benign: kind and causing no harm

A CLOSER LOOK

The anti-salt tax campaign

In 1930 Gandhi organised a 24-day march to Dandi where he and his followers made salt from seawater in defiance of the British salt monopoly. Gandhi was arrested and more than 80,000 Indians gaoled for the civil disobedience the action provoked.

Extension

Undertake some research into the views and contributions of other nationalist leaders such as Subhas Chandra Bose and Jawaharlal Nehru (see page 174) in the years 1914 to 1947. These leaders did not share Gandhi's rejection of violence nor his vision for a predominantly rural and agricultural future for India.

ACTIVITY

Evaluating historical extracts

Summarise Sharp's view in Extract 2 in your own words. From what you have read so far, how far do you agree with this interpretation?

EXTRACT 3

Gandhi's beliefs and methods were ultimately failures. Most of his Congress colleagues accepted non-violence as a political tactic against the British Raj, but they did not believe in it as a way of life. Gandhi's philosophical writings on non-violence were often dismissed as ideas too lofty for ordinary mortals. During the Second World War, Congress rejected Gandhi's talk of defending India non-violently against the Japanese. Gandhi wrote about the duties of citizens and the state, but said little about the political structure of an independent India. He believed in decentralising power as much as possible; India would remain primarily a rural society with its base in agriculture and with minimal industrialisation. These ideas made little impression on the framers of the Indian constitution. In 1947, little heed was paid to the Gandhian approach to government.

Adapted from *In Search of Gandhi: Essays and Reflections* by B.R. Nanda (2004)

ACTIVITY

Evaluating historical extracts

According to Nanda in Extract 3, in what ways could Gandhi be viewed as a failure?

STUDY TIP

Think about Gandhi's strategies for putting pressure on the British and how effective they were. You will need to evaluate each extract with respect to Gandhi's strengths and limitations not simply as an inspirational figure but a leader of an 'independence movement'. Use your own knowledge to criticise the arguments in each extract.

 PRACTICE QUESTION

Evaluating historical extracts

Using your understanding of the historical context, assess how convincing the arguments in Extracts 1, 2 and 3 are, in relation to Gandhi's contribution to the independence movement in India in the years 1919 to 1947.

ACTIVITY

Extension

1. Hold a class debate arguing for and against the motion: 'Gandhi's leadership was crucial to the achievement of Indian independence in 1947'.
2. Investigate the careers of other nationalist leaders in the Empire. The activities of Saya San in Burma in the 1930s might be a good starting point.

ACTIVITY

Extension

Read works by H.G. Wells, George Bernard Shaw and E.M. Forster which give a critical picture of colonial administrators. George Orwell's *Burmese Days* (1934) is also worth a look.

The role and influence of colonial administrators

Colonial administrators faced a tough job both in the years of war and in the difficult inter-war period. It fell to their lot to collect taxes and maintain stability and order in the face of growing nationalist movements seeking, at the least, more representation, and at the worst, as in the case of India, full independence from colonial rule.

Administration responded to the changed circumstances at both imperial and colonial levels. In 1925 the Colonial Office was split into two departments: the Dominions Office, with its own Secretary of State (this also took responsibility for a small number of other territories, most notably Southern Rhodesia) and the Colonial Office itself. This meant that three cabinet members were responsible to Parliament for the good governance of the Commonwealth and Empire: the Secretary of State for the Colonies, the Secretary of State for India and the Secretary of State for the Dominions.

Beneath the three secretaries of state were the permanent officials at Whitehall, and below them, spreading across the Empire, the administrative services which backed up and exercised imperial power. The Dominions recruited and appointed their own civil services, but the British Crown still continued to appoint the governor-generals. However, after the Statute of Westminster in 1931 when the Dominions became autonomous, the Governor-General in the Dominions ceased to be an imperial official and instead became merely the representative of the Crown.

The colonial services were unified in 1930, so that individuals were no longer appointed directly to individual colonial governments. The quality of recruits generally improved, particularly in Africa, where the future of colonial government looked assured. The bulk of administrators continued to be recruited from similar, if not the same, public schools and the traditional universities. Pay varied enormously. The Governor of Nigeria in 1922, for example could expect a salary of £8250 per annum, whereas a cadet staring work in Kenya earned approximately £200 per annum. The Colonial Office appointments handbook spoke of the qualities looked for: single-mindedness and purpose. Administrators were expected to be honest, responsible and industrious, but they could also be smug and narrow-minded, even if the white racial attitudes that had characterised nineteenth-century administrators had been considerably softened by the 1920s and 1930s. **Lord Lugard** of Nigeria was in no doubt as to the quality of these administrators, claiming in 1922 that the public schools 'have produced an English gentleman with an almost passionate conception of 'playing the game'.

Changes in imperial administration reflected, in part, the developing idea that colonial administration in the less-developed parts of the Empire, principally in Africa, should be a form of '**trusteeship**'; administrators were there to protect native interests, foster the colony's economic growth and 'nurture' it towards greater self-rule.

In 1927 a White Paper written by the Colonial Secretary, Leo Amery, argued in favour of 'trusteeship' with colonists and promoting their interests and a Royal Commission under Sir Edward Hilton Young in 1929 ruled out self-government and federation in East Africa in favour of a policy of 'trusteeship'. In 1931 Lord Passfield went a step further and argued in favour of a '**dual mandate**' to reconcile African interests.

However, developing the colonies, in Africa, India or elsewhere, usually meant bringing young and ambitious Western-educated indigenous elites into positions of authority – whether as clerks, managers, civil servants or members of representative institutions. Such a policy obviously came at a risk and may, indeed, have lessened the attractions of colonial service for young Britons by the later 1930s. By 1945, there were actually more Indians than white British in the Indian Civil Service.

Administrators in India

Some of the more prominent colonial administrators in the years 1914 to 1947 included:

Edwin Montagu (1879–1924) who was Secretary of State for India from 1917 to 1922. Together with Lord Chelmsford (1868–1933), who served as Viceroy of India from 1916 to 1921, he was responsible for reforms which led

Fig. 3 *Orwell's* Burmese Days *gives a critical view of colonial administrators*

CROSS-REFERENCE

Lord Lugard is profiled in Chapter 8, page 79.

KEY TERM

trusteeship: a concept whereby colonies had to be ruled in a way that looked after the interests of the indigenous peoples as well as white people; economic development should benefit the indigenous population; this idea was developed further by the UN after the Second World War with the establishment of a Trusteeship Council

KEY TERM

dual mandate: the belief that a colonial power had a double responsibility: to its colonial peoples, it owed material and moral advancement leading to self-government; to the outside world it had the obligation to see that the natural resources of its colonies were developed and exploited

to the Government of India Act of 1919, which gave Indians a limited degree of political representation and control of some aspects of affairs within India itself, subject to the over-riding authority of the British.

Sir Harry Haig (1881–1956) was a lifelong colonial administrator in India, following his appointment as a member of the Viceroy's Executive Council in 1932. Haig was, in many ways, an example of an emergent colonial administrator who was coming to terms with the idea, albeit reluctantly, of Indians as partners in empire. He was, however, an opponent of Gandhi's campaign for Indian independence, describing Gandhi as a 'menace'.

ACTIVITY

Extension

You might like to enlarge your knowledge by finding out more about individual administrators: either those given here or others such as Lord Chelmsford and Justice Sir Sidney Rowlatt.

Fig. 4   *Lord Linlithgow, pictured in around 1930*

Lord Linlithgow (1887–1952) served as Viceroy of India from 1935 to 1943. His seven-year tenure was the longest in the history of the Raj. He was a practical man who actively promoted the further enfranchisement of Indians in the Government of India Act of 1935. He believed that further reform would weaken the more radical elements of nationalism and give rise to 'more responsible' Indian politicians, who would see the wisdom of working with the British towards the longer term goal of self-government. His appeal for unity on the outbreak of the Second World War brought a promise of greater rights in the governance of India for the Indian people; but this was rejected by most Indian politicians. He was an implacable opponent of Gandhi and resorted to suppression during the Indian civil disobedience campaign. Indeed, while he was praised in Britain, Indians blamed him for the division and lack of economic development in their country.

Other influential administrators

Sir Donald Cameron (1872–1948) was, unusually for someone who rose high in colonial service, the son of a sugar-planter from Guiana, who did not attend university, but began his career as a clerk at the Inland Revenue. His career took him from the post of Assistant Colonial Secretary in Mauritius (1904) and Southern Nigeria (1908–24) to Chief Secretary (1923), Governor of Tanganyika (1924–31) and Governor of Nigeria (1931–35). His advancement came partly as a result of his close contacts with **Lord Lugard**, whom he greatly admired, and he is a good example of an administrator who believed in the 'trusteeship' principle. In Nigeria, he promoted exports of ground nuts and palm oil and in Tanganyika, the building of harbours and railways. He sought to advance the colonies economically and supported the entry of indigenous peoples into the civil service but he favoured a gradual path to more self-rule.

William Hailey (Baron Hailey) (1872–1969) was a typical public school/ Oxford administrator who had a long career in the civil service of the Raj (becoming Governor of Punjab in 1924 and the United Provinces in 1928). He was a key participant in the **conferences** leading to the 1935 Government of India Act and officially retired in 1936. However, he travelled over 20,000 miles for the Royal Institute of International Affairs to produce 'an African survey' in 1938 which was so comprehensive and thoughtfully produced that it proved a highly influential study for future British policy, even after the Second World War.

Sir Philip Mitchell (1890–1964) was another typical administrator of the inter-war years, his career showing something of the versatility required in colonial service. After St Paul's School and Oxford his first posting was in Nyasaland in 1912. He subsequently served in Tanganyika (1919–27), becoming Secretary of Native Affairs there (1928) and Chief Secretary (1934). From here he went to Uganda (1935) where he fulfilled the 'trusteeship principle' by extending **Makerere College** and working to create a more educated African elite. His next posting was as Governor of Fiji but in 1944 he returned to Africa as Governor of Kenya.

A CLOSER LOOK

Makerere College

Makerere College was established in 1922 as a technical school with just 14 students studying carpentry, building and mechanics. It expanded to become the prime centre for higher education in East Africa (Uganda) by 1935, offering courses in nursing, agriculture, veterinary science and teacher training, From 1937, it offered post-school certificate courses and in 1949, became a University College affiliated to UCL (in Britain).

The career of **Sir Charles Arden-Clarke (1898–1962)** is typical of that of many who rose to prominence in colonial service. He was born to a missionary family in India, educated at the Rossall School (where colonial service was promoted) and entered colonial service in 1920. He served as a District Officer in Northern Nigeria and as Resident Commissioner in Lagos in 1937 and Basutoland, 1942. He went to Sarawak in 1946, eventually moving to the **Gold Coast** after the war and presiding over the first British African colony to gain independence in 1957.

Sir Andrew Cohen (1909–68) was another public-school/Oxbridge administrator whose interests were in Africa, although he served in Malta during the Second World War. He had considerable sympathy for the plight of the native African peoples and was one of the earliest to understand the need for decolonisation. He cultivated contacts with African nationalists and when

CROSS-REFERENCE
Lord Lugard is profiled in Chapter 8, page 79.

CROSS-REFERENCE
To recap on the conferences of 1930 and 1931 look back to Chapter 13, page 135.

CROSS-REFERENCE
The achievement of independence by the Gold Coast is outlined in Chapter 19, page 181.

appointed Assistant Under-Secretary of State for the Colonial Office in 1947, found himself in a position to influence steps towards greater independence.

Sir Ralph Furse (1887–1973) was not an administrator himself, but he was responsible for improving the recruitment and training of administrators. He was responsible for the 1930 reform of appointments to colonial service and became the director of recruitment in a new personnel division in 1931. His reforms helped establish a standard system of recruitment and training and have led to his being called the 'father of the modern Colonial Service'. By the time of his retirement in 1948, he had considerably improved the quality of those in colonial service.

Summary

Gandhi was a unique nationalist leader whose ideas were the product of both Indian and Western influences. His strategies of peaceful resistance to British rule shaped the attitudes of Indians, British politicians and colonial administrators and ultimately world opinion. British colonial administrators and their strategies evolved during the period for numerous reasons, including a softening (although not total elimination) of racial attitudes; a desire to rule with some measure of consent from the population in 'trusteeship'; and in response to the development of nationalist movements.

ACTIVITY

Look through the details of the various administrators mentioned in this section and identify some common characteristics. Use this information to help write a recruitment advert for the Colonial Service in c1930.

STUDY TIP

It might be helpful to look back to Chapters 10 and 11. You should think about the imperialist attitudes of administrators in the years between 1890 and 1914 and contrast these with the attitudes and behaviour seen in the years from 1919 to 1947. It might be helpful to make a two column plan with contrasts and similarities between administrators in the two eras. Don't forget that you will need to support your arguments about the degree of change with some precise historical references, to individuals, attitudes and actions.

 PRACTICE QUESTION

'The attitude and behaviour of colonial administrators in the years 1919 to 1947 differed greatly from those seen in the years 1890 to 1914.' Assess the validity of this view.

17 Imperialist ideals

EXTRACT 1

In the inter-war years, thousands of British families had friends or relatives who had emigrated to, or served in the Empire as civil servants, teachers, missionaries, engineers, driving locomotives, and as soldiers in the British army. All social classes were influenced in different ways. The churches and Sunday schools provided information about the Empire, as missionaries urged audiences to contribute to medical, educational, and evangelical work throughout the Empire. Missionaries popularised the notion that Western medicine was tackling the most feared tropical diseases in the Empire. The Empire came to the British public in new ways such as through the cinema newsreel and through the press. British people were, for example, well aware of the 1919 Amritsar massacre, which generated much debate. As constitutional reform and eventually decolonisation became imminent, the British people were aware of Asian and African politicians visiting London for Round Table Conferences. Among these was Mahatma Gandhi, who in 1931 stayed in London's East End and visited cotton mills, universities and schools. By these means the Empire became an integral part of British culture.

Adapted from 'The Popular Culture of Empire in Britain' by John M. Mackenzie (1999)

LEARNING OBJECTIVES

In this chapter you will learn about:

- imperialism as represented in popular culture
- representations of empire
- the extent of imperialist ideals.

ACTIVITY

Evaluating historical extracts

According to Mackenzie in Extract 1, in what ways did ordinary people in Britain learn about the Empire in the inter-war years?

Imperialism and popular culture

KEY QUESTION

As you read this chapter, consider the following key question:

How did the Empire influence British attitudes and culture?

Fig. 1 *An Empire Marketing Board poster from around 1930*

Fig. 2 *Another Empire Marketing Board poster from around 1930*

By the twentieth century, the mass of the British people were better equipped than ever before to know about the wider world, Britain's place in it, and the relevance of the British Empire to their lives.

Government promotion of empire

Through mass communication and social organisation, the British population was bombarded by imperial imagery, much of it officially supported by the British government, who were keen to encourage **trade** with the Empire.

The Empire Marketing Board, set up in 1926 following the efforts of Leo Amery, the Secretary of State for Colonies and Dominions, promoted the consumption in Britain of items produced in the Empire through posters and advertising campaigns. The Board became even more active in the 1930s when, following the onset of the Great Depression, international trade declined drastically and the Empire became even more important to the British economy.

Exhibitions were staged, such as the Wembley Exhibition of 1924 to which the British government contributed half the £2.2 million cost. A 0.3-square mile site was purchased at Wembley, North London, and on it pavilions advertising every country in the Empire and a fun fair were erected. There was also a sports stadium, which became the permanent legacy of the exhibition. The exhibition was intended to give visitors an experience of the British Empire 'in miniature'. Over 17 million visitors attended in 1924 and another 9 million in 1925, its final year. Another Empire exhibition in Glasgow in 1938 also proved to be a great success, attracting 12 million and offering a chance to boost the Scottish economy after the Depression.

CROSS-REFERENCE

Trade and commerce and their importance to Britain and the Empire are discussed in Chapter 15, page 149.

Leo Amery is profiled in Chapter 11, page 100.

Fig. 3 *A poster advertising the British Empire Exhibition at Wembley, 1924*

Other ways in which empire was promoted

There were also many non-governmental and private organisations which sought to raise the imperial consciousness of the British public. The BBC, established in 1923, under its first Director General, **John Reith**, took a strong pro-imperial stance and covered as many major imperial events, exhibitions and public celebrations as possible. In particular there were Christmas broadcasts from 1932 which included not only the King's speech, but also various items about the Empire.

The Empire also maintained an important presence in education. It formed a focal point for the teaching of Geography, History and Literature in schools, drawing for the last on the poetry and writing of such pro-imperial writers as **Rudyard Kipling**. The historical study of the Empire became established in universities, with special professorships in Imperial History being created such as the Vere Harmsworth Chair at Cambridge (1919). The universities played an especially important part in training colonial servants, as exemplified by the role of London University's School of Oriental and African Studies, founded in 1917.

Official and institutional sources of imperial awareness were supplemented by popular cultural representations of empire in literature and film. Children's literature in particular celebrated empire and the books of G.A. Henty remained popular. The emergence of the cinema as mass entertainment was another source of imperial culture. Such feature films as *Sanders of the River* (1935) and *The Four Feathers* (1939) used the Empire as a backdrop for adventure, signalling to the public that the Empire was a place of excitement and the playing out of the finer attributes of 'British character'.

KEY PROFILE

John Reith, first Baron Reith (1889–1971)

John Reith was the first Director-General of the BBC from 1927 to 1938 and was from 1940 a Conservative politician. He had strong religious and moral convictions and believed the BBC to be a means of education. He also saw it as a vehicle for supporting the idea of the British Empire.

CROSS-REFERENCE

Rudyard Kipling is profiled in Chapter 11, page 105.

Some composers continued to vaunt the imperial theme. At the 1924 Empire Exhibition, the composer Edward Elgar conducted mass choirs in the singing of 'Land of Hope and Glory' and a new eight-song 'Pageant of Empire' and 'Empire March' were performed. This, however, marked the end of his prolific career as a composer of imperial music. His death, in 1934, almost signified the passing of the 'grand' imperial era. Noel Coward's 1931 song, 'Mad Dogs and Englishmen', may have adopted an imperial note, but it was more gently self-mocking of British ideas about themselves and the Empire.

Commercial advertising from private companies had long used imperial motifs to promote products, and it continued to so in the years between 1914 and 1947. Large traders within the Empire such as the **Co-operative Wholesale Society** celebrated their global and imperial links in their advertising, especially in the CWS's supply of such products as tea, with packets containing collectible cards illustrating places in the Empire.

In addition, there were also the informal links which people had in their everyday lives; relatives who had emigrated to Australia or elsewhere; former missionaries who spoke in Church about their experiences in the Empire, or relatives who had served in the army or navy, bringing them into direct contact with the Empire. These also played a part in disseminating knowledge of the British Empire.

Representations of empire

Between 1914 and 1947, changes in the mass media increased the ways in which empire could be represented to people in Britain; through films and the BBC, for example. There were also some changes in the messages conveyed as explicit jingoism lost its attraction after the horrors of the First World War. The Empire was presented more as a family of nations led by the British: a place of peace and co-operation.

Empire Day celebrations sought to create a sense of belonging to this family of nations, owing allegiance to the same monarch. For this reason, Empire Day was celebrated not just in Britain, but right across the Empire, with participants often wearing their national dress or other costumes representing the different colonies in the Empire. Of course, it is difficult to assess how people responded to these events and the extent to which they received and supported the basic message that the Empire was important for Britain and a great civilising force in the world.

Fig. 4 *Empire Day in Norwich, 1933*

Fig. 5 *An HMV gramophone recording of the Empire Day Message to Children of the British Empire from HM King George V and Queen Mary, recorded at Buckingham Palace, London, in 1923*

SOURCE 1

From Tommy Wray's memories of Empire Day in Leeds in the 1930s:

24th May was Empire Day. We, as children, didn't know what it meant; all we knew was it meant a party in the street.

We would get dressed up, march through the street waving Union Jacks. Then the tables and chairs came out for a feast: custard and jelly, mince pies, buns, cakes and sandwiches. Poor as everyone was they contributed to it; great days.

During the early stages of the Second World War, it was believed to be important to promote positive images of empire, given the importance of the Empire and Commonwealth to the war effort. Ministry of Information films such as *49th Parallel* and *West Indies Calling* stressed the need for tolerance and understanding of other ethnicities in the Empire.

The extent of imperialist ideals

The fact that there was a great deal of pro-imperial propaganda is not of itself proof that it had an influence over the people who consumed it. Indeed, some argue that such strenuous efforts were undertaken to promote empire precisely because so few of the mass of the population were either aware of, or interested in it.

ACTIVITY

Find some more representations of empire from the years 1914 to 1947 and create a wall display. Individuals might like to explain why they have chosen a particular representation and what message it conveys.

Whatever else it may have been, the British Empire was not a 'people's' empire. Those who say that imperialism pervaded British culture during this period, are wrong. There is no direct evidence that the majority of Britons supported the Empire, took an interest in it, or were even aware of it. They were too busy and too poorly educated to care, while the middle classes and upper class imperialists were happy to keep the Empire to themselves. Most people were less affected by empire than by other concerns. The fact of having an empire affected hardly anyone's fundamental view of anything. This is what so bothered the imperial supporters, who thought that the Empire should change people's outlooks. The Empire was merely tolerated, rather than celebrated — and only provided that it did not have a negative impact on people's lives. That was a weakness, as the supporters of empire well knew.

Adapted from *The Absent Minded Imperialists* by Bernard Porter (2006)

ACTIVITY

Evaluating historical extracts

Compare the views expressed in Extract 2 with those in Extract 1. How do they differ?

The impact of imperialism was probably affected also by the **different social groups and classes** to which people belonged. Not all shared the same values and outlook, nor had the same degree of contact with the Empire. This makes it difficult to talk about a British popular culture of empire, because the British population was so diverse.

A CLOSER LOOK

Class differences

Members of the affluent middle classes, with family members employed in colonial service, or others involved in trade with the Empire, were more natural supporters of empire. Many working class people, without relatives serving overseas or any direct and obvious personal interest in the Empire, did not feel that it was either relevant or important to their lives.

It is untrue that most Britons were ignorant of or indifferent to empire; but neither was Britain saturated by imperialism. In the twentieth century, the sources of contact between mother country and colony multiplied, and, as a result, a range of relationships with the Empire developed. There was never a single 'imperial culture' in Britain. In addition, disentangling the 'imperial' from the 'international' is problematic. The dividing line between pride in the Empire and in Britain's broader position as a world power was not clear. The monarchy and the military can be seen as twin pillars of popular imperial sentiment. Yet both appealed to patriotism irrespective of their connection with the Empire. Similarly, the growth of imperial news coverage can be too readily accepted as evidence of enthusiasm for empire when a thirst for mere sensationalism may explain the demand for such reporting.

Adapted from *The Empire Strikes Back?* by Andrew Thompson (2005)

STUDY TIP

You will need to consider the arguments put forward in the extracts about how different social groups in Britain experienced empire and how the Empire was presented in the mass media and through popular culture. Use your own contextual knowledge to evaluate each extract.

 PRACTICE QUESTION

Evaluating historical extracts

Using your understanding of the historical context, assess how convincing the arguments in Extracts 1, 2 and 3 are, in relation to British awareness of and interest in the Empire between 1918 and 1947.

Summary

ACTIVITY

Summary

List the various ways in which different British social groups might be affected by the Empire.

Industrial workers	Middle classes (teachers, managers, doctors, lawyers, businessmen)	Aristocrats/ extremely wealthy	Children	Women

 PRACTICE QUESTION

To what extent were different social groups in Britain affected by the Empire in the years 1914 to 1947?

STUDY TIP

You could use your summary chart to evaluate the different ways in which different social groups were affected by the Empire, and look for specific evidence to support your conclusions about the extent to which each group you include was affected. Remember that the question asks 'to what extent' so you need to consider how widespread the impact of the Empire actually was.

18 Relations with indigenous peoples

LEARNING OBJECTIVES

In this chapter you will learn about:

- protest and conflict
- colonial identity
- the development of nationalist movements.

KEY QUESTION

As you read this chapter, consider the following key questions:
- How did the indigenous peoples respond to British rule?
- How important was the role of individuals and groups and how were they affected by developments?

CROSS-REFERENCE

The nationalist leaders referred to in this extract are discussed as follows:

Gandhi: Chapter 16, pages 153–156.

Kwame Nkrumah: Chapter 19, page 181.

Jomo Kenyatta: Chapter 22, page 211.

CROSS-REFERENCE

Events in Ireland are outlined in Chapter 13, page 125.

EXTRACT 1

The British generally held in contempt those who were displaced by the occupation of their lands. They were forced to negotiate with them in order to secure British interests, but they discounted leaders of political parties as self-serving trouble-makers. Colonial societies, so the argument ran until at least the 1940s, were not nations but collections of peoples; colonies were best administered by British rulers in collaboration with their natural leaders. Self-appointed nationalists were seen as a special-interest group. Not only did British colonial administrations choose not to recognise the possibility of connections between sporadic protests, which they managed to subdue, and nationalist movements to which they were eventually obliged to transfer power, they also disparaged the significance of any kind of opposition (using terms like banditry or mutiny) and constructed a demonology of principal opponents. Winston Churchill sneered at **Gandhi** as the 'naked fakir', Sir Charles Arden-Clarke (Governor of the Gold Coast) referred to **Kwame Nkrumah** as 'our local Hitler' and Sir Patrick Renison (Governor of Kenya) called **Jomo Kenyatta** 'a leader unto darkness and death'.

Adapted from 'Power, Authority and Freedom' by A.J. Stockwell (1996)

ACTIVITY

Evaluating historical extracts

1. With reference to Extract 1, what is Stockwell's view of the British attitude to protest and nationalism in the colonies?
2. As you read this chapter, you should reflect on whether you feel this view is a fair one or not.

Protest and conflict

The years between 1914 and 1947 saw a number of protests across the Empire, marking the growing strength of nationalist movements and, to some extent, Britain's failure to address issues that had arisen before 1914. Some marginal concessions to representation had been granted in India before the First World War, but in Africa, very little had been done to create effective administrations or realise the economic potential of the colonial territories. Elsewhere, too, the ingredients for conflict were not far below the surface.

Ireland

In the last days of peace in Europe, the British government was already facing the prospect of civil war in Ireland where a religious divide between the six Protestant counties of the north and the majority Catholic south was threatening to wreck the 1912/13 Home Rule Bill granting Irish independence. In March 1914, British soldiers at Curragh mutinied, refusing to take action to enforce Home Rule on the hostile north. Conflict occurred as both sides armed themselves: the 'Ulster Volunteers' versus the 'National Volunteers' in the south. There were three deaths and many casualties in July 1914 and Home Rule had to be suspended for the duration of the war.

Protest escalated during the war and a southern pro-independence organisation, Sinn Féin ('We Ourselves') organised an unsuccessful rising in

Dublin during Easter 1916. In 1919, the frustrations caused by the delays to Irish Home Rule led members of Sinn Féin, who won a majority of the Irish seats at Westminster in the 1918 general election, to establish an Irish assembly in Dublin. They declared an Irish Republic and their Irish Republican Army (IRA) began a guerrilla war against the British, who reinforced the Royal Irish Constabulary with the '**Black and Tans**' – to oppose them.

The Black and Tans

The 'Black and Tans' were a force of temporary policemen who were recruited to assist the Royal Irish Constabulary (RIC). Many were British First World War veterans and the improvised uniforms they initially wore, composed of mixture of British Army khaki and RIC uniforms of rifle green, gave them their nickname.

Fig. 1 *A suspected Irish nationalist is searched by 'Black and Tans', 1920*

This conflict ended in 1921 with the signing of the Anglo-Irish Treaty, which created the Irish Free State, as a self-governing Dominion within the British Empire. The six northern counties promptly used their legal right to 'opt out'. However, the conflict was not over since Eamon de Valera, one of the principal Irish leaders, refused to accept the treaty – partly because the Irish Free State was not a republic and partly because it involved splitting the country. This brought a further Irish civil war, which ended in 1923 with the defeat of Valera and the republicans. Southern Ireland was subsequently treated as a Dominion, gaining equality of status in the 1931 Statute of Westminster. Valera was still not satisfied, however, and his protest continued. He refused to attend the Imperial Conference of 1937 and drew up a new constitution which effectively turned Ireland into a republic – Eire. Eire adopted a position of neutrality in the Second World War (the only Commonwealth country to do this) and in 1948 separated itself entirely from the rest of Britain in the Republic of Ireland Act. The Irish had certainly shown that British imperialism could be successfully challenged.

Extension

Produce a flow chart of developments in Ireland from 1912 to 1947. Use chapters 12 and 13 to help you.

India

There was also conflict in India both during and in the aftermath of the First World War. Although the mainstream political leadership in India was overwhelmingly loyal, sending men and money, there were anti-British outbursts in Bengal and Punjab. Moreover the expatriate Indian population, particularly in the USA, Canada and Germany, headed by the Ghadar Party, tried to encourage uprisings in India, with Irish Republican, German and Turkish help. A number

CROSS-REFERENCE

For the 1919 Government of India Act, look back to Chapter 14, page 135.

A CLOSER LOOK

The Amritsar massacre

The British government claimed that 379 were killed and 1200 wounded in this massacre but the Indian National Congress put the number of deaths as high as 1000 with over 1500 wounded. Dyer was censured and he resigned but public opinion in Britain was divided and some prominent Britons spoke out in his defence.

of failed attempts were made to provoke mutiny in the British Indian Army. These included the 1915 Ghadar Conspiracy and the Singapore Mutiny – a seven-day mutiny of Indian sepoys against the British in Singapore.

Further protest was evoked when the **1919 Government of India Act** failed to satisfy the nationalist demands for independence and fear of further uprisings led to the recommendations of the 1919 Rowlatt Acts, which allowed for political cases to be tried without juries and provided for the internment of suspects without trial. This produced a state of extreme tension, particularly in the Punjab region.

Conflict came to a head in the 1919 **Amritsar (or Jallianwallah Bagh) massacre** in the Punjab, after rioting had brought British deaths and the near breakdown of civil order in the region. British Army troops, commanded by Brigadier-General Reginald Dyer, fired upon a crowd containing a mixture of Indians, who had gathered to protest at against the arrest of two nationalist leaders, and Sikh pilgrims, who had gathered in the public gardens of Jallianwallah Bagh adjacent to a sacred site, the Golden Temple, in order to celebrate the Sikh New Year.

This bloodbath provoked a huge reaction; Indian Congress politicians claimed that the way the British had dealt with protest, by shooting into the crowds, showed that the British no longer possessed any moral authority to rule. The action also galvanised Gandhi's Non-Co-operation Movement of 1920–22.

Fig. 2 *This painting depicts the Amritsar massacre, 1919*

ACTIVITY

Evaluating historical extracts

What interpretation of the part of the British in the Amritsar massacre is offered by Paxman in Extract 2?

EXTRACT 2

Dyer's decision at Amritsar in 1919 fitted a pattern – as demonstrated perhaps most graphically by the behaviour of British authorities after the Indian Mutiny and in the Sudan – of using devastating force to impose their will. But in the Jallianwallah Bagh, Dyer had been facing defenceless civilians. In trying to justify his actions afterwards, the general used a particularly telling expression. He had not attempted to clear the Bagh peacefully because 'then they would all come back and laugh at me and I considered I would be making myself a fool'. The true reason for his action was not strength but fear. There were debates in the House of Commons in which much humbug was spoken by people who might have known better – including a retired Brigadier who talked of how the British Empire rested on prestige. Amritsar had laid bare a brutal truth about empire. As Gandhi put it, 'We do not want to punish Dyer. We have no desire for revenge. We want to change the system that produced Dyer.'

Adapted from *Empire* by Jeremy Paxman (2012)

Further conflict occurred in the Chauri Chaura incident of 1922, in the Gorakhpur district of the United Province. Here, violence erupted among a large group of protesters participating in the Non-Cooperation Movement and the police opened fire. The demonstrators attacked and set fire to a police station, and three civilians and 23 policemen were killed. The Indian National Congress called for an end to the Non-Cooperation Movement on the national level as a direct result of this incident.

The discontent continued to simmer for the next 25 years with outbreaks of conflict and protest erupting in what was to become an increasingly political campaign for independence. Thanks to Gandhi's belief in non-violence, the conflict was probably less bloody than it might otherwise have been, but the emergence of the Muslim League in the 1930s brought a new and **increasingly militant** element into the struggle. Non-violent campaigning, however, was relatively easily contained by the British (hence the failure of Gandhi's 1942 **'Quit India' campaign**) although in the aftermath of the Second World War, the situation in India became grave. A wave of violence swept the country as Hindus and Muslims fought for ascendancy and rejected the British offer of Dominion status, as put forward by Stafford Cripps in 1942. India finally received its independence in 1947 amidst scenes of mounting communal violence. 400,000 died during the conflict that had led to **partition**.

CROSS-REFERENCE

An example of growing militancy is the emergence of the Indian National Army (INA), led from 1943 by Subhas Chandra Bose, which is outlined in Chapter 13, page 126.

CROSS-REFERENCE

The partition of India into India and Pakistan is described in Chapter 19, page 175.

A CLOSER LOOK

The Quit India Movement, 1942

The All-India Congress proclaimed a mass campaign of civil disobedience in 1942 demanding 'an orderly British withdrawal' from India. The British (supported by the All India Muslim League, the Princely States and many businessmen) responded by imprisoning almost the entire INC leadership until 1945. Sporadic small-scale violence took place around the country but the campaign failed because of the heavy-handed suppression, its weak coordination and the lack of a clear-cut programme of action.

The Middle East

In **Egypt** there was a countrywide revolution by Egyptians and Sudanese against the British occupation in 1919, after the British exiled the nationalist leader Saad Zaghlul and other members of his party. There was widespread civil disobedience, rioting, demonstrations and strikes encompassing all classes of society – men, women, Muslim and Christian. There were attacks on British military bases, civilian facilities and personnel, in which Egyptian villages were burnt and railways destroyed. At least 800 Egyptians were killed and 1,600 wounded. Following the British 'Milner report', Egypt was granted independence in 1922, but relations remained strained. Britain refused to recognise full Egyptian sovereignty

CROSS-REFERENCE

More detail on Egypt's progress towards independence is to be found in Chapter 13, page 121.

British withdrawal from the Middle East is covered in Chapter 13, pages 123–124.

Tensions in the Middle East in the 1920s and 1930s and the British response are discussed in Chapter 14, page 132.

Haganah: an underground Jewish militia in Palestine (1920–48) that became the national army of Israel after the partition of Palestine in 1948

Stern Gang: a militant Zionist terrorist organisation (officially Lohame Herut Yisra'el 'Fighters for the Freedom of Israel') founded in 1940 by Avram Stern

over Sudan, or to withdraw all its forces. Even after a further treaty in 1936, Britain retained troops in the Suez area.

There were tensions also in Palestine and these escalated in the 1930s as more Jews, fleeing Nazism, entered the country. Arab protests mounted and the inter-racial violence increased as the Jews formed the **Haganah**, to protect themselves.

More militant Jewish nationalists formed secret units such as the **Stern Gang,** which waged open war on both the British and Arabs. By 1945 there was open conflict between the two communities which the British proved unable to control. In 1947, the British announced their departure, leaving it to the United Nations to sort out the troubles.

Colonial identity

It is almost impossible to define 'colonial identity', since it is not something tangible that can be clearly identified or measured but is an abstract concept; even its existence is subject to question. The term suggests that, among peoples who had for decades or more been subject to British imperial rule, there emerged a clear sense of being 'a colonial'.

Of course, colonisation affected the way peoples saw themselves and the world, both geographically and culturally. The British colonisers had adopted deliberate policies, often aimed at 'civilising' those they were colonising. British/European ideals – religious, cultural, and social – and British economic demands were forced upon the indigenous peoples to varying degrees. Some of those peoples cooperated, collaborating in the hope of benefiting from new opportunities, whilst others resisted, never really accepting a foreign culture imposed through overwhelming power.

However, colonised peoples were not merely passive victims. Colonialism involved complex cultural encounters whereby both the colonisers and the colonised forged new ways of thinking of themselves. The way colonial peoples reacted to British rule was, in large measure, dictated by the way they had been treated. Very broadly, people in areas that had enjoyed economic growth and prosperity under British rule tended, on the whole, to see themselves positively, whereas those who associated rule with hardships and deprivation had a more negative attitude.

ACTIVITY

Extension

Investigate other examples of protest and conflict in the years 1914 to 1947. Protest in Cyprus would provide a good starting point. You could also look at the Dominions – particularly Canada and South Africa.

The experiences and facilities provided by the British moulded colonial identity and, to some extent, the experience of protest and the rise of the nationalist movements in the inter-war years was a reaction to the British failure to recognise the aspirations and needs of colonial people. Ultimately, it was the British colonisers, with their keenness to extend Western education and develop regions economically, who created the national consciousness that was to challenge the whole concept of empire.

Fig. 3 *Empire Day is celebrated in the Bahamas, May 1914*

However, this is not quite the whole story because those same British colonisers, perhaps surprisingly, also managed to create a huge sense of loyalty – quite often pride – among those who were part of this great Empire. Despite the protest and emergent nationalism, there remained a strong attachment to British institutions and to the Crown in the years between 1914 and 1947 – as evidenced by the support given by the Empire and Dominions in both World Wars. The Coronation of George VI in 1937 was widely celebrated and covered by 23 hours of continuous broadcasting in Canada. Empire Day and other festivals brought people out on the streets. Millions tuned in to the monarch's Christmas message. Even many nationalist leaders tempered their political demands with expressions of loyalty to the British Crown.

The development of nationalist movements

During the inter-war years, Britain faced nationalist movements right across the Empire – Irish, Greek, Turkish, Arab, Egyptian, Persian, Afghan, Indian, Chinese and West African. Education, economic development and the spread of communications had all helped foster new ideas about nation, race and religion. The First World War had also helped to undermine the imperial idea. The **collapse of the European empires** encouraged a sense of national identity and liberation from rule by 'others', and the partial success of the Irish nationalists inspired counterparts elsewhere.

Nationalists and anti-imperialists believed that the future lay with independent nation states in Asia and Africa, just as much as in Europe.

Indian nationalism

The Indian Congress Movement, which was already well-established before the First World War, grew in the post-war years, in reaction to **Britain's failure to offer the Indians a satisfactory constitutional arrangement in 1918**. After 1918, the movement fell under the leadership of **Gandhi**, who guided

> **ACTIVITY**
>
> Was there a British colonial identity? Discuss the concept with a partner and share your views with the rest of your group.

> **A CLOSER LOOK**
>
> **The collapse of empires**
>
> The Russian revolutions of 1917 had demonstrated the political power of the masses and the war had destroyed the Austro-Hungarian Empire, creating new nation states such as Czechoslovakia, Poland and Yugoslavia. The collapse of the Ottoman Empire had raised the hopes of Arab nationalists, although France and Britain had thwarted their ambitions by obtaining League of Nations mandates in the area (see Chapter 14, page 141).

CROSS-REFERENCE

Britain's failure to agree a satisfactory constitutional agreement with India in 1918 is discussed in Chapter 13, page 128.

The role and influence of Gandhi is discussed in detail in Chapter 16, pages 153–156.

A CLOSER LOOK

Differences between Gandhi and Nehru

Nehru was a committed socialist, who strongly believed that the government of the newly independent India should seek to industrialise and modernise the country through state economic planning. Gandhi, on the other hand, looked to a 'village-India' of social and racial equality.

CROSS-REFERENCE

The activities of Bose and the Indian National Army during the Second World War are introduced in Chapter 13, page 126.

A CLOSER LOOK

Communism had established itself in India in the early 1920s but a British ban had made the organisation of its disparate groups difficult. It was not until the 1930s that Communist organisations became more active, aided by industrial changes and the formation of the All India Trades Union Congress. Some Communists joined the Congress Socialist Party in 1934 and worked as the left wing within Congress, whereas others sought a national revolutionary uprising.

You might like to find out more about the various Communist groups operating in India and consider whether their activities helped or hindered the cause of Indian nationalism.

it towards peaceful protest and civil disobedience, for example boycotting elections in the 1920s. Increasingly prominent, however, was **Jawaharlal Nehru**, a fellow lawyer who became a close ally and friend, although **the two leaders' views** on India's future were very different; Nehru sought modernisation and industrialisation, Gandhi an agricultural, rural-based society. Nehru also diverged from Gandhi over his support for the British during the Second World War and he was only reluctantly pulled into Gandhi's 'Quit India' campaign from 1942.

KEY PROFILE

Jawaharlal Nehru (1889–1964) was the Westernised son of a wealthy Brahmin lawyer. He returned to India in 1912 and joined the Indian National Congress in 1919, becoming a strong ally of Gandhi. He was elected as the INC president in 1928 and imprisoned during the anti-salt tax campaign. Re-elected as president in 1936, he supported Britain in 1939, although he gave reluctant support to Gandhi's 1942 'Quit India' campaign and was consequently imprisoned until 1945. He again became president in 1946 and India's first Prime Minister in 1947 at independence. He died in office.

Fig. 4   *Nehru was educated at Harrow and Cambridge*

Indeed, Gandhi's views were far from universally accepted by all Indian nationalists. The 'Untouchables' leader, the British-educated lawyer Dr B.R. Ambedkar, for example, criticised Gandhi's refusal to reject the caste system completely, even though Gandhi did call for equality between the castes. There were also divisions over strategies and tactics. Nehru's rival for the leadership of the Congress Party in the 1930s, **Subhas Chandra Bose**, wanted the INC to adopt a more militant line. In 1939, Bose allied himself with Britain's enemies, Germany and Japan, and, in 1943, formed the **Indian National Army**.

KEY PROFILE

Subhas Chandra Bose (1897–1945) was an Indian Congress politician. He was president in 1938 and 1939 but broke with the Congress leadership over support for the British in 1939. He was placed under house arrest by the British but escaped and fled to Germany. In 1943, in Japanese-held Sumatra, he established the Indian National Army in Japanese-held Sumatra. He intended to lead the forces to free India but he died in a Japanese plane crash in August 1945.

Whilst the Congress party was overwhelmingly Hindu in support, a second nationalist group, the All India Muslim League, also promoted nationalism in the inter-war years. Originally formed in 1906 and working in co-operation with Congress, it had been the junior partner in the nationalist struggle. However, under **Muhammad Ali Jinnah's** leadership it grew more vociferous in its representation of India's substantial Muslim minority. Jinnah disagreed with Gandhi's tactics and campaigned for the establishment of safeguards for the Muslims in the movement for independence.

KEY PROFILE

Muhammad Ali Jinnah (1876–1948) was a prominent member of the Congress Party and an active member of the Muslim League which he led from 1913. Initially he favoured Hindu–Muslim political co-operation, but he resigned from the Congress Party in 1920, disagreeing with the policy of non-violent protest, and by 1940 he had come to believe that there should be a separate Muslim state. Following his efforts to create Pakistan, he was appointed as the country's first Governor-General in 1947.

Fig. 5   *Jinnah trained as a barrister*

In 1930, Dr Muhammad Iqbal, a European-educated Muslim poet and philosopher from the Punjab, suggested that a Muslim nation-state might be fashioned from the North West India states of Punjab, the North-West Frontier Province, Sind and Baluchistan. The Muslim nationalist Choudry Rahmat Ali proposed the name '**Pakistan**' in 1933. However, the League was not initially united in its desire for partition and Jinnah rejected the idea of an independent Pakistan until 1940.

Thus Indian nationalism, in spite of its shared goal to oust the British, was far from a unified force and sharply divided on what an independent India should look like, and how this should be achieved.

A CLOSER LOOK

Some believe that the name **Pakistan** is a play on the first letters of the state's proposed constituent provinces: P (Punjab) A (Afghania – another name for North-West Province) K (Kashmir) S (Sind) and stan (from last letters of Baluchistan).

EXTRACT 3

Nationalism was never a single and unified movement. Inevitably there were competing ideas as to what a nation was within a colonial arena. The ways in which imperialism had redrawn political and cultural boundaries over the years and favoured some groups over others had clouded and complicated issues. How was a nation to be defined after years of colonial rule that had brought together hitherto separate peoples? In India, for example, differences in that vision were by no means confined to religion, although the violence that erupted so dramatically between Hindus and Muslims in the 1940s was certainly a dominant factor. But we should remember that Gandhi, so frequently depicted in popular culture as the hero of twentieth-century Indian nationalism, had many detractors in India, and his rejection of class-based protest was not popular everywhere. Colonial rule had blurred cultural, ethnic and religious boundaries with ruthless insensitivity.

Adapted from *The British Empire: Sunrise to Sunset* by Philippa Levine (2013)

ACTIVITY

Evaluating historical extracts

Summarise in one sentence Levine's view of the problems of nationalism in colonial countries, as given in Extract 3.

African nationalism

The inter-war period also saw the first stirrings of African nationalism. It was more diverse than Indian nationalism, reflecting the variety of British colonial administrations and African cultures.

West Africa

In West Africa, the colonies of Nigeria, Gambia, Sierra Leone and the Gold Coast already had legislative councils by 1914, although their powers were limited and African representation minimal. This prompted a group of political activists from all these territories to hold a meeting in Accra to found the National Congress of West Africa in 1919. These activists were dominated by the educated elite in the Gold Coast, and the movement was supported by the swelling numbers of the black middle class lawyers, teachers and doctors, many of whom were European educated.

The Congress's demands for greater representation were initially ignored. However, some concessions were granted in the 1920s, although the nationalists were outnumbered by appointed (rather than elected) African chiefs from the interior of the colonies on the legislative councils. Nevertheless, with the spread of education, and as colonial administrations decided to try to win local support for the Empire by increasing new employment opportunities, a new, young and even more radical group of nationalist leaders emerged in the 1930s.

The West African Students' Union (WASU), founded in 1925 helped bring together students from various West African countries studying in London, and, at a time of political flux in Europe and growing nationalism in India, inspired greater radicalism among its members. Among them were men such as **Nnamdi Azikiwe** and **Kwame Nkrumah** from the Gold Coast, both of whom would emerge as significant post-war nationalist figures.

The Second World War accelerated these trends, as it brought faster economic development to the West African colonies, and in 1945, a Pan African Congress was convened in Manchester, England which called for the 'autonomy and independence' of black Africa.

East Africa

Harry Thuku developed the first East African political protest movements. He was initially involved in the formation of the Young Kikuyu, a non-militant organisation set up to recover Kikuyu lands that had been lost when Kenya became a British Crown Colony in 1920. In 1921, he went on to found the East African Association, a larger and more representative organisation. Jomo Kenyatta joined in 1922 and the movement gradually broadened into a campaign for African rights and representation as the East Africa Association. The Second World War had a profoundly radicalising effect and Thuku helped establish the Kenya African Study Union, which, in 1946, became, the Kenya African Union. In 1947 Jomo Kenyatta became its president and it played a crucial role in the post-war decolonisation.

CROSS-REFERENCE

For the role and influence of Nnamdi Azikiwe and Kwame Nkrumah after 1947, look ahead to Chapter 22, pages 210 and 209 respectively.

KEY PROFILE

Harry Thuku (1895–1970) was born into an influential Kikuyu family. Missionary educated, he joined the Kikuyu Association, but left, disillusioned with the organisation's reluctance to use direct and illegal methods to resist British rule. In 1921 he helped found the East Africa Association, only to be imprisoned in 1922 for his involvement in a demonstration which turned violent. He was released in 1931 and in 1932 he became president of the Kikuyu Central Association.

CROSS-REFERENCE

The role and influence of Jomo Kenyatta between 1947 and 1967 is discussed in Chapter 22, page 209.

ACTIVITY

Extension

Divide into groups to investigate Greek, Turkish, Arab, Persian, Afghan and Chinese nationalist movements within the British Empire in the years 1914 to 1947. Make a chart to record your findings on these, as well as the Indian and West African movements.

Summary

The years between 1914 and 1947 saw a good deal of violence as well as the challenge of emergent nationalist movements. These years were a time when colonial identity seemed to be changing. Yet, the Empire held together and in the Second World War, colonial peoples were largely supportive of Great Britain.

PRACTICE QUESTION

Evaluating historical extracts

Using your understanding of the historical context, assess how convincing the arguments in Extracts 1, 2 and 3 are, in relation to conflict and protest in the years 1914 to 1947.

 PRACTICE QUESTION

'The nationalist movements in India and Africa in the years 1918 to 1947 failed to achieve their objectives because the British were too powerful.' Assess the validity of this view.

19 Decolonisation in Africa and Asia

LEARNING OBJECTIVES

In this chapter you will learn about:

- decolonisation in West, East and South Africa

- decolonisation in Singapore and Malaysia.

KEY QUESTION

As you read this chapter, consider the following key question:
Why did the British Empire grow and contract?

EXTRACT 1

The rapidity with which decolonisation occurred between 1945 and 1967 suggests that while decolonisation was the product of changes at the international, domestic British and colonial levels, it was the international ones – particularly the Second World War – that triggered further changes that destroyed the old pre-war relationships of the imperial powers with their empires. In the British case, involvement in the war drove them to changes in colonial policy that created new political conditions which made the colonies harder to rule. Meanwhile the international and domestic British side effects of the war (especially the emergence of the anti-colonial powers, USA and the Soviet Union) encouraged colonial resistance to the old colonial powers. It made it harder for the British to reassert authority without imposing unwelcome financial and political burdens on the home government, as well as jeopardising wider international interests outside the Empire. A 'vicious circle' of imperial decline was set in motion, and the imperial system unravelled.

Adapted from *Britain and Decolonisation* by John Darwin (1988)

ACTIVITY

Evaluating historical extracts

In Darwin's view, what factors contributed to the end of the British Empire? As you read this chapter, consider whether the evidence supports his view.

ACTIVITY

Study Fig. 1 – a photograph of the signing of the agreement which granted Malaya independence in 1957. While it symbolises the end of the Empire in Malaya, in what ways might it be seen as presenting the British Empire in a positive light?

Fig. 1 *Malaya is granted independence in 1957*

The years between 1947 and 1967 saw the dismantling of the British Empire, as former colonies were granted – or won – their independence. This was not a process which affected the British alone; the empires of other European powers also came to an end, notably those of France in Asia and Africa and the Netherlands in Southeast Asia. In this respect, British decolonisation was part of a much wider international phenomenon.

Reasons for decolonisation

- **The economic impact of the Second World War**. All of the imperial powers emerged from the war economically much poorer than they entered it. None could really afford to fight a series of prolonged colonial wars, fighting against **insurgent** nationalist movements.
- **The changed international situation**. The new dominant powers, the USA and USSR, were both hostile to imperialism. Since Britain and other colonial powers were heavily dependent on the USA for defence and economic support, they were susceptible to American pressure to speed up decolonisation.
- **The emergence of powerful nationalist movements in the colonies**. Movements to secure independence from the European empires and establish free independent states appeared in all parts of the world. The strategies employed to secure these aims varied, but all posed a challenge to the imperial governments.
- **Changing priorities in Europe**. By the 1950s, Western Europe was experiencing a dramatic post-war economic recovery, with full employment and rising living standards. This made it less dependent on colonial support. The emergence of the **EEC** from 1957 (which Britain joined in 1973) helped refocus trade within Europe itself. As a result, from the 1950s, support for empire, especially among powerful business interests, dwindled in all the main European imperial powers.
- **Specific problems**. Neither Britain nor the other imperial powers immediately 'gave up' on their empires after the Second World War. The decolonisation of India and Burma and the withdrawal from Palestine in the late 1940s came in response to specific problems in those regions, based on the belief that the benefits of holding onto these possessions were outweighed by the costs that their possession would incur. Decisions to abandon empire were often forced by specific developments rather than being the product of an immediate post-war shift in thinking.

ACTIVITY

Make a spider diagram to show reasons for decolonisation after the Second World War. As you study the rest of the chapter (and Chapter 20), try to add some sub-branches to your diagram to provide examples to support your main factors and record specific factors within different states.

KEY TERM

insurgent: displaying armed hostility to established authority; an individual rebel is known as 'an insurgent'

CROSS-REFERENCE

To recap on the immediate impact of the Second World War, look back to Chapter 13, page 126; the economic impact is further discussed in Chapter 15, page 149–151.

There was some softening of the US stance in the circumstances of the Cold War. For more on the impact of international relations on decolonisation see Chapter 19, page 178.

The rise of nationalist movements between 1945 and 1947 is covered in Chapter 18, pages 173–176.

The emergence of the EEC and relations between Britain and Europe are explored in Chapter 20, pages 199–200.

The British withdrawal from India, Palestine and Burma in the late 1940s is discussed in Chapter 13, pages 128–132.

KEY TERM

EEC: European Economic Community; a free trade community originally comprising France, Germany, Belgium, Luxembourg, the Netherlands and Italy

Africa

Britain's post-war imperial policy placed emphasis upon developing the African colonies so that they could contribute significantly to Britain's post-war economy. British policy was enshrined in the creation of the **Colonial Development Corporation** and the African colonies were earmarked for extensive development initiatives. However, the British underestimated the effects of economic development. The Second World War had already accelerated the economic growth of most of the African colonies in response to the needs of the war effort and this, together with a measure of industrialisation in some colonies and the expansion of towns and cities, enabled new **nationalist ideas** to thrive and spread.

CROSS-REFERENCE

The Colonial Development Corporation is discussed in Chapter 21, page 206.

Nationalist movements in Africa are discussed in Chapter 24, page 234.

Case studies of the following African nationalist leaders are to be found in Chapter 22, as follows:

- Kwame Nkrumah (Gold Coast/ Ghana), page 209
- Dr Nnamdi Azikiwe (Nigeria), page 210
- Jomo Kenyatta (Kenya) page 209
- Apolo Milton Obote (Uganda), page 212
- Nelson Mandela (South Africa), page 213.

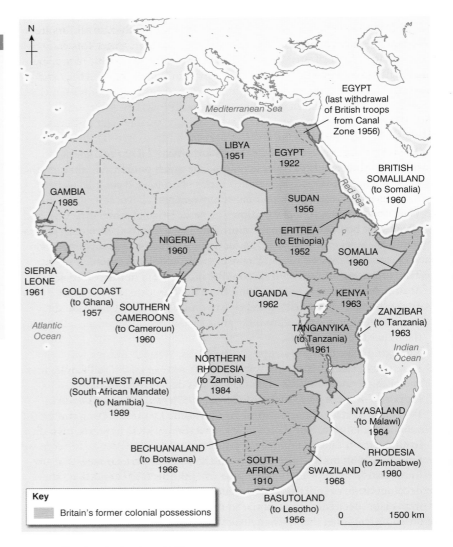

Fig. 2 *The decolonisation of Africa*

West Africa

In 1947, **Andrew Cohen**, Head of the Africa Department in the Colonial Office in London, described the Gold Coast as the most advanced African colony in terms of the political maturity of its people and their fitness to rule themselves. However, even he did not envisage that independence for its people would be feasible for at least a generation, and he warned that elsewhere it would take much longer, despite the emergent African nationalist movements.

The Gold Coast

To some degree, British colonial administrators had anticipated during the war that the rise of an educated African elite would mean allowing some degree of African political representation. However, the British wanted any change to be gradual and managed in a way that did not impair British economic and political interests.

In 1946 the Burns Constitution was drawn up in the Gold Coast (named after Sir Alan Burns, Governor-General 1942–47). This established a Legislative Council of 12 British nominees and 18 elected African members. This was a breakthrough. However, final power still remained in the hands of the British Governor and a wave of unrest spread across the country, as protests against British colonial rule gathered momentum.

CROSS-REFERENCE

There is a case study of Andrew Cohen in Chapter 22, page 215.

The Convention People's Party (CPP) was founded by Kwame Nkrumah in 1949 and pressurised the British administration to make further concessions; the Legislative Council was enlarged and renamed the Legislative Assembly, and the number of people who could vote for it increased, but still the British Governor retained ultimate power.

Although Nkrumah was gaoled in 1950, the CPP won two thirds of the seats in the Legislative Assembly in 1951 and it became clear to Burns that the CPP would have to be brought into government in order to bring the troubles under control. Nkrumah was therefore released and given the position of Prime Minister from 1952, with members of the CPP taking posts as government ministers.

This elected government was given extensive control over internal affairs, and Nkrumah's popularity and standing grew. In 1956, a **plebiscite** in the neighbouring British Mandate of Togoland delivered an overwhelming vote in favour of unification with the Gold Coast. The support for independence was such that in 1957 new elections were held on full adult **suffrage**. The country became fully independent on 6 March 1957 as Ghana, the name of an ancient African state on the edge of the Sahara Desert. But Nkrumah proved a divisive figure and in the years that followed he was forced to become increasingly authoritarian to hold onto power.

Nigeria

There was a similar momentum to independence in Nigeria after the war, although the situation was much more complex. In 1946 the 'Richards Constitution' was drawn up (named after Sir Arthur Richards, Governor 1943–48). As in the Gold Coast, the new arrangements allowed for greater African representation, but with the Governor-General and the Executive Council, which the Governor appointed, retaining ultimate power. The country was **regionally and ethnically divided** and the British took the view that any move towards an independent Nigeria should take the form of a federation of separate regional states. Thus although an expanded Legislative Council was created to discuss issues affecting the whole country, three assemblies for each of the three major regions (West, East and South) were also established, to debate local matters and to advise the British governors in these regions.

However, greater pressure for change from nationalist movements forced the British to amend the constitution. The Macpherson Constitution of 1951 (named after the next Governor-General, 1948–55) extended the right to vote and created a National Council of Ministers, answerable to a 185-seat Federal House of Representatives. This stimulated the growth of Nigerian political parties, which began to compete in elections to the new House. However, the regions were also strengthened, with each region being allowed its own government as well as an elected assembly. The Federal House of Representatives could not over-rule these regional governments. The effect was to exacerbate tensions between the different ethnicities rather than ease them.

New political parties were established representing different ethnic groups and regions and the British found themselves being pushed along the path of granting concessions more quickly than they had originally envisaged. Following further revisions of the constitution and federal elections in 1954, a government was formed consisting of three British officials together with nine ministers drawn from the various regional political parties in order to strike a balance at the national level between the different regions. However, more power was increasingly devolved to the various regional governments and following federal elections in 1959 moves were made towards full independence for the country in October 1960.

Similar tensions manifested themselves in Sierra Leone and Gambia and as the 1950s progressed the British concluded that independence was the best

KEY TERM

plebiscite: a direct vote by all the members of the electorate in a country on an important public question such as a change in the constitution

suffrage: the right to vote in elections. Full adult suffrage means that all adults can vote

ACTIVITY

Create a poster such as Nkrumah and the CPP might have issued before the 1957 elections.

CROSS-REFERENCE

There is a map showing ethnic divisions in Nigeria in Chapter 24, page 237.

ACTIVITY

Draw a flow chart to record the steps to Nigerian independence between 1946 and 1960.

ACTIVITY

Extension

Find out more about the steps towards independence in Sierra Leone and Gambia. What similarities are there between developments in the West African countries?

option. Sierra Leone became independent in 1961 and Gambia in 1965. In all cases, demands for reform compelled British colonial administrations to introduce reforms much faster than they had originally hoped or intended.

East Africa

Progress towards independence was much more violent in parts of East Africa where rapid economic growth brought urbanisation, greater political consciousness, political activism, nationalism and labour disputes. During the years of war, the population of Nairobi in Kenya increased by a half, while the populations of Dar-es-Salaam and Mombasa both doubled and the high inflation, poor housing and overcrowding which followed fuelled protests.

Initially the British saw this region as being ideal for **economic development**, with a view to generating large dollar-earning exports. Perhaps the greatest symbol of these aspirations was the ill-fated Tanganyika Groundnut Scheme of 1946. The failure of this scheme provoked East African peasants into supporting the nationalist movements.

A CLOSER LOOK

The Tanganyika Groundnut Scheme

In 1946, Britain and many countries experienced a severe shortage of cooking fats. From this emerged the idea of growing in Tanganyika large quantities of groundnuts (peanuts) which could be processed into cooking oil and sold to the world economy. The project involved massive investment in tractors, equipment and the construction of a railway to transport the crop. However, the terrain proved too difficult to cultivate and the scheme was abandoned in 1951 having cost £49 million. Furthermore, the land was turned into an uncultivatable dust bowl.

Long-simmering Kikuyu grievances at their treatment by white settlers exploded into violence, when white people sought to mechanise farming and displace the peasant growers. The move prompted many of the most desperate among the Kikuyu to resort to violence and led to the Mau Mau uprising between 1952 and 1956. The British crushed the rebellion with great ruthlessness and successfully divided the Kikuyu people; but in doing so, they weakened their moral authority and support for the nationalists increased. Tanganyika was granted independence as Tanzania in 1961. Uganda followed in 1962 and Kenya in December 1963.

Southern and central Africa

In southern Africa, the white minority had enjoyed full control over South Africa's internal affairs since 1931 following the granting of Dominion status by the **Statute of Westminster**. This meant that their increasingly divisive racial policies had become firmly entrenched. In 1948 the Afrikaner Nationalist party won power, and implemented the policy of **apartheid**, segregating races in all walks of life. In practice, non-white people were treated very poorly and opposition to apartheid emerged, led primarily by the African National Congress. Throughout the 1950s and 1960s, the South African state responded with brutal suppression of all protests; 69 protestors were killed by the police at **Sharpeville** in March 1960.

CROSS-REFERENCE

The contribution of East Africa to the British economy is discussed in Chapter 21, page 206.

CROSS-REFERENCE

The Mau Mau rebellion is covered in detail in Chapter 24, pages 233–235.

CROSS-REFERENCE

The Statute of Westminster in 1931 is discussed in Chapter 14, pages 139–140.

Apartheid and opposition to it, including the Sharpeville massacre of 1960, are covered in Chapter 23, page 227.

KEY TERM

apartheid: originally coming from an Afrikaans word which means 'separateness', this came to represent a policy of discrimination and segregation on grounds of race

Fig. 3 *Apartheid in evidence in Cape Town, South Africa, 1967*

International opinion became increasingly critical of South Africa, and relations with Britain grew strained. This was not just about apartheid. From 1948, South Africa had pressed, unsuccessfully, for the British to hand over adjacent lands administered by the British Colonial Office (Bechuanaland, Basutoland and Swaziland) to South Africa. The British refused and in 1961 the South African white population voted to become a Republic and to leave the Commonwealth.

ACTIVITY

Extension

You might like to read *Cry, My Beloved Country* by Alan Paton, written in 1948 about 'a black man's country under white man's law.' Look at also for more modern novels based on the apartheid era in South Africa.

A CLOSER LOOK

The British granted independence to the southern African territories administered by Britain in the later 1960s. Basutoland gained independence as Lesotho on 4 October 1966; Bechuanaland gained independence as Botswana on 30 September 1966; Swaziland gained independence on 6 September 1968.

The British tried to counter-balance South African influence by building up other colonial possessions in the region. These included
- Northern Rhodesia – a mineral rich (copper) province
- Southern Rhodesia – an agriculturally rich territory with a substantial white settler population
- Nyasaland –a relatively economically undeveloped territory.

During the Second World War the administrations of these three territories had worked together to assist the war effort, and the British came to the view that a joint administration – effectively creating one consolidated colonial state – would provide an effective counter-weight to South Africa. Thus, the idea of a **Central African Federation** (CAF) of the three territories emerged.

The CAF was created in 1953. Its constitution included some protection for African rights: discriminatory legislation against Africans could be vetoed by

KEY CHRONOLOGY

Colonial independence in southern and central Africa

1953	Central African Federation is created
1961	South Africa leaves the Commonwealth, becomes a republic
1963	Central African Federation dissolved
1964	Northern Rhodesia (as Zambia)
1964	Nyasaland (as Malawi)
1965	Ian Smith illegally declares Southern Rhodesia to be independent (UDI) – as 'Rhodesia'
1966	Basuto (as Lesotho); Bechuanaland (as Basuto)
1968	Swaziland
1969	Rhodesia – as (white-controlled) republic; guerrilla war with African nationalist movements begins

CROSS-REFERENCE

The establishment and failure of the Central African Federation are discussed in more detail in Chapter 24, pages 238–239.

Britain. There was also some limited provision for African representation in the new Federal Assembly – but powerful African nationalist movements emerged in all three territories, led by Africans who were suspicious of Britain's intentions. The white governors of the CAF responded fiercely. Nationalist leaders were arrested and imprisoned: actions which brought increasing disorder.

By the end of the 1950s, in line with its policies elsewhere in Africa, Britain had concluded that decolonisation was necessary. In 1960–61, the British government ordered the release of nationalist leaders in Northern Rhodesia and Nyasaland and drew up new constitutions for these territories which paved the way for majority rule and independence. In 1963, the CAF was formally dissolved, and in 1964 **Kenneth Kaunda** led Northern Rhodesia to independence as Zambia, and **Dr Hastings Banda** led Nyasaland to independence as Malawi.

Southern Rhodesia embarked on a very different path. There, the white settlers were determined to avoid being absorbed into an independent African-dominated country. In 1961, when the CAF looked doomed, a large section of the white population switched their support to the new Rhodesian Front Party, which was dedicated to achieving independence for Southern Rhodesia – but under white control. It won the elections in that year and in 1965 the Prime Minister of Rhodesia, **Ian Smith**, illegally declared Southern Rhodesia (which he referred to simply as 'Rhodesia') to be independent. British **sanctions** proved unsuccessful, and in 1969 Rhodesia became a republic and the country was plunged into a long **guerrilla war** between the ruling white people and African nationalists.

CROSS-REFERENCE

Kenneth Kaunda and Dr Hastings Banda are profiled in Chapter 24, page 239.

CROSS-REFERENCE

Ian Smith is profiled in Chapter 24, page 240.

KEY TERM

sanctions: refusing to trade with another country

A CLOSER LOOK

The **guerrilla war** was only ended by negotiation at the end of the 1970s, paving the way for African majority rule and the creation of the modern state of Zimbabwe in 1979.

ACTIVITY

Draw a diagram to show the different paths to independence followed by the Rhodesias and Nyasaland. Can you explain why each developed differently?

EXTRACT 2

In February 1957, Harold Macmillan became Prime Minister. He was not committed to the Empire as Churchill and Eden had been. He was a political adventurer, able to change course if it served his purpose. He aimed above all to secure the friendship of the United States, and, equally, to avoid conflict with African nationalism. He requested a balance sheet that would indicate whether each colony was a liability or an asset. But the economic and military issues were too complex for this to be done. Macmillan, however, decided independently that the Empire was an undesirable burden and that he could only get back on good terms with the Americans by showing that Britain no longer possessed an aggressively imperialist mentality. He recognised too that international sentiment was now against colonialism. While the British could cope with limited colonial insurgency, they could not deal with major colonial warfare. The British Parliament and public would not tolerate it, nor would the economy sustain it.

Adapted from 'The Dissolution of the British Empire' by Wm Roger Louis (1999)

KEY PROFILE

Harold Macmillan (1894–1986) was an Oxford-educated Conservative, who had first entered politics in the 1920s. He was Prime Minister between 1957 and 1963, and presided over a time of post-war prosperity. He was succeeded by Alec Douglas-Home (1963–64) but both leaders' 'Edwardian style' appeared at odds with a more modern form of politics, represented by Labour under Harold Wilson, who came to power in 1964.

Evaluating historical extracts

What reasons does Extract 2 give for the change in British policies towards the colonies under Macmillan (Prime Minister 1957–63)?

Asia

As in Africa, the years between 1947 and 1967 saw the abandonment of most of Britain's colonial possessions in Asia. The contrast in British attitudes towards Burma (which Britain rapidly abandoned after the war) and Malaya and Singapore, which the British were initially determined to keep control of, is, however, striking.

Fig. 4 *The decolonisation of Asia*

Burma

The British decided to grant independence to Burma shortly after the war, following the violent activities of the nationalists and the ascendancy of the AFPFL, led by **Aung San**. Although Clement Attlee, had originally planned a programme of measured and slow steps to independence, the breakdown of order hastened British withdrawal. Talks took place between Aung San and Attlee's government in London in January 1947 and it was agreed that elections for a **Constituent Assembly** would take place in April 1948. These produced a huge AFPFL majority. However the different factions within the

CROSS-REFERENCE

Nationalist activity in Burma (including a key profile of Aung San and information on the AFPFL) is outlined in Chapter 13, pages 131–132.

Constituent Assembly: a body elected to draw up a constitution for a state

KEY CHRONOLOGY

Steps to independence – Malaya and Singapore

1946	UMNO created
1948	Federation of Malaya established
1948	State of Emergency declared
1955	Elections in Malaya and Singapore
1957	Malaya granted independence
1958	Self-government granted to Singapore
1963	Creation of Malaysia (including Singapore)
1965	Singapore expelled from federation and becomes independent state.

KEY TERM

UMNO: United Malays National Organisation

MCA: Malay Chinese Association

MCP: Malayan Communist Party

SPP: Singapore Progressive Party

PAP: People's Action Party (Singapore)

AFPFL could not agree on Burma's future path and in July 1947 Aung San and six of his cabinet ministers were assassinated by a rival political faction. Consequently, the achievement of independence for Burma in January 1948 was not the quiet and measured withdrawal the British had envisaged. Instead, it brought the eruption of civil war and the Burmese completely turned their backs on Britain, even rejecting the idea of joining the British Commonwealth.

Fig. 5 *Aung San at Downing Street in 1947*

Singapore and Malaya

In stark contrast with policy in Burma, the British regarded Malaya and Singapore as crucially important to their post-war economic and imperial strategies. Malaya, as a major producer of rubber, promised to be an important earner of dollars after the war, while Singapore (which had a major naval and military base on the island) was regarded as being militarily and strategically important to Britain's wider interests in Asia.

ACTIVITY

In pairs or small groups, research one of the various parties in Malaya and Singapore and create a one-page illustrated manifesto for it. Each 'party' could then present itself to the rest of the group.

The Malay Peninsula

The British faced a number of serious problems when they tried to re-establish control in the Malay Peninsula in 1945. The Peninsula suffered from ethnic tensions between the Chinese and Indians and the Malay peoples. The United Malays National Organisation (**UMNO**) was created in March 1946 to fight for the rights of the Malay peoples. The Chinese, on the other hand, were represented by the Malay Chinese Association (**MCA**) or the Malayan Communist Party (**MCP**). The Chinese were prominent in labour unions and involved in a series of strikes between 1945 and 1948.

A CLOSER LOOK

The Malaysian Chinese

There had been a large wave of Chinese immigration to Malaya in the late nineteenth century, encouraged by the British who needed labour for the tin mines and rubber plantations. More Chinese arrived during the Chinese Civil War (c1927–50) and by 1947 the Chinese comprised 38.4 per cent of the population compared with 49.5 per cent Malays. By 1957, the Chinese comprised 45 per cent, although this fell to 36 per cent in 1961. The Chinese developed their own communities and schools and flourished in business and commerce, enjoying one of the highest standards of living among the minority demographic groups in the Malay Peninsula.

By 1947, **ethnic tensions** were running so high that the British colonial administration had to abandon its original plan (drawn up by Edward Gent in 1944) to create a 'Malay Union'. This would have awarded equal Malay citizenship all ethnic groups while keeping Singapore as a separate Crown Colony.

CROSS-REFERENCE

A case study of the following nationalist leaders and their various political and ethnic sympathies can be found in Chapter 22, pages 208–209: Onn bin Ja'afar, Tunka Abdul Rahman, Chin Peng and Tan Cheng Lock.

A CLOSER LOOK

Ethnic divisions had been exploited by the Japanese occupiers during the Second World War exacerbating the tensions between the Chinese, who suffered badly at the hands of the occupying Japanese, and Malay peoples.

In June 1947 the British produced a new scheme, which offered a much more restricted definition of Malay citizenship (including proven competence in the Malay and English languages, which was discriminatory against many of the Chinese). The new arrangements, creating the Federation of Malaya, were enacted in January 1948 and established:

- the 'Federation of Malaya Executive Council', with seven official and seven unofficial members, headed by the British High Commissioner. This held the real power.
- the '**Federation of Malaya Legislative Council**' of 62 members representing the various states and other groups. This became an elected body in 1955.
- governments within the individual Malay states to which some of the financial powers of the central Colonial Administration were devolved

The new Federation of Malaya was beset by problems. This was partly the result of the difficult post-war economic circumstances and partly the product of Chinese grievances. The British were so frightened by the potentially damaging impact on of rebel attacks on rubber plantations that they declared a **State of Emergency** in June 1948. This empowered the colonial authorities to use military force and additional sweeping legal powers to arrest suspects and to impose order on the country. Troubles raged between 1948 and 1952, and saw the assassination of Sir Henry Gurney, the British High Commissioner, in October 1951. By 1952, order had been restored, and the British believed that their hold on Malaya had been secured.

ACTIVITY

The War of the Running Dogs by Noel Barber (1971) is a good gripping read about the Malayan Emergency.

A CLOSER LOOK

Following elections in 1955, 28 members of the **Federation of Malaya Legislative Council** (including all the chief ministers of the various states) were Malays, 14 Chinese, six Indians and 14 Europeans.

KEY TERM

State of Emergency: this involves the suspension of normal constitutional procedures during a situation of particular national danger

CROSS-REFERENCE

Ethnic tensions in Malaya are covered in Chapter 24, pages 235–236.

Fig. 6 *British troops on patrol during the Malayan Emergency*

The fear of a nationalist **military rebellion** was all the more real to the British since the French had been defeated by a similar nationalist military movement in their colony of Indo-China (Vietnam) at Dien Bien Phu in 1955.

However, the British position became increasingly untenable. To keep support during the State of Emergency, the British had made promises of Malay independence. They had even promoted the Malay Chinese Association (MCA), which also wanted independence, but with equal rights for the Chinese, in an attempt to win over the Chinese population. However, between 1952 and 1954, both the Malays and Chinese united against British rule and together won 81 per cent of the votes in the federal elections of 1955. The British feared that if they resisted Malay independence much longer, there would be a violent **military rebellion**.

The Reid Commission led by Lord William Reid was established in 1955 to draw up a new democratic constitution and in 1957, an independent Malaya was created. A continuing British military presence in nearby Singapore was accepted and Malaya also continued to collaborate economically with Britain, remaining in the Sterling Area. In a sense, the British had exchanged colonial rule for informal influence, which still offered the prospect of meeting their key economic hopes.

In 1963, Malaya united with Singapore, Sabah (North Borneo) and Sarawak to form Malaysia. However, less than two years later in 1965, Singapore was expelled from the federation. Thereafter, Malaysia forged its own path.

Singapore

Singapore, as an island which had long enjoyed a high degree of internal control over its own affairs and had a predominantly Chinese population (brought in by the British), was treated separately from the rest of the Malay Peninsula.

During 1947 and 1948, it was given its own government, with an Executive and Legislative Council. However, although six of the 25 seats on the Legislative Council were elected, only British subjects (c23,000 people or 10 per cent of the population) had the vote.

As in the Federation of Malaya, the government in Singapore struggled to contain communist insurgency. In addition to arrests and imprisonments, an attempt was made to win the loyalty of the population by enlarging the Legislative Council to 32 seats, with 25 of these chosen by an electorate of c300,000 in 1953.

The first elected Council had been dominated by the Singapore Progressive Party (**SPP**), a conservative group favouring businessmen, but in 1955, the

SPP won only three seats and several new left-wing parties emerged, including the Labour Front (ten seats), the People's Action Party (**PAP**) (three seats) and the United Malays National Organisation/Malay Chinese Association (**UMNO/MCA**) alliance (three seats).

This new left-wing grouping sought discussions with the British about self-rule. Their first leader, David Marshall, was unsuccessful but his successor in 1956, Lim Yew Hock, impressed the British by taking strong action against the communists and thus persuaded Britain, in 1957, to implement full internal self-government for Singapore, although the island would remain part of the Empire. This led to the State of Singapore Act in 1958.

In 1959, Lee Kuan Yew of the PAP (a party with some communist leanings) came to power and although the fears of Singapore's businessmen, and of Britain, proved unfounded, the British decided, in 1963, that Singapore's future would be best assured as part of the Federation of Malaya – which became 'Malaysia' that year. This scheme proved unworkable, however, as race riots between Chinese and Malays led to a breakdown in public order. In August 1965 Singapore was expelled from Malaysia and became a fully independent state in its own right.

CROSS-REFERENCE

UMNO and the MCA are discussed in Chapter 24, page 236.

Summary

ACTIVITY

Summary

Use the table below compare the progress made towards independence by different colonies between 1947 and 1967. Use one of the given phrases to indicate which stage you think each colony had reached by the date concerned:
1. direct colonial rule with no representation at all for the indigenous peoples
2. direct colonial rule with some very limited representation for the indigenous peoples
3. direct colonial rule with considerable representation/involvement for the indigenous peoples
4. complete self-rule within the British Empire
5. complete independence.

Country	1947	1950	1955	1960	1965	1967
Gold Coast (Ghana)						
Nigeria						
Kenya						
Tanganyika						
South Africa						
Central African Federation						
Burma						
Malaya						
Singapore						

Once you have completed the exercise try to identify the main reasons why the pace of change was different in each country.

EXTRACT 3

After the Second World War, a consensus emerged on British aims during the subsequent two decades of decolonisation: withdrawal from India should not appear to be forced by weakness, nor the first step in the dissolution of the Empire. Whatever the outcome, it would be presented to the public as the deliberate result of British policy. To the world at large, the British would be seen as remaining in control of events. The British aimed to control their own destiny, presiding over the rebirth of the Imperial system rather than its dissolution. They would reshape the old Imperial structure into a new framework of more or less equal partners. They would secure the collaboration of moderate nationalists by yielding control before the initiative passed to extremists. Influence would thus be retained by transferring power. Nationalism would be channelled into constructing nations in harmony with British interests. British imperialism would be sustained by means other than domination. It would be a 'managed decline'.

Adapted from 'The Dissolution of the British Empire' by Wm. Roger Louis (1999)

STUDY TIP

Each extract provides different reasons given in each extract for British decolonisation. Summarise each of the three arguments put forward and assess how convincing each is by applying your own contextual knowledge. Try to provide an overall summary conclusion.

 PRACTICE QUESTION

Evaluating historical extracts

Using your understanding of the historical context, assess how convincing the arguments in Extracts 1, 2 and 3 are, in relation to British decolonisation in the years 1947 to 1967.

STUDY TIP

To answer this question you need to consider the extent to which the British were able to control the manner and speed of their departure from their colonies, and the extent to which they were forced to leave before they had really planned to.

 PRACTICE QUESTION

'The British did not withdraw from their Empire between 1947 and 1967. They were pushed out of it.' Assess the validity of this view.

The Second World War and its immediate aftermath may have stimulated a revival in Britain's imperial creativity, but it was much too late. For all the idealism invested in the Commonwealth, it could not make the Empire a competitive option, although the British extricated themselves from Empire with real skill. Although British colonial rule in Africa was more purposeful in promoting economic development and in the provision of health and education in its last phases than it had ever been in the past, there is nothing to suggest that the British government or the British electorate were prepared to commit the resources that would have made any very significant impact on African problems. Nor could British colonial officials long retain the authority to impose their solutions on these problems in the political climate that was emerging after the Second World War. In short, it is hard to see the end of Empire as premature. A world that had been shaped by empires had outgrown even the largest of those empires.

Adapted from 'Empire in Retrospect' by P.J. Marshall (1996)

ACTIVITY

What does Marshall believe to have been the main driving force behind British colonial policy after the Second World War? As you read this chapter, look for other influences on colonial policy.

LEARNING OBJECTIVES

In this chapter you will learn about:

- British colonial policy and administration

- the Suez crisis and its impact

- international relations

- the Commonwealth.

KEY QUESTION

As you read this chapter, consider the following key questions:
- What influenced imperial policy?
- How important was the role of key individuals and groups and how were they affected by developments?

A CLOSER LOOK

The Commonwealth

Almost all of Britain's former colonies joined the British Commonwealth, the voluntary association which had originally been founded for the self-governing Dominions, although South Africa left in 1961. A new but short-lived Commonwealth Office was created in 1966. However, its functions were transferred to the Foreign Office in 1968 (which thus became the Foreign and Commonwealth Office).

Colonial policy and administration

Fig. 1 *A local election in a Gold Coast village, 1951*

CROSS-REFERENCE

To recap on the establishment of the Commonwealth, look back to Chapter 14, pages 139–140.

A CLOSER LOOK

Sir Ralph Furse, as Director of Colonial Services, reformed and professionalised colonial service. When he retired in 1948, only 66,000 of the 250,000 employees of the British Colonial Office were from Britain. More indigenous peoples were brought into administration and colonial service ceased to be a career option with its own training courses in 1954, being replaced by 'Her Majesty's Overseas Civil Service'.

The post-war years saw a change in British colonial policy in the wake of international, domestic and colonial upheavals. Despite the loss of India, Palestine and Burma in 1947 and 1948, in the 1950s (and particularly during the years of Churchill's premiership, 1951–55) there was a belief that Britain's future prosperity lay in trade with the Empire and **Commonwealth** rather than with Europe. It was felt that the Empire was important in the re-establishment of Britain's 'Great Power' status.

Colonial administrators thus found themselves taking on a rather different role in the 1950s. No longer were they just concerned with keeping order and balancing budgets but they were required to raise colonial production and modernise economies at speed. This often involved rapid improvements in agriculture, as well as steps towards industrialisation. The administration thus took on a new aggressive edge, sometimes known as 'economic colonialism'. The administrators' task was, above all, to protect trading commodities, guard vital supplies and destroy insurgents – particularly those associated with communism.

Since colonial administrators were required to be more proactive, this sometimes meant giving less, rather than more power to traditional indigenous leaders. In areas such as Kenya and the Rhodesias, for example, where Britain had formerly relied on devolving power to the tribal chiefs under the watch of a British official, this arrangement was no longer practical. Similarly, it was no longer possible to rely on the Malay sultans in the conditions of the Malayan Emergency. As Britain began to force economic change – advancing credit, sending in experts and settlers in a 'second colonial occupation' – local chieftains were case aside and the British colonial officials had to fall back on their own monopoly of force.

However, even as they sought to harness and develop the Empire, British leaders acknowledged the need to widen representative government and develop timetables for self-rule. Policy-makers believed that victory in war had vindicated Britain's superior political system and, given the emergent nationalism within the colonies, the British were ready (or perhaps were forced) to respond.

ACTIVITY

Look back to Chapters 18 and 19 and find examples to support the idea of a 'managed' colonial policy whereby the native inhabitants of the colonies were initially given a greater say over the management of their own territories in the years after the Second World War.

The Empire had already undergone a good deal of administrative transformation by 1947 and more followed in the 1950s. The White Dominions had been fully independent since 1931 and indigenous peoples – particularly in the more advanced areas where the native elites had received a European education – acquired an increasing say in the management of their own territories. The creation of legislative assemblies in the Gold Coast, Nigeria, the Central African Federation, Kenya, Malaya and elsewhere were all presented as gradual stepping stones towards the creation of fully independent states, even where representation of indigenous peoples was limited and constitutionally constrained by governors or other officers. In this way, the British government suggested that it 'managed' decolonisation on British terms.

The 'wind of change'

The idea of managed decolonisation was seen as consistent with a speech made by Harold Macmillan in 1960, in which he made it clear that Britain would grant independence to its African territories. His speech became known as the 'wind of change'. However, the interpretation put upon both the speech and government policy can be questioned.

The 'wind of change' speech

The speech given by British Prime Minister Harold Macmillan in Cape Town, South Africa on 3 February 1960 warned the White South African Parliament that, 'The wind of change is blowing through this continent and whether we like it or not, this growth of national consciousness is a political fact.' The significance of Macmillan's words may have been exaggerated by the press but the speech certainly appeared to suggest a shift in Conservative thinking and to signal Britain's intention to withdraw from its colonies. It was met with some surprise and accusations of betrayal by British Conservatives.

ACTIVITY

Find out more about Macmillan's 'Wind of Change' speech and the various reactions to it. Different groups could look at: a) the context and the speech itself, b) reaction in South Africa c) reaction within Britain and d) reaction from Black African nationalists. Use this information to create a diagram to illustrate the speech and its impact.

EXTRACT 2

A legend proclaims that, from October 1959 onwards, Macmillan and Iain Macleod, whom he appointed as Colonial Secretary, had decided to end British rule in Africa at maximum speed and hand over power to African nationalists; that their tough-minded liberalism averted disaster for Britain. In fact, neither had any clear view about how to proceed and each harboured doubts about the rapid transfer of power. What happened in Africa was not in the plan. The British had retained the appearance of power up to the point of departure, but not its reality. The influence they expected to yield while conceding instalments of political power quickly dribbled away. They discovered that no halfway house could be found between rule and abdication. Once the British decided that they could not risk using force, they had few cards to play against a determined opponent. They displayed, nonetheless, considerable skill in masking their weakness and in devising the institutional machinery that allowed a peaceful withdrawal.

Adapted from *Unfinished Empire* by John Darwin (2013)

ACTIVITY

Evaluating historical extracts

What is Darwin's view of the British management of decolonisation as given in Extract 2?

Colonial administrators tried to convey the idea of working in collaboration with nationalist movements to prepare colonies economically and politically for independence. However, the reality was not always quite like this. British claims to have the best interest of the colonial peoples at heart did not necessarily ring true and withdrawal was all too often bumpy. Although much skill was used to suggest that decolonisation came as a British 'gift', for which the countries concerned were duly grateful, the pace of change set by the British rarely satisfied the nationalists and in practice the British were often compelled to move much faster than they had originally intended.

CROSS-REFERENCE

British rule in Egypt c1865–90, including the importance of the Suez Canal, is covered in Chapter 1, pages 6. The granting of independence to Egypt is outlined in Chapter 13 page 125.

KEY TERM

Arab League: an organisation of North African and Middle Eastern Arab countries formed in 1945

KEY PROFILE

Colonel Gamal Abdel Nasser (1918–70) was an Egyptian soldier who organised a military coup in Egypt in 1952. He took over the reins of power in 1954, and became President of Egypt from 1956 until his death. He was renowned as a Middle Eastern Arab leader and a ferocious opponent of Western imperialism.

The Suez crisis and its impact

Fig. 2 *British Army guns near the canal zone during the Suez Crisis*

Developments in Egypt, 1947–56

By 1947, Britain was fearful about communist Russia's ambitions in the Middle East: an important British sphere of interest. Despite the withdrawal from Palestine, Britain still had 10,000 troops in the Suez Canal Zone (as agreed by the 1936 Anglo-Egyptian treaty) as well as control over Aden and Cyprus and air-force bases in Iraq. Britain also financed and provided officers for the Jordanian Army, giving the illusion of a strong presence. However, when the British tried to negotiate with the nationalist **Arab League** to resist communist infiltration, it found that the Arabs were not prepared to support Britain while Britain maintained its Suez garrisons and controlled the Sudan – where its presence was seen as an affront to Egypt, the leading Arab nation.

KEY PROFILE

Fig. 3 *Eden was born into a very conservative family*

Anthony Eden (1897–1977) was educated at Eton and Oxford and, after a distinguished military service record in the First World War, entered Parliament in 1923. He served as Foreign Secretary in 1935–38, in 1940–45, and again in 1951–55. Eden succeeded Churchill as Conservative Prime Minister in April 1955, but was already suffering from poor health. He made a serious tactical mistake in the Suez affair and resigned in January 1957, his reputation in tatters.

The years after 1947 saw constant skirmishing around the Canal Zone and in 1951 King Farouk of Egypt independently renounced the 1936 treaty and proclaimed himself King of the Sudan. In January 1952, however, Farouk himself was overthrown in a military coup by a group of army officers led by **Colonel Nasser**. **Anthony Eden**, Foreign Secretary in Churchill's Conservative government, immediately sought to negotiate with Egypt's new rulers and in 1953 an agreement was made on stages towards Sudanese independence. In 1954, the British also agreed to a phased withdrawal of troops from the Suez Canal Zone over the next 20 months, subject to certain rights of reoccupation in time of war. This concession not only reflected Britain's desire to improve Anglo-Arab relations, but also showed Britain's financial difficulties; the British could ill-afford to maintain their bases and fortify the Suez garrisons sufficiently to resist the constant nationalist guerrilla attacks.

ACTIVITY

Extension

In groups, undertake some research on Colonel Nasser, his ambitions and achievements. Present your findings to the class.

In return, the Egyptians promised the British:
- free access through the Suez Canal
- the maintenance of the former British bases in an operational condition
- to respect the independence of the **Suez Canal Company** (ownership of which would revert to the Egyptian government in 1968).

This settlement led to a constructive period of British diplomacy and Britain engineered the Baghdad Pact between Turkey, Pakistan, Iraq, Britain and Persia in 1955 to repel any Soviet threat to the Middle East. However, Nasser refused to sign this agreement and when the British tried to bring Jordan into the pact, put pressure on Jordan's young King Hussein to remain out. Fearing that the pact threatened Egyptian dominance, Nasser turned to communist Czechoslovakia for arms and signed an alliance with Syria. Anthony Eden, who succeeded Churchill as Prime Minister in April 1955 in the midst of these developments, was alarmed.

In June 1956, Nasser made himself President of Egypt. He was determined to establish Egypt as the leading power in the Middle East and his plans for a new Egypt centred on the construction of the **Aswan High Dam** which he hoped to make the core of a programme of irrigation, flood control and electrification. He had obtained promises of financial aid from both the West and from Russia in 1955, but in July 1956, the USA (followed by Britain and the World Bank) announced that they were withdrawing their funding because of Nasser's continued association with communist powers.

The Suez Canal crisis

On 16 July 1956 Nasser announced the nationalisation of the Suez Canal Company. This was a direct blow to the British government, which held approximately 44 per cent of the shares in the company, and an indirect attack on the position of the British in the Middle East. The British tried to use diplomatic pressure to persuade Nasser to reverse the decision, while preparing for military action in case of failure. The French were also outraged by the nationalisation, and invited Britain to join France in a joint assault on Egypt, in alliance with Israel, which was also affected by Nasser's hard-line attitude towards their state.

Although efforts continued to be made to resolve the issue by diplomacy through the UN, secret Anglo-French military discussions took place and attitudes hardened to a point in October when Eden believed that only the **removal of Nasser from power** would ensure the security of British and French interests in the Middle East.

A CLOSER LOOK

The Suez Canal Company was the company that actually ran the canal. It was a private company owned partly by the British government and partly by private shareholders, most of whom were French. Nasser promised to compensate the company but wanted the canal dues to help finance the Aswan Dam.

CROSS-REFERENCE

The Aswan High Dam was a development of the Aswan Dam which opened in 1902, as outlined in Chapter 8, page 76.

A CLOSER LOOK

Removal of Nasser

In 1956, Eden proclaimed in an emotional and somewhat irrational outburst that he wanted Nasser destroyed (he may even have said 'murdered'). This uncharacteristic declamation has been put down to a serious liver condition from which he suffered and his determination as he (as he judged Nasser to be another Hitler) not to repeat the mistake of the appeasers of the 1930s.

A plan was hatched through 'the Protocol of Sèvres' whereby Israel would attack Egypt on 29 October. On the following day, France and Britain would demand that both sides cease fighting and withdraw troops from the vicinity of the canal. This would be followed by a Franco-British invasion of the Canal Zone on 31 October, to 'defend' it.

The Israelis routed the Egyptian forces and forced them back through the Sinai Peninsula towards the canal, at which point Britain and France intervened in a supposed 'police' action. An Anglo-French force knocked out the Egyptian Air Force and landed at the north end of the canal but the Egyptians put up a solid resistance and blocked the canal with sunken ships.

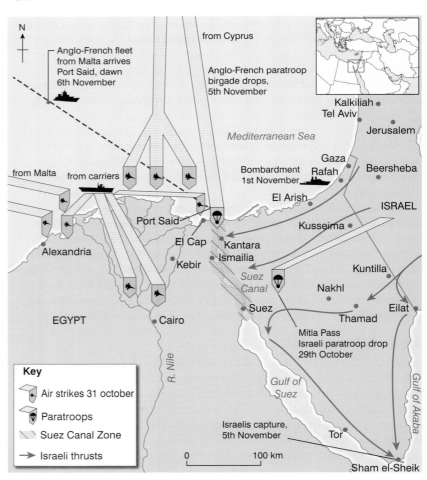

Fig. 4 *Events of the Suez crisis*

The British had miscalculated the international (and particularly the American) reaction. They had embarked on military operations without even informing the USA, and the USA immediately condemned the attack and refused to support sterling in the currency crisis which the war brought upon Britain. Isolated, even within the Commonwealth, the British announced a ceasefire within five days, and both Britain and France began to withdraw troops within weeks. Eden was forced to resign and a **United Nations** force moved in to clear the blocked canal and restore peace.

CROSS-REFERENCE

The United Nations is explained in Chapter 13, page 132.

The consequences of the Suez crisis

The long-term consequences of Suez for British imperial policy were profound. While it did not end Britain's belief in its 'world power' status, nor its commitment to defend residual imperial interests, nevertheless, after Suez, there was a growing realisation across the political spectrum in Britain that the days of empire were numbered.

- Never again would a British government seek to act alone in imperial or international affairs without the approval of, and close consultation with, the USA. In this respect, the illusion that Britain might by means of imperial revival or adjustment restore itself as a major independent power in the world was finally dispelled.
- It suggested to the nationalist movements seeking to achieve independence that if they pushed harder, the British could be forced to surrender. It therefore made Britain's task of containing the independence movements increasingly difficult.
- It called into question the whole credibility of plans to hold onto formal colonies in Africa and elsewhere and encouraged British politicians to accept that it was best to accede to nationalist demands for independence sooner rather than later.
- It dispelled the notion that Britain could 'manage' and control its retreat from Empire in ways that would preserve British power intact.

EXTRACT 3

In 1956, it fell to Anthony Eden to learn the harshest lesson about how the days of Empire were well and truly over. As the British were about to discover, the appearance of dominance in the Middle East was illusory, not so much because of anything observable, but because of a change in world opinion. When the military leader Colonel Gamal Abdel-Nasser seized control of the Suez Canal in July 1956, he brought Britain into a head-on collision with reality. This was the crisis which gave the British Empire its fatal wound. The Egyptian nationalisation of the Suez Canal was not an imperial question but an international one. But there was a sense of imperial anger at work in Britain; Egypt had, after all, spent decades as the Veiled Protectorate. Race played its part too. What finished off British delusions about the country's place in the world was not what happened in Cairo or London, but attitudes in Washington. The Suez blunder was at least as great an imperial blunder as the fall of Singapore. The toothlessness of the British lion had been demonstrated to the world.

Adapted from *Empire* by Jeremy Paxman (2012)

STUDY TIP

Consider the arguments that each author puts forward to explain, justify or criticise British colonial policy in these extracts. Try to summarise the overall view of the author before evaluating and questioning the extract in detail. Try to avoid commenting on the content itself, but use the detail in the extracts together with your own knowledge of the context to support what you write.

(AS LEVEL) PRACTICE QUESTION

Evaluating historical extracts

Using your understanding of the historical context, assess how convincing the arguments in Extracts 1, 2 and 3 are, in relation to British colonial policy in the years 1947 to 1967.

A CLOSER LOOK

The Middle East, 1956–67

Britain's position in the Middle East declined further over the years 1956 to 1967. Iraq left the Baghdad Pact in 1959, after the monarchy had been overthrown in 1958. After years of terrorism and violence between rival Turkish and Greek communities on Britain's Middle Eastern base in Cyprus, the island was granted independence in 1959 (although the British kept some bases). By the mid-1960s, Britain only controlled air bases in Libya and retained a protectorate over a few sheikdoms in the Persian Gulf, Aden and the South Arabian Federation. However, British rule was increasingly resisted by local nationalists, encouraged by the Egyptians, and they evacuated their Aden base in 1967.

A CLOSER LOOK

Cold War

Between c1949 and 1989, the two major super-powers, the USA and the USSR, and their respective allies, were rivals for world dominance. Each represented a different political and economic system: the USA was capitalist, while the Soviet Union was communist. The rivalry brought the constant threat of threat of global war, however. Both sides had nuclear weapons and war could mean global annihilation. Thus, a constant state of tension existed: a 'cold' war as opposed to a 'hot' war of actual fighting.

A CLOSER LOOK

The Truman Doctrine

In March 1947, President Harry S. Truman asked Congress for $400 million in military and economic assistance for Greece and Turkey and established the Truman Doctrine, by declaring, 'It must be the policy of the United States to support free peoples who are resisting attempted subjugation by armed minorities or by outside pressures.' This signalled America's determination to act as a global leader and end its long-standing policy of isolationism.

International relations

Fig. 5   *President Truman signing the authorisation for Marshall Aid, 1947*

Between 1947 and 1967, British imperial policy was moulded by a changed international scene. The USA and USSR had emerged from World War II as 'superpowers' and they were to dictate international developments in the post-war world. Nevertheless the emergence of a state of **Cold War** between the US-dominated capitalist West and the USSR-led communist East initially gave a renewed impetus to British imperialism.

Despite American anti-imperialist attitudes, it suited the USA to have a strong Britain, in a position to resist communist advances in all quarters of the globe. America was therefore prepared to turn a blind eye to the post-war re-imposition of British control over its colonies (even indirectly financing it through low interest loans) – particularly where this involved driving out communist insurgents.

In the Balkan area, the USA was even prepared to step in when the British support for the monarchists fighting communists in Greece could no longer be sustained because of financial considerations. By the **Truman Doctrine** of 1947, the USA pledged its help to countries 'resisting subjugation' (implying communist subjugation) and provided financial and military aid to prop up Greece and Turkey as Britain withdrew from the region.

However, as the state of Cold War hardened from 1947, the USA became more fearful of communist expansion in areas such as the Middle East and Africa and believed that the best way of **preventing** communism becoming an attractive option to nationalist movements was to build up these countries as stable and economically prosperous areas – dependent not on Britain but on American loans, capitalist practices and world trade. Britain was in no position to resist such an attitude.

Britain had emerged from the Second World War as a strong ally of the USA and liked to think of itself as an equal partner (despite Suez their association was referred to as a **'special relationship'**), Britain was, in practice, limited by its financial and military dependence on the USA. The US **Marshall Plan** of 1948–52, for example, provided Britain with $3.3 billion of support, while it was the USA's economic pressure that forced Britain and France to end their invasion of Egypt in 1956. It was clear by the 1960s that, without US backing, the British were in no position to combat nationalist independence movements.

Britain also relied on the North Atlantic Treaty Organisation (**NATO**) of 1949 and America's nuclear capacity (despite developing its own nuclear weapons from 1952) for defence. Britain co-operated with the USA in the Korean War of 1950–53, but, despite a United Nations mandate, the command was American.

A CLOSER LOOK

USA/UK co-operation over defence

The Anglo-American Mutual Defence Agreement signed in 1958 provided American assistance for the development of a British nuclear arsenal. In April 1963, US President John F. Kennedy and Harold Macmillan signed the Polaris Sales Agreement. The USA agreed to supply Britain with Polaris ballistic missiles for use in Royal Navy submarines.

Britain's weakness and reliance on the USA became increasingly obvious. Even Britain's relations with its old 'White' Dominions were affected by changes in Britain's global position after 1945. Whereas the Dominions had previously looked to Britain as guarantors of their safety; they increasingly turned to the USA. The formation of the South East Asia Treaty Organisation (**SEATO**) in 1954, bringing together Australia, France, New Zealand, Pakistan, the Philippines, Thailand, Britain and the USA in the wake of the Korean War, was an acknowledgement of the need for an American-led protective alliance.

Until the 1960s, Britain's hopes of reconstituting and preserving its Empire kept it apart from the **European Economic Community (EEC)**, which brought Belgium, France, Italy, Luxembourg, the Netherlands and West Germany together in an economic union in 1957. By the time Britain realised that its economic future lay more with Europe than with the Empire, the French under de Gaulle conspired to keep Britain out. British membership of EEC was vetoed twice in 1963 and 1967 and Britain only joined in 1973.

International affairs thus had a major impact on Britain's imperial role – in both bolstering and weakening British commitment. From the mid-1960s, Britain tried to adopt a role as the guardian of Western interests 'East of Suez': an area from East Africa to Australia and including the Persian Gulf and former British Malaya and Borneo. Occasionally, British

KEY TERM

'special relationship': a close political and diplomatic association which stemmed from the shared cultural and historical heritage of the United States with its former 'master', Britain

Marshall Plan: a programme of US economic aid for the reconstruction of post-Second World War from Europe 1948 to 1952

KEY TERM

NATO: the North Atlantic Treaty Organisation, set up in 1949 as an inter-governmental organisation but with an American Supreme Allied Commander

SEATO: the Southeast Asia Treaty Organisation, set up in 1954, was a counterpart to NATO for the collective defence of South East Asia against communism. It did not, however, have a joint command

CROSS-REFERENCE

The EEC is introduced in Chapter 19, page 179.

leaders still spoke of India as falling within a British sphere of influence, but this was little more than an illusion. In January 1968 Labour Prime Minister Harold Wilson announced that British troops would be withdrawn from major military bases in South East Asia, the Persian Gulf and the Maldives in a final acknowledgement that Britain's days as a 'world policeman' were over.

The Commonwealth

Fig. 6 *Queen Elizabeth II poses with Commonwealth ministers at Buckingham Palace, 1962*

The Commonwealth had originally been conceived in the 1920s as an 'exclusive club' of White Dominions enjoying a high degree of domestic self-rule. It was given increased status by the Statute of Westminster of 1931 which established legal self-rule for the Dominions. By implication these were now part of the 'British Commonwealth of Nations', a status which implied theoretical equality with Britain, although in practice **much of the real power continued to reside in London**.

Originally, implicit in Commonwealth status was acceptance of the sovereignty of the British monarch over all countries in the Commonwealth (a principle which led to the exclusion of Ireland when it became a republic in 1949). However, the meaning of the Commonwealth evolved significantly in the period after the Second World War, when independence for India, Pakistan and Burma revived the issue of Commonwealth membership. The British came to see Commonwealth as a way of surrendering the costs of formal imperial control whilst maintaining informal ties which would help protect Britain's global economic interests and influence. However, not all former colonies thought the same way.

Both India and Pakistan joined in 1947, although Burma refused to join in 1948, maintaining its hostility to Britain. Nehru's decision to declare India a Republic led to a change the rules for Commonwealth membership in April 1949. Membership was broadened so as to allow a wider range of regimes to join – most importantly republics. The British monarch became a 'symbol of the free association of its independent member nations and as such, the 'Head of the Commonwealth'. This was subtly but crucially different to claiming that the monarch enjoyed royal authority over each former colony.

The Commonwealth served a purpose in allowing some continuation of British global power by means other than formal empire. Britain liked to think of the Commonwealth as a family of 'friendly' nations around the world, which could lend critical and qualified support, or even mediate in disputes, as **Robert Menzies**, Prime Minister of Australia, attempted to do over **Suez**. The Commonwealth thus became a body of 'free and equal' states, with no legal obligation to one another but united by their history and their shared 'British' values of democracy and human rights. It thus acquired an idealistic purpose to uphold the 'rule of law', although the scale and extent of its power remained questionable.

Membership of the Commonwealth to 1967

Country	Joined
Australia	December 1931
Barbados	November 1966
Botswana	September 1966
Canada and Newfoundland	December 1931
Cyprus	March 1961
The Gambia	February 1965
Ghana	March 1957
Guyana (formerly British Guiana)	May 1966
India	August 1947
Ireland	December 1931; left April 1949
Jamaica	August 1962
Kenya	December 1963
Lesotho	October 1966
Malawi	July 1964
Malaysia	August 1957
Malta	September 1964
New Zealand	December 1931
Nigeria	October 1960
Pakistan	August 1947
Sierra Leone	April 1961
Singapore	August 1965
South Africa	December 1931; left May 1961
Dominion of Ceylon (Sri Lanka)	February 1948
Tanganyika (became Zanzibar, then Tanzania from 1964)	December 1961
Trinidad and Tobago	August 1962
Uganda	October 1962
Zambia	October 1964

A CLOSER LOOK

Menzies and Suez

Although the Panama Canal was more important to Australia and New Zealand than Suez, by 1956, the Australian Prime Minister Robert Menzies and New Zealand's Sidney Holland still gave support to Britain in the early weeks after Nasser's seizure of the Suez Canal, based on past wartime solidarity, to protect a 'lifeline' to Britain. Holland hinted that New Zealand might send troops to assist Britain and in August, Menzies travelled to London, joined in Cabinet discussions and spoke on the BBC. Menzies subsequently led a mission to negotiate with Nasser in September 1956 which failed.

ACTIVITY

1. Re-order the chart above horizontally, according to the date when each former colony joined the Commonwealth.
2. Divide these countries between the members of your group. Research the factors that brought each country its independence and, pooling information, provide a few brief details below your time line.

Summary

In the years 1947 to 1967, colonial policy and administration was mainly concerned with managing Britain's remaining Empire in a way that would maximise its economic value to Britain, assure its loyalty and assist in moves towards independence. Britain's international position had changed and while it took time for the British to accept that their future lay less with the Empire than with Europe, they conceived a means to preserve something of their old

Empire through the development of the British Commonwealth. Britain's last attempt to flaunt its imperial muscle really took place in 1956, in the Suez affair, but after the humiliating climb-down that followed, Britain was forced to come to terms with its loss of status and accept the 'wind of change'.

STUDY TIP

You will need to define what is meant by 'changed international circumstances' and also consider other factors which affected the break-up of the British Empire after 1945, with reference to earlier chapters. Look at a range of specific examples of decolonisation to evaluate how far the international scene influenced British policies.

PRACTICE QUESTION

'The break-up of the British Empire in the years 1945 to 1967 was the result of changed international circumstances.' Assess the validity of this view.

21 Trade and commerce

EXTRACT 1

Far from being abandoned after 1947, the Empire was repositioned in Africa, Malaya and, informally, in the Middle East. These regions were sources of vital supplies and contributed through their dollar earning. Britain's new colonial policy needs to be interpreted with Britain's economic priorities in mind. By forming the Colonial Development Corporation in 1947, Britain hoped to promote the production of food and other raw materials urgently needed at home and use the colonies to earn dollars on the world market. It is no coincidence that the areas over which the British most wanted to maintain imperial control were the regions of greatest economic value in the period of post-war reconstruction.

Adapted from *British Imperialism* by P.J. Cain and A.G. Hopkins (2001)

ACTIVITY

Evaluating historical extracts

1. What do Cain and Hopkins suggest, in Extract 1, about British attitudes to the Empire in the aftermath of the Second World War?
2. As you read this chapter, consider the importance of economic factors in the post-war history of the British Empire.

LEARNING OBJECTIVES

In this chapter you will learn about:

- trade and commerce
- post-war reconstruction.

KEY QUESTION

As you read this chapter, consider the following key questions:
- What influenced imperial policy?
- What part did economic factors play in the development of the British Empire?

Trade and commerce

Fig. 1 *The Royal Docks in London early 1950s, where a thriving trade with the Commonwealth took place*

Between 1947 and 1967 there was a dramatic change in the importance of Empire as a supplier of British imports and a market for British produce. Until the 1960s, the Empire and Commonwealth were extremely important for Britain's international trading position. They provided essential imports of food and raw materials at a time when Britain's reserves of foreign exchange were too limited to source imports from many other parts of the world. A great deal of British investment also went to the Empire. In 1956 approximately 58 per cent of all overseas investments in the UK in shares and securities were in Empire companies and governments. However, from the 1960s, other parts of the world, and especially Western Europe, became more important to Britain, as seen in the charts below.

	1948		1954		1960		1965	
Imports	£m	%	£m	%	£m	%	£m	%
World	2077	100	3379	100	4655	100	5763	`00
Common-wealth	933	44.9	1634	48.3	1510	32.4	1720	29.8
Western Europe	427	20.5	818	24.2	1136	24.4	1762	30.6

Table 1 *British imports 1948–65*

	1948		1954		1960		1965	
Exports	£m	%	£m	%	£m	%	£m	%
World	1639	100	2755	100	3789	100	4897	100
Common-weath	757	46.1	1333	48	1353	35.7	1365	27.9
Western Europe	407	24.8	776	28	1009	26.6	1593	32.5

Table 2 *British exports 1948–65*

ACTIVITY

In pairs or small groups, discuss the following questions:
1. What happened to trade with the Commonwealth in the years 1948 to 1965? What trends can you discern regarding the rate of growth or shrinkage?
2. Imagine it is 1960, and you are a junior official in the civil service. You have been asked for your opinion about how important trade with the Commonwealth and Western Europe are to Britain and what you anticipate future trends will be. What would you say? (Try to use your contextual knowledge from Chapters 20 and 21 to explain your thinking)

ACTIVITY

Evaluating historical extracts

According to Extract 2, what change took place in Britain's attitude to trade with the colonies from the mid-1950s?

EXTRACT 2

From the mid 1950s to mid 1960s the trading ties between the colonies and Britain declined as Britain edged closer to Western Europe and North America. International trade in manufactured goods and services became more valuable than that in raw materials and food. The colonies consequently became less attractive to British exporters looking for markets with higher incomes. There was also more competition for Britain from other industrial countries who were supplying goods to Britain's colonies and ex-colonies by the 1960s. Britain's decision to apply for membership of the EEC both reflected its rapidly expanding trade with nearby Europe the decline of that with its far flung imperial trading partners. It also reinforced this trend, even though Britain's entry to Europe was delayed until 1973.

Adapted from *Colonialism and Development: Britain and its Tropical Colonies, 1850–1960* by Michael Havinden and David Meredith (1993)

The European economy recovered from **the war** much more quickly and impressively than might have been expected. This was partly thanks to **US Marshall Aid**, the continuing support offered by the USA and the climate of liberal democracy which favoured private enterprise. Advances in science and technology as well as changes in industrial relations also played their part. The result was that by the mid-1950s there was full employment throughout Europe, growth rates were high and living standards, at least in the West, were rising rapidly.

The British, trusting to their traditional reliance on the Empire, had chosen not to join the EEC in 1957 and had, instead, set up their own rival trading bloc of European non-EEC members–EFTA (the European Free Trade Association). However, the EEC flourished and the British were increasingly torn between a future based on a Commonwealth of global trade links and one in which trade and economic relations with Europe would become the basis of future policy.

With exports to Europe outstripping those to Empire in the early 1960s, Britain applied for membership in 1963 and again in 1967, only to be rejected partly because the British insisted on special concessions being allowed for British commerce with the Commonwealth. However, the **sterling devaluation of 1967** destroyed the old 'Sterling Area' by weakening international faith in the value of sterling and hit at Britain's global imperial pretensions. Eventually Britain was to join in 1973.

CROSS-REFERENCE

The economic impact of the Second World War and policies adopted from 1945 to 1947 are discussed in Chapter 15, pages 149–150.

CROSS-REFERENCE

US Marshall Aid is outlined in Chapter 20, page 199.

A CLOSER LOOK

The sterling devaluation, 1967

In 1967, Harold Wilson's Labour government announced that it was lowering the exchange rate so the pound became worth $2.40, down from $2.80; this was a cut of just over 14 per cent. The decision was taken reluctantly, in the face of a balance of payments crisis (Britain was spending more on imports than it was gaining from exports). It was designed to cut Britain's deficit by making British exports cheaper (although it made imports dearer).

Fig. 2 *Newspaper headlines announce the sterling devaluation*

Post-war reconstruction

The USA's economic predominance after the Second World War made that country the main supplier of commodities to the wider world. However, in order to buy vitally needed goods, Britain needed to earn dollars and build up foreign exchange reserves with which to pay for imports.

The British initially met this challenge by continuing rationing at home, to cut the cost of food imports, and prioritising British industrial production for the export rather than the domestic market. They also tried to develop the productive and export capacities of the colonies, particularly in Africa, where the relative under-development of local resources offered huge opportunities

KEY TERM

Hard Currency Pool: a collective pool of dollars earned by the Sterling Area

CROSS-REFERENCE

The Tanganyika Groundnuts Scheme is covered in Chapter 19, page 182.

The State of Emergency in Malaya is discussed in Chapter 19, page 187.

ACTIVITY

Evaluating historical extracts

According to Extract 3, in what ways could Britain be accused of failing to formulate an effective economic policy for its colonies in the post-war years?

for growth. This was in order both to increase dollar reserves from colonial sales and to ensure a steady supply of goods to Britain from within the sterling area, thus saving precious reserves of dollars and other scarce foreign currencies.

The Colonial Development and Welfare Acts of 1940 and 1945 were used to expand agricultural production and promote new technology in the colonies and, in 1948, the Colonial Development Corporation was set up to co-ordinate major projects and develop self-sustaining agriculture, industry and trade. It was renamed the Commonwealth Development Corporation (CDC) in 1963.

Colonies in:	1946	1950	1956
West Africa	£43.1	£167.1	£228.5
East Africa	£30.5	£75.7	£123.4
Central Africa	£32.0	£86.4	£181.7
Asia	£191.4	£819.6	£815.1
Pacific	£2.6	£5.6	£8.8
Caribbean	£20.0	£63.8	£127.5
TOTAL	£319.6	£1218.2	£1485.0

Table 3 *Value of exports from British colonies 1946–56 (£ millions)*

Not all the colonial development schemes were successful. The Tanganyika Groundnuts Scheme launched in 1948, for example, was an abject failure. However, Malay rubber proved a crucial dollar earner, and as a member of the Sterling Area, Malaya became a major contributor to the **Hard Currency Pool**. This helps explain why the British would not countenance immediate independence for Malaya, and responded so fiercely to the communist terrorist attacks against economic targets there in 1948.

The impact of Britain's policies of post-war reconstruction was to prove long-lasting – as suggested in Extract 3.

EXTRACT 3

British colonial development policies remained 'Empire-centred' until the late 1950s and 1960s, and one effect was to sustain the pattern of economic activity that had been established in the late nineteenth century well into the post-war era. As a result, many Commonwealth countries still relied on a narrow range of primary produce for two-thirds to three-quarters of their commodity exports even in the mid-1960s. Furthermore, a relatively small number of Commonwealth producers remained major world suppliers of particular raw materials and foodstuffs, with Britain an important market. The most intense imperial trade relationships were in meat and dairy produce, especially between New Zealand and Britain. The dominance of the export sector in primary produce in the economies of Britain's colonies and ex-colonies in West Africa, South Asia, and South-East Asia showed the limitations of British colonial economic policies.

Adapted from 'Imperialism and After: The Economy of the Empire on the Periphery' by B.R. Tomlinson (1999)

Summary

Britain remained heavily reliant on trade and commerce with the Empire and Commonwealth until the 1960s. Policies were put in place to develop colonial agriculture and industry, and it was assumed that such colonial development would benefit and support the British economy. However, Britain's trade with Europe and the USA also grew strongly and by 1967 a clear change of direction away from the Empire had already taken place.

 A **LEVEL** | **PRACTICE QUESTION**

Evaluating historical extracts

Using your understanding of the historical context, assess how convincing Extracts 1, 2 and 3 are, in relation to British economic policies affecting the colonies, Empire and Commonwealth between 1947 and 1967.

 A **LEVEL** | **PRACTICE QUESTION**

To what extent were trade and commerce with the Empire and Commonwealth of major importance to Britain in the years 1947 to 1967?

22 Attitudes to empire – the role and influence of individuals

LEARNING OBJECTIVES

In this chapter you will learn about:

- the role and influence on attitudes to empire of nationalist leaders

- the role and influence of colonial administration.

ACTIVITY

Evaluating historical extracts

Summarise Easton's view in Extract 1 in a sentence.

KEY QUESTION

As you read this chapter consider the following key question:
- What influenced imperial policy?
- How important was the role of key individuals and groups and how were they affected by developments?

CROSS-REFERENCE

The events that led to independence in the Malay Peninsula and Singapore are covered in Chapter 19, page 187.

EXTRACT 1

It would be a mistake to think that the European powers gave independence to their colonies after the Second World War. There were certainly international pressures which helped bring about decolonisation, as well as domestic considerations within the imperial nations. But independence was wrested from the grasp of the imperialists – not freely surrendered. It was the nationalists who held the whip hand for once – not the imperialists. The winning of independence by the former colonies was in a very large measure the work of the nationalists in the colonies themselves. Their 'positive action' and agitation, including in some instances armed insurrection, gradually made it clear to the colonial powers that, in the existing state of world opinion, it was not worth their while to attempt to hold the colony by force and that it was better to retreat with the best face possible, salvaging what they could and trying to retain as much good will as possible for the post-independence era.

Adapted from *The Rise and Fall of Western Colonialism* by Stewart C. Easton (1964)

Colonial development and decolonisation after 1947 were influenced by both the nationalist leaders campaigning for greater indigenous involvement in government or independence, and the colonial administrators in London and in the colonies themselves, tasked with ruling and guiding colonial development.

The role and influence of nationalist leaders

The years after the Second World War brought economic developments and social change, including new educational opportunities in the colonies. Nevertheless, a growth in skills, knowledge and understanding of the wider world among the elites, coupled with a higher purchasing power (which outstripped the supply of food and other necessities, so causing inflation) among the wider indigenous population, were fatal ingredients for dissatisfaction with imperial rule. Nationalist leaders emerged who were ready to challenge British domination.

Case study: nationalist leaders and groups in the Malay Peninsula

Onn bin Ja'afar (1895–1962) was the founder of the United Malays National Organisation (UMNO). This campaigned to rally the Malays against the Malayan Union, established by the British in 1946 to unite British possessions (except Singapore). He became UMNO's president in May 1946. Drawing on the hostility of many of the traditional Malayan rulers he organised rallies and amassed sufficient public support to force a British climb-down in favour of the 'Federation of Malay States' in 1948. One of his supporters was Tunku Abdul Rahman (1903–90), a law student who first studied in England and was to become Malaya's first Prime Minister after independence in 1957.

Nationalist leaders in the Malay Peninsula were driven by ideology and race. Onn faced opposition from Malayan Communists (members of the MCP) under Chin Peng (1924–2013), a middle-class Chinaman who had been awarded an OBE by the British for his services in wartime. He was also opposed by Tan Cheng Lock (1883–1960), a well-to-do Chinese businessman educated in Singapore who led the Malaysian Chinese Association (MCA), formed in 1949. Tan was fiercely anti-communist and was trusted by the British colonial officials. He fought for constitutional change and inter-ethnic co-operation.

However, nationalism in Malaya brought the 'Malayan Emergency', a violent guerrilla war between 1948 and 1960 between armed forces of the British Commonwealth and the Malayan National Liberation Army (MNLA), the military arm of the Malayan Communist Party (MCP).

Tan decided that partnership with UMNO (in 1954) was the best way of protecting the Malaysian Chinese and both Onn and Tan participated in the successful negotiations for independence from the British in 1957.

Case studies: nationalist leaders in Africa

West Africa: Kwame Nkrumah

Kwame Nkrumah (1909–72), from the African Gold Coast, was, in many respects, typical of many post-war nationalist leaders. Educated in a Catholic mission school and a government teacher training college, he was the direct product of colonial institutions. Studying in the capital, Accra, he was exposed to radical Western ideas, and while continuing his studies at various universities in the USA in the 1930s and 1940s he became involved in radical Black activism and deeply politicised. In 1945 he went to London, where he helped to organise the fifth Pan-African Congress in Manchester and by 1947 he already had such an international reputation that he was invited, on his return to the Gold Coast, to become General Secretary of the United Gold Coast Convention (UGGC), established by the wealthy lawyer J.B. Danquah with the goal of national independence.

Briefly imprisoned in 1948, Nkrumah built on his growing popularity to form a new political group, the Convention People's Party (CPP). Such was its success that he became Prime Minister between 1953 and 1957, during which time he moved the Gold Coast towards full independence as Ghana in 1957. Ghana became a Republic in 1960 and Nkrumah held power until a military coup in 1966 (later revealed to have been backed by the American CIA). He lived the last six years of his life in exile in Guinea.

Nkrumah became a figurehead for African nationalism throughout the continent. He gathered a coterie of African, Caribbean and Black American intellectuals and politicians around him and helped to coordinate various African independence movements.

His political philosophy encompassed a number of key ideas, which spread and were shared not only by other African nationalists, but also by intellectuals in the more advanced countries, including Britain itself. These included:

- pan-Africanism – a belief that African peoples should work together politically for their collective common good. Nkrumah was a founder member of the **Organisation of African Unity** in 1963.
- Marxist socialism – a belief in the redistribution of wealth to give the poor control over their own destinies. Although he did not align himself with the communist world or the USSR, Nkrumah argued that the British Empire served the interests of the international capitalists, who were responsible for the poverty, inequality and oppression throughout Africa; and that British rule was an exploitative and outdated form of government which was holding Africa back.
- popular nationalism – Nkrumah associated himself with the demands for change emerging from below.

CROSS-REFERENCE

The events that led to independence for the African colonies are covered in Chapter 19, pages 178–184.

KEY TERM

Organisation of African Unity: An organisation representing states across Africa dedicated to improving the life of Africans. It was disbanded in 2002 and replaced by a new organisation with many of the same aims – the African Union

- responsible leadership – despite his radical ideas, Nkrumah understood the importance of developing a working relationship with the British to gain their confidence and support, in order to establish a stable state.

West Africa: Dr Nnamdi Azikiwe

Fig. 1 *Azikiwe was also a member of the Queen's Privy Council*

Like Nkrumah, **Dr Nnamdi Azikiwe of Nigeria (1904–96)** enjoyed a Western education in Nigeria followed by further study in the USA, where he was exposed to radical ideas. He developed a strong sense of African nationalism, working as a journalist, first briefly in the Gold Coast and from 1937 in Lagos, Nigeria. He emerged as a champion of Nigerian nationalism in the 1940s, helping to create the National Council of Nigeria and the Cameroons (NCNC) in 1944 and becoming its leader.

The demands of developing a nationalist movement in Nigeria were much greater than in the Gold Coast. Nigeria was starkly divided on religious and **ethnic** grounds. The north, containing about half the population, was largely Muslim, and dominated by the Hausa and Fulani; the west was dominated by the Yoruba and the east by the Ibo. The result was that several different nationalist political groups emerged: the NCNC which was dominated by the Ibo, the 'Yoruba Action Group', and the Northern People's Congress (NPC) which was largely based in the Muslim north.

The creation of an independent Nigeria demanded a federal solution which meant that Azikiwe had to be able to work with both his nationalist rivals and the British to create a viable and stable Nigerian state. It took all of Azikiwe's bargaining skills to prevent the colony from sliding into anarchy and breaking up – but he secured independence in 1960 and by negotiating a deal with the NPC was able to establish Nigeria's first government with himself as President. As in the case of Nkrumah, his ability to compromise and to win the trust of a variety of committed nationalists from the various nationalist communities, as well as the British, was crucial in facilitating the peaceful transition to independence. Crucially, he, more than anyone, was able to persuade the British that it was possible for the various regional ethnic groups to work successfully within a federal system, and that British imperial rule was not essential to avoid ethnic conflict and civil war.

East Africa: Jomo Kenyatta

Jomo Kenyatta (c1891–1978) was a member of the Kikuyu from British East Africa. The son of illiterate parents, he was educated in a Scottish missionary school – paying his way by working for white settlers. He worked as a clerk in Nairobi in the 1920s and became interested in politics, joining the Kikuyu Central Association (KCA) which had been set up to defend the Kikuyu land-holdings that were being encroached upon by white settlers. A visit to London in 1929 turned into a 17-year stay (with a brief visit to Moscow following a short-lived interest in communism). In England he developed his education, authored books including *Facing Mount Kenya* and grew determined to fight for the independence of his country. He returned home in 1946 to become principal of Kenya's teachers' college and, in 1947, became president of the Kenya Africa Union (KAU). From 1948 to 1951 he toured and lectured around the country campaigning for the return of land given to white settlers and for independence within three years.

However, hostility to white people led to the emergence of the **Mau Mau rebellion** in 1951, a radical anti-colonial movement. This led to the banning of the KAU and the declaration of a State of Emergency in 1952. As the acknowledged leader of the Kikuyu, who were at the centre of the Mau Mau revolt, Kenyatta was arrested in October 1952 and accused of 'managing and being a member' of the Mau Mau Society. Kenyatta's defence lawyer argued that the white settlers were trying to scapegoat Kenyatta and that there was no evidence tying him to the Mau Mau (which was probably true), but he was nevertheless sentenced in 1953 to seven years' imprisonment with hard labour.

A CLOSER LOOK

One of Jomo Kenyatta's famous sayings is: 'When the Missionaries arrived, the Africans had the land and the Missionaries had the Bible. They taught us how to pray with our eyes closed. When we opened them, they had the land and we had the Bible'.

A CLOSER LOOK

Even Kenyatta himself was uncertain as to his date of birth. No formal birth records of native Africans were kept in Kenya at that time.

CROSS-REFERENCE

For more details on the Mau Mau rebellion, look ahead to Chapter 24, pages 233–235.

There were public meetings and petitions organised to demand his release and in May 1960 (while still in goal) he was elected the leader of the Kenya African National Union (KANU), the successor to KAU, whilst still in gaol. The State of Emergency was lifted in January 1960 and after release in 1961, he immediately began negotiations with the British which led to Kenya gaining independence in December 1963. Initially, Kenyatta served as Prime Minister, but in 1964, the country became a Republic and Kenyatta became President; a position he held for 14 years until his death.

Kenyatta brought about a gradual Africanisation of the government, keeping many colonial civil servants in their positions until they could be gradually replaced by Kenyans. However, while he helped forge a relatively prosperous capitalist state and oversaw a peaceful land reform process, he failed to mould Kenya into a homogeneous multi-ethnic state. He ensured Kikuyu dominance over other groups and placed several of his Kikuyu tribesmen in the most powerful state and security offices, where they (like Kenyatta himself) enjoyed a wealthy life-style and persecuted political opponents. Kenyatta created a one-party state in 1964 and had the Constitution amended to expand his own powers in 1966.

EXTRACT 2

There emerged a new style of African leadership in the east of the continent after 1945. The first stage began soon after the war when the earlier leadership of illiterate workers was replaced by younger, more educated men in the cities, such as Mombasa and Nairobi. A similar change followed more slowly in the rural areas, where the chiefs lost out to a newer, younger generation of leaders: the school teachers, the clerks and the traders who were outside the traditional authority structure. The second stage occurred in the 1950s, with the appearance of a new type of politician, the nationalist, with a strong, more specific anti-colonial commitment. Many still in their twenties, they were better educated than the earlier leaders. Some had been abroad for part of their education. The majority of these new leaders were the second generation of the emergent elite: teachers, cooperative officials, trade unionists, clerks, and some professional men. These were the men who built the political parties; who edited the party newspapers; and who moulded rural and urban discontent into a base from which they demanded power.

Adapted from 'East and Central Africa' by Cherry Gertzel (1984)

Central Africa: Apolo Milton Obote

Fig. 2 *Obote, President of Uganda, 1966–71*

Apolo Milton Obote (1925–2005) was the son of a tribal chief from southern Uganda. He was educated at a Protestant missionary school and Makarere University. He went to Kenya as a construction worker in the 1950s and there became politicised. He had socialist political ideas and, returning to Uganda in 1956, he joined the Uganda National Congress (UNC). In 1957 he was elected to the Colonial Legislative Council. Obote manoeuvered between different political factions and party amalgamations and, in 1962, was appointed by the Governor-General, Sir Walter Coutts, as Prime Minister of an independent Uganda. In 1963 the position of Governor-General was replaced by the ceremonial presidency of Mutesa, the King of Buganda, but Obote held the real power.

Obote ruled in an increasingly arbitrary way, with his power maintained by the Ugandan military, under the control of Idi Amin. Kenyans were forced out of leadership positions and in 1966, following accusations of gold-smuggling, he suspended the constitution and declared himself President. Several members of his cabinet, who were leaders of rival factions, were arrested and detained without charge and Mutesa was forced to flee into exile. In 1967, Obote's power was cemented when the parliament agreed a new constitution which abolished the federal structure established on independence.

Obote was overthrown by Idi Amin in 1971, but regained power after Amin was in turn overthrown in 1979. His second rule was marred by repression and by the deaths of many civilians as a result of civil war. Obote serves as an example of a nationalist leader whose apparently genuine commitment to his people's freedom became tainted by power, leading to post-colonial violence and corruption.

South Africa: Nelson Mandela

Fig. 3 *Mandela giving a speech to the African National Congress*

Nelson Mandela (1913–2013) was a different type of nationalist: one who was determined to achieve equal rights for black people and end the apartheid regime established in South Africa in 1948. He came from the Xhosa tribe and Thembu royal family and was educated by Methodist missionaries who gave him the name Nelson. He became involved in anti-colonial politics whilst studying law at Fort Hare and the Witwatersrand universities. He helped to form the youth league of the African National Congress (ANC) in 1944 and rose through the ranks. He supported the radical mass-based policy, the 'Programme of Action', in 1949 and in 1952 was chosen to head the 'Defiance Campaign' of civil disobedience against unjust laws.

ACTIVITY

Find out more about the activities of Spear of the Nation (Umkhonto weSizwe). You could create a poster for this organisation, showing its beliefs and methods.

A CLOSER LOOK

Mandela established South Africa's first black law firm in 1952, representing disenfranchised black people. It was his involvement in the ANC, however, that led to arrests and a treason trial (1956–61), during which the ANC was banned in 1960. Nelson Mandela became a national figure, speaking out for a national strike at an 'All in Africa Conference', although the strike never actually came about.

Mandela was influenced by Marxism and secretly joined the South African Communist Party (SACP) and sat on its Central Committee. In association with the SACP he co-founded the militant Umkhonto weSizwe (Spear of the Nation) in 1961, which became the ANC's armed wing and led a sabotage campaign against the apartheid government.

Nelson Mandela secretly left South Africa in 1962, travelling around Africa and visiting England to gain support for his armed struggle. He received military training in Morocco and Ethiopia and returned to South Africa in July 1962 – only to be promptly arrested, charged with leaving the country without a permit and inciting workers to strike. He was convicted and sentenced to five years' imprisonment. However, while he was in prison, a police raid on the ANC's Rivonia hideout brought a further conviction. In October 1963, Nelson Mandela and his colleagues were again prosecuted in the Rivonia Trial, where he gave his most famous speech on 20 April 1964:

SOURCE 1

I have fought against white domination, and I have fought against black domination. I have cherished the ideal of a democratic and free society in which all persons live together in harmony and with equal opportunities. It is an ideal which I hope to live for and to achieve. But if needs be, it is an ideal for which I am prepared to die.

In June 1964 Nelson Mandela and seven others were sentenced to life imprisonment on Robben Island, off Cape Town. Mandela served 27 years in prison but he was eventually to emerge in 1990, after an international campaign in his support, to be hailed as a great moral champion and inspirational leader. He became President in 1994, serving until 1999.

CROSS-REFERENCE

Another example of a nationalist leader is Ian Smith in Southern Rhodesia, who is profiled in Chapter 24, page 240. You might like to find out more about the career, beliefs and actions of Ian Smith; your findings will help you with the activity below.

ACTIVITY

Extension

When Nelson Mandela died in 2013, many newspapers published obituaries and tributes to him. Find some of these online to read.

ACTIVITY

The nationalist leaders featured here represent only a small fraction of those that fought for a cause within the former British Empire. You might like to look back at the list of colonies which achieved independence in the years 1947 to 1967 given in Chapter 20 and find out something about other nationalist groups and leaders. Beginning with the leaders featured here and adding in any further examples you find, complete a chart like that below. Discuss the similarities and differences between the leaders.

Leader			
Education			
Politicisation and membership of political groups			
Beliefs and personal qualities			
Achievements			
Comments on significance			

The role and influence of colonial administrators

EXTRACT 3

There are grounds for doubting whether nationalism, however powerful and decisive it may have been in certain cases, really was the crucial determining factor in accelerating imperial retreat generally. The growth of nationalism alone was never the whole story. An alternative way of explaining imperial retreat has been to see it as a political choice taken by post-war governments under the pressure of domestic (often economic) constraints and calculations of national interest. In this sense Britain simply drifted away from her old imperial role; the 'will to rule' gradually slackened and public indifference reinforced the effects of economic decline. The idea that during the 1940s and 1950s there was a sharp change of attitude in Britain towards empire and the burdens of an imperial role, and that this played a key part in disengagement from colonial responsibilities, helps to explain the end of the British Empire.

Adapted from *Decolonization since 1945* by John Springhall (2001)

ACTIVITY

Evaluating historical extracts

According to Extract 3, how important were British attitudes towards the colonies for the end of Empire?

British colonial administrators faced a difficult task in the years after 1947. They had to be tough, remarkably politically astute and able to judge a fast changing public mood. They were required to implement changes which previously had seemed unthinkable and willing and able to deal with a vast array of frequently aggressive nationalist leaders, sometimes in an atmosphere of intimidation or violence. The colonial administrators were frequently the uncomfortable 'go-betweens' who had to deal with rapid changes in attitudes, not only among the nationalists and colonial populations, but also among politicians and officials within the Colonial Office in London. It is little wonder that many colonial administrators have been seen as imperfect or failures – such was the extreme difficulty of the tasks they had to undertake.

CROSS-REFERENCE

The establishment of the Central African Federation is outlined in Chapter 19, page 183.

Case study: Sir Andrew Cohen

Sir Andrew Cohen (1909–68) enjoyed a largely successful time as a colonial administrator. He had enjoyed a very different start in life from those of most of the nationalist leaders with whom he was to find himself in discussion. Born into a prominent Anglo-Jewish family, he had a public school education and took a double first in Classics at Cambridge in 1931. He entered the Civil Service and almost immediately transferred to the Colonial Office where, except for a brief spell during the Second World War, he concentrated on African affairs. In 1947 he was appointed Assistant Under-Secretary of State for the Colonial Office's African division.

Cohen knew that decolonisation would have to come about and thought hard about how best to undertake it. He was deeply concerned by the treatment of Africans in the colonies, and strongly believed in listening to the nationalists, and he cultivated contacts in both West and central Africa. He believed in devolving power to indigenous officials with their superior knowledge of local affairs and his Cohen Report of 1947 set out a new direction for colonial policy, mapping a route, through gradual reform, by which they could eventually emerge as independent, democratic and stable nations.

He was seriously concerned about the possible effects of apartheid, which was spreading north from South Africa, and proposed the confederation of Rhodesia and Nyasaland as the **Central African Federation**. (This was carried out in 1953, although it proved unsuccessful and was dissolved in 1963.)

Cohen and Buganda

Between 1953 and 1955, there was major unrest in Buganda following a British proposal to set up an East African Federation. The Bagandan people felt this would destroy their own culture and their Kabaka (King) Mutesa II called for the separation of Buganda from the rest of Uganda. Cohen tried to provide reassurances but deported the Kabaka in 1953. This set off a storm of protest and Cohen declared a state of emergency. Further negotiations produced the 1955 Buganda agreement whereby the Kabaka was restored. The Kabaka became a leading player in deciding how an independent Uganda would be governed, and the country's first President in 1962.

In 1952, Cohen was appointed Governor of Uganda where he served until 1957. Here, he brought Africans into government and encouraged the development of political parties as well as expanding the University of Makerere. His handling of Buganda has been questioned, but he helped to lay the groundwork for Uganda's independence in 1962.

Although most African nations progressed much faster towards independence than Cohen originally thought possible or prudent, his leadership helped to provide a blueprint against which progress could be measured and judged.

Case study: Sir John Macpherson

Sir John Macpherson (1898–1971) is remembered for managing the transition to independence in Nigeria. A Scot, educated at Edinburgh University, he had served in the Malayan Civil Service from 1921 to 1937, and in various posts in the Caribbean, Palestine and the USA before becoming Governor of Nigeria. As the seventh Governor General from 1948 to 1955, he moved the colonial administration towards reform, opening the higher levels of the colonial administration to Nigerians, and organising a major conference in 1951 to open discussions on a constitution which could accommodate the different regions and their competing political authorities.

The federal 'Macpherson Constitution' of 1951 stimulated political parties but failed to work effectively in the face of competing interests. This left the Colonial Secretary, Oliver Lyttleton, to approve a new constitution allowing for greater regional autonomy in 1954. Nevertheless, Macpherson had helped to ensure that, notwithstanding the wrangling between the regional factions, an independent Nigeria emerged in 1960, which did not collapse into separatism, anarchy or civil war.

Case study: Sir Charles Arden-Clarke

Fig. 4 *Arden-Clarke, Governor of the Gold Coast, 1949–57*

Sir Charles Arden-Clarke (1898–1962), born in India, the son of a Church of England missionary, and educated at the Rossall School, declined a scholarship to Cambridge in favour of entry, into colonial service in 1920. He had various appointments in Africa before becoming Governor of the Gold Coast in 1949. As a colonial administrator he was of a similar mould to Macpherson: a man who increasingly saw his role as a facilitator of self-rule and independence, rather than a barrier to it. The part he played not only in securing the release of Nkrumah from prison in 1951, but also in bringing him into government, was central in diffusing what had become a volatile situation in the wake of riots, strikes and imprisonments in West Africa. Arden-Clarke skilfully managed relations between Nkrumah and Ashanti politicians who were concerned about the domination of an intellectual elite in a new Ghanaian state.

Arden-Clarke proved a skilled and practical politician in dealing with highly complex and swiftly changing situations. Sometimes he had to rein Nkrumah in, even though his strategy was very much based on working closely with him. For example, he delayed the timetable for independence to allow for a third general election under colonial rule in 1956, in order for Nkrumah to demonstrate that he carried the support of the people, despite growing Ashanti criticism of him. When independence came in 1957, Arden-Clarke was held in such high regard that he was asked by the Ghanaian government to become the country's first honorary 'Governor-General'. In the event, the job did not suit him and he retired to England shortly afterwards to act as an advisor on African and colonial affairs.

EXTRACT 4

Decolonisation should perhaps be seen as a 'struggle for who should rule' rather than a 'struggle against colonial rule'. Many nationalists who sought to lead former colonial states to independence came to realise that the trickiest hurdle in their path was not the British but other nationalists. In decolonisation, partnerships were often forged between nationalists and British colonial officials where regional interests threatened to fragment the former colony. In Ghana, Nkrumah had to seek the aid of the governor, Sir Charles Arden-Clarke, to counter the Ashanti and the Northern Territories.

Adapted from *Decolonisation: The British Experience since 1945* by Nicholas White (2014)

ACTIVITY

Write an obituary for one of the colonial administrators mentioned in this section – or for another you are interested in. Remember that an obituary provides a reflection on an individual's life work and an overall summary of their contribution to 'progress', usually interspersed with some anecdotes from their life. Have a look at some modern obituaries in a newspaper for inspiration.

Summary

Attitudes to empire were shaped by the nationalist leaders and colonial administrators as much as – and possibly more than – the Colonial Office, media or government in London. These leaders share certain characteristics, one of which was a belief in and commitment to a cause. Both sides were concerned for their country and its peoples and both had to accept some sort of compromise in shaping imperial policies at a time of change.

 PRACTICE QUESTION

Evaluating historical extracts

Using your understanding of the historical context, assess how convincing Extracts 2, 3 and 4 are, in relation to the role of individuals in the transition of British colonies in Africa to independence in the years 1947 to 1967.

STUDY TIP

In order to answer this question you will need to identify the arguments that each extract puts forward and ask yourself: to what extent did nationalist leaders depend upon colonial officials to guide their countries to independence? What was the relative importance of nationalist leaders and colonial administrators? Use your own knowledge to explain the extracts and draw conclusions about each.

STUDY TIP

Think about the nationalist leaders and colonial administrators you have studied and try to combine this knowledge with information from earlier chapters about decolonisation and colonial policy. This question is asking you to assess who was 'in the driving seat' and you will need examples of the behaviour and decisions of individual leaders and administrators to support whatever argument you put forward.

 PRACTICE QUESTION

'Nationalist leaders and colonial administrators shaped the British government's relationship with its Empire, in the years 1947 to 1967.' Assess the validity of this view.

23 Post-colonial ties

Before the Second World War, racial thinking was shaped by the geographical separation between empire and **metropole**. Black and Asian people, although British subjects, were seen as belonging in the Empire, not Britain. In the 1950s and 1960s as the Empire collapsed, migration ended this racial separation but produced no vision of a multi-racial Britain. This exposed the fragility of the multi-racial Commonwealth ideal. Attitudes in the mid twentieth century were diverse, but the arrival of black and Asian migrants, coinciding with increasing awareness of loss of imperial power, produced a response which generally saw them as a threat to Britishness. They were widely regarded as people who did not belong in Britain and one of their key experiences was that of the outsider. Commonwealth migration, nevertheless, produced a multi-racial Britain and religious pluralism.

Adapted from 'The Empire Comes Home: Commonwealth Migration to Britain' by Wendy Webster (2011)

ACTIVITY

Evaluating historical extracts

With reference to Extract 1, explain what is meant by:
a) 'belonging in the Empire, not Britain'
b) the 'multi-racial commonwealth ideal'
b) a 'threat to Britishness'
c) a 'multi-racial Britain and religious pluralism'.
Before reading this chapter, discuss the potential results of increased migration from the old Empire and Commonwealth to Great Britain. When you have read the chapter, you can assess how many of your ideas were correct.

Even during its last 20 years, the Empire still had a considerable impact on British society. Political, economic and cultural ties remained strong even as decolonisation accelerated in the 1960s.

LEARNING OBJECTIVES

In this chapter you will learn about:

- post-colonial political and economic ties
- migration
- the residual impact of empire and cultural ties
- popular culture.

KEY QUESTION

As you read this chapter, consider the following key questions:
- What influenced imperial policy?
- How did the Empire influence British attitudes and culture?
- How important was the role of key individuals and groups and how were they affected by developments?

Post-colonial political and economic ties

Fig. 1 *The 1964 Commonwealth prime ministers conference*

Politically, Britain still maintained strong ties with its former colonies. Britain was proud of creating new 'nation-states' with their representative institutions and practices. Parliaments, ministries, wigged judges and British-style legal systems were all legacies of the British Empire. More practically, in the new states, former colonial officials stayed on as expatriate advisers in some of the key positions.

Furthermore, the growth and development of the Commonwealth, with its emphasis on a shared political tradition, helped maintain political ties. Regular Commonwealth Conferences, attended by prime ministers or presidents, took place at least once every two years and there was a major Commonwealth Economic Conference in 1952. All meetings except one took place in London, however, reinforcing the view that Britain 'dominated' the Commonwealth, much as it had the British Empire. (The only meeting outside London was a special meeting in January 1966 in Lagos, to coordinate policies towards Rhodesia).

Just as the Empire had been deemed to make Britain 'Great', so the Commonwealth helped to bolster Britain's international position in the post-colonial world, providing a strong and wide-ranging diplomatic network and ensuring Britain's membership of key international bodies. Britain's place on the United Nations Security Council, for example, can be seen as a reflection of Britain's status acquired through empire and maintained through Britain's world-wide influence.

Although the Commonwealth was not a military alliance, Britain continued to maintain a military with a 'global reach' and recruited citizens from Commonwealth nations, all of whom (with residency requirements) remained eligible to serve in the British forces. Britain even retained a remnant of the old Indian Army in the brigade of Gurkhas.

Above all, the Queen remained as a symbol of the Commonwealth and personally reinforced the connections through regular Commonwealth visits, sometimes with other members of the royal family, to all countries. The establishment of a Commonwealth Secretary General and his Secretariat in 1965 permitted the co-ordination of many Commonwealth activities, while the Queen also held her own regular meetings with Heads of Government from Commonwealth countries. Citizens of the Commonwealth remained eligible for British honours and many listened avidly to the monarch's annual **Christmas Day** message.

A CLOSER LOOK

The royal Christmas Day broadcast

The tradition of a Royal Christmas Day Broadcast began with George V in 1932, when he gave a two and a half minute-long 'wireless' broadcast, scripted by Rudyard Kipling and at the behest of Sir John Reith, to inaugurate the new British Empire service (subsequently the British World Service). Since then, a Christmas Day message reflecting current issues and concerns has been delivered by the British monarch to the people of the United Kingdom and the Commonwealth almost every year.

Another major legacy of the Empire was Britain's status as a globalised economy. The City of London remained as one of the world's major financial centres, the headquarters of banking, insurance and investment companies. The conventions of international trade and law had been spawned during the years of imperial rule and Britain's imperial connections had given rise to multi-national companies with branches around the world. Britain thus emerged from empire with a vast overseas investment portfolio and important trading links that continued to be of major importance – particularly given Britain's exclusion from the EEC until 1973. Certainly, the British government made every effort to keep ex-colonies within the Sterling Area and it could be said that, in this regard Britain replaced its 'formal' empire with a return to the old 'informal' one of trading links and economic ties.

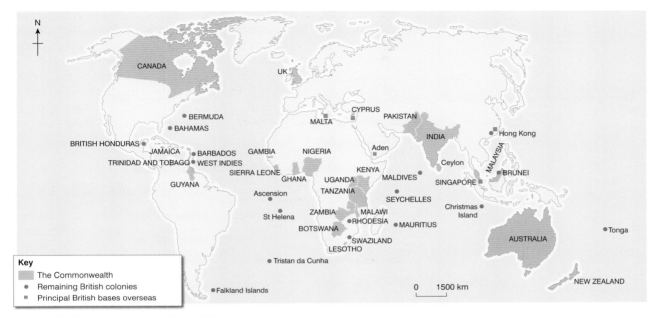

Fig. 2   *The British Commonwealth, 1967*

Migration

Movement from Britain to the Empire and Commonwealth

The experiences of wartime, the continuation of rationing until as late as 1954 and the increasing demand for labour in countries such as Australia, Canada and New Zealand, which offered better prospects, encouraged a post-war surge in emigration from Britain.

Between 1946 and 1957 approximately 1 million people left Britain for the Dominions, representing a marked acceleration of pre-war levels. This intensified the range and depth of personal contacts between ordinary British people and the White Dominions. A mass observation survey in 1948 showed that around 25 per cent of the population of Britain were **in contact with relatives** in the Dominions.

It is difficult to know how far this informal, almost invisible, contact between Britain and the Dominions raised awareness of the Empire and the Commonwealth in Britain. It must have had some impact in widening people's horizons, if only in extending their knowledge of the specific countries to which their friends and relatives had gone.

There continued to be a flow of administrators, civil servants and senior army officers who left Britain to experience the Empire at first hand. Such men were drawn from the upper ranks of society and had generally been through a public school system which instilled belief in, and prepared them for, imperial rule. Of those lower down the social order, the only groups likely to encounter the Empire and Commonwealth at first hand were men who were required to do **National Service** and became involved in one of the late colonial wars, perhaps in Kenya, Malaya or at Suez.

A CLOSER LOOK

Money was regularly transferred from those in Britain to **friends and family overseas** and vice versa. It is estimated that such movements of money amounted to about £12 million in 1959 – about £1 billion in current values.

KEY TERM

National Service: between 1939 and 1960, young British men aged 17–21 years were required to undertake military service for up to 18 months

By the late 1950s, improved living standards and full employment within Britain helped curb the flood of people to the Dominions, and they increasingly looked to other sources of skilled labour around the world. The abolition of National Service in 1960 closed off another outlet for travel and as decolonisation gathered pace, the movement of British people tended to be from the Empire and ex-Empire to Britain, as colonial servants and soldiers were repatriated. By the late 1960s, direct personal experience of the Empire among the British had become rarer.

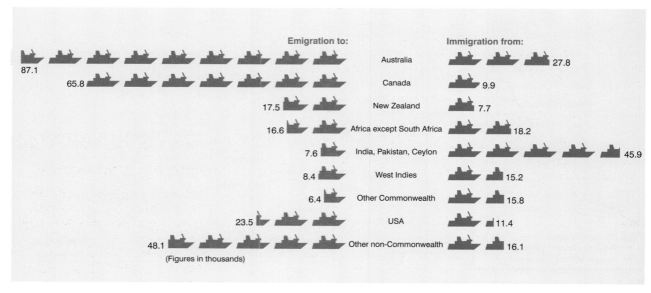

Fig. 3 *Patterns of emigration and immigration from and to Britain in 1967 (figures in thousands). What does this diagram show about patterns of emigration from Britain and immigration into Britain in 1967?*

ACTIVITY

Draw a diagram to show why people left Britain for the Empire and Commonwealth between c1946 and 1958. When you have read the next section, create another to show what attracted people from the Empire and Commonwealth to come to Britain in the same period.

Movement from the Empire and Commonwealth to Britain

Fig. 4 *The arrival of the* Empire Windrush *from Jamaica in June 1948, carrying immigrants*

A CLOSER LOOK

Immigration before 1947

There had been relatively small numbers of colonial immigrants settling in Britain since the late nineteenth century, especially sailors from Asia and the Caribbean. Although large numbers of Indian soldiers had been billeted in Britain during the First World War, their stay had been temporary, so there had been relatively little direct exposure to the Empire for most Britons.

Although most of those who chose to move to Britain before the early 1950s were European (often fleeing persecution), thereafter there was a huge growth in the immigration of people from the colonies. Immigrants came especially from the Caribbean in the 1950s, from Pakistan and India in the 1960s and from Kenya in 1967 as Kenyatta (who wanted Kenya to be a purely African state) pressurised the Asian Kenyans, many of whom held British passports, to leave.

In recognition of the Empire's war-time contribution, the British Nationality Act was passed in 1948, giving full British citizenship, including the right of free entry into Britain, to every inhabitant of the Empire and Commonwealth.

As the British economy recovered from its war-time dislocation, there was plentiful and well-paid work for the unskilled in the booming British factories and the British government actively encouraged immigration. There were successful recruitment drives to encourage unskilled workers to take up a work in public transport and the National Health Service, and in 1956 London Transport took on nearly 4000 new employees – mostly from Barbados. Some of these chose to put down roots and sent for their wives, children and girlfriends to join them; others earned enough to repay their passage (often advanced by a recruiting firm) and returned home. Since there were plenty of jobs available, no action was taken to limit immigration, although equally, none was taken to help migrants settle or find decent accommodation.

A CLOSER LOOK

Immigrants from Jamaica

Although not strictly the first post-war immigrants, the first to attract media interest were the 492 mostly male Jamaican passengers who arrived on the steamship *Empire Windrush* at Tilbury, East London, in 1948. This ship arrived without prior notification and the authorities were hastily forced to house the immigrants in a temporary shelter at Clapham. These immigrants were to form the nucleus of the subsequent immigrant community in nearby Brixton.

A CLOSER LOOK

Numbers of Commonwealth immigrants 1958

115,000 West Indians	An increase from the 17,500 West Indians in 1951. By 1959 West Indian immigration was running at about 16,000 people per year.
55,000 Indians and Pakistanis	In 1949 there had only been 100 Indians in Birmingham but in 1959 there were to be 3000 immigrant arrivals from India and Pakistan.
25,000 West Africans	A drift, mostly of students, from West Africa had begun in the inter-war years and this accelerated after 1945.
10,000 Cypriots	Most of these fled the war from 1955–59 and in 1959, 25,000 Cypriots came to Britain.

Nearly half, particularly the West Indians, lived in London while the 25,000 in and around Birmingham included large numbers of Indians and Pakistanis. There were also 8000 in Manchester and 6000 each in Liverpool and Leeds. Many Asians settled in Oldham and Bradford where the declining textile industries were desperate for cheap unskilled labour.

Mosley and the Union Movement

Oswald Mosley, former leader of the British Union of Fascists, founded the Union Movement (UM) in 1948. He stood on an anti-immigration platform in the 1959 election in Kensington North (which included Notting Hill) and issued pamphlets provocatively featuring black people with spears entering Britain and slogans such as 'Stop coloured immigration' and 'Houses for White people'. He called for assisted repatriation and spread scare stories regarding the criminality and bad behaviour of immigrants. Although he received only 8.1 per cent of the vote, his campaigns increased white extremism.

Notting Hill Carnival

After the racial tensions of the late 1950s, efforts were made to improve community relations and encourage groups to mix socially. The steel band music performed by immigrant Trinidadians became popular in local pubs and in 1964 a local festival, set up by West Indian immigrants, provided the first Notting Hill carnival. The festival developed in subsequent years with spectacular floats, steel drum bands, bright, outlandish costumes and dancing on the streets. It was accompanied by stalls serving typical Caribbean food, particularly jerk chicken, rice and peas and rum punch.

The initial British reaction to this increased exposure to peoples of other races was one of curiosity mingled with uncertainty. Indifference was more common than intolerance in the very early fifties, but, as the post-war boom slackened, prejudice and anxieties that were never far below the surface grew. Worries about the dilution of British cultural and national identity were coupled with a concern to protect houses and jobs and it was the Commonwealth immigrants who bore the brunt of job redundancies. Immigrants also found themselves in the poorest houses in the least desirable parts of towns and as these immigrant communities grew, they were seen as threatening by local residents.

1958 saw gangs of 'Teddy boy' youths attacking black people and violent riots broke out in Nottingham and Notting Hill, London. Oswald Mosley's anti-immigration **Union Movement** also increased its activities and in a survey in 1962, 90 per cent of the British population supported legislation to curb immigration and 80 per cent agreed that there were too many immigrants in Britain already.

In the three years between 1960 and 1962 more migrants arrived in Britain than in the whole of the twentieth century to that point. Immigration ran at just over 50,000 per year between 1962 and 1965, and by c1967 Britain's black population was nearly 1 million.

Fig. 5 *Immigrants were not always welcomed, but here London students are trying to demonstrate goodwill to immigrants in 1961*

Whilst there was some assimilation and interchange of culture – the development of the **Notting Hill Carnival** being the best example – more often the British turned their backs on the immigrant communities or actively campaigned against them. A survey in North London in 1965 showed that one in five objected to working with black people or Asians; half said they would refuse to live next door to a coloured person and nine out of ten disapproved of mixed marriages. Such attitudes were mild compared with the more extreme **racists** – characterised by Alf Garnett in the hit TV series *Till Death Do us Part* which appeared on British TV screens from 1965. His constant swearing about 'bloody coons' won him a cult following, even though the writer's intention had been to satirise ignorant bigotry. A group of Conservative MPs from the West Midlands, encouraged by pressure groups such as the Birmingham Immigration Control Association formed in 1960, pushed for political action, arguing that unless something was done, Britain would cease to be a European nation and become a mixed Afro-Asian society.

A CLOSER LOOK

Racist attitudes

Racist attitudes were strongest among those working class communities that found themselves living in or near predominantly immigrant communities. In the East End of London, the Bengalis who had settled in some of the city's poorest housing were subjected to campaigns of violence which rendered certain streets 'no go' areas, especially at night. Girls were kicked going to school, stones flung and eggs and tomatoes hurled. It was not even safe to wait at a bus stop or to go shopping. From Bradford to Luton 'paki-bashing', which referred to attacks on anyone with black skin, became an all-too-common occurrence.

The **1962 Commonwealth Immigrants Act** was an attempt to control the escalating immigration. Free immigration for former colonial subjects was ended, even when they held a British passport. Instead, a work permit (voucher) scheme was put in place. Although this did not explicitly discriminate against black or Asian workers, it had the same effect. The Irish were exempt and most white immigrants had skills which enabled them to obtain vouchers. The unskilled black applicants, however, found it difficult to obtain permits and in the 12 months following the Act only 34,500 arrived in Britain. The Act was both unfair and difficult to operate, but it received massive public support; opinion polls suggested 70 per cent.

A CLOSER LOOK

The 1962 Commonwealth Immigrants Act

This act divided would-be immigrants into three groups:
1. those with employment in the UK already arranged
2. those with skills or qualifications that were in short supply in the UK
3. all others who were placed on a waiting list, with ex-servicemen at the top.

A system of quotas was drawn up whereby a limited number of entry vouchers would be issued annually, starting with categories A and B and so limiting the numbers in the C category.

As immigrants feared they would be unable to return if they left Britain, the Act had the effect of encouraging immigrants to put down roots in Britain and

A CLOSER LOOK

Race Relations Board, 1965

The Race Relations Board was set up to consider all aspects of race relations. It compiled statistics, produced reports and held 'hearings'. However, it could not compel witnesses to attend and although it handled 982 complaints in its first year, 734 were dismissed through lack of evidence. Over half of those upheld were about racial stereotypes in advertising rather than direct examples of discrimination.

A CLOSER LOOK

On the radio, *Caribbean Voices*, first broadcast in 1946, was a weekly programme which focused on the literary output of the Caribbean region. It helped authors find publishers, assisted them when they arrived in Britain, and provided them with work as readers. In the 1960s it featured other migrant writers too.

ACTIVITY

Create a two column timeline. In the first column indicate the key phases of immigration and record incidents of racial tension and assimilation; in the second note political events and legislation relating to immigration and race between 1947 and 1967.

bring their families over (which was still permissible). Issues of immigration featured strongly in the 1964 general election campaign and in Smethwick, which had c6000 recent immigrants in its population of 70,000 giving it the highest concentration of immigrants in any county borough in England, Peter Griffiths (Conservative) managed to win the seat from Patrick Gordon Walker (then the Labour Shadow Foreign Secretary), by using the slogan, 'If you want a nigger for a neighbour, vote Labour'. Harold Wilson, the new Labour Prime Minister, called such campaigning a 'disgrace to British democracy', but it was clear that many voters shared Griffiths' view.

The new Labour government reduced the quota of vouchers and barred children over 16 from entering Britain as family members. However, some attempt was made to reduce tensions with the passing of the 1965 Race Relations Act which forbade discrimination in public places 'on the grounds of colour, race or ethnic or national origins'. Although discrimination in housing and employment were excluded and incitement to race hatred was not made a criminal offence, other complaints could be made to a **Race Relations Board** which would conciliate between the two sides.

The impact of Commonwealth immigration by 1967 was clearly mixed. On the negative side, immigration had provoked fierce racial sentiments, challenging British claims of toleration and freedom of expression. However, more positively, some assimilation was underway and beginning to turn Britain into a more multi-racial society. Much depended on where white Britons lived, but, through the media, if not direct contact, white people became more familiar with black faces and 'foreign' ways. TV dramas like *Emergency Ward 10* and *Z Cars* began to feature black people, whilst the appearance of Asian corner-shops and Chinese take-aways helped to transform British tastes.

Life for the Commonwealth immigrants was not easy. West Indians, who were English-speaking and shared the predominant Christian religious background of the native British, were generally more easily assimilated. Indians and Pakistanis, who were often very hard-working and whose children were higher achievers in school, were neverthless regarded as more alien. Some cultural traditions did not easily fit in a country which pre-war had been almost exclusively Christian. To cite just one example, the Islamic interdict on the consumption of alcohol kept Muslims out of the local public house and yet this was very often the centre of white British working class culture. Barriers of language, disparities in education, employment, housing and the application of the justice system were all issues that future governments would have to address.

A CLOSER LOOK

Commonwealth immigrant attitudes

In a survey in Nottingham in the early 1960s, Robert Davison found that 87 per cent of the Jamaicans said they felt 'British' before they came to England and 86 per cent were happy for their children to feel 'English'. However, among the Indians and Pakistanis only 2 per cent had felt 'British' before arrival and only 6 per cent wanted their children to feel English.

The residual impact of empire and cultural ties

Familiarity with and interest in 'empire' declined in Britain through the 1950s and 1960s as the British moved into the era of decolonisation. Society became more subject to Americanisation and interest in Europe was fuelled as much by charter flight holidays as by political concerns about joining the EEC. Symbolically, 'Empire Day' (24 May) was abolished in 1962.

Such attitudes can be seen in Extract 2:

EXTRACT 2

Although the imperial message was still conveyed to Liverpool schools after 1945 through films and lecturers sent by the Imperial Institute, and though prizes were still awarded for essays on imperial and Commonwealth themes, much of the impetus had waned by the mid-1950s. The 1953 Coronation was effectively the last great imperial event in Liverpool. An amnesia about empire seemed to set in. Even Labour, finally in control of the council in 1955, seems to have taken little interest in imperial affairs. Its Toxteth branch passed no resolutions regarding colonies in the 1950s, and woke up to events in Africa only with the Sharpeville massacre of March 1960. Nor did members show interest in the conditions of Liverpool's black community, itself a legacy of empire. It is therefore tempting to accept the argument that imperial propaganda was generated by a few enthusiasts, and appealed only to relatively few of the population.

Adapted from 'Transmitting Ideas of Empire: Representations and Celebrations in Liverpool, 1886–1953' by Murray Steele (2008)

ACTIVITY

Evaluating historical extracts

What can be learnt from Extract 2 about public attitudes to the Empire in Liverpool in the 1950s?

Nevertheless, there remained, at least through the 1950s, a strong patriotic current that had been nurtured by victory in the Second World War and the belief that Britain had – almost single-handedly – brought about Hitler's defeat in Western Europe. This helped nurture support for some sort of imperial links, perhaps imparting the nostalgic idea of the 'family' to be nurtured by the mother country (even though, ironically, the war had helped those countries to 'grow up' and, in some cases, to shun such mothering).

Fig. 6 *Australian swimmers try on the robes of Ghanaian athletes at the Commonwealth Games, 1958*

KEY TERM

diaspora: the spread of peoples from their original homeland

The associations forged by imperial rule did not entirely disappear and just as the Commonwealth reinforced political and economic ties, so too did it become a medium for maintaining cultural links. The Empire had left a British **diaspora** of c10 million spread around the world, who often clustered in vibrant ex-patriate communities and maintained English traditions and contacts. Furthermore, peoples in former British colonies continued to bear and use

ACTIVITY

Create a poster to show the use of the Union Jack in the flags of former colonies.

A CLOSER LOOK

The British Empire and Commonwealth Games took place from 1954 (replacing the British Empire Games which had been held since 1930). They were an international, multi-sport event involving athletes from the Commonwealth countries.

ACTIVITY

Listen to some of the music mentioned here that is associated with the British imperial tradition. Why do you think it continued to appeal to audiences in 1967 (and later) after much of the British Empire had been dismantled?

anglicised names, live in anglicised communities with neo-Gothic churches and British-style railway stations, and speak variants of the English language. The Union Jack was retained in the corner of many flags, from Fiji to New Zealand, and was still hoisted as a mark of solidarity and respect in many corners of the globe. The Anglican Church had more members in Africa than in Britain itself, while the Boy Scout movement maintained its ties across the former Empire.

Perhaps the most obvious residual impact of empire was in sport. Poker, football, racket sports, snooker and even croquet were all exported across the Empire while rugby had been firmly established in such countries as New Zealand and South Africa (as well as Fiji, Tonga and Samoa), and cricket in India and Australia (among others), where the public school-educated colonial administrators had ensured their spread. Sporting competitions were one way in which the British continued to be regularly reminded of the former Empire and the **Commonwealth Games** brought nations together every four years.

In Britain too, reminders of the imperial past were never far away. Words like bungalow, dinghy, verandah and pyjamas (from India), and safari, mumbo-jumbo and zombie (from Africa) had entered the English language and colonial contacts remained strong in British public schools, the military and in some professions. Royal pageantry preserved some of the traditions of the imperial past and the Empire still featured in **honours** and the awarding of the British Empire Medal.

A CLOSER LOOK

Imperial royal honours

In descending order of precedence these are:
- Knight/Dame Grand Cross of the Most Excellent Order of the British Empire (GBE)
- Knight/Dame Commander of the Most Excellent Order of the British Empire (KBE or DBE)
- Commander of the Most Excellent Order of the British Empire (CBE)
- Officer of the Most Excellent Order of the British Empire (OBE)
- Member of the Most Excellent Order of the British Empire (MBE)
- The British Empire Medal (BEM)

Another reminder of Britain's imperial past appeared in 1954 in the second half of the 'last night of the proms', when Sir Malcolm Sargent established the tradition of using this for a rendering of patriotic British music. Performances of Edward Elgar's 'Pomp & Circumstance March No. 1' (to part of which 'Land of Hope and Glory' was sung), Henry Wood's 'Fantasia on British Sea Songs', culminating in Thomas Arne's 'Rule, Britannia!', Hubert Parry's 'Jerusalem' (a setting of a poem by William Blake) and the British national anthem (followed by the non-programmed 'Auld Lang Syne' sung by the promenaders at the end of the concert) certainly demonstrated an imperial spirit on at least one night of the year.

Popular culture

The demise of empire weakened the appeal of imperial topics in the media. Children's stories and comics, for example, abandoned formerly popular imperial themes and the ground-breaking boy's comic *Eagle*, published between 1950 and 1969, explicitly informed its writers that foreigners were not to be depicted as either enemies or villains and that at least one child in any group of children should be from an ethnic minority.

In the cinema, mass audiences no longer welcomed overtly patriotic films in a post-war Britain dealing with retreat, economic decline and decolonisation. Fewer films used the Empire as a backdrop, although a wide range of formats, including romances, comedies, adventure-stories and even horror films sometimes did. Among the films that conveyed imperial messages were:

- *North West Frontier* (1959) which concerned a British officer's attempt to protect a Hindu prince from a murderous Muslim uprising. It hinted strongly that the Empire in India had been necessary to preserve order.
- *Guns at Batasi* (1964) based on the dilemmas faced by a British officer leading troops which faced turmoil in a newly independent colony. The message was about the role the British played in containing internal divisions within the colonies.
- *Lawrence of Arabia* (1962), which told the adventures of Lawrence, a British First World War hero, in the Middle East. Lawrence was depicted as torn between loyalty to King and Empire, and to his Arab allies with whom he collaborates to defeat the Turks. This film had a more critical view of empire.

Television replaced radio as the main medium for the spread of popular culture in the post-war era.Here, documentaries enabled the public to become more aware of other countries and cultures, but there was equally some lampooning of traditional imperial attitudes in the 1960s satire boom – seen, for example in **That Was the Week**, *That Was*, a satirical comedy programme hosted by David Frost which ran between 1962 and 1963.

Race and immigration were also the subject of 1960s comedy programmes, such as *Till Death us Do Part* and comedians used popular music to ridicule immigrant communities, as did Lance Percival in his 1967 record *Maharajah of Brum*. Much theatre and TV comedy freely used racist stereotyping and the Black and White Minstrels' show was a popular light entertainment show that ran from 1958 until the late 1970s.

While 'attitudes' are always difficult to define, still less substantiate with concrete evidence, it is probably fair to say that British society became more open and less deferential in the 1960s. There are, of course, many reasons for such changes and these are not exclusive to Britain. However, there are those who (as seen in Extract 3) have identified a link between changes in popular attitudes and the decline of empire.

ACTIVITY

Try to view at least part of some of these films or look at episodes of the TV programmes mentioned here. You could discuss the messages they convey and how they put these across.

CROSS-REFERENCE

Till Death us Do Part is introduced earlier in this chapter, on page 225.

KEY TERM

Angry Young Men: this refers to a number of British playwrights and novelists of the early 1950s whose work was marked by irreverence towards the Establishment and disgust at the survival of class distinctions and privilege

EXTRACT 3

What then happened to those values, such as 'duty', 'loyalty', 'hierarchy', and 'authority', previously considered to be the social bedrock of empire, yet now increasingly called into question? It is tempting to link the erosion of these values to the process of decolonisation. After all, within scarcely a generation the whole hierarchical embrace of empire had been dismantled, such that the British aristocracy could no longer credibly claim to be the national and imperial ruling class by hereditary right. It could be argued that Suez changed attitudes toward military authority, ushering in a willingness to challenge old, deferential values. Among those who felt that Suez epitomised what was wrong with post-war Britain were the 'Angry Young Men' of the post-war era. Most famously, John Osborne and Alan Sillitoe captured the pessimism and disillusionment of the late 1950s and early 1960s, and especially the lack of opportunities for the working class. For both men, Suez provided a licence to rail against the arrogance and ineptitude of Britain's ruling class.

Adapted from 'Social Life and Cultural Representation: Empire in the Public Imagination' by Andrew Thompson with Meaghan Kowalsky (2011)

ACTIVITY

Evaluating historical extracts

In pairs, discuss the view put forward in Extract 3. Can you think of any reason or evidence to criticise this view?

Summary

STUDY TIP

You should aim to focus upon the way in which the Empire affected Britain, particularly in the form of immigration from the Commonwealth in the years 1947 to 1967. You need to identify the very particular views conveyed in each extract and relate these to the debates outlined in this chapter.

 PRACTICE QUESTION

Evaluating historical extracts

Using your understanding of the historical context, how convincing are Extracts 1, 2, and 3, in relation to the legacy of the Empire for British society between 1947 and 1967.

STUDY TIP

An answer to this question should aim to bring together the material you have studied in earlier chapters on the Empire after 1947, as well as the detail covered in this chapter on the impact of immigration, migration and continuing contacts with the Commonwealth and Empire. You should reflect on the extent to which cultural ties were maintained. Remember – Empire could still be an influence on popular culture – even if it only provoked a reaction against Britain's imperial past.

 PRACTICE QUESTION

In the years 1947 to 1967 most white Britons showed little interest in the Empire'. Assess the validity of this view.

24 Relations with indigenous peoples

EXTRACT 1

The devolution of colonial power, whether achieved by armed struggle or negotiation, was the result of two complementary forces: increasingly popular anti-imperialism which was articulate and often threatening; and decreasing European means and will to power. Everywhere anti-imperialism formed the basis of colonial nationalism. It gave political cohesion to diverse ethnic and social groups within each colony; it provided for ideological unification and it explained in simple terms to the colonial peoples their poverty and backwardness. Once the imperial jewels like India had demonstrated the possibilities of anti-imperialist action, colonial politics elsewhere inclined more and more towards future independence and nationhood. The political change was effected by two means: guerrilla war (which was more the exception than the rule) and colonial party politics (an external appendage of Western liberal democracy). The chief agency of political change was negotiation between the colonial administration and the emergent national political party. Thus, the British converted the most vociferous national party into the majority party and its leader eventually became Prime Minister.

Adapted from 'Europe recalls her Legions' by Raymond Bette (1970)

ACTIVITY

Evaluating historical extracts

According to Extract 1, what part did anti-imperialist national independence movements play in challenging British rule in its Empire?

Challenges to colonial rule in Africa and Asia

The disruptive consequences of the Second World War are hard to overestimate. In South East Asia the effects of this were perhaps most stark. The rapid Japanese victories and conquests of Malaya and Burma destroyed Asian notions of British invincibility, and left a strong conviction among many indigenous groups that British power was vulnerable, even after it had been reinstated.

Similar processes were evident in Africa, where rapid economic development was generated during the war years by the need to provide raw materials and food to support the British war effort. Thus major cities such as Nairobi and Mombasa in East Africa, and Accra and Lagos in West Africa, grew rapidly in the immediate post-war period, and became major theatres of industrial conflict and anti-British agitation.

An important factor was the return to the colonies of men who had served in imperial and Commonwealth forces during the war. They felt an entitlement to be treated well after their sacrifices in the imperial cause, and they possessed the military skills to cause serious trouble if they were so inclined.

LEARNING OBJECTIVES

In this chapter you will learn about:

- challenges to colonial rule in Africa and Asia
- the growth of nationalist movements and reactions to them
- the Mau Mau rebellion
- nationalism in Rhodesia.

KEY QUESTION

As you read this chapter, consider the following key questions:
- How did the indigenous peoples respond to British rule?
- How important was the role of key individuals and groups and how were they affected by developments?
- What influenced imperial policy?

The growth of nationalist movements

The years 1947 to 1967 saw the emergence of mass nationalist movements across Asia, Africa and elsewhere. These demanded, at first, greater representation, and, subsequently, independence from imperial rule. Of course, the economic, social and political conditions varied across the Empire, but certain common factors propelling these movements can be discerned across the two continents.

- **The legacy of war:** much of the British Empire had been affected by the Second World War – either through direct fighting and/or occupation or by sending troops to support the British war effort. Black soldiers had fought alongside white and the colonies expected some reward. Britain's seeming reluctance to continue the process begun in India, Palestine and Burma in the 1940s brought disillusionment and impatience.

- **Economic and social discontent:** despite the rapid post-war economic growth of some colonies, local people were not always sufficiently skilled to benefit from the job opportunities and some developments came at the expense of traditional farming and employment. In places there was competition for land between foreign interests and indigenous farmers and when British projects failed (as in the **Tanganyika Groundnuts Scheme**) it was the local peoples that suffered. Elsewhere (for example on the Gold Coast or in Kenyan cities, such as Nairobi), there was a surplus of educated youth, unwilling to take manual employment – the product of efforts to improve educational opportunities for indigenous peoples.

CROSS-REFERENCE

The Tanganyika Groundnuts Scheme is described in Chapter 19, page 182.

Fig. 1   *A mill in Burma that was destroyed by RAF bombers*

CROSS-REFERENCE

For the events that led to independence in the Malay Peninsula and Singapore, Gold Coast and Nigeria, look back to Chapter 19, pages 187, 188 and 181 respectively.

The motivations of the nationalist leaders in these countries are explored in Chapter 20, pages 197 and 192.

- **Ethnic and religious rivalries:** tensions between ethnic groups within colonies fuelled the nationalist movements. Some ethnic groups felt discriminated against when the British favoured other groups in the running of colonial government. British acceptance that the definition of 'Malay nationality' be restricted to those of **Malay** ethnicity in 1949, for example, encouraged the discontented Chinese to support nationalist attacks upon Europeans. Similarly, the political mobilisation of the Ashanti in the **Gold Coast**, and of the Yoruba and Northern Muslims in **Nigeria**, was in response to suspicions that other ethnic groups were being favoured.

- **Charismatic and Western-educated leaders**: key figures able to unite different ethnic groups and factions behind the drive for independence were crucial for the emergence of the nationalist independence movements. **Nkrumah** in the Gold Coast, **Azikiwe** in Nigeria, **Lee Kuan Yew** in Singapore, **Aung San** in Burma and **Kaunda** in Zambia are all examples of

Western-educated leaders. Some actually travelled to Britain, Europe or the USA, others attended Western schools and institutions in the colonies, but all learnt to think and criticise, absorbing political ideas about nationalism, liberalism, socialism and Marxism which challenged imperial rule.

- **Mass political parties**: nationalist movements relied on strength of numbers in support of their cause. By showing that they had a mass (and organised) following, leaders put the British in a difficult moral position. Given their strong belief in democracy and ideas of self-determination, they were obliged to bow to respectable political organisations. The creation of parties also enabled the dissemination of ideas and the opportunity to compete for power, once democratic elections were instituted. The CPP in the Gold Coast, AFPFL in Burma, ANC in Rhodesia and South Africa and UMNO and MCA in Malaya all used mass mobilisation and mass action to achieve their aims.

CROSS-REFERENCE

For details on the nationalist leaders, see the following:

Nkrumah – Chapter 18, page 168, Chapter 19, page 181 and Chapter 22, page 209.

Azikiwe – Chapter 22, page 210.

Lee Kuan Yew – Chapter19, page 189

Aung San – Chapter 13, pages 131–132 and Chapter 19, page 186.

Kaunda - in Chapter 19, and later in this chapter, on page 239.

Nationalist movements and reactions to them

Case study: Kenya and the Mau Mau

ACTIVITY

Create a spider diagram to show the factors that influenced the growth of nationalist movements in the British colonies after 1947.

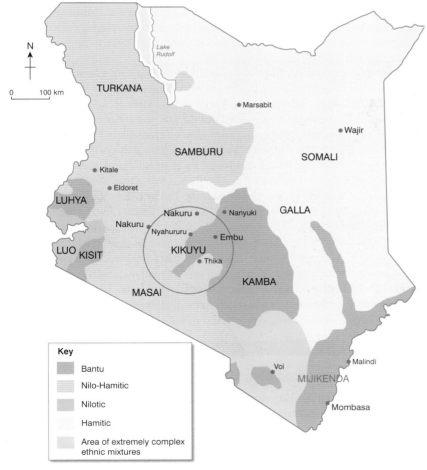

Fig. 2 *Ethnic divisions in Kenya; the Kikuyu occupied one of the most fertile areas in the centre of Kenya (circled)*

The Mau Mau was a Kenyan movement largely confined to the **Kikuyu** people. The Kikuyu suffered from a shortage of land (which had been taken by white settlers) and from unemployment and poor conditions in the towns.

A CLOSER LOOK

Kikuyu grievances

The Kikuyu had found themselves progressively squeezed off land in the 'White Highlands' to accommodate an expanding number of white settlers. They were confined to reservation lands which were inadequate for their needs. Evictions (sometimes violent) added to growing Kikuyu concerns that their communities were falling apart. Kikuyus and others who had migrated to the cities were also enraged by what was happening in the Highlands. Anger was most acute among the young, poor and landless.

Although the movement dated back to the 1940s, it was only in 1952 that a major insurrection shook British colonial rule. This showed the vulnerability of a regime based on privileged white settlers who were determined that post-war Kenya would be dominated politically and economically by them, with no concessions to the black majority. The attitude of colonial administrators under the governor, Sir Philip Mitchell, who announced in 1948 that self-government would not be possible in the near future, fuelled Kenyan frustrations.

In 1952, there was an escalation of murders by Mau Mau – some of white farmers, but more of fellow Kikuyu (many of them Christians) who had refused to take the Mau Mau oath. The Chief of Kikuyu, Waruhiu wa Kungu, spoke out against the atrocities, but he himself was assassinated in October 1952. Reports that the Mau Mau were taking ritualistic oaths of allegiance, committing them to extreme violence against whites people, fuelled a panic among the white settlers and prompted a fierce backlash.

Such violence put the British in a difficult position. Guerrilla tactics were not easy to deal with and a new British Governor, **Sir Evelyn Baring**, resorted to declaring a State of Emergency (1952). This suspended all black African political rights and the Mau Mau were treated as political terrorists. Black leaders, including Jomo Kenyatta (it would seem wrongly in his case) were imprisoned for conspiring with the Mau Mau. Thousands of British troops were taken to Kenya to stamp out the insurrection, which placed the British in an awkward moral position as the white outsider using force to impose its will on the majority black indigenous population.

The British employed a huge repressive machine – from recruiting a 'home guard' of loyal Kikuyu to using British ground troops, aided by helicopters and planes. The Mau Mau really stood little chance against the superior British forces, although they managed to hold out for five years. Kikuyu villages were uprooted and relocated, cutting the Mau Mau off from their sources of support in the White Highlands, and the Mau Mau were gradually cornered in the forests below Mount Kenya and destroyed through military force.

There were atrocities on both sides, but it was those that were committed by the British that had the greater repercussions. The British hanged suspects on the least excuse and interned thousands in 'rehabilitation camps' where they systematically interrogated the inmates to sift out the Mau Mau sympathisers. Torture was used to force admissions of complicity and guilt and between 1952 and 1956, 11–12,000 people were killed and 81,000 detained. The appalling conditions in the camps were highlighted in 1959 when **atrocities at the Hola Camp**, in which 11 inmates had been killed, came to light. The British press reported the incidents and although the State of Emergency was not lifted until 1960, the British government was left embarrassed and shocked.

KEY PROFILE

Sir Evelyn Baring (1903–73) was a member of the prosperous London banking family, and the younger son of Evelyn Baring, Lord Cromer, the first Consul-General of Egypt (see Chapter 4 for his Key Profile). Baring had been Governor of Southern Rhodesia before becoming Governor of Kenya.

ACTIVITY

Extension

You can read more about the Hola atrocities in Caroline Elkins' *Imperial Reckoning: The Untold Story of Britain's Gulag in Kenya* (2005).

A CLOSER LOOK

The Hola Camp atrocities, 1959

The Hola Camp in Kenya housed tough Mau Mau prisoners who would not relinquish their Mau Mau oaths. The camp commandant decided to force 88 of the most unco-operative, who refused to obey orders, to perform manual labour or join rehabilitation schemes to undertake work. When they resisted, they were beaten by the guards. Eleven of the detainees died outright; the remaining 77 sustained serious injuries. When the *East African Standard* reported the incident, it quoted an official report which suggested that ten men had died from drinking contaminated water. The truth emerged over the following weeks when an examining doctor discovered that the 11 deaths had been caused by lung congestion and haemorrhage following multiple bruises and other injuries.

Fig. 3 *Mau Mau suspects being arrested in 1954*

Macmillan's **'wind of change'** speech of 1960 and the shift in policy towards African independence was undoubtedly (although not exclusively) linked to the Mau Mau insurrection. The new Governor of Kenya, Sir Patrick Renison, paved the way for a move to independence and black majority rule, which was granted in 1963, whereupon 1500 remaining Mau Mau guerrillas laid down their arms.

The Mau Mau rebellion had shown that colonial governments were poorly equipped to deal with large-scale insurrection and caused deep apprehension. However, how far it was a typical 'nationalist' rising has been questioned.

CROSS-REFERENCE

Macmillan's 'wind of change' speech is discussed in Chapter 20, page 193.

ACTIVITY

Evaluating historical extracts

1. According to Extract 2, what were the main characteristics of the Mau Mau rebellion?
2. Write a newspaper editorial from the 1950s about the Mau Mau insurgency. Choose your date carefully. You may wish to condemn the Mau Mau or to expose British atrocities.

EXTRACT 2

The Mau Mau was a nationalist, anti-colonial peasant movement. In Mau Mau there were no revolutionary intellectuals. As a result, the Mau Mau lacked the focus and discipline of a revolutionary party. In the Mau Mau revolt, there was a direct challenge to the social order, which was colonial and racist. To this end, it could be argued that Mau Mau agitated for the abolition of the colonial system. The revolt strove for an independent future free of colonial control. Yet most of the participants were peasants who wanted their own land to live on and farm and who wanted to enjoy prosperity. But to strive for an independent future did not necessarily mean that Mau Mau activists had a common concrete idea as to the shape of this future. This remained one of their major weaknesses.

Adapted from *Mau Mau and Kenya* by Wunyabari O. Maloba (1998)

CROSS-REFERENCE

The situation in the Malay Peninsula is covered in Chapter 19, page 187 and Chapter 20, page 192.

The role of the nationalist leaders, including Onn bin Ja'afar, is examined in Chapter 22, pages 208–209.

Case study: the Malay States

The activities of the nationalist organisations of the Malay states exemplify some of the characteristics of the indigenous independence movements and show, in particular, how issues of race and ethnicity complicated the fight for independence. The principal Malay nationalist organisation, the UMNO, initially co-operated with the British to defeat the Communists who were attempting to establish control in the area after the war, but it opposed British ideas of a Malayan Union and after the British agreed to the establishment of the Federation of Malaya in 1949, giving semi-autonomous power to the region, it focused on political independence.

Make a list of the methods used and difficulties faced by: a) the Mau Mau and b) the nationalist movements in Malaya in their respective struggles for independence. In the light of your findings, consider the relative merits of violence and peaceful negotiation.

CROSS-REFERENCE

The background to the racial divisions in the Malay Peninsula is outlined in Chapter 19, page 187.

A CLOSER LOOK

The assassination of Sir Henry Gurney

In October 1951, Guerney, was being driven in his Rolls Royce, with his wife and private secretary, in a convoy including an armoured scout car, a police wireless van, and a Landrover with six Malayan policemen in its open back. Despite some engine trouble with the wireless van, Gurney had continued his journey, but 60 miles north of Kuala Lumpur, the convoy was fired upon by 38 Malayan Communist Party guerrillas who killed the chauffeur, injured Gurney and five of the six policemen and punctured tyres. As Gurney left his car, the guerrillas assassinated him. His wife and secretary survived.

However, Malaya's path to full independence was complicated by the position of the non-Malays (particularly the ethnic Chinese) in the region and the British decision that 'Malay nationality' be restricted to those of Malay ethnicity in 1949 aggravated the situation. Ja'afar left the UMNO in 1951 to form his own Independence of Malaya Party (IMP) having failed to broaden his party's ethnic membership. Although under Tunku Abdul Rahman the UMNO increased its power through alliances, underlying friction remained. Co-operation with the MCA (the Malayan Chinese Association) in 1954 and the MIC (Malayan Indian Congress) in 1955 ensured electoral success but did not resolve the issues of a **racially divided peninsula**.

The British co-operated with the UMNO because it offered a positive programme of action (extending primary schooling for example) and was ready to combat the very different tactics adopted by the militant independence movements such as the Malayan Races Liberation Army (MRLA) and Malayan Communist Party (MCP), the latter of which was supported by many Chinese influenced by the spread of communism in China itself. The militants' attacks on farms and police stations, their strike activity and disruption of transport and communication systems provoked the 'Malayan Emergency': an instance of British desperation. The MCP and several other left-wing political groups were declared illegal in 1948; but it took five years to defeat the insurrection, and in 1951, **Sir Henry Gurney**, the High Commissioner in Malaya, was shot dead in his official Rolls Royce by guerrillas.

The British anxiety was partly the result of fears of communism and partly because they were concerned to protect a valuable economic resource – the tin and rubber industry. Malaya was also a prime strategic asset. To restore stability, they had to depend on the local indigenous elite, and to gain this meant offering the promise of staged self-government. Once the Emergency was past, Tunku became the first Chief Minister of Malaya in 1955. However, when his discussions with Chin Peng, the MCP Secretary-General, broke down, Tunku had to turn to London to support a deal that would lead to full independence in August 1957.

Independence did not end internal strife. The underlying differences between the UMNO and MCA surfaced and many of the Chinese broke with their former allies. Ethnic troubles plagued the politics of the new state and although Tunku (in accordance with British wishes) created Malaysia in 1963, consisting of Singapore, Sabah and Sarawak (Brunei pulled out after an armed revolt there) this did not last. Friction in Singapore because of the strain in race relations led to riots in 1964, and in 1965 Singapore was expelled from the union. British hopes of retaining influence and interests in the area were thus weakened.

Case study: Nigeria

Ethnic division also plagued moves to independence in Nigeria, an area that prospered economically after the Second World War. Nigeria was an artificial creation, made up of diverse peoples and regions, and nationalism there derived more from pan-Africanism than from any sense of a common Nigerian nationality. The north was an Islamic area under emirs; here nationalist sentiments were decidedly anti-Western. In the west was an economically advanced and ambitious community that sought independent control. Southern nationalism was more influenced by European ideas, professional organisations of teachers, lawyers and traders and independent Christian churches. Nigeria had had an elected Legislative Council since 1922, which had helped stimulate political thinking, and wartime service by Nigerians in Ethiopia, Palestine, Morocco, Sicily and Burma reinforced the nationalism of the younger generation – particularly the educated intellectuals.

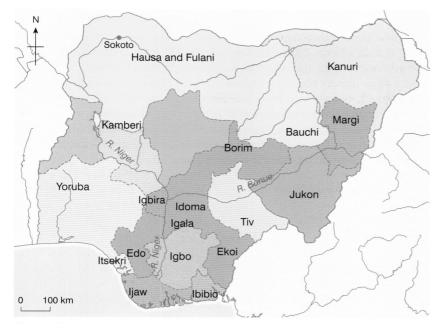

Fig. 4 *Ethnic divisions in Nigeria*

In the post-war period, several major nationalist independence parties emerged, but these were sharply drawn on the basis of regionalism and ethnicity.

- **The National Council of Nigeria and the Cameroons (NCNC).** This was dominated by the Igbo, under the commanding personality of Azikiwe, a man who owned a string of newspapers through which he could argue the nationalist cause. This party had the widest appeal.
- **The Action Group.** This was dominated by the Yoruba which resisted the concept of unitary government and represented the comparatively economically advanced Western Region. Despite divisions arising from conflict within the Yoruba community, its leader Awolowo proved a formidable debater and political campaigner. This group sought autonomous states within a federal structure, and was even prepared to support the severance of a mid-west state from the Western Region.
- **The Northern People's Congress (NPC).** This was dominated by the Hausa and Fulani and led by Western-educated northern Muslims with the assent of the emirs. The most powerful figure in the party was Ahmadu Bello, the *sardauna* (war leader) of Sokoto. Bello wanted to protect northern social and political institutions from southern influence and insisted on maintaining the territorial integrity of the Northern Region, including those areas with non-Muslim populations. However, peasant disaffection and rivalry among Muslim factions proved problematic.

In all three Nigerian regions, there were other minority parties representing the special interests of ethnic groups which made negotiations with the British government over constitutional changes a difficult exercise in compromise and political expediency. The co-operation that emerged was more the result of necessity in the face of an overall goal, than the product of an emerging sense of national identity.

Three constitutions were drawn up in consultation with the British from 1946 to 1954 amidst considerable political controversy as ethnic divisions intensified. Political activists in the southern areas sought self-government in order to promote educational opportunities and economic development. In the north, the emirs demanded firm control on economic and political change and made it clear that any action by the south would be seen as a challenge to the primacy

CROSS-REFERENCE

The role and influence of Azikiwe is discussed in Chapter 22, page 210.

Two examples of nationalist movements, one in Asia and one in Africa, have been provided in this section. Try to research some of the many more and include at least one from an area outside Asia and Africa. You could divide into small groups to do this and prepare a PowerPoint presentation for your class. Some suggestions of countries to look at are:

Asia: Singapore
Africa: the Gold Coast and Zambia
Europe: Cyprus
Americas: Trinidad and Tobago

of the emirates. Furthermore, the differences between the Yoruba and the Igbo grew more acute as they competed for control. Also, as the British granted more power to local officials and politicians, they rivalled one another for patronage over government jobs, funds for local development, market permits, trade licences, government contracts, and even scholarships for higher education.

The South, Western and Eastern regions became formally self-governing under the parliamentary system in 1957 and similar status was acquired by the Northern Region in 1959. However, while this 'grant' of a federal constitution by the British may have looked like a peaceful transition to self-rule, it actually shrouded considerable division that was to haunt Nigeria in the years to come.

Case study: Rhodesia

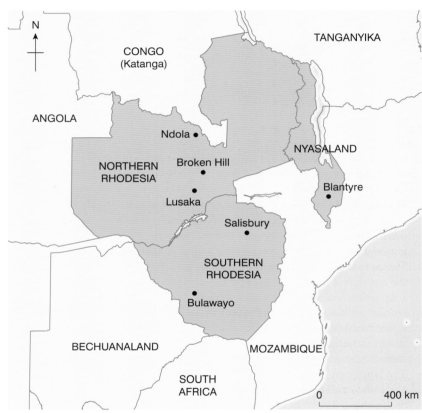

Fig. 5 *Map of Rhodesia*

The constitution of Southern Rhodesia is sometimes referred to as 'colour-blind'. It allowed black people to vote, but only if they met stringent education and property requirements, which the majority did not.

Another part of British colonial Africa with a substantial number of white settlers and a resentful black majority was the Rhodesias (North and South). In both Rhodesias there was much black resentment at low pay and few rights, which had intensified due to the increase in number of white settlers following the end of the Second World War. The 129,000 white settlers (many wealthy farmers) of Southern Rhodesia, who had been granted self-government in 1923, were intent on preserving white power whilst the 36,000 white settlers of Northern Rhodesia (mostly involved in the copper mining industry) also wanted white control, despite Northern Rhodesia's separate status as a Protectorate, directly ruled from London.

Since the mineral wealth of Northern Rhodesia seemed likely to tempt the Southern Rhodesian politicians to extend their influence, the British tried to forestall such a situation by creating a Federation of Rhodesia and Nyasaland in 1953. Known as the Central African Federation (CAF), each of the three areas within it was to have its own legislature and government. It was hoped that this would protect Africans in Northern Rhodesia and Nyasaland from the discriminatory **Southern Rhodesian laws**. However, the Southern white people tried to use the Federation to reinforce their own political leadership and to give the white Northern Rhodesians the same political influence. This left Nyasaland at the centre of a storm. It had very few white people and had resisted the Federation in 1953.

Black African nationalist congress parties emerged in both Northern Rhodesia and Nyasaland and in 1959, **Dr Hastings Banda** of Nyasaland returned from the Gold Coast (where he had been working as a doctor) to lead a campaign to end the Federation. The Governor of Nyasaland, Sir Robert Armitage, fearing the collapse of British authority, promptly declared a State of Emergency and banned the Nyasaland African Congress (NAC) and imprisoned its leaders (including Hastings Banda and **Kenneth Kaunda**). Around 1300 people, many of whom were members of the Congress parties (such as Harry Nkumbula of the Zambian (Northern Rhodesian) African National Congress) were also detained without trial and over 2000 were imprisoned for offences related to the Emergency. Reinforcements from Northern and Southern Rhodesia were used to round up activists and 51 were killed by troops or the police, including 20 in an incident at **Nkata Bay**.

Kenneth Kaunda (b. 1924) was the son of the first African missionary in Northern Rhodesia and had a varied career as an army instructor, schoolteacher, mine-worker and choirmaster before entering politics in the 1950s. In 1953, he became secretary-general of the ANC in Northern Rhodesia. He formed the Zambian (North Rhodesian) African National Congress (ZANC) in 1958 and in 1960 became president of the United National independence Party (UNIP). He encouraged a 'Cha-Cha-Cha' campaign of civil disobedience against the British and led Zambia (Northern Rhodesia) to independence, becoming its President from 1964 to 1991.

A specially convened British Commission of 1959 concluded that the Emergency had been an overreaction. It denounced Nyasaland for employing illegal and unnecessary force and endorsed the opinion that the majority of Nyasaland Africans were bitterly opposed to federation.

A CLOSER LOOK

The publication of the British Commission report in 1959 coincided with that on maltreatment at the Hola Camp in Kenya. It shook Macmillan's government by highlighting the dangers of Emergency rule.

Macmillan and Ian Macleod, his new Colonial Secretary from October 1959, had little choice but to agree to break up the Federation. However, the UNIP (United National Independence Party) led by Kenneth Kaunda in Northern Rhodesia contested the British proposals of 1961 and there was continuing violence as a solution was hammered out. Ultimately in 1964:
- Northern Rhodesia became the new African state of Zambia (under Kaunda) with provision for the emergence of a Black African majority government. It became a member of the Commonwealth.
- Nyasaland became Malawi (under Banda) – also with black majority rule and as a member of the Commonwealth.
- Southern Rhodesia under Ian Smith as Prime Minister retained a white-dominated government and in 1965 declared UDI – a **Unilateral Declaration of Independence** – as 'Rhodesia'.

A CLOSER LOOK

Nkata Bay, March 1959

Prisoners detained in Northern Rhodesia were waiting in Nkata Bay for a lake steamer to take them to the south. A local Congress leader tried to secure their release and encouraged a large crowd to gather at the dockside. The District Commissioner, fearing the situation was getting out of control, ordered troops to open fire on the crowds.

KEY PROFILE

Fig.6   *Banda studied medicine in the USA and Scotland*

Dr Hastings Banda (1898–1997) was born in Nyasaland and educated by missionaries. He worked in London, becoming a nationalist before spending five years in Kenya and one on the Gold Coast. In 1959 he returned home and involved himself in politics. He became Prime Minister on independence in 1963 and through the establishment of Malawi in 1964. He was President from 1966 to 1994: a period marked by violence and political assassination.

KEY TERM

Unilateral Declaration of Independence: a declaration of independence from imperial rule without the normal two-sided negotiations and legal procedures expected to establish this

Fig. 7 *Smith served in the RAF during the Second World War*

Ian Smith (1919–2007) was a white Southern Rhodesian, educated in South Africa. He was elected to the Southern Rhodesian Parliament in 1948. He supported the British-proposed federation with Northern Rhodesia and Nyasaland, but when this broke down, helped form the Rhodesian Front Party (RF). He became Prime Minister in 1964 on an anti-black rule programme. He issued UDI in 1965 and remained in power until 1979, refusing to negotiate any compromise.

ACTIVITY

Create a flow chart to show the development of the Rhodesias/ Nyasaland from their inauguration as British colonies in the nineteenth century until 1967. Highlight the key developments and turning points. (You will need to refer back to Chapters 1, 7 and 19 to help you in this).

STUDY TIP

You need to look carefully at the reasons given in each extract not only about the successes of the nationalist movements but also about their weaknesses and the ways in which they were and were not important. Weigh up the ideas the extracts present and use your own knowledge to evaluate what they say.

A CLOSER LOOK

Smith and the White Rhodesian Front

A hard-line white settler movement, the Rhodesian Front (RF) – initially led by the Prime Minister Winston Field, but dominated by his deputy, Ian Smith – had emerged in Southern Rhodesia. The RF rejected the British demand for majority rule or some sort of white/black power-sharing as the price of independence. Southern Rhodesia had its own small army and was therefore in a position to ignore the British demands. The dominant white leadership simply imprisoned black African nationalists such as members of the Zimbabwe African National Union (ZANU) and Zimbabwe African People's Union (ZAPU), led Robert Mugabe and Joshua Nkomo.

UDI was rejected as illegal and unconstitutional by Britain, the United Nations and most of the rest of the world, but Smith defiantly pursued his own line. Britain imposed sanctions, but they proved of little use since South Africa refused to cooperate. The affair revealed Britain's embarrassing impotence. Whilst claiming a world role, it proved unable to deal with rebels in its own ex-colony. Britain also received a torrent of criticism from the Commonwealth (where other nations accused the British of betraying Commonwealth ideals). Apart from Britain's malaise, UDI triggered a 15-year long civil war between white people and black nationalists in what Smith called 'Rhodesia'. This finally culminated in the establishment of black African majority rule and the creation of Zimbabwe in 1980: it was the last British African colony to achieve independence.

EXTRACT 3

The significance of nationalist movements in bringing about the end of empire can be questioned. Until local crises blew up, policy towards specific colonies was mainly determined by Britain's economic and national needs, while plans for individual territories were shaped by reasoned assessments for the security, economic viability social cohesion and political maturity of each. Increasingly, however, events forced the British to compromise – ultimately to abandon – staged progress, measured programmes and long-term planning. But even then authorities were influenced more by the dangers of lawlessness on a colony than by the force of nationalists' demands. Left to themselves, the British would probably have proceeded slowly – worrying about whether colonies were important from a British point of view and setting a leisurely programme for them to evolve towards independence. But outbreaks of violence and disorder increasingly forced the pace. In general violence was not deliberately instigated by the nationalists. But nationalist movements did benefit from unrest since the British did not want to hold out for long against violence.

Adapted from 'Power, Authority and Freedom' by A.J. Stockwell (1996)

 PRACTICE QUESTION

Evaluating historical extracts

Using your understanding of the historical context, assess how convincing the arguments in Extracts 1, 2 and 3 are, in relation to the importance of nationalist movements in bringing about independence from British imperial rule in the years 1947 to 1967.

Summary

The degree to which nationalist movements contributed to the end of empire can certainly be questioned, but they cannot be ignored. Nationalist movements posed a clear challenge to British authority. Such movements were sometimes violent – as in the case of the Mau Mau – but more often emerged from developed political groups, led by charismatic leaders, working within the imperial system. They railed against injustice but they were also the product of imperial rule. They grew out of the expansion of education and educational opportunities and were stimulated by the post-war growth in colonial economies. Both factors produced the leadership and national consciousness needed for movements to succeed. Most nationalist movements did, however, have to cope with ethnic and racial divisions as well as regional diversity. Side by side with the nationalists' struggles for independence, therefore, there were often equally vigorous struggles between the nationalists themselves and these sometimes boiled over once independence was achieved.

ACTIVITY

Summary

Consider the aims of the various nationalist movements you have looked at. Complete the table to record details of their aims, methods, the British response and their success. Five have been supplied to get you started.

Nationalist movement	Aims	Methods	British response	Success
Mau Mau				
The United Malays National organisation (UMNO)				
The National Council of Nigeria and the Cameroons (NCNC)				
The Nyasaland African Congress (NAC)				
Rhodesian Front (RF)				

PRACTICE QUESTION

To what extent did Britain retain the initiative in negotiations with indigenous peoples in negotiations leading to the independence of former colonies in the years 1947 to 1957?

STUDY TIP

This question is asking you to determine how far Britain was able to act as the 'leader' in negotiations leading to independence – moving at its own pace and achieving the terms it wanted – and how far indigenous peoples, through their nationalist movements and leaders, actually dictated the pace and details of change. In answering the question you should aim to draw on a variety of examples and ensure you provide some evidence on both sides. You should, however, reach an overall conclusion.

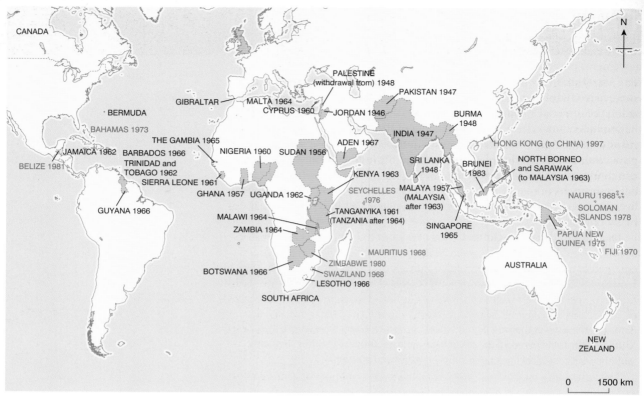

Fig. 5 *The end of the British Empire in 1967 with dates of independence; dates in red are post-1967*

Conclusion

For nearly a century after 1857, the phrase, 'the Empire on which the sun never sets' – implying an empire that was so extensive that there was always at least one part of it enjoying daylight – was popularly used to describe the nations and peoples over which Britain exerted its sovereignty. British world maps with the Empire shaded in a contented glow of red were published and pored over by officials, businessmen and schoolchildren. It is hard to think of a more powerful visual way of reinforcing the imperial mindset. Visual demonstrations of the geographical extent of Britain's global influence helped bolster a sense of British superiority and 'right' to rule other peoples, that was rarely questioned before the 1920s.

Of course, this Empire did not last and the sun did indeed set after the Second World War so that, between 1947 and 1967, many new nation states emerged and the British were forced to rethink their role in the changing world. However, even during and after decolonisation, the legacy of empire was such that the experience left its mark – both positive and negative. Today, the legacy of empire can be seen and heard constantly – in the daily news, in current demographics and conflicts in Africa and Asia and in the complex affairs of the Middle East. It is also present in international commerce and in the food, sport and language that are adopted in many different parts of the world.

The years between 1857 and 1967 were both years of imperial achievement and innovation and years of atrocity and oppression. There was much about empire, particularly the attitudes to and treatment of native peoples, that is abhorrent to the modern mind. Yet, another legacy of empire – the Commonwealth, which is committed to the cause of world peace, human rights, equality, democracy and economic development – suggests that the Empire had some positive outcomes. That two such differing impressions exist is evidence of the varied and incoherent nature of the Empire and how it has meant (and continues to mean) different things to different people at different times.

Evaluating British imperialism is not straightforward and, as this book has shown, it is all too easy to view developments from a twenty-first-century perspective and to be ultra-critical of British actions. It must be remembered that the development of empire was not unique to Britain, even if the British possessions were the most extensive of all the European nations. The expansion and control of empire was not purely the result of greed and military conquest, nor was it solely driven by a selfish search for trade and resources. Clearly that was part of the process but there was much more besides and the 'moral' motives alleged in publications of the nineteenth century were genuinely held by many of a religious disposition. To attribute the British Empire to rampant greed is to forget that the Empire was rarely cost-effective. Nor was empire always imposed on unwilling peoples; it relied on collaboration with colonials and direct support from colonies that actually facilitated imperial expansion. Adding to the complexities of interpretation, it is also important to remember that for most of the Empire's history, imperial peoples exhibited as much, if not more, patriotism and loyalty to their British monarch than those living within the British Isles themselves.

This is not to absolve Britain from all blame in forcing its control over other peoples and for the way in which it ran its empire. The acceptance of British dominance, readiness to embrace inequality in government, attitudes to race and an imperial ideology which accepted empire as 'natural' are all seen as unacceptable today. Certainly atrocities were committed – from the crushing of the Indian Mutiny to the Boer War and the action against the Mau Mau. Imperialism could often bring out the worst in the nation. It is therefore unsurprising, perhaps, that imperial controversy still rages. When, in 2011, a life-size bronze sculpture of the Welsh explorer Henry Morton Stanley (born in Denbigh in 1841) was commissioned to go in front of the Denbigh Library Museum and Gallery, 50 eminent people, including Jan Morris whose writings have been used in extracts in this book, signed a letter of protest against the statue. They argued that Stanley's expeditions had contributed to the 'racism' of today. The sculptor Nick Elphick countered the criticism by saying: 'I think it's wrong to judge people by our own understanding today, because they were brought up very differently.' Having studied this book, it is hoped that you feel able to engage with issues such as this from a standpoint of historical knowledge and understanding.

Fig. 1 *The statue of Sir Henry Morton Stanley in Denbigh High Street, Wales*

Through your reading of this book, you should now be able to answer the key questions that were posed in the introduction. None of these have 'easy' answers but by seeking to address them you will come to appreciate many of the issues which affected the growth, development and decline of the Empire during the years 1857 to 1967, and which continue to affect the present-day world. You should understand the complexity of interests and ideas which played a role in developments and the forces which restricted the decision-makers' freedom of manoeuvre. You should, in short, be in a position to form judgements of your own about the issues, events and developments which this book explores and in so doing, appreciate the importance of the Empire, both historically and in shaping lives in the twenty-first century.

Glossary

A

Afrikaner: this term gradually replaced the use of 'Boer' to denote an Afrikaans-speaking person in South Africa, descended from the predominantly Dutch settlers there

Anglicans: members of the Protestant (non-Catholic) Church of England; the established Christian Church of Great Britain with the monarch, at its head

Angry Young Men: British playwrights and novelists of the early 1950s whose work was marked by irreverence towards the Establishment and disgust at the survival of class distinctions and privilege

apartheid: originally coming from an Afrikaans word which means 'separateness', this came to represent a policy of discrimination and segregation on grounds of race

Arab league: an organisation of North African and Arabian Arab countries formed in 1945

Ashanti: an ethnic group which had once possessed a large Empire along the Gulf of Guinea

B

Bantu: a general label for the 300–600 ethnic groups in Africa who speak Bantu languages; they inhabit a geographical area stretching east and southward from Central Africa across the African Great Lakes region down to Southern Africa

bellicosity: an aggressive attitude suggesting an eagerness to fight

benign: kind or causing no harm

Boers: Dutch population which settled in South Africa in the late 1600s

C

cabinet minister: one of a committee of senior ministers responsible for controlling government policy

caste: a particular social position according to traditional Hindu hierarchy

chartered companies: a trading company would gain status, legal rights and privileges on award of a royal charter; such a company would be granted permission to rule indirectly within their territory of operation

client state: an area with its own ruler but with strong British influence which restricted that ruler's independence politically, militarily and economically

coalition government: a government combining a number of different political parties

Commonwealth: an association consisting of the UK together with states that were previously part of the British Empire, and its dependencies

constituent assembly: a body elected to draw up a constitution for a state

consul general: Britain's highest governmental representative in an overseas territory; the Consul General speaks on behalf of his state in the country in which he is located

cornucopia: literally means, a 'horn of plenty'; in other words, an abundant supply of good things

Crown Colony: a colony ruled directly by an appointee of the British crown and accountable to the Colonial Office

D

Dervish: members of a Muslim order committed to the defence of the faith through frenzied attack

diaspora: the spread of peoples from their original homeland

dominion: a British-settler colony with self-governing powers, albeit with the British monarch as head of state

dual mandate: the belief that a colonial power had a double responsibility: to its colonial peoples, it owed material and moral advancement leading to self-government; to the outside world it had the obligation to see that the natural resources of its colonies were developed and exploited

durbar: a public reception held by an Indian prince or British Viceroy

dyarchy: a system of rule where power is divided between two centres of authority

E

effective occupation: a European power which could demonstrate that it had a local treaty agreement, an active administration and was able to police the territory it claimed, was recognised as the rightful ruler of that territory

The European Economic Community (EEC): a free trade community originally comprising France, Germany, Belgium, Luxembourg, the Netherlands and Italy

F

federal: a system of government in which several states form a single country but remain independent in internal affairs

free trade: a market system whereby goods are both imported and exported between countries or zones without restriction or imposition of tariffs

G

Ganda: the ethnic group of the Ganda people formed one of the largest and most powerful states in East Africa during the eighteenth and nineteenth centuries

geopolitical: the effects of geography on the politics of a nation; especially how that nation's concerns and interests around the world influence it foreign, economic and defence policies

The gold standard: a system by which the value of the currency was defined in terms of gold, for which the currency could be exchanged

Great Depression: this was a worldwide economic slump beginning in c1873 and lasting until c1896

guerrilla war: war pursued by civilian forces rather than conventional armies, usually against a much stronger conventional army: tactics involve ambushes and raids, rather than full scale battles

H

haganah: an underground Jewish militia in Palestine (1920–48) that became the national army of Israel after the partition of Palestine in 1948

Hard Currency Pool: a collective pool of dollars earned by the Sterling Area

hegemony: dominance by one state over others in the region

I

indigenous: native or born in the area

informal empire: areas influenced, if not ruled, by the British via deals with local rulers

insurgent: displaying armed hostility to established authority; an individual rebel is also known as 'an insurgent'

'invisibles': any export that provides income but does not have a physical presence; examples include insurance, banking services and return on overseas investments

The Jewish National Fund: an international organisation founded in 1901 in Switzerland at the Fifth Zionist Congress: its role

was to buy land in Palestine for Jewish settlement

J

jihadist: a person fighting a holy war

jingoism: Empire-related patriotism, encouraging and celebrating British imperial gains, boasting about Britain's power

K

Khedive: the ruler of Egypt, who exercised authority on behalf of the Ottoman Sultan

L

Lend-Lease: an arrangement during the Second World War by which the US supplied Britain, weapons, food and other necessities

M

Mahdi: an Islamic redeemer – regarded by Shi'ites as the Twelfth Imam (the final successor to the Prophet Muhammad)

mandate: a territory allocated by the League of Nations to a particular country to be governed by that country on the League's behalf

Marshall Plan: a programme of US economic aid for the reconstruction of post-World War II Europe (1948–52)

mercantilism: a system of regulations governing trade

Methodists: a Protestant nonconformist group; this movement had grown strongly in some of England's industrial working class communities in the early nineteenth century

metropole: the parent state of a colony

monopoly: means an exclusive right to control trade

N

National Service: between 1939 and 1960, young British men aged

17–21 years were required to undertake military service for up to 18 months

NATO: the North Atlantic treaty Organisation, set up in 1949 as an inter-governmental organisation but with an American supreme allied commander

non-Conformist: a religious non-Conformist is a member of a Protestant Church which acts independently from the established Church of England

O

Organisation of African Unity: an organisation representing states across Africa dedicated to improving the life of Africans

P

Pax Britannica: Latin for 'British Peace'; the term was used to mirror the Romans' use of 'Pax Romana' meaning a period of peace brought about by the dominant power

plebiscite: a direct vote by all the members of the electorate in a country on an important public question such as a change in the constitution

Princely States: large parts of India that had been bound to the British Crown by treaties and were 'protected' in return

Presbyterians: a Protestant nonconformist denomination deriving from Calvinist ideas of a Church which preferred simple services and has no bishops

protectionist: using tariffs – particularly duties on imported goods to regulate trade

protectorate: an area with its own ruler, but placed under the protection of the British Crown, which controlled it militarily and usually influenced domestic policies through advisers

provincial autonomy: a nation state where there is a central government, but in which the different provinces are constitutionally given a measure of control of their own affairs

puppet ruler: a ruler who has to act as directed by his master

R

Raj: taken from the Hindi term for 'king' or 'rule', formal British rule in India between 1858 and 1947 became known as the British Raj

representative system: a system of government in which citizens vote for an assembly to govern them

responsible government: a system of government similar to that in Britain itself, where areas had their own government ministers who were answerable to their individual elected parliaments

Roman Catholics: those who believed the Pope to be the Head of the Christian Church and did not accept Anglicanism

Round Table Conference: a meeting between all the political groups interested in a controversial question with a view to working out a commonly agreed way forward

S

Satyagraha: 'insistence on the truth'; rejecting violence to combat evil, relying instead upon peaceful protest: the aim is to win by appealing to the moral conscience and compassion of one's opponents

scorched earth policy: this is a military strategy that involves destroying anything that might be useful to the enemy while advancing through (or withdrawing from) an area

SEATO: the South East Asian Asia Treaty Organisation, set up in 1954 was a counter-part to NATO for the collective defence of South-East Asia against communism. It did not, however, have a joint command

secular: means without religious basis; secular authorities here include the legal system,

police, military powers and governments

self-determination: the right of a distinct national or ethnic group of people to determine their own nation-state and form of government

sepoys: Indian soldiers serving in the East India Company Army

'special relationship': a close political and diplomatic association which stemmed from the shared cultural and historical heritage of the United States with its former 'master', Britain

Star of India medal: an order of chivalry founded by Queen Victoria in 1861 with three classes: Knight Grand Commander, Knight Commander, Companion

State of Emergency: this involves the suspension of normal constitutional procedures during a situation of particular national danger

Sterling Area: countries (mostly although not all in the Empire and Commonwealth) that either pegged their currencies to the pound sterling, or used the pound as their own currency: the arrangement was formalised under the Exchange Control Act of 1947 and lasted even after the devaluation of the £ against the US dollar in 1967 precipitated its end

Stern gang: militant Zionist terrorist organization (officially Lohame Herut Yisra'el 'Fighters for the Freedom of Israel') founded 1940 by Avram Stern

suffrage: the right to vote in elections. Full adult suffrage means that all adults can vote

suzerainty: a situation in which a powerful region or people controls the foreign affairs of a tributary vassal state while allowing the subservient nation internal autonomy

T

tariff: a duty or tax paid on goods travelling between countries or zones

trusteeship: a concept whereby colonies had to be ruled in a way that looked after the interests of the native peoples as well as white people: economic development had to benefit native peoples as well as colonial powers

U

Unilateral Declaration of Independence: a declaration of independence from imperial rule without the normal two-sided negotiations and legal procedures expected to establish this

unitary state: a nation state governed by a single centre of power (government), and where that government only devolves as much power as it chooses to do

United Nations: established at the end of the Second World War, this was the successor organisation to the League of Nations: its aim was to maintain world peace and settling international disputes by negotiation

V

veiled protectorate: a state controlled by another in an indirect manner

Viceroy: a ruler exercising direct authority on behalf of the sovereign

Z

zealot: a person who is fanatical and uncompromising in pursuit of their ideals

Zionist: a political belief and movement advocating the creation of a national Jewish homeland based on the historic kingdom of Israel in the Middle East

Bibliography

Students

Brendon, Piers, *The Decline and Fall of the British Empire*, Vintage, 2008

Chamberlain, Muriel, *The Scramble for Africa*, Longman, 1999

Dalziel, Nigel, *The Penguin Historical Atlas of the British Empire,* Penguin, 2006

Darwin, John, *The Empire Project,* Cambridge University Press, 2009

Darwin, John, *Unfinished Empire – The Global Expansion of Britain,* Penguin, 2013

Ferguson, Niall, *Empire: How Britain Made the Modern World,* Penguin, 2004

Jackson, Ashley, *The British Empire, a Very Short Introduction*, Oxford University Press, 2013

James, Lawrence, *The Rise and Fall of the British Empire*, Abacus, 1995

Marshall, P.J. (ed.), *The Cambridge Illustrated History of the British Empire*, Cambridge University Press, 1996

Paxman, Jeremy, *Empire*, Penguin, 2012

Teachers and extension

Brad Faught, C., *The New A-Z of Empire*, Tauris, 2011

MacKenzie, John M. *Propaganda and Empire*, Manchester University Press, 1988

Morris, Jan, *Pax Britannica*, Faber and Faber, 1968

Porter, Andrew (ed.), *The Oxford History of the British Empire*, Oxford University Press, 1999

Stockwell, Sarah (ed.), *The British Empire, Themes and Perspectives,* Blackwell, 2008

Hyam, Ronald, *Understanding the British Empire*, Cambridge University Press, 2010

India

Allen, Charles, *Raj: A Scrapbook of British India 1877–1947*, Penguin, 1979

Brown, Judith, *Modern India*, Oxford University Press, 1994

Copland, Ian, *India 1885–1947*, Routledge, 2001

Misra, Maria, *Vishnu's Crowded Temple: India since the Great Rebellion*, Yale University Press, 2008

Von Tunzelmann, Alex, *Indian Summer: The Secret History of an End of an Empire*, Pocket Books, 2007

Africa

Meredith, Martin, *The State of Africa: A History of the Continent Since Independence*, Free Press, 2005

Osborne, Myles and Susan Kingsley Kent, *Africans and Britons in the Age of Empires 1660–1980*, Routledge, 2015

Pakenham, Thomas, *The Scramble for Africa*, Abacus, 1992

Reid, Richard J., *A, History of Modern Africa*, Wiley-Blackwell, 2009

Robinson, Ronald, John Gallagher and Alice Denny, *Africa and the Victorians: the Official Mind of Imperialism*, I.B. Tauris 2015

Other

Porter, Bernard, *The Absent-Minded Imperialists: Empire, Society and Culture in Britain*, Oxford University Press, 2005

Watts, Duncan, *Joseph Chamberlain and the Challenge of Radicalism*, Hodder and Stoughton, 1992

Articles

Carr, Robert, 'The Evangelical Empire: Christianity's Contribution to Victorian Colonial Expansion', britishempire.co.uk

Hammal, Rowena, 'How Long Before the Sunset? British Attitudes Towards War 1871–1914', *History Review*, Issue 68, Dec 2010

Porter, Bernard, 'Cutting the British Empire Down to Size', *History Today*, Vol 62, Issue 10, Oct 2012

Llewellyn-Jones, Rosie, 'Delhi: Short-Lived Capital of the Raj', *History Today*, Vol 61, Issue 12, Dec 2011

Roberts, Andrew, 'Salisbury: The Empire Builder Who Never Was', *History Today*, Vol 49, Issue 10, Nov 1999

Simpson, Neil, 'An "Informal Empire"?', britishempire.co.uk

Websites

www.britishempire.co.uk
www.africafederation.net

Acknowledgements

The publisher would like to thank the following for permission to use their photographs:

Cover: The Delhi Durbar, 1903 (oil on canvas), MacKenzie, Roderick D. (1865-1941)/Private Collection/Bridgeman Images; **pxv:** The Return Visit of the Viceroy to the Maharajah of Cashmere, 1863 (chromolitho), Simpson, William 'Crimea' (1823-99)/Private Collection/The Stapleton Collection/Bridgeman Images; **p2:** The Keasbury-Gordon Photograph Archive/Alamy; **p5:** Mary Evans Picture Library; **p6:** Barry Iverson Collection/Alamy; **p9:** The Art Archive/Alamy; **p13:** Mary Evans Picture Library; **p17:** The National Archives, London. England/Mary Evans Picture Library; **p18:** Photos 12/Alamy; **p20:** Wikipedia Commons; **p23:** North Wind Picture Archives/Alamy; **p25:** Universal Images Group Editorial/Getty Images; **p27:** Hulton Archive/Getty Images; **p28:** Heritage Auctiions; **p31:** Popperfoto/Getty Images; **p34:** Universal Images Group Editorial/Getty Images; **p37:** Pictorial Press Ltd/Alamy; **p38:** Pictorial Press Ltd/Alamy; **p39:** Hulton Archive/Getty Images; **p42:** Pictures From History/AKG-images; **p43:** (l) The Print Collector/Alamy, (r) Universal Images Group Editorial/Getty Images; **p47:** The LIFE Picture Collection/Getty Images; **p50:** Pictorial Press Ltd/Alamy; **p53:** (l) DINODIA/Age Fotostock, (r) Universal Images Group Editorial/Getty Images; **p55:** De Agostini/Lebrecht Music and Arts; **p60:** Stock Montage, Inc./Alamy; **p63:** Photos 12/Alamy; **p68:** Hulton Archive/Getty Images; **p69:** Wikipedia Commons; **p72:** The Viceregal Palace, Simla, c.1890 (b/w photo), English Photographer, (19th century)/Private Collection/Bridgeman Images; **p75:** Hulton Archive/Getty Images; **p77:** Thomas Cook Archive/Mary Evans Picture Library; **p79:** Mary Evans Picture Library/Alamy; **p81:** Hulton Archive/Getty Images; **p85:** Lordprice Collection/Alamy; **p86:** Archive Photos/Getty Images; **p88:** National Archives; **p91:** Classic Image/Alamy; **p93:** Universal Images Group Editorial/Getty Images; **p94:** Chronicle/Alamy; **p95:** Hulton Archive/Getty Images; **p98:** Mary Evans Picture Library/Alamy; **p102:** Universal Images Group Editorial/Getty Images; **p103:** The Art Archive/Alamy; **p104:** John Frost Newspapers/Mary Evans Picture Library; **p106:** George A. Smathers Libraries, University of Florida; **p108:** Mary Evans Picture Library; **p111:** Illustrated London News Ltd/Mary Evans Picture Library; **p113:** Look and Learn/Illustrated Papers Collection/Bridgeman Art Library; **p114:** Chronicle/Alamy; **p116:** Universal Images Group Editorial/Getty Images; **p126:** David Cole/Alamy; **p129:** By permission of Llyfrgell Genedlaethol Cymru/The National Library of Wales; **p135:** Dinodia Photos/Alamy; **p138:** ullstein bild/Getty Images; **p140:** Hulton-Deutsch Collection/Corbis UK Ltd.; **p142:** Popperfoto/Getty Images; **p145:** The Print Collector /Alamy; **p147:** The National Archives, London. England/Mary Evans Picture Library; **p150:** Pictorial Press Ltd/Alamy; **p151:** Sueddeutsche Zeitung Photo/Mary Evans Picture Library; **p154:** (l) Dinodia Photos/Alamy, (r) Imagno/Mary Evans Picture Library; **p157:** Ulana Switucha/Alamy; **p158:** Hulton Archive/Getty Images; **p161:** The National Archives, London. England/Mary Evans Picture Library; **p162:** The National Archives, London. England/Mary Evans Picture Library; **p163:** Chronicle/Alamy; **p164:** Norwich Evening News 24; **p165:** The Lothians; **p169:** Hulton Archive/Getty Images; **p170:** Yvan Travert/AKG-images; **p173:** The Scout Association/Mary Evans Picture Library; **p174:** Everett Collection Historical/Alamy; **p175:** Gamma-Keystone/Getty Images; **p178:** Bettmann/Corbis UK Ltd.; **p183:** James Davis Photography/Alamy; **p186:** Hulton Archive/Getty Images; **p188:** Trinity Mirror/Mirrorpix/Alamy; **p191:** Gamma-Keystone/Getty Images; **p194:** (t) Hulton Archive/Getty Images, (b) Trinity Mirror/Mirrorpix/Alamy; **p198:** Bettmann/Corbis UK Ltd.; **p200:** Hulton Royals Collection/Getty Images; **p203:** Bettmann/Corbis UK Ltd.; **p205:** Keystone Pictures USA/Alamy; **p210:** Popperfoto/Getty Images; **p212:** The LIFE Picture Collection/Getty Images; **p213:** Gamma-Keystone/Getty Images; **p216:** Popperfoto/Getty Images; **p219:** Keystone Pictures USA/Alamy; **p222:** SSPL/Getty Images; **p224:** Hulton Archive/Getty Images; **p227:** Popperfoto/Getty Images; **p232:** Popperfoto/Getty Images; **p235:** Popperfoto/Getty Images; **p239:** Keystone Pictures USA/Alamy; **p240:** Hulton Archive/Getty Images; **p244:** Ian G Dagnall/Alamy

Artwork by OKS and OUP.

We are grateful to the authors and publishers for use of extracts from their titles and in particular for the following:

Harm J de Blij & Peter O Müller: *Geography: Realms, Regions and Concepts* (10e, Wiley, 2002), copyright © 1971, reproduced by permission of John Wiley & Sons, Inc, via Copyright Clearance Center, Inc. **Piers Brendon:** *The Decline and Fall of the British Empire* (Cape, 2007), reproduced by permission of The Random House Group Ltd. **Judith Brown:** 'India' in Judith Brown & W Roger Louis (Eds): *Oxford History of the British Empire, Volume 4, The Twentieth Century* (OUP, 1999), reproduced by permission of Oxford University Press. **P J Cain:** 'Gentlemanly Imperialism at work: the Bank of England, Canada and the Sterling Area 1932-36' in *Economic History Review* Vol. 49, No 2 (May 1996), copyright © 1996, reproduced by permission of John Wiley & Sons Ltd, via Copyright Clearance Center, Inc. **P J Cain & A G Hopkins:** 'Gentlemanly Capitalism and British Expansion Overseas; New Imperialism 1850-1945', in *Economic History Review*, Vol. 40, No 1 (Feb 1987), copyright © 1987, reproduced by permission of John Wiley & Sons Ltd, via Copyright Clearance Center, Inc; *British Imperialism 1688-2001* (Longman, 2001), copyright © P J Cain & A G Hopkins 1983, reproduced by permission of Taylor & Francis Books UK. **M E Chamberlain:** *Scramble for Africa* (3e, Longman, 2010), copyright © M E Chamberlain 1974, reproduced by permission of Taylor & Francis Books UK. **Linda Colley:** 'Into the belly of the beast', review of Niall Fergusson's book *Empire*, *The Guardian*, 18 Jan 2003, reproduced by permission

of the author. **John Darwin:** *The Empire Project: The Rise and Fall of the British World-System, 1830-1970* (Cambridge University Press, 2009), copyright © John Darwin 2009, reproduced by permission of the publishers; *Britain and Decolonisation: the Retreat from Empire in the post-war world* (Palgrave Macmillan, 1988), reproduced by permission of Palgrave Macmillan; *Unfinished Empire* (Allen Lane, 2012), copyright © John Darwin 2012, reproduced by permission of Penguin Books Ltd. **D K Fieldhouse:** 'The Metropolitan Economics of Empire', in Judith Brown & W Roger Louis (Eds): *Oxford History of the British Empire, Volume 4, The Twentieth Century* (OUP, 1999), reproduced by permission of Oxford University Press. **Niall Ferguson:** *Empire: the rise and demise of the British World Order and the Lessons for Global Power* (Allen Lane, 2002), copyright © Niall Ferguson 2002, reproduced by permission of Penguin Books Ltd. **Cherry Gertzel:** 'East and Central Africa' in Michael Crowder (Ed): *The Cambridge History of Africa*, vol. 8: from c 1945 to c 1975 (Cambridge University Press, 1984), copyright © Cambridge University Press 1984, reproduced by permission of the publishers. **Catherine Hall:** 'Culture and Identity in Imperial Britain', in S E Stockwell (Ed): *The British Empire: themes and perspectives* (Blackwell, 2008), copyright © 2008, reproduced by permission of Blackwell Publishers via Copyright Clearance Center, Inc. **Michael Havinden** and **David Meredith:** *Colonialism and Development: Britain and its Tropical Colonies, 1850-1960* (Taylor & Francis, 1993), copyright © Michael Havinden and David Meredith 1993, reproduced by permission of Taylor & Francis Books UK. **Robert Holland:** 'The British Empire and the Great War', in Judith Brown & W Roger Louis (Eds): *Oxford History of the British Empire, Volume 4, The Twentieth Century* (OUP, 1999), reproduced by permission of Oxford University Press. **Ronald Hyam:** *Understanding the British Empire* (Cambridge University Press, 2010), copyright © Ronald Hyam 2010, reproduced by permission of the publishers. **Stephen Howe:** 'Empire and Ideology', in S E Stockwell (Ed): *The British Empire: themes and perspectives* (Blackwell, 2008), copyright © 2008, reproduced by permission of Blackwell Publishers via Copyright Clearance Center, Inc. **Ashley Jackson:** *The British Empire: A Very Short Introduction* (OUP, 2013), reproduced by permission of Oxford University Press. **Lawrence James:** *The Rise and Fall of the British Empire* (Abacus, 2004), copyright © Lawrence James 1998, reproduced by permission of Little, Brown Book Group Ltd, Hachette UK. **Dane Kennedy:** *Britain and Empire 1880-1945* (Longman, 2002), copyright © Dane Kennedy 2002, reproduced by permission of Taylor & Francis Books UK. **Juhani Koponen:** 'The Partition of Africa: A Scramble for a Mirage?', *Nordic Journal of African Studies* 2: 1 (1993), reproduced by permission of the NJAS. **Philippa Levine:** *The British Empire: Sunrise to Sunset* (Pearson, 2013), copyright © Philippa Levine 2007, reproduced by permission of Taylor & Francis Books UK. **William Roger Louis:** 'The Dissolution of the British Empire', in Judith Brown & W Roger Louis (Eds): *Oxford History of the British Empire, Volume 4, The Twentieth Century* (OUP, 1999), reproduced by permission of Oxford University Press. **J M Mackenzie:** 'Empire and Metropolitan Culture', in Andrew Porter (ed): *Oxford History of the British Empire, Volume 3, The Nineteenth Century* (OUP, 1999); and 'The Popular Culture of Empire in Britain', in Judith Brown & W Roger Louis (eds): *Oxford History of the British Empire, Volume 4, The Twentieth Century* (OUP, 1999), reproduced by permission of Oxford University Press. **P J Marshall** (Ed): *The Cambridge Illustrated History of the British Empire* (Cambridge University Press, 1996), copyright © Cambridge University Press 1996, reproduced by permission of the publishers. **Jan Morris:** *Pax Britannica* (Faber, 1968), copyright © James Morris 1968, reproduced by permission of United Agents (www.unitedagents.co.uk) on behalf of the author. **B R Nanda:** *In search of Gandhi: Essays and Reflections* (OUP, 2002), reproduced by permission of Oxford University Press. **Jeremy Paxman:** *Empire: What ruling the world did to the British* (Penguin, 2011), copyright © Jeremy Paxman 2011, reproduced by permission of Penguin Books Ltd. **Andrew Porter** (Ed): 'Introduction' to *Oxford History of the British Empire, Volume 3, The Nineteenth Century* (OUP, 1999), reproduced by permission of Oxford University Press. **Bernard Porter:** *Absent-minded Imperialists* (OUP, 2004), reproduced by permission of Oxford University Press. **Ronald Robinson, John Gallagher** and **Alice Denny:** *Africa and the Victorians* (I B Tauris. 2015), reproduced by permission of I B Tauris & Co Ltd. **Werner Schlote:** *British Overseas Trade from 1700 to the 1930s* translated by W O Henderson and W H Chaloner (Blackwell, 1952), reproduced by permission of Blackwell Publishers, John Wiley & Sons Ltd. **Gene Sharp:** *Gandhi's Political Significance Today* published on www.mkgandhi.org, reproduced by permission of the Gandhi Peace Foundation. **John Springhall:** *Decolonization since 1945* (Palgrave Macmillan, 2001), reproduced by permission of Palgrave Macmillan. **Murray Steele:** 'Transmitting Ideas of Empire: Representations and celebrations in Liverpool, 1886-1953', in S Haggerty, A Webster, and N J White (Eds): *The Empire in One City: Britain's Inconvenient Imperial Past* (Manchester University Press, 2012), reproduced by permission of the publishers. **Andrew Thompson** with **Megan Kowalsky:** 'Social Life and Cultural Representation: Empire in the Public Imagination', in Andrew Thompson (Ed): *Britain's Experience of Empire in the Twentieth Century* (OUP, 2012), reproduced by permission of Oxford University Press. **Wendy Webster:** 'The Empire Comes Home: Commonwealth Migration to Britain', in Andrew Thompson (Ed): *Britain's Experience of Empire in the Twentieth Century* (OUP, 2012), reproduced by permission of Oxford University Press. **O Maloba Wunyabari:** *Mau Mau and Kenya; an analysis of a peasant revolt* (J Currey, 1998), reproduced by permission of Boydell & Brewer Ltd.

We have made every effort to trace and contact all copyright holders before publication, but if notified of any errors or omissions, the publisher will be happy to rectify these at the earliest opportunity.

Index

A

administration *see* colonial administration

Afghanistan 44

Africa
  administration 136–7
  Bantu people 54–7
  Berlin Conference 18–19
  Boers 27, 54–7
  British expansion 1–10, 59–70
  Brussels Conference 18
  challenges 112–15, 231
  colonial policy 16–20, 136–7
  decolonisation 179–84
  East Africa 63–7, 176, 182,
    211–12
  First World War 121
  imperial consolidation 59–70
  indigenous peoples 112–15, 231,
    233–4, 236–40
  nationalist leaders 209–14, 232
  nationalist movements 175–6
  North Africa 127
  scramble for 16–20, 60–1
  see also individual countries; southern/
    South Africa; West Africa

Afrikaners 68

agriculture 25–6

All India Muslim League 128

American colonies, loss of 1

Amery, Leo 100–1, 124

Amritsar massacre 128, 154, 170

Anglicans 33

Angry Young Men 229

apartheid 182

appeasement 141

Arabi Pasha 46

Arab League 194

Arden-Clarke, Charles 159, 216–17

Argentina 20

Ashantiland 62–3, 91

Asia 178–9, 185–9, 231
  see also Malaya; South East Asia

Asquith, Herbert 103

assassination of Gurney 236

Aswan Dam/High Dam 76, 195

attitudes
  of Commonwealth immigrants 226
  to empire 30–41, 91–7, 153–60,
    208–18
  to imperialism 42–9, 98–110

Attlee, Clement 127

Aung San 131–2, 185–6, 232

Australia 146, 149

Azikiwe, Nnamdi 176, 210, 232

B

Baden-Powell, Robert 107

Balfour, Arthur 123–4

Balfour Declaration 123–4, 139–40

Banda, Hastings 184, 239

Bantu people 54–7

Baring, Evelyn 8–9, 38–9, 76, 95–6, 234

Battle of El Alamein 127

BBC (British Broadcasting
  Company) 163

Beaverbrook, Lord 101, 148

Bechuanaland 56–7

beliefs, Gandhi 155–6

bellicosity 98

Bengal 73, 112

benign methods 155

Berlin Conference 1884-5 18–19, 37,
    45, 60

Black and Tans (police) 168

Boers 27, 54–7

Boer Wars
  First 45
  see also Second Boer war

Bose, Subhas Chandra 126, 174

Britain
  migration from Empire/Common-
    wealth 222–6
  migration to Empire/Common-
    wealth 221–2
  USA, special relationship 199
  world's foremost trading nation 23

British Broadcasting Company
    (BBC) 163

British East India Company 12

British Empire and Commonwealth
    Games 228

British expansion 1–10, 59–70, 119–25

British government 42–6

British public 46–9

British Raj 14, 52, 130

Brussels Conference 1876 18

Buganda 64, 216

Burma 131–2, 185–6

Burton, Richard 32

C

cabinet ministers 11

CAF *see* Central African Federation

Cameron, Donald 159

campaigns 65–6, 112, 153–4

Canada 145

canals/rivers 25

Cape Colony 68–9
  see also South Africa

Carpenter, Mary 53

caste system 16, 155

Cawnpore incident 46

central Africa 182–4, 212–13, 215

Central African Federation (CAF) 183–
    4, 215

challenges 111–15, 231

Chamberlain, Joseph 68–9, 88–9, 91–3,
    115

charismatic leaders 232

chartered companies 6, 28–9

charters 36, 43

China/Chinese 17, 20, 21, 187

Christian imperialism 33–5

Christmas Day broadcast 220

Churchill, Winston 103, 125–6, 168

class differences 166

client states 5

clipper ships 24

coalition government 120

Cohen, Andrew 159–60, 180, 215–16

Cold War 198

colonial administration 93–7, 134–43,
    191–202, 215–17
  administrators 38–40, 93–7,
    156–60, 215–17
  Africa 136–7
  Egypt 71, 75–8
  India 12–15, 71–4, 134–5
  Middle East 137–9

Colonial Development Corpora-
    tion 179

colonial identity 172–3

colonial involvement
  First World War 119, 120–1
  Second World War 126–7

Colonial Office 71

colonial policy 11–21, 71–83, 134–43,
    191–202
  Africa 16–20, 136–7
  China 17, 20, 21
  Commonwealth 191–2, 200–1
  the Dominions 139–40
  Egypt 71, 75–8, 194–7
  imperial defence 141–2
  India 12–16, 71–4, 134–5
  indirect rule 136
  informal empire 20–1
  international relations 79–83,
    198–200
  Middle East 137–9, 198
  native policy 78–9
  Statute of Westminster 137, 139–40

commerce *see* trade

Commonwealth
  attitudes to immigrants 226
  colonial policy 191–2, 200–1
  concept of 139–40
  immigrant numbers 1958 223

migration to Britain   222–6
post-colonial ties   220
Commonwealth Games   228
Commonwealth Immigrants Act,
1962   225
concentration camps   116–17
condominiums   61
confederations   39
conflict   43–6, 168–72
Congo empire   18
Congress Movement, Hindu   128
Conservative party   43–5, 94
consolidation of empire   59–70
Constituent Assembly   185–6
constitutional arrangements, India   173
Consul-General   8
contraction of empire   119, 124–32
Convention People's Party (CPP)   181
Co-operative Wholesale Society   164
cornucopia   22
CPP see Convention People's Party
critics of imperialism   101–2
culture   104–7, 161–4, 226–9
Curzon, George (Viceroy)   72–3, 94–5

D

Darwin, Charles   47–8, 61
decolonisation   178–90
defence   12, 16, 73, 141–2, 199
Denshawai incident   77, 96
dervishes   66, 112
de Valera, Eamon   169
diamonds   27, 35–6
diasporas   227
Disraeli, Benjamin   8, 43–5
Dominions/Dominion status   117, 120,
128, 135, 139–40
dual mandate   157
dyarchy   134
Dyer, Reginald   170–1

E

East Africa   63–7, 176, 182, 211–12
economic issues
British expansion   3
East African development   182
impacts of war   144–52
India and change   53
inter-war year difficulties   141
nationalist movements   232
post-colonial ties   219–21
post-war Britain   127
Eden, Anthony   194–5
education   53, 232–3
Edwardian period   83
EEC see European Economic Community
effective occupation   19
efficiency, national   102–3
Egypt
administration   71, 75–8
Arabi Pasha's revolt   46

British control   8–9
colonial policy   194–7
developments 1947-56   194–5
Gladstone   45
protests/conflict   172
Suez Canal   6–9, 195–7
tourism   76
El Alamein, Battle of   127
Elgar, Edward   105, 164
Empire Day   164–5
ethnic divisions   181, 187, 210, 232
European Economic Community
(EEC)   179, 199
exhibitions   47–9
expansion of empire   1–10, 59–70,
119–25
explorers   3, 4, 30–3

F

Faisal I, King of Iraq   138
Fashoda incident   66, 75, 80
fasts, Gandhi   154–5
Federation of Malaya Legislative Coun-
cil   187
federations   40
female missionaries   34
films   163, 165, 229
First Boer War   45
First World War   83, 119–21, 144–6
France   6
free trade   19, 23, 24, 89
Frere, Bartle   39, 56
Furse, Ralph   160, 192

G

Gallipoli campaign   120
Gandhi, Mohandas (Mahatma)   153–6
beliefs   155–6
campaigns   112, 153–4
Churchill's comment   168
fasts   154–5
importance of   155
inter-war years   128
nationalist movements   173–4
protest/conflict   170–1
Round Table Conferences   135
Gascoyne-Cecil, Robert (Lord Salisbury)   99
geopolitical aspects   141
German fleet/navy   103
Gladstone, William   8–9, 43, 45–6
Gold Coast   159, 175–6, 180–1, 232
gold discoveries   57
Goldie, George   36–8
gold standard   73, 87, 144
Gordon, Charles   10, 48
government
British   42–6
Indian   52–3
Government of India Acts
1858   13

1919   128, 134, 170
1935   128, 135
Great Depression   3, 29, 136, 141, 145,
146
guerrilla war   67, 184
Gurney, Henry   236

H

Haganah   172
Haggard, H. Rider   46
Haig, Harry   158
Hailey, William (Baron)   159
Hard Currency Pool   206
Harmsworth, Alfred (Lord Northcliffe)
104–5
hegemony   45
Hindu Congress Movement   128
Hobhouse, Emily   101
Hobson, John A.   86–7, 101
Hola Campatrocities   234
holocaust   132
Home Rule, Ireland   45–6, 91, 168
honours, royal   228

I

ideals, imperialist   161–7
identity, colonial   172–3
immigration   223–226
see also migration
Imperial Conference   82
imperial consolidation   59–70
imperial exhibitions   47–9
Imperial Federation League   85
imperialist ideals   161–7
imperial policy see colonial policy
imperial preference   100, 148
imperial royal honours   228
India
administration   12–15, 71–4, 134–5
administrators   157–8
British withdrawal   127–30
caste system   16, 155
challenges   112
colonial policy   12–16, 71–4, 134–5
Curzon   72–3, 94–5
defence   12, 16, 73
First World War   120–1, 145
independent states   135
indigenous peoples   50–4, 112
inter-war years   128
nationalist movements   173–5
passage to   7–8
protests/conflict   169–71
provinces   15
Second World War   128
Suez Canal   7–8
tea   26
see also Government of India Acts
Indian Army   16, 17
Indian Mutiny   11, 12, 50–4
Indian National Army   128, 174

Indian National Congress   72–3
Indian Raj   52
indigenous peoples   50–8, 111–18, 168–77, 231–42
  challenges   111–15
  colonial identity   172–3
  nationalist movements   173–6, 232–40
  native policy   78–9
  protest/conflict   168–72
  Second Boer War   115–17
  see also Africa; India
indirect rule   136
individual roles see roles of individuals
industry   27–8
influence   3
  see also roles of individuals
insurgents   179
international relations   17–18, 79–83, 198–200
invisibles/invisible trade   25, 87
Iraq   138–9
Ireland   45–6, 91, 125, 168–9
Isma'il Pasha (the Magnificent)   6–7

J

Jallianwallah Bagh massacre *see* Amritsar massacre
Jamaica   223
Jameson, Leander Starr   68
Jameson raid   68, 81, 91, 93
Jewish National Fund   137
jihadists   10
jingoism   44, 105
Jinnah, Muhammad Ali   128, 174–5

K

Kaunda, Kenneth   184, 232, 239
Kenya   65, 233–5
Kenyatta, Jomo   168, 176, 211–12
Keynes, John Maynard   150
khaki election   99
Khedive of Egypt   6
Kikuyu grievances   233
Kipling, Rudyard   102, 105, 163
Kirk, John   32
Kitchener, Herbert   66–7, 76, 78, 116

L

Labour government, post-war   127
Lawrence, T.E. (Lawrence of Arabia)   123
leadership   208–14, 232–3
League of Nations   121–4, 136, 141
Lee Kuan Yew   232
Lend-Lease   150
Liberal party   45–6, 59–118
Linlithgow, Lord   158
literature   105–6, 163
Livingstone, David   30–1
Lloyd-George, David   103, 119–20

Lugard, Frederick (Lord)   64, 79, 157, 159

M

Mackinnon, William   36
Macmillan, Harold   184, 192–3, 235
Macpherson, John   216
Mahdi (Islamic Redeemer)   10
Mahdist Rebellion   45, 65
Makerere College   159
Malaya
  Malay Peninsula   186–8
  Malaysian Chinese   187
  nationalist leaders/movements   208–9, 232, 235–6
Malayan Communist Party (MCP)   186
Malay Chinese Association (MCA)   186, 189
mandates   121–4, 136, 137–9
Mandela, Nelson   213–14
Marshall Aid/Plan   199, 205
mass political parties   233
Mau Mau rebellion   211, 233–5
MCA *see* Malay Chinese Association
MCP *see* Malayan Communist Party
medals   52, 53
Menzies, Robert   201
mercantilism   23, 89
merchant-imperialists   3
Methodists   33–4
metropoles   84, 219
Middle East   198
  administration   137–9
  British withdrawal   127, 132
  colonial policy   137–9, 198
  protests/conflict   172
migration   27, 221–6
militancy   171, 188
military rebellion   188
Milner, Alfred (Lord)   93, 95, 96–7, 100, 115, 124
mining   26–7
Minto, Viceroy   74
missionaries   4, 33–5
Mitchell, Philip   159
monopolies   12
Montagu, Edwin   157–8
moral factors, expansion   4
Morley–Minto reforms   74
Mosley, Oswald   224
Mountbatten, Louis (Lord)   129
music   105–6
mutinies   12
Mwanga , King of Uganda   64

N

Nasser, Gamal Abdel   194–7
national efficiency   102–3
nationalism   128, 179
nationalist leaders   208–14
nationalist movements   141, 173–6

Africa   175–6, 209–14, 232
  growth of   232–3
  India   173–5
  Malaya   208–9, 232, 235–6
  reactions to   233–42
National Service   221
native Indian troops   16, 17
native policy   78–9
naval fleet, German   103
Nehru, Jawaharial   174
New Zealand   146, 149
Nigeria   38, 63, 181–2, 210, 232, 236–8
Nkata Bay, Rhodesia   239
Nkrumah, Kwame   168, 176, 209–10, 217, 232
non-conformists   33
North Africa   127
Northcliffe, Lord   104–5
Northern Nigeria   38
North-West Frontier Province   94
Notting Hill Carnival   224–5
Nyasaland   67

O

Obote, Apolo Milton   212–13
occupation   5, 9, 19
Onn bin Ja'afar   208–9
Organisation of African Unity   209

P

Pakistan   171, 175
Palestine   123, 132, 137–8
PAP *see* People's Action Party
partition
  Bengal   73, 112
  India and Pakistan   171
party political conflicts   43–6
Pax Britannica   114–15
People's Action Party (PAP)   189
personal influence *see* influence
plebiscite vote   181
policy *see* colonial policy
political conflicts   43–6
politicalties   219–21
pooling of sovereignty   100
popular culture   104–7, 161–4, 228–9
post-colonial ties   219–30
post-war reconstruction   205–6
power-sharing   128
Presbyterians   33
press, popular   104–5
promotion of empire   162–4
protectionism   23
protests   168–72
provinces   15, 94, 132
public, British   46–9
puppet rulers   8

Q

Quit India Movement   171

R

Race Relations Board   **226**
racial divisions   **236**
racism   **47, 225**
raids   **68, 91**
railways   **24–5, 53, 64, 91**
Raj   **14, 52, 130**
Reform Act 1867   **44**
regional divisions   **181**
Reith, John   **163**
religious rivalries   **232**
representations of empire   **107–9, 164–5**
residual impact of empire   **226–9**
rhetoric   **101**
Rhodes, Cecil   **35–6, 57, 93, 115**
Rhodesia   **67, 238–40**
rivers/canals   **25**
roles of individuals   **30–41, 91–7,
     153–60, 208–18**
  colonial administrators   **38–40,
     93–7, 156–60, 215–17**
  in the empire   **30–41**
  explorers   **30–3**
  missionaries   **33–5**
  nationalist leaders   **208–14**
  traders   **35–8**
  see also Gandhi
Roman Catholics   **33**
Round Table movement   **100, 128, 135**
royal charters   **36**
royal honours   **228**
Royal Niger Company   **91**
Russia   **80**

S

Salisbury, Lord   **99**
sanctions   **184**
satyagraha (insistence on truth)   **155**
'scorched earth' policy   **113, 116**
scramble for Africa   **16–20, 60–1**
Second Boer War   **69**
  causes   **115–16**
  Chamberlain   **91–2**
  consequences   **116–17**
  the Dominions   **139**
  media   **105**
Second World War   **125–8**
  colonial involvement   **126–7**
  impacts   **149–51, 179**
  India   **128**
  nationalist movements   **232**
  reconstruction after   **205–6**
  recovery from   **205**
secular authorities   **33**
self-determination   **122**
sepoys   **12, 51**
settlement, definition   **5**
settlements, white   **12, 78, 136–7**
sharing of powers   **128**
ships/shipping   **24**

Simon Commission   **134–5**
Simon, John   **134**
Singapore   **186, 188–9**
Smith, Ian   **184, 240**
social classes   **166**
social Darwinism   **61**
social discontents,   **232**
social reformers   **34, 53**
society, India   **52–3**
Somaliland   **67, 112**
South East Asia   **126–7, 199**
southern/South Africa
  British expansion   **67–9**
  decolonisation   **182–4**
  nationalist leaders   **213–14**
  Union of   **117**
  see also Boer Wars; Boers; Transvaal
'special relationship', Britain/USA   **199**
Speke, John Hanning   **32–3**
Spicer, Howard Handley   **107**
Stanley, Henry   **31, 48**
Star of India medal   **52, 53**
State of Emergency   **187**
Statute of Westminster   **137, 139–40,
     182**
sterling   **146, 205**
Stern Gang   **172**
strategic factors   **3, 82–3**
Sudan   **9–10, 65–7, 113–15**
Suez Canal/crisis   **6–9, 195–7, 201**
suffrage   **181**
Sultan, Turkey   **75**
supporters of imperialism   **99–101**
suzerainty   **95**
swadeshi movement   **89**
'Swing to the East' concept 1

T

Tan Cheng Lock   **209**
Tanganyika   **182, 232**
tariffs   **8**
tea   **26**
That Was the Week That Was TV pro-
     gramme   **229**
Thuku, Harry   **176**
tourism, Egypt   **76**
trade   **22–9, 84–90, 144–52, 203–7**
  debates over   **88–9**
  expansion of empire   **3**
  First World War   **144–6**
  free   **19, 23, 24, 89**
  infrastructure   **24–5**
  inter-war years   **146–9**
  investment in empire   **86–8**
  products   **25–8**
  Second World War   **149–51**
  traders   **35–8**
  value of   **147–9**
Transvaal   **44, 57, 68–9, 96, 115–17**
tropical Africa   **62–7**

Truman Doctrine   **198**
trusteeship   **157**

U

Uganda   **64, 91**
Uitlanders   **115**
UMNO see United Malays National
     Organisation
Unilateral Declaration of Independ-
     ence   **239**
Union Movement   **224**
unitary states   **132**
United Malays National Organisation
     (UMNO)   **186, 189, 208–9**
United Nations   **132**
United States of America (USA)   **199,
     205**

V

veiled protectorates   **8–9**
Viceroys of India   **13–14, 72–4, 94–5**
Vimy Ridge battle   **120**
voting rights   **115**

W

war *see* Boer Wars; World Wars
West Africa   **62–3, 113**
  decolonisation   **180–2**
  nationalism   **175–6, 209–10**
West Griqualand   **55–6**
White Dominions   **120**
White Rhodesian Front   **240**
white settlements   **12, 78, 136–7**
'wind of change' speech   **192–3, 235**
World Wars see First World War; Second
     World War

Y

youth   **106–7**

Z

Zanzibar   **63, 113**
zealots   **67**
zionists   **123–4**
Zulus   **40, 44–5, 56**

Topics available from *Oxford AQA History for A Level*

Tsarist and Communist Russia 1855-1964
978 019 835467 3

Challenge and Transformation: Britain c1851-1964
978 019 835466 6

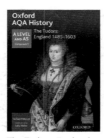

The Tudors: England 1485-1603
978 019 835460 4

Stuart Britain and the Crisis of Monarchy 1603-1702
978 019 835462 8

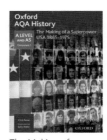

The Making of a Superpower: USA 1865-1975
978 019 835469 7

The Quest for Political Stability: Germany 1871-1991
978 019 835468 0

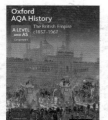

The British Empire c1857-1967
978 019 835463 5

Industrialisation and the People: Britain c1783-1885
978 019 835453 6

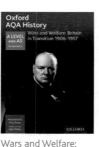

Wars and Welfare: Britain in Transition 1906-1957
978 019 835459 8

The Cold War c1945-1991
978 019 835461 1

Democracy and Nazism: Germany 1918-1945
978 019 835457 4

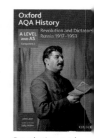

Revolution and Dictatorship: Russia 1917-1953
978 019 835458 1

Religious Conflict and the Church in England c1529-c1570
978 019 835471 0

International Relations and Global Conflict c1890-1941
978 019 835454 3

The American Dream: Reality and Illusion 1945-1980
978 019 835455 0

The Making of Modern Britain 1951-2007
978 019 835464 2

The Crisis of Communism: the USSR and the Soviet Empire 1953-2000
978 019 835465 9

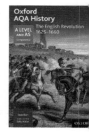

The English Revolution 1625-1660
978 019 835472 7

France in Revolution 1774-1815
978 019 835473 4

The Transformation of China 1936-1997
978 019 835456 7

Order online at **www.oxfordsecondary.co.uk/aqahistory**

OXFORD